Wiley 11th Hour Guide for 2018 Level I CFA Exam

Thousands of candidates from more than 100 countries have relied on these Study Guides to pass the CFA® Exam. Covering every Learning Outcome Statement (LOS) on the exam, these review materials are an invaluable tool for anyone who wants a deep-dive review of all the concepts, formulas, and topics required to pass.

Wiley study materials are produced by expert CFA charterholders, CFA Institute members, and investment professionals from around the globe. For more information, contact us at info@efficientlearning.com.

Wiley 11th Hour Guide for 2018 Level I CFA Exam

WILEY

Published by John Wiley & Sons, Inc., Hoboken, New Jersey.

Prior to 2014, the material was published by Élan Guides.

Published simultaneously in Canada.

For general information on our other products and services or for technical support, please contact our Customer Care Department within the United States at (800) 762-2974, outside the United States at (317) 572-3993 or fax (317) 572-4002.

Wiley publishes in a variety of print and electronic formats and by print-on-demand. Some material included with standard print versions of this book may not be included in e-books or in print-on-demand. If this book refers to media such as a CD or DVD that is not included in the version you purchased, you may download this material at http://booksupport.wiley.com. For more information about Wiley products, visit www.wiley.com.

ISBN 978-1-119-43523-5; 978-1-119-43525-9 (epub) (ebook); 978-1-119-43524-2 (epdf)

Contents

Foreword

Wiley 11th Hour Guide for 2018 Level I CFA Exam is a concise and easy-to-understand review book that is meant to supplement your review for the CFA Level I exam. It becomes extremely difficult to go through the entire curriculum in the last few weeks leading up to the exam, so we have condensed the material for you. You must remember, though, that this book is not meant to be a primary study tool for the exam. It is designed to help you review the material in an efficient and effective manner so that you can be confident on exam day.

About the Authors

Wiley's Study Guides are written by a team of highly qualified CFA charterholders and leading CFA instructors from around the globe. Our team of CFA experts work collaboratively to produce the best study materials for CFA candidates available today.

Wiley's expert team of contributing authors and instructors is led by Content Director Basit Shajani, CFA. Basit founded online education start-up Élan Guides in 2009 to help address CFA candidates' need for better study materials. As lead writer, lecturer, and curriculum developer, Basit's unique ability to break down complex topics helped the company grow organically to be a leading global provider of CFA Exam prep materials. In January 2014, Élan Guides was acquired by John Wiley & Sons, Inc., where Basit continues his work as Director of CFA Content. Basit graduated magna cum laude from the Wharton School of Business at the University of Pennsylvania with majors in finance and legal studies. He went on to obtain his CFA charter in 2006, passing all three levels on the first attempt. Prior to Élan Guides, Basit ran his own private wealth management business. He is a past president of the Pakistani CFA Society.

There are many more expert CFA charterholders who contribute to the creation of Wiley materials. We are thankful for their invaluable expertise and diligent work. To learn more about Wiley's team of subject matter experts, please visit: www.efficientlearning.com/cfa/why-wiley/.

Study Session 1: Ethical and Professional Standards

ETHICS AND TRUST IN THE INVESTMENT PROFESSION
Cross-Reference to CFA Institute Assigned Reading #1

Ethics describes a system of principles, beliefs, and values that guide (or society believes should guide) our behavior. **Principles** are fundamental truths that form the basis for a chain of reasoning leading to beliefs about cause and effect and the way things should and shouldn't be.

Standards of conduct serve as benchmarks for the minimally acceptable behavior required of members of a group. They serve to clarify the organization's **code of ethics**, which lays out its beliefs regarding obligatory and forbidden conduct.

Professionals use specialized knowledge and skills in service to others. A profession's code of ethics publicly communicates the shared principles and expected behaviors of a profession's members. It helps foster confidence in members of the profession.

Challenges to Ethical Behavior

- **Overconfidence bias:** People being more likely to overestimate the morality of their own behavior, particularly in situations that they have not faced before.
- **Situational influences:** External factors, such as environmental or cultural elements, that shape a person's thinking, decision making, and behavior such as the bystander effect (where people are less likely to intervene in an emergency when others are present).
- Focusing on the immediate rather than long-term outcomes or consequences of a decision.

Some ethical behavior may be illegal. New laws designed to reduce or eliminate conduct that adversely affects the markets can create opportunities for different, but similarly problematic, conduct.

Ethically sound decisions are almost always better than law from an equity standpoint, but almost always require good judgment and active consideration of stakeholders' interests from the stakeholder perspective.

Ethical Decision-Making Frameworks

An ethical decision-making framework is a tool for analyzing the potential alternative actions and consequences of a decision. It raises awareness of different perspectives, improves decision-making, and helps avoid unanticipated ethical consequences.

A general ethical decision-making framework is shown below:

- Identify: Facts of the situation, ethical/legal obligations to stakeholders, and potential conflicts of interest.
- Consider: Potential alternatives, situational influences, and guidance external to the situation.
- Decide and act.
- Reflect: Why did or why didn't the decision yield the expected result?

ET

CODE OF ETHICS AND STANDARDS OF PROFESSIONAL CONDUCT; GUIDANCE FOR STANDARDS I–VII

Cross-Reference to CFA Institute Assigned Readings #2 & 3

All CFA Institute members and candidates enrolled in the CFA Program are required to comply with the Code of Ethics and the Standards of Professional Conduct (Code and Standards). The CFA Institute Bylaws and Rules of Procedure for Proceedings Related to Professional Conduct (Rules of Procedure) form the basic structure for enforcing the Code and Standards.

The Rules of Procedure are based on the following two principles:

1. Fair process.
2. Maintaining confidentiality of process.

The CFA Institute Board of Governors is responsible for implementing the Professional Conduct Program (PCP) through the Disciplinary Review Committee (DRC).

The CFA Institute Designated Officer, through the Professional Conduct staff, carries out professional conduct inquiries. Circumstances which can initiate an inquiry include:

- Information disclosed on the annual Professional Conduct Statement.
- Written complaints received by Professional Conduct staff.
- Questionable conduct as publicized by the media or any other source.
- A violation report submitted by a CFA examination proctor.

Once an inquiry is initiated, the Professional Conduct staff undertakes an investigation which can include:

- Requesting a written explanation.
- Interviewing related person(s).
- Collecting any supporting documents.

The information collected is reviewed by the Designated Officer, who may conclude that:

1. No disciplinary action is needed
2. A cautionary letter needs to be issued
3. Proceedings need to be continued.

If it is concluded that there has been a violation of the Code and Standards, the Designated Officer can propose a disciplinary sanction. The member or candidate has the right to accept or reject the decision. A rejection would require the matter to be referred to a hearing by a panel of CFA Institute members. Sanctions by CFA Institute may include condemnation by peers, consequences for current or future employment or suspension from the CFA program.

The adherence of investment professionals to ethical practices benefits all market participants.

- Clients are reassured that investment professionals they hire prioritize their interests.
- Investment professionals benefit from the more efficient and transparent operation of the market that promotes integrity.

Sound ethics is fundamental to capital markets and the investment profession as it increases investors' confidence in global financial markets. Ethics is also of paramount importance because of the interconnectedness of global financial markets, which gives rise to the issue of market sustainability. It is imperative that top management foster a strong culture of ethics not just among CFA charter holders and candidates but among all staff members who are involved directly or indirectly with client relations, the investment process, record keeping, and beyond.

However, new challenges continually arise for members and candidates in applying the Code and Standards. This is because ethical dilemmas are not unambiguously right or wrong and require a bit of judgment.

The CFA Institute Code of Ethics plays an integral role in maintaining the integrity of CFA Institute members and upholding professional excellence. All CFA Institute members and CFA candidates must abide by this code and are encouraged to notify their employers of any violations. Violations may result in disciplinary sanctions by CFA Institute, which may include revocation of membership, candidacy in the CFA program and the right to use the CFA designation.

The Code of Ethics requires all members and candidates to:

- Act with integrity, competence, diligence, respect, and in an ethical manner with the public, clients, prospective clients, employers, employees, colleagues in the investment profession, and other participants in the global capital markets.
- Place the integrity of the investment profession and the interests of clients above their own personal interests.
- Use reasonable care and exercise independent professional judgment when conducting investment analysis, making investment recommendations, taking investment actions, and engaging in other professional activities.
- Practice and encourage others to practice in a professional and ethical manner that will reflect credit on themselves and the profession.
- Promote the integrity of, and uphold the rules governing, capital markets.
- Maintain and improve their professional competence and strive to maintain and improve the competence of other investment professionals.

Standards of Professional Conduct:

I. Professionalism

A. Knowledge of the Law
B. Independence and Objectivity
C. Misrepresentation
D. Misconduct

II. Integrity of Capital Markets

A. Material Nonpublic Information
B. Market Manipulation

III. Duties to Clients

A. Loyalty, Prudence and Care
B. Fair Dealing
C. Suitability
D. Performance Presentation
E. Preservation of Confidentiality

IV. Duties to Employers

A. Loyalty
B. Additional Compensation Arrangements
C. Responsibilities of Supervisors

V. Investment Analysis, Recommendations and Actions

A. Diligence and Reasonable Basis
B. Communication with Clients and Prospective Clients
C. Record Retention

VI. Conflicts of Interest

A. Disclosure of Conflicts
B. Priority of Transactions
C. Referral Fees

VII. Responsibilities as a CFA Institute Member or CFA Candidate

A. Conduct as Participants in CFA Institute Programs
B. Reference to CFA Institute, the CFA Designation, and the CFA Program

The best way to prepare for Ethics is to thoroughly read the Standards themselves, along with related guidance and examples.

INTRODUCTION TO THE GLOBAL INVESTMENT PERFORMANCE STANDARDS (GIPS®)

Cross-Reference to CFA Institute Assigned Reading #4

Individual and institutional investors typically use past investment performance to gauge a fund manager's ability and to make investment decisions. Questions relating to the accuracy and credibility of the data used to present investment performance make comparisons difficult.

The GIPS standards aim to provide clients and prospective clients with comparable and representative investment performance data. They establish an industry-wide, standard approach for calculation and presentation of investment performance. This forces complying firms to avoid misrepresentation and to communicate all relevant information that prospective clients should know to make informed investment decisions. Compliance with GIPS standards for any firm is *voluntary* and not required by any legal or regulatory authorities. However, only investment management firms that actually manage assets can claim compliance. Plan sponsors and consultants cannot claim to comply with GIPS if they do not manage any assets. They can only endorse the standards or require their investment managers to comply with them. Further, compliance is a firm-wide process that cannot be achieved on a single product or composite. In order to claim compliance, the firm needs to comply with all requirements of GIPS standards; there is no such thing as partial compliance to GIPS.

The GIPS standards benefit two main groups—investment management firms and prospective clients.

The GIPS standards require the use of composites. A composite is formed by combining discretionary portfolios into one group that represents a particular investment objective or strategy. A composite representing a particular strategy, must include **all** discretionary portfolios managed according to that strategy.

To ensure that the firm does not include only its best performing funds when presenting its investment performance, the GIPS standards require that the criteria for classifying portfolios into composites be decided before performance is known (i.e., on an ex-ante basis), not after the fact.

Firms that claim compliance with GIPS standards are responsible for ensuring that they really are compliant and that they maintain their compliant status going forward. After claiming compliance, firms may hire an independent third party to verify that they are compliant to add credibility to their claim.

Verification assures that the investment manager is compliant with GIPS standards on a firm-wide basis. Verification needs to be performed on the entire firm rather than specific composites. Verification tests:

- Whether the investment firm has complied with all the composite construction requirements on a firm-wide basis; and
- Whether the firm's processes and procedures calculate and present performance information according to GIPS standards.

Verification is optional, and it cannot be performed by the firm itself.

THE GIPS STANDARDS

Cross-Reference to CFA Institute Assigned Reading #5

Objectives of GIPS

- To establish investment industry's best practices for calculating and presenting investment performance that promote investor interests and instill investor confidence.
- To obtain worldwide acceptance of a single standard for the calculation and presentation of investment performance based on the principles of fair representation and full disclosure.
- To promote the use of accurate and consistent investment performance data.
- To encourage fair, global competition among investment firms without creating barriers to entry.
- To foster the notion of industry "self-regulation" on a global basis.

Overview

GIPS standards have the following key features:

- GIPS standards are ethical standards to ensure full disclosure and fair representation of investment performance. In order to claim compliance, firms must adhere to all the requirements of the GIPS standards.
- Apart from adhering to the minimum requirements of the GIPS standards, firms should try to adhere to the recommendations of the GIPS standards to achieve best practice in the calculation and presentation of performance.
- Firms should include all actual, discretionary, and fee-paying portfolios in at least one composite defined by investment mandate, objective, or strategy in order to prevent firms from cherry-picking their best performance.
- The accuracy of performance presentation is dependent on the accuracy of input data. The underlying valuations of portfolio holdings drive the portfolio's performance. Therefore, it is essential for these and other inputs to be accurate. The GIPS standards require firms to adhere to certain calculation methodologies and to make specific disclosures along with the firm's performance.
- Firms must comply with all requirements of the GIPS standards, including any updates, Guidance Statements, interpretations, Questions & Answers, and clarifications published by CFA Institute and the GIPS Executive Committee, which are available on the GIPS website as well as in the GIPS Handbook.

The GIPS standards do not address every aspect of performance measurement or cover unique characteristics of each asset class. However, they will continue to evolve over time to address additional areas of investment performance.

Fundamentals of Compliance

The fundamentals of compliance include both recommendations and requirements.

Requirements

- Firms must comply with all the requirements of the GIPS standards, including any updates, Guidance Statements, interpretations, Questions & Answers, and clarifications published by CFA Institute and the GIPS Executive Committee, which are available on the GIPS website as well as in the GIPS Handbook.
- Firms must comply with all applicable laws and regulations regarding the calculation and presentation of performance.
- Firms must not present performance or performance-related information that is false or misleading.
- The GIPS standards must be applied on a firm-wide basis.
- Firms must document their policies and procedures used in establishing and maintaining compliance with the GIPS standards, including ensuring the existence and ownership of client assets, and must apply them consistently.
- If the firm does not meet all the requirements of the GIPS standards, it must not represent or state that it is "in compliance with the Global Investment Performance Standards except for…" or make any other statements that may indicate partial compliance with the GIPS standards.
- Statements referring to the calculation methodology as being "in accordance," "in compliance," or "consistent with" the GIPS standards, or similar statements, are prohibited.
- Statements referring to the performance of a single, existing client portfolio as being "calculated in accordance with the GIPS standards" are prohibited, except when a GIPS-compliant firm reports the performance of an individual client's portfolio to that particular client.
- Firms must make every reasonable effort to provide a compliant presentation to all prospective clients. Firms must not choose whom they present a compliant presentation to. As long as a prospective client has received a compliant presentation within the previous 12 months, the firm has met this requirement.
- Firms must provide a complete list of composite descriptions to any prospective client that makes such a request. They must include terminated composites on their list of composite descriptions for at least five years after the composite termination date.
- Firms must provide a compliant presentation for any composite listed on their list of composite descriptions to any prospective client that makes such a request.
- Firms must be defined as an investment firm, subsidiary, or division held out to clients or prospective clients as a distinct business entity.
- For periods beginning on, or after 1 January 2011, total firm assets must be aggregate fair value of all discretionary and non-discretionary assets managed by the firm. This includes both fee-paying and non-fee-paying portfolios.
- Total firm assets must include assets assigned to a sub-advisor provided that the firm has discretion over the selection of the sub-advisor.

- Changes in a firm's organization must not lead to alteration of historical composite performance.
- When the firm jointly markets with other firms, the firm claiming compliance with the GIPS standards must ensure that it is clearly defined and separate from the other firms being marketed, and that it is clear which firm is claiming compliance.

Recommendations

- Firms should comply with the recommendations of the GIPS standards, including recommendations in any updates, Guidance Statements, interpretations, Questions & Answers, and clarifications published by CFA Institute and the GIPS Executive Committee, which will be made available on the GIPS website as well as in the GIPS Handbook.
- Firms should be verified.
- Firms should adopt the broadest, most meaningful definition of the firm, encompassing all geographical offices operating under the same brand name regardless of the actual name of the individual investment management company.
- Firms should provide to each existing client, on an annual basis, a compliant presentation of the composite in which the client's portfolio is included.

Historical Performance Record

Firms are required to present a minimum of five years of GIPS-compliant historical investment performance. If the firm or composite has been in existence for less than five years, the presentation should include performance since inception. After initiating compliance with GIPS standards, the firm must add one year of compliant performance each year, so that the firm eventually presents a (minimum) performance record of 10 years.

Firms may link non-GIPS-compliant performance records to their compliant history as long as the non-compliant record is not for data after January 1, 2000. In such a case the firm must disclose the period of non-compliant data and disclose how the performance presentation differs from GIPS standards.

Firms that manage private equity, real estate, and/or wrap fee/separately managed account (SMA) portfolios must also comply with Sections 6, 7, and 8, respectively, of the Provisions of the GIPS standards that became effective as of 1 January 2006.

The effective date for the 2010 edition of the GIPS standards is 1 January 2011. Compliant presentations that include performance for periods that begin on or after 1 January 2011 must be prepared in accordance with the 2010 edition of the GIPS standards. Prior editions of the GIPS standards may be found on the GIPS website.

Implementation of GIPS Standards

In countries where laws and regulations regarding performance presentation do exist, firms are encouraged to adhere to GIPS in addition to their local laws. In case of a conflict, local laws are applicable and firms are required to disclose the conflict.

Nine Major Sections of the GIPS Standards

The nine major sections of the GIPS standards are:

0. Fundamentals of compliance which discusses issues pertaining to definition of a firm, documentation of policies and procedures, maintaining compliance with any updates and ensuring proper reference to claim of compliance with GIPS and references to verification of GIPS.
1. Input data which specifies standards for input data to be used to calculate investment performance. For periods beginning on or after 1 January 2011, all portfolios must be valued in accordance with the definition of fair value and the GIPS Valuation Principles.
2. Calculation methodology includes definitions of specific methods for return calculations of portfolios and composites.
3. Composite construction: Composites should be constructed to achieve consistency and fair presentation. Details were discussed in LOS 3b.
4. Disclosures Requirements for disclosure of information pertaining to a firm's policies and performance presentation.
5. Presentation and reporting: Performance presentation must be according to GIPS requirements.
6. Real estate standards must be applied to present performance relating to real estate investments.
7. Private equity: GIPS Private Equity Valuation Principals must be used to value private equity investments, except for open-end and evergreen funds.
8. Wrap Fee/Separately Managed Account (SMA) Portfolios: Firms must include the performance record of all wrap fee/SMA portfolios in appropriate composites in accordance with the firm's established portfolio inclusion policies.

Study Session 2: Quantitative Methods—Basic Concepts

QM

THE TIME VALUE OF MONEY

Cross-Reference to CFA Institute Assigned Reading #6

Interest rates can be thought of in three ways:

- The minimum rate of return that you require to accept a payment at a later date.
- The discount rate that must be applied to a future cash flow to determine its present value.
- The opportunity cost of receiving money today as opposed to saving it for a certain period and earning a return on it.

Interest rates are composed of the real risk-free rate plus compensation for bearing various risks.

- The real risk-free rate is the single-period return on a risk-free security assuming zero inflation. With no inflation, every dollar holds on to its purchasing power, so this rate purely reflects individuals' preferences for current versus future consumption.
- The inflation premium is added to the real risk-free rate to reflect the expected loss in purchasing power over the term of a loan. The real risk-free rate plus the inflation premium equals the nominal risk-free rate.
- The default risk premium compensates investors for the risk that the borrower might fail to make her payments on time in full.
- The liquidity premium compensates investors for any difficulty they might face in converting their holdings readily into cash at close to the most recent market price. Securities that trade infrequently or with low volumes require a higher liquidity premium than those that trade frequently with high volumes.
- The maturity premium compensates investors for the higher sensitivity of the market values of longer term debt instruments to changes in interest rates.

Present Value versus Future Value

- Present value (PV) is the current worth of sum of money or stream of cash flows that will be received in the future, given the interest rate.
    - For a given discount rate, the *longer* the time period till the future amount is received, the *lower* the present value.
    - For a given time period, the *higher* the discount rate, the *lower* the present value of an amount.
- Future value (FV) is the value of a sum of money at a specified date in the future.
    - For a given interest rate, the future value *increases* as the number of periods *increases.*
    - For a given number of periods, the future value *increases* as the interest rate *increases.*

Since PV and FV are separated in time, remember the following that we can add sums of money only if they are being valued at exactly the same point in time.

QM

Annuities

- An annuity is a series of recurring periodic level payments.
- An ordinary annuity is an annuity where the cash flows occur at the end of each compounding period.
- An annuity due is an annuity where cash flows occur at the beginning of every period. Problems relating to annuities due can either be solved in [BGN] mode or by converting the value of an ordinary annuity to that of an annuity due.

$$PV_{\text{Annuity Due}} = PV_{\text{Ordinary Annuity}} \times (1 + r)$$
$$FV_{\text{Annuity Due}} = FV_{\text{Ordinary Annuity}} \times (1 + r)$$

Perpetuities

A perpetuity is a never ending series of level payments, where the first cash flow occurs one period from now (at t = 1).

$$PV = \frac{PMT}{I/Y}$$

The Effects of Compounding Frequency

- As the number of compounding periods *increases*, the future value of the investment *increases.*
- As the number of compounding periods *increases*, the present value of the investment *decreases*.
- The effective annual rate *rises* as compounding frequency *increases.*

Loan Payments and Amortization Schedules

Loan amortization is the process of retiring a loan obligation through predetermined equal monthly payments. Each of these payments includes an interest component, which is calculated on the principal outstanding at the beginning of the period, and a principal repayment component. The principal component increases with the passage of time, and the interest component declines over time in line with the decreasing amount of principal outstanding.

The principal outstanding at any payment date equals the present value of the remaining payments discounted at the periodic discount rate.

The Cash Flow Additivity Principle

The additivity principle states that the present value of any stream of cash flows equals the sum of the present values of the individual cash flows. If we have two streams of cash flows, the sum of the present values of the two streams at any point in time is the same as the present value of the two series combined by adding cash flows that occur at the same point in time. The cash flow stream can also be divided in any desired manner, and the present value of the pieces will equal the present value of the series.

DISCOUNTED CASH FLOW APPLICATIONS
Cross-Reference to CFA Institute Assigned Reading #7

Net Present Value

The net present value (NPV) of an investment equals the present value of all expected inflows from the project minus the present value of all expected outflows. The rate used to discount all cash flows is the appropriate cost of capital, which reflects the opportunity cost of undertaking the particular investment, and compensates investors for various risks inherent in the project.

- Positive NPV projects increase shareholder wealth and should be accepted.
- Negative NPV projects decrease shareholder wealth and should be rejected.
- For mutually exclusive projects (where only one project can be chosen from several options) the project with the highest, positive NPV should be chosen as it would add the most value to the firm.

Internal Rate of Return (IRR)

The internal rate of return (IRR) of a project is the discount rate that equates the project's NPV to zero. Effectively, it is the discount rate that equates the present value of all inflows from a project to the present value of all project-related outflows. Calculating IRR only requires forecasts of cash flows in the future; there is no need for externally generated market data to determine appropriate discount rates. An important thing to remember regarding IRR is that it assumes that all cash flows from the project will be reinvested at the IRR.

- Projects for which the IRR *exceeds* the required rate of return should be accepted.
- Projects for which the IRR is *lower* than the required rate of return should be rejected.

NPV versus IRR

In deciding whether a single project should be undertaken, IRR and NPV will offer the same recommendation.

- If IRR is *greater* than the required rate of return, NPV is *positive.*
- If IRR is *less* than the required rate of return, NPV is *negative.*

When only one of two or more projects can be accepted, the projects are said to be mutually exclusive. For mutually exclusive projects, NPV and IRR may offer conflicting conclusions. This can happen in two scenarios:

- When the projects' initial cash outlays are different.
- When there is a difference in timing of the cash flows across the projects.

NPV assumes that interim cash flows from the project will be reinvested at the required rate of return, whereas IRR assumes that they will be reinvested at the IRR. When choosing between mutually exclusive projects, use the NPV rule if the recommendations of the NPV and IRR rules conflict.

Measures of Portfolio Return

- The holding period yield (HPY), also known as holding period return, is simply the return earned on an investment over the entire investment horizon.
- The money-weighted rate of return is simply the internal rate of return of an investment.
- The time-weighted rate of return measures the compounded rate of growth of an investment over the stated measurement period.
  - It is not affected by cash withdrawals or contributions to the portfolio.
  - It is basically the geometric mean of subperiod returns.
  - The time-weighted rate of return is preferred because it is not affected by the timing and amount of cash inflows and outflows.
  - Decisions regarding contributions and withdrawals from a portfolio are usually made by clients. Since these decisions are not typically in investment managers' hands, it would be inappropriate to evaluate their performance based on money-weighted returns. If a manager does have discretion over withdrawals and contributions of funds in a portfolio, money-weighted return might be a more appropriate measure of portfolio performance.

Money-Weighted versus Time-Weighted Rates of Return

- If funds are deposited to the investment portfolio prior to a period of superior performance, the money-weighted return will be *higher* than the time-weighted return.
- If funds are deposited into the investment portfolio just before a period of relatively poor performance, the money-weighted return will be *lower* than the time-weighted return.

Market Yields

The bank discount yield is a quoting convention used primarily for quoting Treasury bills. It annualizes the discount on the instrument as a percentage of *par or face value* over a *360-day* period.

$$r_{BD} = \frac{D}{F} \times \frac{360}{t}$$

Yields presented on a bank discount basis do not hold much meaning to investors for the following reasons:

- Investors want to evaluate returns on the amount invested to purchase the instrument; BDY calculates returns based on par value.
- Returns are based on a 360-day year; not a 365-day year.
- BDY assumes simple interest. In doing so, it ignores interest earned on interest (compound interest).

The holding period yield equals the return realized on an investment over the entire horizon that it is held (which can either be till maturity or sale). It is an *unannualized* return measure.

$$HPY = \frac{P_1 - P_0 + D_1}{P_0} = \frac{P_1 + D_1}{P_0} - 1$$

The effective annual yield is an *annualized* return measure that accounts for *compounding* over a *365-day* period.

$$EAY = (1 + HPY)^{365/t} - 1$$

We can also convert an EAY to HPY using the following formula:

$$HPY = (1 + EAY)^{t/365} - 1$$

The money-market yield is the holding period yield annualized on a *360-day* year. Further, it does *not* consider the effects of compounding. It is different from the bank discount yield as it is based on the *purchase price*, not par value.

$$R_{MM} = \frac{360 \times r_{BD}}{360 - (t \times r_{BD})}$$

And, more conveniently:

$$R_{MM} = HPY \times (360 / t)$$

A relatively simple way to get through problems on market yields is to first calculate the HPY and then convert it into the required return measure.

- The HPY is the actual unannualized return an investor realizes over the investment period.
- The EAY is the HPY annualized on a *365-day* year *with* compounding.
- The money-market yield is the HPY annualized on a *360-day* year *without* compounding.

The bond equivalent yield (BEY) is simply the semiannual discount rate multiplied by two. This convention comes from the U.S. where bonds are quoted at twice the semiannual rate because coupon payments are made semiannually.

STATISTICAL CONCEPTS AND MARKET RETURNS
Cross-Reference to CFA Institute Assigned Reading #8

A **population** includes *all* the members of a particular group. It is usually very costly and time consuming to obtain measurements for each member of the population. Therefore, information about a small subset of the population, called a **sample**, is collected and conclusions about the population are drawn from the information obtained from the sample.

Types of Scales

QM

- Nominal scales categorize or count data but do not rank them.
- Ordinal scales sort data into categories that are ranked according to certain characteristics. However, they tell us nothing about the magnitude of the difference between categories.
- Interval scales rank observations such that the difference between scale values is equal so that values can be added and subtracted meaningfully.
- Ratio scales have all the characteristics of interval scales and have a true zero point as the origin. Therefore, meaningful ratios can also be computed with ratio scales.

Methods of Presenting Data

- A frequency distribution is a tabular illustration of data categorized into a relatively small number of intervals or classes.
- The relative frequency for an interval is the proportion or fraction of total observations that are represented by a particular interval.
- The cumulative absolute frequency or cumulative frequency for an interval is the number of observations that are less than the upper bound of the interval. Alternatively, it is the sum of the frequencies of all intervals less than and including the said interval.
- The cumulative relative frequency for an interval is the proportion of total observations that are less than the upper bound of the interval.
- A histogram is used graphically to represent the data contained in a frequency distribution.
- A frequency polygon also graphically illustrates the information in a frequency distribution. The coordinates or points of a frequency polygon are the frequency of each interval plotted against the midpoint of the interval.

Measures of Central Tendency

The arithmetic mean is the sum of all the observations in a data set divided by the total number of observations. The arithmetic mean of a sample is the best estimate of the value of the next observation.

- All observations are used in the computation of the arithmetic mean.
- All interval and ratio data sets have an arithmetic mean.
- The sum of the deviations from the arithmetic mean always equals zero.
- An arithmetic mean is unique—a data set only has one arithmetic mean.

The median is the value of the middle item of a data set once it has been sorted into an ascending or descending order. The advantage of using the median is that, unlike the mean, it is not sensitive to extreme values. However, the median does not use all the information about the size and magnitude of the observations and only focuses on their relative positions.

The mode of a data set is simply its most frequently occurring value. A data set that has one mode is said to be unimodal, while one that has two modes is said to be bimodal. It is also possible for a data set to have no mode, where all values are different and no value occurs more frequently than others. For grouped data, the **modal interval** is the interval with the highest frequency. The mode is the only measure of central tendency that can be used with nominal data.

The weighted mean is calculated by assigning different weights to observations in the data set to account for the disproportionate effect of certain observations on the arithmetic mean. The arithmetic mean assigns equal weights to every observation in the data set, which makes it very sensitive to extreme values.

The geometric mean is used to average rates of change over time or to calculate the growth rate of a variable over a period. In order to calculate the geometric mean for returns data, we must add 1 to each return observation (expressed as a decimal) and then subtract 1 from the result.

$$R_G = \left[\sqrt[n]{(1+R_1)\times(1+R_2)\times\ldots\times(1+R_n)}\right] - 1$$

Important Relationships Between the Arithmetic Mean and Geometric Mean

- The geometric mean is always less than, or equal to the arithmetic mean.
- The geometric mean equals the arithmetic mean only when all the observations are identical.
- The difference between the geometric and arithmetic mean increases as the dispersion in observed values increases.

The harmonic mean is used in the investment management arena to determine the average cost of shares purchased over time. It may be viewed as a special type of weighted mean where the weight of an observation is inversely proportional to its magnitude.

$$\text{Harmonic mean: } \bar{X}_H = \frac{N}{\sum_{i=1}^{N} \frac{1}{x_i}}$$

Mathematically, unless all the observations in the data set are identical (equal in value), the harmonic mean will always be less than the geometric mean, which itself will be less than the arithmetic mean.

QM

Quantiles

A quantile is a value at, or below which a stated proportion of the observations in a data set lie. Examples of quantiles include:

- quartiles, which divide the distribution in quarters or four equal parts.
- quintiles, which divide the distribution into fifths.
- deciles, which divide the data into tenths.
- percentiles, which divide the distribution into hundredths.

Measures of Dispersion

Dispersion is the variability or spread of a random variable around its central tendency.

The range is one of the most basic measures of variability of data. It is simply the difference between the highest and lowest values in a data set.

$$\text{Range} = \text{Maximum value} - \text{Minimum value}$$

The mean absolute deviation (MAD) is the average of the *absolute* values of deviations of observations in a data set from their mean.

$$\text{MAD} = \frac{\sum_{i=1}^{n} |X_i - \bar{X}|}{n}$$

The variance is the average of the squared deviations around the mean. The standard deviation is the positive square root of the variance. While the variance has no units, the standard deviation has the same units as the random variable.

Population Variance and Standard Deviation

$$\sigma^2 = \frac{\sum_{i=1}^{n} (X_i - \mu)^2}{n}$$

$$\sigma = \sqrt{\frac{\sum_{i=1}^{n} (X_i - \mu)^2}{n}}$$

Sample Variance and Standard Deviation

$$s^2 = \frac{\sum_{i=1}^{n}(X_i - \bar{X})^2}{n-1}$$

$$s = \sqrt{\frac{\sum_{i=1}^{n}(X_i - \bar{X})^2}{n-1}}$$

The mean absolute deviation (MAD) will always be less than or equal to the standard deviation. This is because, by squaring all deviations from the mean, the standard deviation attaches a greater weight to larger deviations from the mean.

The semivariance is the average of squared deviations *below* the mean, while the semideviation is the positive square root of the semivariance. The target semivariance refers to the sum of the squared deviations from a specific target return and its square root.

Chebyshev's Inequality

Chebyshev's inequality gives an approximate value for the proportion of observations in a data set that fall within k standard deviations from the mean.

$$\text{Proportion of observations within k standard deviations from mean} = 1 - 1/k^2$$

The advantage of Chebyshev's inequality is that it holds for samples and populations and for discrete and continuous data regardless of the shape of the distribution.

Coefficient of Variation

The coefficient of variation, which is the ratio of the standard deviation of the data set to its mean, is used to compare the relative dispersions of data sets. A lower coefficient of variation is better.

$$CV = \frac{s}{X}$$

Remember: The CV measures risk per unit of return.

QM

Sharpe Ratio

The Sharpe ratio is the ratio of excess return over the risk-free rate from an investment to its standard deviation. It basically measures excess return per unit of risk. Portfolios with higher Sharpe ratios are more attractive.

The Sharpe ratio measures excess return per unit of risk.

$$\text{Sharpe ratio} = \frac{\overline{r}_p - r_f}{\sigma_p}$$

Issues with the Sharpe Ratio

All other factors remaining the same:

- For portfolios with positive Sharpe ratios, the Sharpe ratio decreases if we increase risk. A portfolio with a higher positive Sharpe ratio offers a better risk-adjusted return.
- For portfolios with negative Sharpe ratios, the ratio increases (to a negative number closer to zero) if we increase risk. With negative Sharpe ratios we cannot always assume that the portfolio with the higher Sharpe ratio (closer to zero) offers a better risk-adjusted performance. If the standard deviation of two portfolios with negative Sharpe ratios is the same, the one with the higher ratio offers the better risk-adjusted performance.

The standard deviation (which is used in the Sharpe ratio as a measure of risk) is an appropriate measure or risk only for investments and strategies that have approximately symmetric distributions. Use of the Sharpe ratio to evaluate the performance of hedge funds and option strategies (that have an asymmetric returns distribution) would give inaccurate results.

Symmetrical versus Nonsymmetrical Distributions

A distribution is said to be **symmetrical** about its mean when each side of the distribution is a mirror image of the other. Loss and gain intervals exhibit the same frequencies for a symmetrical distribution (e.g., the frequency of a loss between 2% and 5% is identical to the frequency of a gain between 2% and 5%). For a symmetrical distribution, the mean, median and mode are equal.

When a distribution is not symmetrical, it is said to be skewed. Skewness can be negative or positive.

- A distribution that is positively skewed (or skewed to the right) has a long tail on the right side. It contains some observations that are much larger in value than most of the observations in the data set. For positively skewed distributions, the mode is less than the median, which is less than the mean. The mean is affected the most by the extreme values (outliers) in the tail on the right side, and is "pulled" towards them.
- A negatively skewed distribution (skewed to the left) has a long tail on the left side. It contains outliers that are much smaller in value than the majority of observations in the distribution. For a negatively skewed distribution, the mode is greater than the median, which is greater than the mean. The mean is "pulled" lower by the outliers in the tail on the left side of the distribution.

Sample Skewness

$$S_K \approx \frac{1}{n}\frac{\sum_{i=1}^{n}(X_i - \bar{X})^3}{s^3}$$

where:
s = sample standard deviation

Some researchers believe that all other factors remaining the same, investors should prefer positive skewness i.e., portfolios that have a higher probability of earning relatively large profits.

- When the distribution is positively (right) skewed, sample skewness is positive because the numerator of the formula above is a positive number (the average of deviations above the mean is larger than that of deviations below the mean).
- When the distribution is negatively (left) skewed, sample skewness is negative because the numerator of the formula above is a negative number (the average of deviations below the mean is larger than that of deviations above the mean).
- Sample skewness of zero indicates that the data set follows a symmetrical distribution.
- Absolute values of skewness greater than 0.5 suggest that the data set is significantly skewed.

Kurtosis

Kurtosis measures the extent to which a distribution is more or less peaked than a normal distribution. A normal distribution has a kurtosis of 3. Excess kurtosis equals the kurtosis of the distribution minus the kurtosis of the normal distribution (3).

- A *leptokurtic* distribution is *more* peaked and has *fatter* tails than a normal distribution and has an excess kurtosis greater than zero. A leptokurtic distribution has a greater proportion of small deviations from the mean and a greater proportion of large deviations from the mean compared to a normal distribution.
- A *platykurtic* distribution is *less* peaked and has *thinner* tails than a normal distribution. Its excess kurtosis is less than zero.
- A *mesokurtic* distribution is identical to a normal distribution and has an excess kurtosis of zero.

Sample Kurtosis uses standard deviations to the fourth power, and is calculated as:

$$K_E \approx \frac{1}{n}\frac{\sum_{i=1}^{n}(X_i - \bar{X})^4}{s^4} - 3$$

where:
s = sample standard deviation

For a sample size greater than 100, a sample excess kurtosis of greater than 1.0 would be considered unusually high.

Geometric versus Arithmetic Mean

For reporting historical returns, the geometric mean is more appropriate because it equals the rate of growth an investor would have to earn each year to match the actual cumulative investment performance. The geometric mean is an excellent measure of past performance. The arithmetic mean can distort evaluation of past performance.

- If we want to gauge performance over a single period, the arithmetic mean should be used because the arithmetic mean is the average of one-period returns.
- If we want to estimate returns over more than one period, we should use the geometric mean as it measures how investment returns are linked over time.

To calculate expected equity risk premiums (in a forward-looking context) use of the arithmetic mean is more appropriate.

- Uncertainty in cash flows or returns causes the arithmetic mean to be larger than the geometric mean. The more the uncertainty, the greater the divergence between the two.

Studies have shown that the geometric mean return approximately equals the arithmetic mean minus half the variance of returns.

PROBABILITY CONCEPTS

Cross-Reference to CFA Institute Assigned Reading #9

- A random variable is one whose possible values or results are *uncertain.*
- An outcome is the observed value of a random variable.
- An event could be a single outcome or a set of outcomes.
- Mutually exclusive events are events that cannot happen simultaneously. The occurrence of one precludes the occurrence of the other.
- Exhaustive events cover the range of *all possible outcomes* of an event.

A probability is a number between 0 and 1 that reflects the chance of a certain event occurring. A probability of zero means that it is impossible for the event to occur, while a probability of 1 means that an event will definitely occur and the outcome is not random.

There are two basic defining principles of probability:

1. The probability of any event, E, is a number between 0 and 1.
2. The sum of the probabilities of mutually exclusive and exhaustive events equals 1.

Methods of Estimating Probabilities

An empirical probability estimates the probability of an event based on its frequency of occurrence in the past.
A subjective probability draws on subjective reasoning and personal judgment to estimate the probability of an event.
An a priori probability is based on formal analysis and reasoning.

Probabilities Stated as Odds

The odds *for* an event are stated as the probability of the event occurring to the probability of the event not occurring. Odds *for* an event, E, are stated as P(E) to [1 – P(E)].

If the odds *for* are given as "a to b" then:

$$P(E) = \frac{a}{(a+b)}$$

The odds *against* an event are stated as the probability of an event not occurring to the probability of the event occurring. Odds *against* an event, E, are stated in the form of [1 – P(E)] to P(E).

QM

If the odds *against* are given as "a to b" then:

$$P(E) = \frac{b}{(a+b)}$$

- Given the odds for an outcome, the odds against the outcome are simply the *reciprocal* of the odds for.
- Given the odds against an outcome, the odds for the outcome are simply the *reciprocal* of the odds against.

The Dutch Book Theorem states that if the probabilities reflected in the stock prices are not consistent, they give rise to profit opportunities. As investors take positions to take advantage of such opportunities, the inconsistency is eventually eliminated.

Conditional versus Unconditional Probabilities

Unconditional or marginal probabilities estimate the probability of an event irrespective of the occurrence of other events. They can be thought of as stand-alone probabilities and answer questions like "What is the probability of a return on a stock above 10%?" or "What are the chances of getting a 3 on a roll of a die?"

Conditional probabilities express the probability of an event occurring *given* that another event has occurred. The questions answered are like "What is the probability of the return on a stock being more than 10%, *given* that the return is above the risk free rate?" or "What is the probability of rolling a 3, *given* that an odd number is rolled." Conditional probabilities are computed using joint probabilities.

- A *joint probability,* P(AB), answers questions like, "What is the probability of *both* A **and** B happening?"
    - If A and B are mutually exclusive events, the joint probability P(AB) equals zero. This is because mutually exclusive events cannot occur simultaneously.
    - If A is contained within the set of possible outcomes for B, P(AB) = P(A)

Mathematically, conditional probability is expressed as:

$$P(A|B) = \frac{P(AB)}{P(B)} \text{ given that } P(B) \neq 0$$

The multiplication rule for probability calculates joint probabilities using a conditional probability.

$$P(AB) = P(A \mid B) \times P(B)$$

The addition rule for probabilities is used to calculate the probability of A or B occurring.

$$P(A \text{ or } B) = P(A) + P(B) - P(AB)$$

Given that A and B share some outcomes, if we simply add P(B) to P(A) we would be double counting the shared outcomes. Therefore, we subtract the joint probability from the sum of the probabilities of A and B.

If the events are mutually exclusive, the joint probability of A and B, P(AB), equals zero, so P(A or B) would simply equal P(A) + P(B).

Dependent versus Independent Events

With two dependent events, the occurrence of one is related to the occurrence of the other. For example, the probability of doing well on an exam is related to the probability of preparing well for it.

Two events are independent if the occurrence of one does *not* have any bearing on the occurrence of the other. For example, the probability of doing well on an exam is unrelated to the probability of there being 5 trees in the park nearby.

When two events are independent:

$$P(A|B) = P(A) \text{ or equivalently, } P(B|A) = P(B)$$

- With independent events, the word *and* implies multiplication, and the word *or* implies addition.

$$P(A \text{ or } B) = P(A) + P(B) - P(AB)$$

$$P(A \text{ and } B) = P(A) \times P(B)$$

QM

The Total Probability Rule for Unconditional Probabilities

The total probability rule expresses the unconditional probability of an event in terms of conditional probabilities for mutually exclusive and exhaustive events.

$$P(A) = P(AS) + P(AS^C)$$

$$P(A) = P(A \mid S) \times P(S) + P(A \mid S^c) \times P(S^c)$$

The probability of Event A, P(A), is expressed as a weighted average in the total probability rule. The weights applied to the conditional probabilities are the probabilities of the scenarios. For example, the weight attached to the conditional probability, P(A|S), is the probability of scenario S, P(S).

Expected Value

The expected value of a random variable is the probability-weighted average of all possible outcomes for the random variable.

$$E(X) = \sum_{i=1}^{n} P(X_i)X_i$$

$$E(X) = P(X_1)X_1 + P(X_2)X_2 + \text{ ...... } P(X_n)X_n$$

Variance

If variance is zero, there is no dispersion in the distribution. In this case, the outcome is certain, and the variable is not a random variable.

$$\sigma^2(X) = E\{[X - E(X)]^2\}$$

$$\sigma^2(X) = \sum_{i=1}^{n} P(X_i)[X_i - E(X)]^2$$

Standard deviation is the positive square root of the variance. The variance has no units while the standard deviation is expressed in the same unit as the expected value and the random variable itself.

Total Probability Rule for Expected Value

Similar to the total probability rule for stating unconditional probabilities in terms of conditional probabilities, the total probability rule for expected value states (unconditional) expected values in terms of conditional expected values.

$$E(X) = E(X \mid S)P(S) + E(X \mid S^c)P(S^c)$$

$$E(X) = E(X \mid S_1) \times P(S_1) + E(X \mid S_2) \times P(S_2) + \; .... \; + E(X \mid S_n) \times P(S_n)$$

Covariance Vol 1, pg 434

Covariance is a measure of the extent to which two random variables move together.

$$\text{Cov}\,(R_i, R_j) = E\{[R_i - E(R_i)][R_j - E(R_j)]\}$$

The covariance between the returns on Asset I and Asset J can also be calculated as:

$$\text{Cov}(R_i R_j) = \sigma(R_i)\sigma(R_j)\rho(R_i, R_j)$$

Properties of Covariance

- Covariance is a similar concept to variance. The difference lies in the fact that variance measures how a random variable varies with itself, while covariance measures how a particular random variable varies with another.
- Covariance is symmetric, i.e., Cov(X,Y) = Cov (Y,X).
- Covariance may range from positive infinity to negative infinity. Variance on the other hand, is always positive.
- The covariance of X with itself, Cov(X,X) equals the variance of X, Var(X).

Interpretation of Covariance

- When the covariance of returns of two assets is *negative*, it means that when the return on one asset is above its expected value, the return on the other tends to be below its expected value. There is an *inverse* relationship between the two variables.
- When the covariance of returns of two assets is *positive*, it means that when the return on one asset is above its expected value, the return on the other also tends to be above its expected value.
- Covariance of returns is zero if the returns are unrelated.

QM

Limitations of Covariance

- Because the unit that covariance is expressed in depends on the unit that the data is presented in, it is difficult to compare covariance across data sets that have different scales.
- In practice, it is difficult to interpret covariance as it can take on extreme large values.
- Covariance does not tell us anything about the strength of the relationship between the two variables.

Correlation Coefficient

The correlation coefficient measures the strength and direction of a linear relationship between two random variables. It is obtained by dividing the covariance between two random variables by the product of their standard deviations.

$$\text{Corr}(R_A, R_B) = \rho(R_A, R_B) = \frac{\text{Cov}(R_A, R_B)}{(\sigma_A)(\sigma_B)}$$

Properties of the Correlation Coefficient

- It measures the strength of the relationship between two random variables.
- It has no unit.
- It lies between –1 and +1.

Interpretation of the Correlation Coefficient

- A correlation coefficient of +1 indicates a perfectly positive correlation between two random variables.
- A correlation coefficient of –1 indicates a perfectly negative correlation between two random variables.
- A correlation coefficient of zero indicates no linear relationship between two random variables.

A shortcoming of the correlation coefficient is the fact that it does not specify which factor or variable *causes* the linear relationship between the two variables.

Expected Return of a Portfolio

$$E(R_p) = \sum_{i=1}^{N} w_i E(R_i) = w_1 E(R_1) + w_2 E(R_2) + \ldots + w_N E(R_N)$$

Variance of a 2-Asset Portfolio

$$Var(R_p) = w_A^2\sigma^2(R_A) + w_B^2\sigma^2(R_B) + 2w_Aw_BCov(R_A, R_B)$$

$$Var(R_p) = w_A^2\sigma^2(R_A) + w_B^2\sigma^2(R_B) + 2w_Aw_B\rho(R_A, R_B)\sigma(R_A)\sigma(R_B)$$

Variance of a 3-Asset Portfolio

$$\begin{aligned} Var(R_p) = {} & w_A^2\sigma^2(R_A) + w_B^2\sigma^2(R_B) + w_C^2\sigma^2(R_C) \\ & + 2w_Aw_BCov(R_A, R_B) + 2w_Bw_CCov(R_B, R_C) + 2w_Cw_ACov(R_C, R_A) \end{aligned}$$

To calculate the variance for a portfolio containing *n* different assets we would require *n(n-1)/2* unique covariances.

Finally, the expected value of the products of uncorrelated random variables equals the product of their expected values.

E(XY) = E(X)E(Y) if X and Y are uncorrelated.

Bayes' Formula

By using Bayes' formula, we can reverse the "given that probability" P(A|B) and convert it into P(B|A) using P(A) and P(B). Bear in mind that you will probably have to use the total probability rule to calculate P(B).

$$P(B|A) = \frac{P(A|B) \times P(B)}{P(A)}$$

$$P\text{ (Event | Information)} = \frac{P\text{ (Information | Event)} \times P\text{(Event)}}{P\text{ (Information)}}$$

QM

Counting Problems

- Factorials are used when there is only one group and we are simply arranging a given set or group of n items. Given n items, there are n! ways of arranging them.
- The labeling formula is used for three or more groups of predetermined sizes. Each item must be labeled as a member of one of the groups.
- The combination formula is used when there are only two groups of predetermined sizes and crucially, the order or rank of labeling is NOT important.
- The permutation formula is used when there are only two groups of predetermined sizes and the order or ranking IS important.

Study Session 3: Quantitative Methods—Application

QM

COMMON PROBABILITY DISTRIBUTIONS

Cross-Reference to CFA Institute Assigned Reading #10

Discrete versus Continuous Random Variables

- A discrete random variable is one that can take on a countable number of values. Each outcome has a specific probability of occurring, which can be measured.
- A continuous random variable is one for which the number of possible outcomes cannot be counted (there are infinite possible outcomes) and therefore, probabilities cannot be attached to specific outcomes.

The **probability distribution** of a random variable identifies the probability of each of the possible outcomes of a random variable.

A **probability function p(x)**, expresses the probability that "X." the random variable takes on a specific value of "x." A probability function can also be stated as P(X=x).

A **probability density function (pdf)**, which is denoted by f(x), is used to determine the probability that the outcome lies within a specified range of possible values. It is used to interpret the probability structure of continuous random variables.

A **cumulative distribution function (cdf)**, or distribution function, expresses the probability that a random variable, X, takes on a value *less than or equal to* a specific value, x. It is the sum of the probabilities of all outcomes that are less than or equal to the specified value, x. A cdf is denoted by $F(x) = P(X \le x)$.

QM

The Discrete Uniform Distribution

A discrete uniform distribution is one in which the probability of each of the possible outcomes is identical. The best example of a uniform distribution is the probability distribution of the outcomes from the roll of a fair die, for which the probability of each outcome is 1/6.

The Continuous Uniform Distribution

A continuous uniform distribution is described by a lower limit, *a*, and an upper limit, *b*. These limits serve as the parameters of the distribution. The probability of any outcome or range of outcomes outside this interval is 0. Being a continuous distribution, individual outcomes also have a probability of 0. The distribution is often denoted as U(*a,b*).

The probability that the random variable will take a value that falls between x_1 and x_2, that both lie within the range, *a* to *b*, is the proportion of the total area taken up by the range, x_1 to x_2.

$$P(x_1 \leq X \leq x_2) = \frac{x_2 - x_1}{b-a}$$

Remember that $P(X^3\ x)$ is the same as $P(X > x)$ or this distribution because it is a continuous distribution where $P(X = x)$ equals zero.

The Binomial Distribution

A binomial random variable is the number of successes (X) from a Bernoulli trial that is carried out "n" times. A Bernoulli experiment is an experiment that has only 2 possible outcomes which are labeled "success" and "failure." Further, these two outcomes are mutually exclusive and collectively exhaustive.

The probability of x successes in *n* trials is given by:

$$P(X=x) = {}_nC_x (p)^x (1-p)^{n-x}$$

- The **expected value** of a binomial random variable (X) is given by:

$$E(x) = n \times p$$

- The **variance** of a binomial random variable is given by:

$$\sigma^2 = n \times p \times (1\text{-}p)$$

Binomial Trees

Binomial trees may be drawn to illustrate possible stock price movements. Binomial stock price models are extensively used in option pricing.

The Normal Distribution

- It is completely described by its mean and variance.
- It is symmetric about the mean (skewness = 0).
- Kurtosis = 3.
- Any linear combination of jointly, normally distributed random variables is also normally distributed.

Skewness and the Binomial Distribution

- If the probability of success is 0.50, the binomial distribution is symmetric.
- If the probability of success is less than 0.50, the binomial distribution is skewed to the right.
- If the probability of success is more than 0.50, the binomial distribution is skewed to the left.

Tracking Objectives, Tracking Errors, and Portfolio Risk

Tracking error is a measure of how closely a portfolio's returns match the returns of the index to which it is benchmarked. It is the difference between the total return on the portfolio (before deducting fees) and the total return on the benchmark index.

Tracking error = Gross return on portfolio – Total return on benchmark index

Calculating Probabilities Using the Standard Normal Distribution

This standard normal distribution is a normal distribution that has been standardized so that it has a mean of zero and a standard deviation of 1. To standardize an observation from a normal distribution, its standardized value or *z-score* must be calculated. This is done by subtracting the mean of the population from the observed value of the random variable, and dividing the result by the standard deviation.

z-score = (observed value – population mean) / standard deviation = $(x - \mu) / \sigma$

Essentially the z-value represents the number of standard deviations away from the population mean, an observed value of a random variable lies.

QM

Confidence Intervals

A confidence interval represents the range of values within which a certain population parameter is expected to lie in a specified percentage of the time.

Shortfall Risk and Safety-First Ratio

Shortfall risk is the probability that a portfolio's value or return, $E(R_P)$, will fall below a particular target return (R_T) over a given period.

Roy's safety-first criterion states that an optimal portfolio minimizes the probability that the actual portfolio return, R_P, will fall below the target return, R_T.

The safety-first ratio (SF Ratio) is similar to the Sharpe Ratio. The Sharpe Ratio is a special case of the SF Ratio, where the threshold level is the risk-free rate.

$$\text{Shortfall ratio (SF Ratio) or z-score} = \frac{E(R_p)-R_T}{\sigma_p}$$

Portfolios with *higher* SF Ratios are *preferred* to those that have a *lower* SF ratio; *higher* SF Ratio portfolios have a *lower* probability of not meeting their target returns.

The Lognormal Distribution

A random variable, Y, follows the lognormal distribution if its natural logarithm (ln Y) is normally distributed. Three important features differentiate the lognormal distribution from the normal distribution:

1. It is bounded by zero on the lower end.
2. The upper end of its range is unbounded.
3. It is skewed to the right (positively skewed).

The lognormal distribution is frequently used to model the distribution of asset prices because it is bounded on the left by zero.

Discretely compounded returns are based on discrete or defined compounding periods, such as 12 months or 6 months. As the compounding periods get shorter and shorter, the effective annual rate (EAR) rises. With continuous compounding, the effective annual rate is given as:

$$EAR = e^{r_{cc}} - 1 \qquad r_{cc} = \text{continuously compounded annual rate}$$

The expression for calculating the continuously compounded rate, r_{cc}, is given as:

$$r_{cc} = \ln(\text{EAR} + 1)$$

Simulation

Monte Carlo simulation generates random numbers and operator inputs to synthetically create probability distributions for variables. It is used to calculate expected values and dispersion measures for random variables, which are then used for statistical inferences.

Investment Applications

- To experiment with a proposed policy before actually implementing it.
- To provide a probability distribution to estimate investment risk.
- To provide expected values of investments that can be difficult to price.
- To test models and investment tools and strategies.

Limitations

- Answers are as good as the assumptions and model used.
- Does not provide cause-and-effect relationships.

Historical simulation assumes that the distribution of the random variable going forward depends on its distribution in the past. This method of forecasting has an advantage, in that the distribution of risk factors does not need to be estimated. However, it faces the following limitations:

- A risk factor that was not represented in historical data will not be considered in the simulation.
- It does not facilitate "what if" analysis if the "if" factor has not occurred in the past. Monte Carlo simulation can be used for "what if" analysis.
- It assumes that the future will be similar to the past.
- It does not provide any cause-and-effect relationship information.

SAMPLING AND ESTIMATION

Cross-Reference to CFA Institute Assigned Reading #11

- In a simple random sample, each member of the population has the same likelihood of being included in the sample.
- In systematic sampling, every *k*th member in the population is selected until the desired sample size is reached.
- Stratified random sampling: Stratification is the process of grouping members of the population into relatively homogeneous subgroups, or strata, before drawing samples. The strata should be mutually exclusive and collectively exhaustive. Random sampling is applied within each stratum and the size of the sample from each stratum is based on the size of the stratum relative to the population. This often improves the *representativeness* of the sample by reducing sampling error.

QM

Sampling error is the difference between a sample statistic and the corresponding population parameter.

Sampling error of the mean = sample mean – population mean = $\bar{x} - \mu$

Time-Series versus Cross-Sectional Data

- Time-series data consists of observations measured over a period of time, spaced at uniform intervals. The monthly returns on a particular stock over the last 5 years are an example of time-series data.
- Cross-sectional data refers to data collected by observing many subjects (such as individuals, firms or countries/regions) at the same point in time. The returns of individual stocks over the last years are examples of cross-sectional data.

Longitudinal versus Panel Data

- Longitudinal data refers to data collected over time about multiple characteristics of the same observational unit. The various economic indicators—unemployment levels, inflation, and GDP growth rates (multiple characteristics) of a particular country (observational unit) over a decade (period of time) are examples of longitudinal data.
- Panel data refers to data collected over a time about a single characteristic of multiple observational units. The unemployment rate (single characteristic) of a number of countries (multiple observational units) over a time are examples of panel data.

The Central Limit Theorem

The important properties of the central limit theorem are:

- Given a population with *any* probability distribution, with mean, μ, and variance, σ^2, the sampling distribution of the sample mean x, computed from sample size *n* will approximately be *normal* with mean, μ (the population mean), and variance,

σ^2/n (population variance divided by sample size), when the sample size is greater than or equal to 30.

- No matter what the distribution of the population, for a sample whose size is greater than or equal to 30, the sample mean will be normally distributed.

$$\bar{x} \sim N\left(\mu, \frac{\sigma^2}{n}\right)$$

- The mean of the population (m) and the mean of the distribution of sample means are equal.
- The variance of the distribution of sample means equals σ^2/n, or population variance divided by sample size.

Standard Error of Sample Mean

The standard deviation of the distribution of sample means is known as the **standard error** of the statistic (σ_x).

When the population variance is known, the standard error of sample mean is calculated as:

$$\sigma_{\bar{x}} = \sigma / \sqrt{n}$$

Practically speaking, population variances are almost never known, so we estimate the standard error of the sample mean using the sample's standard deviation.

$$s_{\bar{x}} = \frac{s}{\sqrt{n}}$$

Point Estimates versus Confidence Intervals

A point estimate involves the use of sample data to calculate a single value that serves as an approximation for an unknown population parameter. For example, the sample mean, x, is a point estimate of the population mean, μ.

A confidence interval uses sample data to calculate a range of possible (or probable) values that an unknown population parameter can take, with a given probability of $(1-\alpha)$. α is called the level of significance, and $(1-\alpha)$ refers to the degree of confidence that the relevant parameter will lie in the computed interval. For example, a calculated interval between 100 and 150, at the 5% significance level, implies that we can be 95% confident that the population parameter lies between 100 and 150.

A (1-α)% confidence interval has the following structure:

Point estimate ± (reliability factor × standard error)

Desirable Properties of an Estimator

- Unbiasedness.
- Efficiency.
- Consistency.

QM

Characteristics of Student's t-Distribution

- It is symmetrical.
- It is defined by a single parameter, the degrees of freedom, (df), where degrees of freedom equal sample size minus one (n-1).
- It has a lower peak than the normal curve, but fatter tails.
- As the degrees of freedom increase, the shape of the t-distribution approaches the shape of the standard normal curve.

As the degrees of freedom increase, the t-distribution curve becomes more peaked and its tails become thinner (bringing it closer to a normal curve). Therefore, the confidence interval for a random variable that follows the t-distribution will become narrower when the degrees of freedom increase for a given significance level.

The t-distribution is used in the following scenarios:

- It is used to construct confidence intervals of a normally (or approximately normally) distributed population whose variance is *unknown* when the sample size is small ($n < 30$).
- It may also be used for a non-normally distributed population whose variance is unknown if the sample size is large ($n \geq 30$).

When the population is *normally* distributed we:

- Use the z-statistic when the population variance is known.
- Use the t-statistic when the population variance is not known.

When the distribution of the population is *nonnormal* the construction of an appropriate confidence interval depends on the size of the sample:

- If the population variance is known and the sample size is large we use the z-statistic. This is because the central limit theorem tells us that the distribution of the sample mean is approximately normal when sample size is large.
- If the population variance is not known and sample size is large, we can use the z-statistic or the t-statistic. However, in this scenario the use of the t-statistic is encouraged because it results in a more conservative measure.
- This implies that we cannot construct confidence intervals for nonnormal distributions if sample size is less than 30.

When Sampling from a:	Small Sample n < 30	Large Sample n > 30
Normal distribution with known variance	z-statistic	z-statistic
Normal distribution with unknown variance	t-statistic	t-statistic*
Non-normal distribution with known variance	not available	z-statistic
Non-normal distribution with unknown variance	not available	t-statistic*
* *Use of z-statistic is also acceptable*		

Sample Biases

Data-Mining Bias

Data mining is the practice of extensively searching through a data set for statistically significant relationships till a pattern "that works" is discovered. In the process of data mining, large numbers of hypotheses about a single data set are tested in a very short time by searching for combinations of variables that might show a correlation.

Warning signs that data mining bias might exist are:

- Too much digging warning sign.
- No story, no future warning sign.

The best way to avoid data-mining bias is to test the "apparently statistically significant relationships" on "out-of-sample" data to check whether they hold.

Sample Selection Bias

Sample selection bias results from the exclusion of certain assets from a study due to the unavailability of data.

Some databases use historical information and may suffer from a type of sample selection bias known as **survivorship bias**. Databases that only list companies or funds currently in existence suffer from this bias.

Look-Ahead Bias

An analyst may not have complete information at the time of testing. Look-ahead bias arises if the analyst uses an assumed figure instead. The actual figure may be different from the one used in the study.

Time-Period Bias

Time-period bias arises if the sample data is drawn from a certain time period. The results obtained from the study of such a data set will be time-specific.

QM

HYPOTHESIS TESTING

Cross-Reference to CFA Institute Assigned Reading #12

Steps in Hypothesis Testing

- State the hypothesis.
- Select the appropriate test-statistic.
- Specify the level of significance.
- State the decision rules.
- Calculate the sample statistic.
- Make a decision regarding the validity of the hypothesis.

Null versus Alternative Hypotheses

- The null hypothesis (H_0) generally represents the status quo, and is the hypothesis that we are *interested in rejecting*. This hypothesis will not be rejected unless the sample data provides sufficient evidence to suggest otherwise.
- The alternate hypothesis (H_A) is the statement that will only be accepted if the sample data provides convincing evidence of its truth. It is the conclusion of the test if the null hypothesis is rejected. *The alternate hypothesis is essentially the statement whose validity we are tying to evaluate.*

One-Tailed versus Two-Tailed Tests

Under one-tailed tests, we assess whether the value of the population parameter is either *greater than, or less than* a given hypothesized value. Hypotheses for one-tailed hypotheses tests are structured as:

- $H_0 : \mu \leq \mu_0$ versus $H_a : \mu > \mu_0$; when determining whether the population mean is *greater* than a hypothesized value.
- $H_0 : \mu \geq \mu_0$ versus $H_a : \mu < \mu_0$; when determining whether the population mean is *less* than a hypothesized value.

The following rejection rules apply when we are trying to determine whether the population mean is *greater* than the hypothesized value.

When we want to ascertain whether the population mean is *greater* than the hypothesized mean, we compare the test statistic to the *positive* critical value.

- Reject H_0 when:
  Test statistic > positive critical value
- Fail to reject H_0 when:
  Test statistic ≤ positive critical value

The following rejection rules apply when we are trying to determine whether the population mean is *lower* than the hypothesized value.

- Reject H_0 when:
  Test statistic < negative critical value
- Fail to reject H_0 when:
  Test statistic ≥ negative critical value

When we want to ascertain whether the population mean is *less* than the hypothesized mean, we compare the test statistic to the *negative* critical value.

Under two-tailed tests, we assess whether the value of the population parameter is *simply different from* a given hypothesized value. Hypotheses for two-tailed hypotheses tests are structured as:

$$H_0 : \mu = \mu_0$$
$$H_a : \mu \neq \mu_0$$

The following rejection rules apply for two-tailed hypothesis test

- Reject H_0 when:
  Test statistic < lower critical value
  Test statistic > upper critical value
- Fail to reject H_0 when:
  Lower critical value ≤ test statistic ≤ Upper critical value

Type I versus Type II Errors

- Type I error: Rejecting the null when it is actually true.
- Type II error: Not rejecting the null when it is actually false.

The significance level (α) represents the probability of making a Type I error. A significance level of 5% means that there is a 5% chance of rejecting the null when it is actually true.

If we were to fail to reject the null hypothesis given the lack of overwhelming evidence in favor of the alternate, we risk a Type II error- *failing to reject the null hypothesis when it is false.*

Sample size and the choice of significance level (probability of Type I error) together determine the probability of a Type II error.

The power of a test is the probability of *correctly* rejecting the null hypothesis when it is false.

$$\text{Power of a test} = 1 - P(\text{Type II error})$$

Errors in Hypothesis Testing

Decision	H_0 is true	H_0 is false
Do not reject H_0	Correct decision	Incorrect decision **Type II error**
Reject H_0	Incorrect decision **Type I error** Significance level (α)	Correct decision Power of the test = 1-P(Type II error)

- The *higher* the power of the test, the *better* is it for purposes of hypothesis testing.
- An *increase* in the power of a test comes at the cost of *increasing* the probability of a Type I error.
- The only way to *decrease* the probability of a Type II error given the significance level is to *increase the sample size.*

Confidence Intervals versus Hypothesis Tests

- In a confidence interval we state that the population parameter lies within the interval, which represents the "fail-to-reject-the-null region" with a (1– α) level of confidence.
- In a hypothesis test, we examine whether the population parameter lies in the rejection region, or outside the interval, at the α level of significance.

P-Values and Hypothesis Tests

The p-value is the smallest level of significance at which the null hypothesis can be rejected. It is the probability of obtaining a critical value that would lead to the rejection of the null hypothesis.

- If the p-value is *less* than the required level of significance, we can *reject* the null hypothesis.
- If the p-value is *greater* then the required level of significance, we *fail to reject* the null hypothesis.

Hypothesis Tests Concerning a Single Mean

The t-test is used when the variance of the population is unknown *and* either of the conditions below hold:

- The sample size is large.
- The sample is small, but the underlying population is normally distributed or approximately normally distributed.

Summary of Hypothesis Tests on the Mean of a Single Population

Type of test	Null hypothesis	Alternate hypothesis	Reject null if	Fail to reject null if	P-value represents
One-tailed (upper tail)	$H_0 : \mu \leq \mu_0$	$H_a : \mu > \mu_0$	Test statistic > critical value	Test statistic ≤ critical value	Probability that lies above the computed test statistic.
One-tailed (lower tail)	$H_0 : \mu \geq \mu_0$	$H_a : \mu < \mu_0$	Test statistic < critical value	Test statistic ≥ critical value	Probability that lies below the computed test statistic.
Two-tailed	$H_0 : \mu = \mu_0$	$H_a : \mu \neq \mu_0$	Test statistic < Lower critical value Test statistic > Upper critical value	Lower critical value ≤ test statistic ≤ Upper critical value	Probability that lies above the positive value of the computed test statistic *plus* the probability that lies below the negative value of the computed test statistic.

The t-statistic for hypothesis test concerning the mean of a single population is:

$$\text{t-stat} = \frac{\bar{x} - \mu_0}{s/\sqrt{n}}$$

In a t-test, the sample's t-statistic is compared to the critical t-value with degrees of freedom (n-1) at the desired level of significance.

The z-test is used to conduct hypothesis tests of the population mean when the population is normally distributed and its variance is known.

$$\text{z-stat} = \frac{\bar{x} - \mu_0}{\sigma/\sqrt{n}}$$

The z-test can also be used when the population's variance is unknown, but the sample size is large.

$$\text{z-stat} = \frac{\bar{x} - \mu_0}{s/\sqrt{n}}$$

QM

In a z-test, the z-statistic is compared to the critical z-value at the given level of significance.

Hypothesis Tests Concerning the Mean of Two Populations

Population distribution	Relationship between samples	Assumption regarding variance	Type of test
Normal	Independent	Equal	t-test with pooled variance
Normal	Independent	Unequal	t-test with variance not pooled
Normal	Dependent	N/A	t-test with paired comparisons

Hypothesis Tests Concerning the Variance

Hypothesis tests for the variance of a normally distributed population involve the use of the chi-square distribution where the test statistic is denoted as χ^2. Three important features of the chi-square distribution are:

- It is asymmetrical.
- It is bounded by zero. Chi-square values cannot be negative.
- It approaches the normal distribution in shape as degrees of freedom increase.

The chi-square test statistic with n-1 degrees of freedom is calculated as:

$$\chi^2 = \frac{(n-1)s^2}{\sigma_0^2}$$

Hypotheses related to the equality of the variance of two populations are tested with an F-test. This test is used under the assumptions that:

- The populations from which samples are drawn are normally distributed.
- The samples are independent.

The test statistic for the F-test is given by:

$$F = \frac{s_1^2}{s_2^2}$$

Features of the F-distribution:

- It is skewed to the right.
- It is bounded by zero on the left.
- It is defined by two separate degrees of freedom.

The rejection region for any F-test, whether it be one-tailed or two-tailed, always lies in the right tail. This unique feature makes the F-test different from other hypothesis tests.

Hypothesis Test Concerning	Appropriate test statistic
Variance of a single, normally distributed population	Chi-square stat
Equality of variance of two independent, normally distributed populations	F-stat

Parametric versus Nonparametric Tests

A parametric test has at least one of the following two characteristics:

- It is concerned with parameters, or defining features, of a distribution.
- It makes a definite set of assumptions.

A non-parametric test is not concerned with a parameter, and makes only a minimal set of assumptions regarding the population. Non-parametric tests are used when:

- The researcher is concerned about quantities other than the parameters of the distribution.
- The assumptions made by parametric tests cannot be supported.
- When the data available is ranked. For example, non-parametric methods are widely used for studying populations such as movie reviews that receive one to five stars based on people's preferences.

The Spearman rank correlation coefficient is calculated on the ranks of two variables within their respective samples.

Statistically versus Economically Meaningful Results

Even though a trading strategy that is being studied provides a statistically significant return of greater than zero (based on the hypothesis test) it does not guarantee that trading on this strategy would result in economically meaningful returns. The returns may not be economically significant after accounting for taxes, transaction costs and risks inherented in the strategy.

TECHNICAL ANALYSIS

Cross-Reference to CFA Institute Assigned Reading #13

Technical analysis is a security analysis technique that involves the examination of past market trends (using data such as prices and trading volumes) to predict the future behavior of the overall market and of individual securities.

Technical analysis is based on the following:

- Supply and demand determine prices in real time.
- Changes in supply and demand cause changes in prices.
- Prices can be projected with charts and other technical tools.

Principles and Assumptions

- Technicians suggest that market trends and patterns reflect irrational human behavior.
- Technicians believe that the market reflects collective investor knowledge and sentiment.
- Technical analysis is the only tool available to investors to forecast future prices for assets that do not have underlying financial statements or associated income streams.
- Technicians believe that security price movements occur before fundamental developments occur or are reported.

Technical versus Fundamental Analysis

- Technical analysis uses only trading data, which includes market price and volume information. Fundamental analysis uses external information (e.g., financial reports, industry and macroeconomic analysis) and also incorporates social and political variables.
- The data used by technical analysts is more concrete and reliable. The financial statements used by fundamental analysts are subject to manipulation by management.
- Fundamental analysis is more conceptual as it aims to determine the theoretical long-term (intrinsic) value of a security. Technical analysis is more practical as it studies actual trading patterns to evaluate the market price of a security.
- Technical analysis has been in use for a longer period in investment decision-making. Fundamental analysis is a relatively new field.

Drawbacks of Technical Analysis

- Technicians only study market movements and trends, which can change without warning. Further, it may take some time for a clear, identifiable trend to emerge.
- Technicians expect trends to repeat themselves so a change in investor psychology may be missed by them.
- Application of technical analysis is limited in markets that are subject to significant outside manipulation and in illiquid markets.

Construction and Interpretation of Technical Analysis Charts

Charts

Charts are used to illustrate historical price information, which is used by technicians to infer future price behavior. The choice of charts is governed by the purpose of the analysis.

Line Charts

- A line chart is a simple graphical display of prices over time.
- Charts plot closing prices as data points, and have a line connecting these points.
- Time is plotted on the horizontal axis and prices are plotted on the vertical axis.
- Line charts provide a broad overview of investor sentiment, and the information they provide can be analyzed quickly.

Bar Charts

- A bar chart presents four pieces of information- opening price, highest and lowest prices and the closing price for each time interval.
- A short bar indicates low price volatility, while a longer bar indicates high price volatility.
- For each time interval, the top of the line shows the highest price, while the bottom of the line shows the lowest price. The cross-hatch to the left indicates the opening price, while the cross-hatch to the right indicates the closing price.

Candlestick Charts

- A candlestick chart provides the opening and closing prices, and highs and lows during the period.
- Further, it also clearly illustrates whether the market closed up or down.
- The body of the candle is shaded if the closing price was lower than the opening price, and the body is clear if the closing price was higher than the opening price.

Point and Figure Chart

To construct a point and figure chart, a box size and a reversal size must first be determined.

- The box size refers to the minimum change in price that will be represented by a box on the chart.
- The reversal size determines when a new column will be created on the chart.
- The vertical axis measures discrete movements in price.
- Box and figure charts are useful as they highlight the prices at which trends change (when the columns change), as well as price levels at which the security most frequently trades (congestion areas).

Scale

The vertical axis on a charts can be constructed with a linear (arithmetic) scale or a logarithmic scale.

- A linear scale is more appropriate when the data fluctuate within a narrow range.
- In a logarithmic scale, percentage changes are plotted on the vertical axis. They are more appropriate when the range of data is larger.
- Time is plotted on the horizontal axis.

Volume

Volume is used by technicians as a barometer of the strength of a trend.

- If a security's price is increasing with increasing volumes, it shows that more and more investors are purchasing the stock at higher prices. This indicates that the trend is expected to continue as the two indicators "confirm" each other.
- If a security's price is rising with declining volumes (the two indicators are diverging), it suggests that the trend is losing momentum as fewer investors are willing to buy at higher prices.

Time Intervals

Short term investors may create charts with intervals less than a minute long, while longer term investors may use charts with intervals as long as one year.

Relative Strength Analysis

Relative strength analysis is used to evaluate the relative performance of a security compared to a stated benchmark by plotting the ratio of the security's price to the benchmark index over time.

- An upward-sloping line indicates outperformance.
- A downward-sloping line suggests underperformance.

Trend, Support, Resistance Lines, and Changes in Polarity

Trend analysis assumes that investors tend to behave in herds and that trends usually continue for an extended period of time.

An uptrend occurs when a security's price makes higher highs and higher lows.

- Higher highs occur when each high lies above the previous high, and when the price declines (there is a retracement) each subsequent low is higher than the prior low.
- To illustrate an uptrend, the technician connects all the lows on the price chart with a straight line.
- Major retracements (that drag the security's price significantly below the trend line) indicate that the uptrend is over and that the price may decline further.
- There are more ready buyers for a security than there are sellers and traders are willing to pay a higher price for the security over time.

A downtrend is indicated by lower highs and lower lows on the price chart.

- A technician connects all the highs on the chart to illustrate the downtrend.
- Major breakouts above the trend line may indicate that the downtrend is over and that the security's price could rise further.
- In a downtrend, sellers are willing to accept lower and lower prices for the security, which indicates negative investor sentiment regarding the asset.

During a sideways trend, there is a relative balance between demand and supply.

- Typically, options positions are more profitable than long or short positions on the security itself during a sideways trend.

Trend analysis involves the use of support and resistance levels.

- A support level is defined as the price at which there is sufficient buying interest in the stock to arrest the price decline.
- A resistance level is the price at which enough selling activity is generated to prevent any further increase in price.

Support and resistance levels may be horizontal or sloped lines.

The change in polarity principle asserts that once the price rises above the resistance level, it becomes the new support level. Similarly, once the price falls below a support level, it becomes the new resistance level.

Chart Patterns

Chart patterns are formations on price charts that look like recognizable shapes. Recurring chart patterns can be used to predict future prices because these patterns essentially represent collective investor sentiment over a given time period.

Reversal Patterns

Reversal patterns indicate the end of a prevailing trend.

Head and Shoulders

A head and shoulders pattern follows an uptrend in the price of a security. It is composed of three parts:

Left shoulder: The left shoulder consists of a strong rally with high volumes.
Head: The price starts to rise again, and this time records a higher high than the one reached in the left shoulder. However, volumes in this rally are lower.
Right shoulder: The right shoulder is similar to the left shoulder, but with lower volumes.

Note that the neckline may not always be a perfectly horizontal line.

Volume is very important in analyzing head and shoulders patterns. The fact that the high of the "head" is higher than the "high" of the left shoulder, but has lower volumes indicates that investor interest is waning.

When one indicator is bullish (rising price) while another is bearish (lower volumes) it is known as a **divergence**.

- Once a head and shoulders pattern has formed, prices are expected to decline (the uptrend that preceded the head and shoulders pattern is expected to reverse).
- Once the price falls below the neckline (which previously acted as a support level), it becomes the new resistance level (change in polarity principle).

Inverse Head and Shoulders

- A downtrend in prices precedes an inverse head and shoulders pattern.
- The price characteristics of each of the three segments of the head and shoulders pattern are reversed in an inverse head and shoulders pattern, but the volume characteristics are the same.

Setting Price Targets with Head and Shoulders Patterns

Once the neckline has been breached in the head and shoulders pattern, the price is expected to decline by an amount equal to the distance between the top of the head and the neckline.

$$\text{Price target} = \text{Neckline} - (\text{Head} - \text{Neckline})$$

Typically, the stronger the rally preceding the head and shoulders pattern, the more pronounced the expected reversal.

Setting Price Targets for Inverse Head and Shoulders Patterns

Inverse head and shoulders patterns are preceded by a downtrend. Therefore, prices are expected to rise or break out above the neckline after the right shoulder has been formed.

Price target = Neckline + (Neckline – Head)

Double Tops and Bottoms

A double top occurs when an uptrend in prices reverses twice at approximately the same price level (two highs are recorded at roughly the same level). Usually, the first top has a higher volume.

For a double top, the price target (where the reversal will end) is established at a level that is lower than the valley (the low recorded between the two tops) by an amount that equals the distance between the tops and the valley.

The more significant the sell-off after the first top (deeper the valley) and the longer the time period between the two tops, the more significant the formation is considered to be.

A double bottom indicates the reversal of a downtrend. It occurs when, following a recent downtrend, prices fall to a certain level, rise for a bit, then fall back to the same level and rise again.

For double bottoms, the price is expected to rise above the peak between the two bottoms by approximately an amount equal to the distance between the bottoms and the peak.

Triple Tops and Bottoms

A triple top consists of three peaks at roughly the same level, while a triple bottom occurs when three troughs are formed at roughly the same price level.

- Triple tops and bottoms are rare, but when they occur, they indicate more significant reversals than double tops and double bottoms.
- Generally speaking, the greater the number of times the price reverses at a given price level, and the longer the period over which the pattern is formed, the more significant the expected reversal.

QM

Continuation Patterns

A continuation pattern is used to confirm the resumption of the current market trend.

Triangle Patterns

A triangle pattern is formed when the range between highs and lows over a period narrows down on the price chart. The line connecting the highs over the period eventually meets the line connecting the lows, forming a triangle.

An ascending triangle is formed when the trend line connecting the highs is horizontal while the trend line connecting the lows is upward-sloping.

- Ascending triangles form during an uptrend.
- Eventually the share price is expected to rise.

A descending triangle suggests that the stock price will continue to decline.

- The line connecting the highs is downward-sloping, while the line connecting the lows is horizontal.

In a symmetrical triangle, the line connecting the highs is downward-sloping, while the line connecting the lows is upward-sloping.

- Such a formation suggests that buyers are becoming more bullish as they continue to buy at higher prices than before, but sellers are becoming increasingly bearish as they sell at successively lower prices.
- After the formation, the trend ends up in the same direction as the trend that preceded the triangle formation.

More about Triangle Patterns

- The height of the triangle (also known as **measuring implication**) equals the distance between the two trend lines at the start of the formation.
- Once the price breaks through one of the trend lines, analysts expect the price to move further by roughly the measuring implication.
- Usually, the breakout from the triangle occurs between halfway and three-fourths of the way into the pattern; not at the end of the pattern.
- The longer the triangle pattern, the more significant and volatile the subsequent price movement is expected to be.

Rectangle Patterns

When the two trend lines (one that connects the highs and the other that connects the lows) are both horizontal, a rectangle pattern is formed. Once a breakout occurs, the trend in prices is the same as the trend that preceded the rectangle formation.

Flags and Pennants

Flags and pennants form over a much shorter time interval (usually on a daily price chart over a week) compared to triangles and rectangle patterns.

A flag is formed when two trend lines are parallel to each other (similar to country flags or parallelograms).

- Typically, the slope of the trend lines is opposite to that of the prevailing trend.

A pennant is basically a triangle that is formed over a relatively short span of time (typically over a week).

- For both flags and pennants, the expectation is that the trend that preceded the formation will continue after the pattern.
- The breakout beyond the trend line is expected to roughly equal the distance between the start of the trend and the flag or the pennant.

Common Technical Analysis Indicators

Price-Based Indicators

Price-based technical indicators incorporate current and historical market price information.

Moving Average

A moving average is the average of the closing price over a given number of periods. Moving averages smooth out short term price fluctuations and therefore, give a clearer picture of a market trend.

- A simple moving average uses the arithmetic mean, weighing each price equally in computing the average.
- An exponential moving average attaches a greater weight to recent prices in computing the average.

Applications of Moving Averages

- Generally, a stock that is in a downtrend tends to trade below its moving average, while one in an upward trend will typically trade above its moving average.
- Moving average trend lines can also act as support or resistance levels.
- When the short term moving average intersects the long term moving average from below, the formation is referred to as a *golden cross* and is a bullish sign.
- When the short term moving average intersects the long term moving average from above, it forms a *dead cross* which is a bearish signal.

Bollinger Bands

Bollinger bands consist of a simple moving average plus upper and lower bands that are calculated by adding and subtracting a specific number of standard deviations from the moving average.

Applications of Bollinger Bands

- A contrarian technical strategy based on Bollinger bands aims to sell the security when it reaches the upper band and purchase the security when it touches the lower band. The assumption here is that the security will continue to trade within the bands.
- A long-term investor may purchase the security once it has broken out significantly above the upper band, or short the security once it has fallen significantly below the lower band.

Momentum Oscillators

Momentum oscillators are used to identify changes in market sentiment. They are calculated in such a manner that they either fluctuate within a range (usually between 0 and 100) or hover around a number (such as 0 or 100).

- It is easy to identify extreme highs and lows on oscillators, and these extremes indicate that market buying/selling activity is more aggressive than historical levels.
- Technicians focus on whether oscillators and price data are moving in the same direction (convergence) or in different directions (divergence).
- When the price forms a new low, but the momentum oscillator is not at its lowest, the formation is a divergence. It implies that the downtrend is weakening and is expected to end soon.

Applications of Momentum Oscillators

- The oscillator range for a security can be used to determine the strength of a trend. Oversold conditions suggest that bearish market sentiment will end soon, while overbought conditions signal that the bullish market sentiment may soon change.
- They may signal a trend reversal when they reach historical highs or lows.
- They can be used to make short-term trading decisions in non-trending markets.

Momentum or Rate of Change Oscillator

A momentum oscillator (rate of change (ROC) oscillator) is calculated as follows:

$$M = (V - Vx) \times 100$$

where:
M = momentum oscillator value
V = last closing price
V*x* = closing price *x* days ago, typically 10 days

- When the momentum oscillator value crosses zero into positive territory in an uptrend (when prices are also rising) it is a bullish signal.
- When it crosses zero into negative territory in a downtrend (when prices are falling), it is a bearish signal.
- Crossovers that occur in the opposite direction of the trend are ignored because technicians who use oscillators first consider the general trend when making trading decisions.

The base value for an oscillator can also be set at 100. In this case, the oscillator is calculated as:

$$M = \frac{V}{Vx} \times 100$$

Relative Strength Index

A relative strength index (RSI) compares a security's gains with its losses over a given time period.

$$RSI = 100 - \frac{100}{1 + RS}$$

$$\text{where } RS = \frac{\Sigma \text{ (Up changes for the period under consideration)}}{\Sigma \text{ (|Down changes for the period under consideration|)}}$$

- The RSI lies between the 0 and 100.
- A value above 70 typically represents an overbought situation, while a value below 30 usually indicates an oversold situation.
- Less volatile stocks may trade in a narrower range.
- The RSI range for any stock does not need to be symmetrical around 50.

QM

Stochastic Oscillator

A stochastic oscillator is based on the assumption that in an uptrend, the stock price tends to close near the high of its recent range, while in a downtrend it tends to close around its recent low.

The stochastic oscillator lies between 0 and 100 and is usually calculated using 14-day price data. It is composed of two lines, %K and %D.

$$\%K = 100\left(\frac{C - L14}{H14 - L14}\right)$$

where:
C = last closing price
L14 = lowest price in last 14 days
H14 = highest price in last 14 days

%D (signal line) = Average of the last three %K values calculated daily.

Applications of Stochastic Oscillators

- Generally speaking, when the stochastic oscillator is greater than 80, it usually indicates that the security is overbought and should be sold. A value lower than 20 indicates that the security is oversold and should be purchased. However, analysts should consider the absolute level of the two lines in light of their historical range.
- Crossovers between the two lines can also give trading signals similar to crossovers of moving average lines. When the %K (smoothed line) crosses %D from below, it is a short-term bullish signal, and if it crosses %D from above, it is a bearish signal.

Moving Average Convergence/Divergence Oscillator

The moving average convergence/divergence oscillator (MACD) is the difference between the short term and long term moving average of a security's price. The MACD is composed of two lines:

- The MACD line, which is the difference between two exponentially smoothed moving average lines (typically over 12 and 26 days).
- The signal line, which is the exponentially smoothed moving average of the MACD line (typically over 9 days).

The MACD is compared with its historical levels to determine whether market sentiment regarding the security is different from what it usually is. The indicator itself moves around 0 and has no limits.

Applications of the MACD Oscillator

- Crossovers of the MACD line and the signal line may indicate a change in trend (similar to crossovers of moving averages and the stochastic oscillator).
- When MACD line moves outside its historical range, it indicates a weakening in the current trend.
- Convergence (which suggests that the trend will continue) occurs when the MACD and price move in the same direction, while divergence (which suggests that the trend will reverse) occurs when the MACD and price move in opposite directions.

Sentiment Indicators

Sentiment indicators evaluate investor activity looking for signs of bullishness or bearishness.

Opinion Polls

A number of companies conduct regular polls of investors and investment professionals to gauge market sentiment. Technicians compare the data (which is also presented graphically) with recent market highs, lows and inflection points to establish relationships that might be useful in predicting future market direction.

Calculated Statistical Indices

- A high **put-call ratio** indicates that the market is bearish, while a low ratio suggests that the market is bullish.
- The **VIX** rises when investors fear a market decline.
- **Margin debt levels** are very strongly correlated with the movement in the market.
- The **short interest ratio** may be interpreted in two ways. A high ratio may suggest that:
  - There is overall a negative outlook on the security and one should expect the price to decline.
  - The effect of short sales has already been factored into the current market price. When these short sellers cover their positions, the price of the stock will rise.

Flow of Funds Indicators

Technicians also look at the potential demand and supply for securities in making trading decisions.

Arms Index

$$\text{Arms Index} = \frac{\text{Number of advancing issues / Number of declining issues}}{\text{Volume of advancing issues / Volume of declining issues}}$$

- When the market is in balance, the arms index is close to 1.
- Values above 1 indicate that there is more activity in declining stocks, and that the market is in a selling mood.
- Values below 1 indicate that there is more activity in advancing stocks and that market sentiment is currently bullish.

Margin Debt

Margin loans may increase stock purchases, while declining margin balances may force the selling of stocks.

Mutual Fund Cash Positions

- Contrarians buy when mutual funds' cash positions are high and sell when their cash positions are low.
- The average cash percentage of mutual funds has historically hovered around 6.8%.

New Equity Issuance

When the new equity issuance indicator is high, the market is usually near its peak and is likely to decline in the future.

Secondary Offerings

While these offerings do not increase the number of shares outstanding, they do increase the number of shares available for trading (the free float). Therefore, secondary offerings affect the supply of shares just like IPOs.

Cycles

Over time, technicians have observed recurring cycles in the markets, only some of which can be logically explained. By identifying different cycles, technicians look to predict the market's future direction.

Kondratieff Waves

Nikolai Kondratieff suggested that economies went through a 54-year economic cycle. His theory was mainly derived from economic cycles and commodity prices, but similar cycles have also been seen in equity prices during the time of his work.

18-year cycle

The 18-year cycle is usually mentioned in real estate markets though it can also be observed in equities and other markets.

Decennial Pattern

The decennial pattern traces the average annual stock returns (based on the DJIA) according to the last digit of the year. The DJIA has historically performed poorly in years ending with a 0, while the best ones have been years that end with a 5.

Presidential Cycle

Historically, it has been observed that the third year (of the four-year U.S. Presidential term) boasts the best stock market performance. The stock market has done reasonably well in the fourth year as well. One explanation for this is that politicians up for re-election inject stimuli into the economy to increase their popularity.

Elliott Wave Theory and Fibonacci numbers

Elliott Wave Theory

In 1938, R. N. Elliott proposed that the market moves in regular cycles or waves.

- In a bull market, the market moves up in five waves (called **impulse waves**) in the following pattern: 1 = up, 2 = down, 3 = up, 4 = down and 5 = up.
- The impulse wave is followed by a corrective wave that has three components: a = down, b = up and c = down.
- The same pattern is reversed in a bear market.
- Each wave can be broken into smaller waves. Starting with the largest "grand supercycle" which takes place over centuries, waves can be broken down into supercycles, cycles, and subcycles which take place over shorter and shorter intervals.

> The Fibonacci Sequence starts with the numbers 0, 1, 1, and then each subsequent number in the sequence is the sum of the two preceding numbers: 0, 1, 1, 2, 3, 5, 8, 13, . . .

Elliot discovered that market waves followed patterns that were ratios of numbers in a **Fibonacci sequence**.

- Positive price movements would take prices up by a factor equal to the ratio of a Fibonacci number to its preceding number.
- Negative price movements would reverse prices by a factor of a Fibonacci number to the next number.
- Elliot wave theory is used along with Dow Theory, trend analysis, pattern analysis and oscillator analysis to forecast market movements.
- Its biggest advantage is that it can be applied in short-term trading as well as long-term economic analysis.

Intermarket Analysis

Intermarket analysis refers to the technique of combining analysis of different markets to identify trends and reversals of trends. It is based on the principle that markets for different categories of securities (stocks, bonds, currencies, commodities, etc.) are interrelated and influence each other, and asserts that these relationships are strengthening with increasing globalization. Some of the relationships that have been observed between different asset classes are:

- Stock prices and bond prices tend to move in the same direction. Therefore, rising bond prices are a positive for stocks.
- Declining bond prices are a signal of commodities prices possibly rising.
- A strong dollar usually results in lower commodity prices.

Applications of Intermarket Analysis

- Technicians often use relative strength analysis to identify **inflection points** in a particular market and then look for a change in trend in a related market.
- Given technical observations regarding the business cycle at any time, relative strength analysis can be used to identify potentially lucrative investments from within the equity market.
- Intermarket analysis can also be used to identify which countries one should invest in.

Study Session 4:
Economics—Microeconomics and Macroeconomics

EC

EC

TOPICS IN DEMAND AND SUPPLY ANALYSIS

Cross-Reference to CFA Institute Assigned Reading #14

Demand Concepts

Demand is defined as the willingness and ability of consumers to purchase a given amount of a good or a service at a particular price.

The law of demand states that as the price of a product increases, consumers will be willing and able to purchase less of it, and as the price decreases, they will be willing and able to purchase more of it (i.e., price and quantity demanded are inversely related).

The **demand function** uses quantity demanded as the dependent variable in capturing the relationship between own-price and quantity demanded. The **inverse demand function** makes price the dependent variable in capturing the relationship between own-price and quantity demanded. The **demand curve** is based on the inverse demand function.

The slope of the demand curve equals the coefficient on quantity demanded in the inverse demand function. The slope of the demand curve is also the reciprocal of the coefficient on own-price in the demand function.

Changes in Demand versus Movements along the Demand Curve

- When own-price changes, there is a **movement along the demand curve** or a change in quantity demanded.
- When there is a change in anything else that affects demand (i.e., a change in any of the factors assumed constant in the demand function), there is a **shift in the demand curve** (because the intercept term in the inverse demand function changes) or a change in demand.

Demand Elasticities

The own-price elasticity of demand is calculated as:

$$ED_{Px} = \frac{\%\Delta QD_x}{\%\Delta P_x}$$

$$ED_{Px} = \frac{\%\Delta QD_x}{\%\Delta P_x} = \frac{\Delta QD_x / QD_x}{\Delta P_x / P_x} = \left(\frac{\Delta QD_x}{\Delta P_x}\right)\left(\frac{P_x}{QD_x}\right)$$

Slope of demand function

Coefficient on own-price in market demand function

We look at the absolute value of own-price elasticity of demand when classifying how sensitive quantity demanded is to changes in price:

- If own-price elasticity of demand equals 1, demand is said to be unit elastic.
- If own-price elasticity of demand equals 0, demand is said to be perfectly inelastic.
- If own-price elasticity of demand equals ∞, demand is said to be perfectly elastic.
- If the absolute value of price elasticity of demand lies between 0 and 1, demand is said to be relatively inelastic.
- If the absolute value of price elasticity of demand is greater than 1, demand is said to be relatively elastic.

While the slope of the demand curve remains constant along a downward-sloping linear demand curve, the ratio of price to quantity is different at each point along the demand curve (unless the demand curve is perfectly elastic or perfectly inelastic).

- At relatively low prices (relatively high quantities), the ratio of price to quantity is relatively low so own-price elasticity of demand (absolute value of ED_P) is low and demand is relatively inelastic.
- At relatively high prices (relatively low quantities), the ratio of price to quantity is relatively high so own-price elasticity of demand (absolute value of ED_P) is high and demand is relatively elastic.
- Demand is unit elastic at the midpoint of the demand curve, relatively elastic above the midpoint, and relatively inelastic below the midpoint.

Factors That Affect Price Elasticity of Demand

Availability of close substitutes: If a consumer can *easily* switch away from a good, her ability to respond to a price increase (by reducing consumption of the good) is *high*, and demand for that product would be *relatively elastic.*

Proportion of income spent on the good: If a relatively *small* proportion of a consumer's income is spent on a good (e.g., soap), she will not significantly cut down on consumption if prices increase. Demand for such a good will be *relatively inelastic*.

Time elapsed since price change: The *longer* the time that has elapsed since the price change, the *more elastic* demand will be.

The extent to which the good is viewed as necessary or optional: The *more* the good is seen as being necessary, the *less elastic* its demand is likely to be.

Own-Price Elasticity of Demand and Total Expenditure/Total Revenue

- If demand is relatively elastic, a decrease in price will result in an increase in total expenditure, and an increase in price will result in a decrease in total expenditure.
- If demand is relatively inelastic, a decrease in price will result in a decrease in total expenditure, and an increase in price will result in an increase in total expenditure.
- If demand is unit elastic, a decrease or an increase in price will result in no change in total expenditure.

Total Expenditure/Revenue Test

- If the price cut *increases* total revenue, demand is relatively elastic.
- If the price cut *decreases* total revenue, demand is relatively inelastic.
- If the price cut *does not change* total revenue, demand is unit elastic.

Total Revenue and Price Elasticity

- If the demand curve facing a producer is relatively elastic, an *increase* in price will *decrease* total revenue.
- If the demand curve facing a producer is relatively inelastic, an *increase* in price will *increase* total revenue.
- If the demand curve facing a producer is unit elastic, an *increase* in price will *not change* total revenue.

Note that no producer would knowingly set a price that falls in the inelastic region of the demand curve.

Income Elasticity of Demand

Income elasticity of demand measures the responsiveness of demand for a particular good to a change in income, holding all other things constant.

$$ED_I = \frac{\%\Delta QD_x}{\%\Delta I} = \frac{\Delta QD_x / QD_x}{\Delta I / I} = \left(\frac{\Delta QD_x}{\Delta I}\right)\left(\frac{I}{QD_x}\right)$$

$$E_I = \frac{\%\text{ change in quantity demanded}}{\%\text{ change in income}}$$

If income elasticity is *greater* than 1, demand is income elastic, and the product is classified as a *normal good*.

- As income *rises*, the percentage increase in demand *exceeds* the percentage change in income.
- As income *increases*, a consumer spends a *higher proportion* of her income on the product.

If income elasticity lies *between* zero and 1, demand is income inelastic, but the product is still classified as a *normal good*.

- As income *rises*, the percentage increase in demand is *less* than the percentage increase in income.
- As income *increases*, a consumer spends a *lower proportion* of her income on the product.

If income elasticity is *less* than zero (negative), the product is classified as an *inferior good*.

- As income *rises*, there is a *negative* change in demand.
- As income *increases*, the amount spent on the good *decreases.*

When income changes, there is a shift in the demand curve (change in demand).

Cross-Price Elasticity of Demand

Cross elasticity of demand measures the responsiveness of demand for a particular good to a change in price of *another* good, holding all other things constant.

$$ED_{Py} = \frac{\%\Delta QD_x}{\%\Delta P_y} = \frac{\Delta QD_x / QD_x}{\Delta P_y / P_y} = \left(\frac{\Delta QD_x}{\Delta P_y}\right)\left(\frac{P_y}{QD_x}\right)$$

$$E_C = \frac{\text{\% change in quantity demanded}}{\text{\% change in price of substitute or complement}}$$

EC

For **substitutes**, the numerator and denominator of the cross elasticity formula head in the *same* direction. Therefore, cross elasticity of demand for substitutes is *positive.*

- *A high* value for cross elasticity indicates that the two products are very *close* substitutes.
- For substitutes, an increase in the price of another good results in an increase in demand (shift in demand to the right).

For **complements**, the numerator and denominator of the cross elasticity formula head in *opposite* directions. If the price of one good increases, demand for the other falls. Therefore, the cross elasticity of demand for complements is *negative*.

- A *high* absolute value for cross elasticity indicates that the two products are very *close* complements.
- For complements, an increase in price of another good results in a decrease in demand (shift in demand to the left).

Substitution and Income Effects

The law of demand states that when the price of a good falls, quantity demanded increases, and when the price rises, quantity demanded decreases. There are two main reasons for this:

The substitution effect: If the good becomes cheaper compared to other goods, more of the good gets substituted for other goods in the consumer's consumption basket. The substitution effect always goes in the opposite direction of the price change.

The income effect: If the consumer's real income increases (in terms of the quantity of goods and services that can be purchased with the same dollar income), then, if the good is a normal good (which most goods are), the increase in real income (due to the decrease in its price) leads to an increase in quantity purchased.

Normal Goods

For **normal goods** (e.g., restaurant meals, which most people tend to buy more of when their incomes rise), the substitution and the income effects reinforce one another.

Inferior Goods

If a good is an **inferior good**:

- The substitution effect of a change in price will be the same as for a normal good (i.e., a decrease in price of the good will cause the consumer to buy more of the good).
- However, the income effect will be the opposite of what it is for a normal good. For an inferior good, the increase in real income resulting from a decline in the good's price will cause the consumer to buy less of this good.

Overall, for an inferior good (e.g., margarine, which most people buy less of as their incomes rise), the income effect mitigates the substitution effect of a price change.

Note that:

- The substitution effect of a change in the price will always go in the direction opposite to that of the price change. If the price increases, less will be consumed, and if the price decreases, more will be consumed.
- The income effect of that same price change, however, depends on whether the good is normal or inferior.
    - For a normal good, the income effect reinforces the substitution effect, both leading to a negatively sloped demand curve.
    - For an inferior good, the income effect and the substitution effect work in opposite directions.

Giffen and Veblen Goods

For Giffen goods and Veblen goods, the demand curve is actually upward sloping.

A **Giffen good** is a special case of an inferior good where the negative income effect of a decrease in price of the good is so strong that it outweighs the positive substitution effect. Therefore, for a Giffen good, quantity demanded actually falls when there is a decrease in price, which makes the demand curve upward sloping.

Note the following:

- All Giffen goods are inferior goods because the income effect and substitution effect work in opposite directions.
- However, not all inferior goods are Giffen goods.
    - For inferior goods, the income effect partially mitigates or offsets the substitution effect.
    - For Giffen goods, the income effect outweighs the substitution effect.

With status goods such as expensive jewelry, the high price itself adds to the utility from the good, such that the consumer values the item more if it has a higher price. Such goods are known as **Veblen goods**.

Giffen Goods versus Veblen Goods

- Giffen goods **are inferior goods**. They are not status goods. An increase in income would reduce demand for them (due to negative income elasticity of demand).
- Veblen goods **are not inferior goods**. An increase in income would not lead to a decrease in demand.

Supply Analysis: The Firm

EC

Short Run versus Long Run

- In the **short run**, at least one factor of production is fixed. Usually we assume that labor is the only variable factor of production in the short run.
- In the **long run**, quantities of all factors of production can be varied.

Total, Average, and Marginal Product of Labor

Total product (TP) is the maximum output that a given quantity of labor can produce when working with a fixed quantity of capital units.

- TP provides insight into the company's size relative to the overall industry.
- It does not show how efficient the firm is in producing its output.
- In the initial stages, total product *increases at an increasing rate*. Later, as more units of labor are employed to work with the fixed quantity of capital, total output *increases at a decreasing rate*, and the slope of the TP curve becomes *flatter*.

Marginal product (MP) (also known as marginal return) equals the increase in total product brought about by hiring one more unit of labor, while holding quantities of all other factors of production constant.

- MP measures the productivity of the individual additional unit of labor.

Average product (AP) equals the total product of labor divided by the quantity of labor units employed.

- AP is a measure of overall labor productivity.
- The lower a firm's AP, the more efficient it is.

Relationship between MP and AP

- MP intersects AP from *above* through the *maximum point* of AP.
- When MP is *above* AP, AP *rises*, and when MP is *below* AP, AP *falls*.

Note the following:

- Total product is simply an indication of a firm's output volume and potential market share.
- Average product and marginal product are better measures of productivity, as they can reveal competitive advantage through production efficiency.
- Average product is the preferred measure of productivity when workers perform tasks collectively, as in that case individual worker productivity is not easily measurable.

Breakeven and Shutdown Analysis

Accounting Profit versus Economic Profit

Accounting profit (also known as **net profit**, **net income**, and **net earnings**) equals revenue less all accounting (or explicit) costs. Accounting costs are payments to nonowner parties for goods and services supplied to the firm, and do not necessarily require a cash outlay.

Accounting profit (loss) = Total revenue – Total accounting costs

Economic profit (also known as **abnormal profit** or **supernormal profit**) is calculated as revenue less all economic costs (economic costs include explicit and implicit costs). Alternatively, economic profit can be calculated as accounting profit less all implicit opportunity costs that are not included in total accounting costs.

Economic profit = Total revenue – Total economic costs

Economic profit = Total revenue – (Explicit costs + Implicit costs)

Economic profit = Accounting profit – Total implicit opportunity costs

Normal profit is the level of accounting profit that is required to cover the implicit opportunity costs that are not included in accounting costs.

Accounting profit = Economic profit + Normal profit

EC

Note that:

- When accounting profit equals normal profit, economic profit equals 0.
- When accounting profit is greater than normal profit, economic profit is positive.
- When accounting profit is less than normal profit, economic profit is negative.

Total, Average, and Marginal Revenue

Revenue	Calculation
Total revenue (TR)	Price times quantity (P × Q), or the sum of individual units sold times their respective prices; Σ(Pi × Qi)
Average revenue (AR)	Total revenue divided by quantity; (TR/Q)
Marginal revenue (MR)	Change in total revenue divided by change in quantity; (ΔTR/ΔQ)

The Demand Curve in Perfect and Imperfect Competition

- In **perfect competition**, each individual firm faces a perfectly elastic demand curve (i.e., it can sell as many units of output as it desires at the given market price).
- In **imperfect competition**, the firm has at least some control over the price at which it sells its output. The demand curve facing the firm is downward sloping, so in order to increase units sold the firm must lower its price.

EC

Total, Average, and Marginal Revenue under Perfect Competition

- MR always equals AR, and they both equal market price.
- If there is an increase in market demand, the market price increases, which results in both MR and AR shifting up and TR pivoting upward as well.

Total, Average, and Marginal Revenue under Imperfect Competition

- As quantity increases, the rate of increase in TR (as measured by MR) decreases.
- AR equals price at each output level.
- MR is also downward sloping, with a slope that is steeper than that of AR (demand).
- TR reaches its maximum point when MR equals 0.

Note that MR equals price plus Q multiplied by the slope of the demand curve.

$$MR = P + Q(\Delta P/\Delta Q) \text{ or } MR = P + Q * \text{Slope of demand curve}$$

- Under perfect competition, the slope of the demand curve is zero. Therefore, MR = P
- Under imperfect competition, the slope of the demand curve is negative. As a result, MR is less than price.

Total, Average, Marginal, Fixed, and Variable Costs

Cost	Calculation
Total fixed cost (TFC)	Sum of all fixed expenses, here defined to include all opportunity costs
Total variable cost (TVC)	Sum of all variable expenses, or per unit variable cost times quantity; (per unit VC × Q)
Total cost (TC)	Total fixed cost plus total variable cost; (TFC + TVC)
Average fixed cost (AFC)	Total fixed cost divided by quantity; (TFC/Q)
Average variable cost (AVC)	Total variable cost divided by quantity; (TVC/Q)
Average total cost (ATC)	Total cost divided by quantity; (TC/Q) or (AFC + AVC)
Marginal cost (MC)	Change in total cost divided by change in quantity; (ΔTC/ΔQ)

Characteristics of Total Cost Curves

- TC and TVC increase at a decreasing rate at low levels of output, and increase at an increasing rate at higher levels of output.
- The difference between TC and TVC equals TFC.

Characteristics of Average Cost Curves

- As output levels rise, AFC continues to fall at a decreasing rate as total fixed costs are spread over more and more units.
- The ATC curve is U-shaped. It falls initially as fixed costs are spread over an increasing number of units. Later, however, the effect of a falling AFC is offset by diminishing marginal returns (increasing AVC) so ATC starts rising.
- The vertical distance between the AVC and ATC curves equals AFC. The vertical distance between the AVC and ATC curves gets smaller as output increases.

Average Cost and Marginal Cost Curves

- MC intersects ATC and AVC from *below* at their respective *minimum* points.
- When MC lies below AVC, AVC falls, and when MC lies above AVC, AVC rises.
- When MC lies below ATC, ATC falls, and when MC lies above ATC, ATC rises.

Short-Run Marginal Cost (SMC) versus Long-Run Marginal Cost (LMC)

- SMC is the additional cost of the variable input (labor) that must be incurred to increase the level of output by one unit.
- LMC is the additional cost of all inputs necessary to increase the level of output, allowing the firm the flexibility of changing both labor and capital inputs in a way that maximizes efficiency.

Marginal Product and Marginal Cost Curves

- A firm's MP curve is linked to its MC curve. Initially, as more labor is hired, MP rises and MC falls.
- At the point where MP reaches its maximum, MC stands at its minimum.
- As output expands further, MP falls and MC rises.

Average Product and Average Variable Cost Curves

- A firm's AP curve is linked to its AVC curve. Initially, as the firm hires more labor, AP rises and AVC falls.
- At the point where AP reaches its maximum, AVC is at its minimum.
- As the firm increases output further, AP falls and AVC rises.

EC

Costs are directly related to input prices and inversely related to productivity.

- If the wage rate were to rise, costs would also rise, but if labor productivity were to improve, costs would fall. This relationship can be captured by the expression: $MC = w/MP_L$.
- Similarly, if wages rise, AVC also rises, but if labor productivity were to improve, AVC would fall. Therefore, $AVC = w/AP_L$.
- As the firm benefits from increasing marginal returns, MP_L increases and MC declines. However, as more and more labor is added to a fixed amount of capital, diminishing marginal returns set in and MP_L falls, causing MC to rise.

Marginal Revenue, Marginal Cost, and Profit Maximization

Profits are maximized when the difference between TR and TC is at its highest. The level of output at which this occurs is the point where (1) marginal revenue equals marginal cost (MC = MR), and (2) MC is not falling.

- When MR > MC, the firm should increase production, as the last unit produced added more to revenue that it did to costs.
- When MR < MC, the firm should reduce production, as the last unit produced added more to costs than it did to revenue.
- Recall that $MC = w/MP_L$, so if MC is falling, MP would be rising. If an additional unit of labor causes MC to fall, the firm would want to add that unit of labor until MC is upward sloping.

Perfect Competition

- The firm's profit-maximizing quantity is the output level where MR (which equals P and AR) equals MC while MC is rising. If P is greater than ATC, the firm makes economic profits. Economic profits are possible in perfect competition only in the short run. In the long run, more firms will enter the industry, taking market prices down to a level where they equal ATC.

Monopoly

- A monopoly faces a downward-sloping demand curve. As a result, the MR and demand curves are not identical. The profit-maximizing level of output occurs at the point where MC equals MR while MC is rising. Once the profit-maximizing level of output has been determined, the optimal price is obtained from the demand curve. If P is greater than ATC, the monopolist earns positive economic profits, and these can continue in the long run due to high barriers to entry.

Breakeven Analysis

A firm is said to break even if its TR equals its TC. At the breakeven quantity of production, price (or AR) equals ATC. This is true under both perfect and imperfect competition. Breaking even implies that the firm is covering all its economic costs (total accounting costs and implicit opportunity costs), so, while it is not earning positive economic profits, the firm is at least covering the opportunity cost of all its factors of production, including capital. In other words, the firm is earning **normal profit**.

The Shutdown Decision

- At price levels below AVC, the firm will not be willing to produce, as continued production would only extend losses beyond simply total fixed costs.
- When price lies between AVC and ATC, the firm will remain in production in the short run, as it meets all variable costs and covers a portion of its fixed costs.
- To remain in business in the long run, the firm must break even or cover all costs (revenues should meet total costs).
- Once prices exceed ATC, the firm makes economic profits.

Short-Run and Long-Run Operating Decisions

Revenue-Cost Relationship	Short-Run Decision	Long-Run Decision
TR = TC	Continue to operate	Continue to operate
TR = TVC but TR < TC	Continue to operate	Exit market
TR < TVC	Shut down	Exit market

Economies and Diseconomies of Scale

A company's **production function** shows how different quantities of labor and capital affect total product.

- Short-run ATC curves are U-shaped.
- The larger the plant, the greater the output at which short-run ATC is at its minimum.

The **long-run average cost (LRAC)** curve illustrates the relationship between average total cost and output when all factors of production are variable. The LRAC curve is also known as a *planning curve* because it shows the expected per-unit cost of producing various levels of output using different combinations of factors of production.

- **Economies of scale** occur in the downward-sloping region of the LRAC curve. They result from mass production and specialization of labor.
- **Diseconomies of scale** occur in the upward-sloping region of the LRAC curve. They result from bureaucratic inefficiencies as effective management, supervision, and communication become difficult.
- In the horizontal portion of the LRAC curve, when an increase in production does not result in any change in average costs, a firm realizes **constant returns to scale**.

Also, note that:

- The **minimum efficient scale** is the smallest quantity of output at which long-run average cost reaches its lowest level.
- In the long run, all firms in perfect competition operate at their minimum efficient scale, as price equals minimum average cost.

THE FIRM AND MARKET STRUCTURES

Cross-Reference to CFA Institute Assigned Reading #15

PERFECT COMPETITION

Characteristics

- There are a large number of buyers and sellers.
- Each seller offers an identical product for sale.
- There are minimal barriers to entry.
- Sellers have no pricing power.
- There is no non-price competition in the market.

Demand in a Perfectly Competitive Market

- The market demand curve is downward sloping.
- The relationship between MR and price elasticity can be expressed as:

$$MR = P[1-(1/E_P)]$$

Optimal Price and Output in Perfectly Competitive Markets

Each firm in perfect competition is very small compared to the size of the overall market. The actions of any firm do not impact market equilibrium. Each firm can sell as much output as it desires at the equilibrium market price.

- Therefore, the demand curve faced by an individual firm is perfectly elastic (horizontal).

Average revenue equals price and marginal revenue. AR = P = MR

The law of diminishing marginal returns dictates the "U" shape of SR cost curves.

Firms always maximize profits at the point where MC equals MR.

- Total revenue equals price times quantity sold.
- Total cost equals AC times quantity sold.
- The positive (negative) difference between the two equals economic profit (loss).
- If the two are equal, the firm only makes normal profit.

In the short run, a firm in perfect competition can make economic profits, economic losses or normal profit.

- In each scenario the firm produces the output level at which MC equals MR.
- Whether it makes a profit or a loss depends on the position of the demand curve relative to its average cost at the profit-maximizing quantity.
- If $P > AC \Rightarrow$ Economic profit
- If $P = AC \Rightarrow$ Normal profit
- If $P < AC \Rightarrow$ Economic loss

In the long run, all firms in perfect competition will only make normal profit.

- In the LR, MC = MR = P = AR = min AC

Schumpeter's take on Perfect Competition

Joseph Schumpeter suggested that perfect competition is more of a long-run type of market structure. In the short run, companies develop new products or processes that give them an edge over competitors but in the long run, as competitors adopt those new products, perfect competition prevails.

MONOPOLY

Characteristics

- There is a single seller of a highly differentiated product, which has no close substitutes.
- There are high barriers to entry.
- The firm has considerable pricing power.
- The product is differentiated through non-price strategies (e.g., advertising).

Factors that Give Rise to Monopolies

- Control over critical sources of production
- Patents or copyrights
- Non-price differentiation leading to pricing-power.
- Network effects, which result from synergies related to increasing market penetration
- Government-controlled authorization.

Demand Analysis in Monopoly Markets

The demand curve faced by the monopoly is effectively the industry demand curve. It is downward-sloping.

- The AR curve is the same as the demand curve.
- The MR curve and the demand curve have the same y-intercept.
- The slope of the MR curve is two times the slope of the demand curve.
- The x-intercept of the MR curve is half of that of the demand curve.
- The MR curve is the derivative of the TR curve with respect to quantity sold.

Supply Analysis in Monopoly Markets

- The monopolist does not have a well-defined supply function that determines optimal price and output.
- The profit-maximizing output level occurs at the point where MR = MC.
- The price is determined from the demand curve (based on the profit-maximizing quantity).

Optimal Price and Output in Monopoly Markets

The profit-maximizing output level equals the quantity at which:

- MC = MR; and
- Profit is unaffected by changes in quantity: $\Delta\pi/\Delta Q_D = 0$

The profit-maximizing level of output always occurs in the relatively elastic portion of the demand curve. Given its cost structure and price elasticity of demand, a monopoly can use the following equation to determine the profit maximizing price.

$$P[1-(1/E_P)] = MC$$

Natural Monopolies

A natural monopoly is an industry where the supplier's average cost is still falling even when it satisfies total market demand entirely on its own.

Regulation of Natural Monopolies

- Marginal cost pricing forces a monopoly to charge a price that equals its marginal cost of production. Under marginal cost pricing, the monopoly makes an economic loss, which the government must subsidize. Alternatively the government may allow the monopoly to discriminate on prices or to engage in two-part pricing to offset losses. Marginal cost pricing is also known as efficient regulation.
- Average cost pricing forces a monopoly to charge a price that equals its average cost of production. This allows the monopoly to earn normal profits.

Price Discrimination and Consumer Surplus

First-degree price discrimination occurs when a monopolist is able to charge each individual consumer the highest price that she is willing and able to pay.

Under perfect price discrimination:

- The MR curve equals the demand curve.
- The profit maximizing level of output increases.
- The entire consumer surplus is eaten up by the producer.
- There is no dead weight loss.
- The more perfectly a monopolist can price discriminate, the more "efficient" the outcome.

In **second-degree price discrimination**, the monopolist offers a variety of quantity-based pricing options that induce customers to self-select based on how highly they value the product (e.g., volume discounts, product bundling).

EC

Third-degree price discrimination can occur when customers can be separated by geographical or other traits. One set of customers is charged a higher price, while the other is charged a lower price (e.g., airlines charge higher fares on one day roundtrip tickets as they are more likely to be purchased by business people).

Factors Affecting Long Run Equilibrium in Monopoly Markets

An unregulated monopoly can earn economic profits in the long run as it is protected by substantial barriers to entry.

For regulated monopolies, such as natural monopolies there are various solutions:

- A marginal cost pricing structure. However, the firm must be provided a subsidy in this scenario.
- An average cost pricing structure.
- National ownership of the monopoly.
- Franchising the monopoly via a bidding war (e.g., selling retail space at railway stations and airports).

MONOPOLISTIC COMPETITION

Characteristics

- There are a large number of buyers and sellers.
- The products offered by each seller are similar, but not identical. They serve as close substitutes to each other.
- Firms try to differentiate their product from the competition through advertising and other non-price strategies.
- There are low barriers to entry and exit.
- Firms have some degree of pricing power.

Demand and Supply Analysis in Monopolistically Competitive Markets

Demand:

- Each firm faces a downward sloping demand curve.
- Demand is relatively elastic at higher prices and relatively inelastic at lower prices.

Supply:

- There is no well-defined supply function.
- Neither the MC nor the AC curve represent the firm's supply curve.
- The firm will always produce at the output level where MC = MR.
- The price that is charged is derived from the market demand curve.

Short Run versus Long Run Equilibrium

- In the short run, a firm in monopolistic competition produces the output level where MC equals MR, and charges the maximum possible price that buyers are willing to pay for its product (determined by the demand curve).
- In the long run, firms in the industry make normal profits, there is no incentive for new firms to enter, or for existing firms to exit the industry.

Monopolistic Competition versus Perfect Competition

- A firm in monopolistic competition generally produces *lower* output and charges a *higher* price than in perfect competition. In perfect competition, price *equals* marginal cost, while in monopolistic competition, price *exceeds* marginal cost. This excess of price over marginal cost is known as *markup.*
- For a firm in monopolistic competition, in the long run, the profit maximizing output level occurs at a point where demand is tangent to the average cost curve, but at a stage where average costs are *still falling.* In perfect competition in the long run, each firm produces an output level where average cost is at its *minimum,* or at its efficient scale of production. Firms under monopolistic competition therefore, have *excess capacity.*

However, monopolistic competition enjoys some support because it offers consumers options to choose from. Product innovation, advertising and brand building are crucial to a firm's success in monopolistic competition.

OLIGOPOLY

Characteristics

- There are a small number of sellers.
- The products offered by sellers are close substitutes for each other. Products may be differentiated by brand (e.g., Coke® and Pepsi®) or be homogenous (e.g., oil).
- There are high costs of entry and significant barriers to competition.
- Firms enjoy substantial pricing power.
- Products are often differentiated on the basis of quality, features, marketing and other non-price strategies.

Demand Analysis and Pricing Strategies in Oligopoly Markets

Pricing interdependence (kinked demand curve model): The demand curve has two contrasting shapes. It is relatively elastic above current prices, and relatively inelastic below current prices This results in a kink in the firm's demand curve and a break in its marginal revenue curve. This break in the MR curve implies that it would take a significant change in costs of production to change the firm's profit-maximizing output level.

The Cournot assumption asserts that each firm determines its profit-maximizing level assuming that other firms' output will not change. In equilibrium, no firm has an incentive to change output. In the long run, prices and output are stable i.e., there is no possible change in output or price that would make any firm better off.

Game theory: Nash equilibrium is achieved when none of the firms in an oligopoly market can increase profits by unilaterally changing its price. Each firm tries to maximize its own profits given the responses of its rivals. Each firm anticipates how its rival will respond to a change in its strategy and tries to maximize its profits under the forecasted scenario. As a result, the firms in the market are interdependent, but their actions are non-cooperative: firms do not collude to maximize profits.

The Stackelberg model (also known as the dominant firm model) assumes that decision-making is sequential. The leader or dominant firm determines its profit-maximizing level of output, the price is determined from the demand curve for its product (the dominant firm is the price-maker) and then each of the follower firms determine their quantities based on the given market price (they are price-takers).

Factors Affecting Chances of Successful Collusion

- There are fewer firms in the industry or if one firm is dominant. Collusion becomes difficult as competition between firms in the industry increases.
- The firms produce similar products.
- The firms have similar cost structures.
- Order size is small and orders are received more frequently.
- There is minimal threat of retaliation from other firms in the industry.
- There is minimal external competition.

Supply Analysis in Oligopoly Markets

- The supply function for a firm in an oligopoly is not well-defined because optimal quantity and price depend on the actions of rival firms.
- The firm produces where MC = MR.
- Equilibrium price comes from the demand curve.

Optimal Price and Output in Oligopoly Markets

There is no single optimal price and output that fits all oligopoly market situations.

- In the kinked demand curve model, the optimal price is the prevailing price (at which the demand curve kinks).
- In the dominant firm model, the leader produces an output level where MC = MR. Followers have little or no power to influence price.
- In the Cournot assumption, each firm assumes that rivals will have no response to any actions on their part. Each firm produces where MC = MR.
- In Nash equilibrium, firms continue to respond to changing circumstances with the aim of maximizing their own profit. Since there is significant interdependence between firms, there is no certainty regarding an individual firm's price and output.

Identification of Market Structure

Econometric Approaches: Estimate the price elasticity of market demand based on time series analysis or cross sectional regression analysis.

N-firm concentration ratio: Computes the aggregate market share of the *N* largest firms in the industry.

- It does not quantify market power.
- It is unaffected by mergers in the top tier.

Herfindahl-Hirschman Index (HHI): Adds up the squares of the market shares of each of the largest *N* companies in the market.

- The HHI equals 1 for a monopoly.
- If there are *M* firms in the industry with equal market shares, the HHI will equal $1/M$.
- Does not account for the possibility of entry, nor does it consider the elasticity of demand. However, it is more useful than the concentration ratio.

AGGREGATE OUTPUT, PRICE, AND ECONOMIC GROWTH
Cross-Reference to CFA Institute Assigned Reading #16

Aggregate output refers to the total value of all the goods and services produced in an economy over a period of time.

Aggregate income refers to the total value of all payments earned by the suppliers of factors of production in an economy over a period of time.

Aggregate expenditure refers to the total amount spent on the goods and services produced in the domestic economy over a period of time.

Gross Domestic Product (GDP)

- Output definition: GDP is the market value of all final goods and services produced within an economy over a period of time.
- Income definition: GDP is the aggregate income earned by all households, companies, and the government in an economy over a period of time.

Criteria for Inclusion in GDP

- Only goods and services produced *during* the measurement period are included.
    - Transfer payments and income from capital gains are excluded.
- Only goods and services whose value can be determined by being sold in the market are included.
    - The value of labor used in activities that are not sold in the market is excluded.
    - By-products of production processes which have no explicit market value are not included.
    - Activities in the underground economy are not included.
    - Barter transactions are not included.
- Only the value of *final* goods and services is included in the calculation of GDP. The value of intermediate goods (that are resold to produce another good) is excluded because the entire value added during the production process is reflected in the selling price of the final good produced (value-of-final-output). GDP can also be measured by summing the value added at each stage of the production and distribution processes (sum-of-value-added).

Nominal versus Real GDP

Nominal GDP = Quantity produced in Year t × Prices in Year t

Real GDP = Quantity produced in Year t × Base-year prices

GDP Deflator

The GDP deflator broadly measures the aggregate change in prices across the overall economy. Changes in the GDP deflator provide a useful measure of inflation.

$$\text{GDP deflator} = \frac{\text{Value of current year output at current year prices}}{\text{Value of current year output at base year prices}} \times 100$$

$$\text{GDP deflator} = \frac{\text{Nominal GDP}}{\text{Real GDP}} \times 100$$

The Components of GDP

$$\text{GDP} = C + I + G + (X - M)$$

Expenditure Approach

GDP = Consumer spending on goods and services
+ Business gross fixed investment
+ Change in inventories
+ Government spending on goods and services
+ Government gross fixed investment
+ Exports – Imports
+ Statistical discrepancy

Income Approach

GDP = National income + Capital consumption allowance
+ Statistical discrepancy

GDP-Related Measures

National income equals the sum of incomes received by all factors of production used to generate final output. It includes:

- Employee compensation
- Corporate and government enterprise profits before taxes
    - Dividends paid to households
    - Corporate profits retained by businesses
    - Corporate taxes paid to the government
- Interest income
- Rent and unincorporated business net income (proprietor's income)
- Indirect business taxes less subsidies

The **capital consumption allowance (CCA)** accounts for the wear and tear or depreciation that occurs in capital stock during the production process. It represents the amount that must be reinvested by the company in the business to maintain current productivity levels. You should think of profits + CCA as the amount earned by capital.

Personal income measures the ability of households to make purchases and includes all income received by households, regardless of whether it is **earned** or **unearned**. It differs from national income in the following respects:

- National income includes income that goes to businesses and the government (e.g., indirect business taxes, corporate income taxes and retained earnings), which personal income does not.
- National income does not include household income that is not earned (e.g., transfer payments).

Personal income = National income
– Indirect business taxes
– Corporate income taxes
– Undistributed corporate profits
+ Transfer payments

Personal disposable income measures the amount of income that households have left to spend or to save after paying taxes.

Personal disposable income = Personal income – Personal taxes

Personal disposable income = Household consumption + Household saving

Household saving = Personal disposable income
– Consumption expenditures
– Interest paid by consumers to businesses
– Personal transfer payments to foreigners

Business sector saving = Undistributed corporate profits
+ Capital consumption allowance

The Equality of Expenditure and Income

$$S = I + (G - T) + (X - M)$$

Based on this equation we can say that domestic private saving can be used for:

- Investment spending (I);
- Financing government deficits (G – T); and/or
- Building up financial claims against overseas economies by financing their trade deficits (lending the domestic economy's trade surplus, X – M).
- If an economy has a negative trade balance, foreign savings will supplement domestic savings and foreigners will build up financial claims against the domestic economy.
- If the government runs a fiscal surplus, the surplus will add to domestic savings.

$$(G - T) = (S - I) - (X - M)$$

A fiscal deficit occurs when government expenditures exceed net taxes, i.e., $G - T > 0$. In order to finance a fiscal deficit:

- The private sector must save more than it invests ($S > I$); and/or
- The country's imports must exceed its exports ($M > X \Rightarrow$ trade deficit) with a corresponding inflow of foreign saving.

EC

Generating the Aggregate Demand Curve

The **aggregate demand (AD)** curve shows the combinations of aggregate income and price level at which the following conditions are satisfied:

- Planned expenditures equal actual (or realized) income/output
- There is equilibrium in the money market

The first condition gives rise to the **IS curve**, while the second gives rise to the **LM curve**. By combining the IS and LM curves, we obtain the **aggregate demand curve**.

Deriving the IS Curve: Relationship between Income and the Real Interest Rate

- Consumption varies positively with income, but negatively with taxes.
- Investment expenditure varies positively with income, and negatively with real interest rates.
- Government expenditure does not vary with income. Taxes vary positively with income. Therefore, the government's fiscal balance varies negatively with income.
- Net exports vary negatively with income, and negatively with domestic price levels.

$$S - I = (G - T) + (X - M)$$

- The fiscal balance (G – T) and the trade balance (X – M) **decline** as income rises.
- The saving-investment differential (S – I), **increases** as income increases.

The point of intersection between these two lines defines the point where aggregate expenditure and aggregate income are equal.

Changes in the level of real interest rates (r) cause shifts in the line representing the saving-investment differential. If the real interest rate falls (rises) the point of intersection between the (S – I) and the (G – T) + (X – M) curves occurs at a higher (lower) level of income.

This **inverse relationship between income and the real interest rate** referred to as the **IS curve**.

The LM Curve

The LM curve shows the combinations of interest rates and real income for which the money market is in equilibrium. Equilibrium in the money market requires that real money demand (M_D/P) equals real money supply (M/P).

EC

Demand for real money (RM_D or M_D/P) is a positive function of real income and a negative function of interest rates. Given the real money supply, an **increase** in real income (which would lead to an increase in real money demand) must be accompanied by an **increase** in interest rates (which would lead to a decrease in real money demand) so that demand for real money remains the same and equilibrium in the money market is maintained.

Therefore, if real money supply is held constant, we can infer a positive relationship between real income (Y) and the real interest rate (r). This **positive** relationship between real income and the real interest rate is illustrated by the **LM curve**.

Changes in real money supply cause shifts in the LM curve. If real money supply increases (decreases), the LM curve would shift to the right (left).

The Aggregate Demand Curve

If money supply is held constant, the only variable that affects real money supply is price. A **decrease** (increase) in the price level leads to an increase (decrease) in real money supply. The increase (decrease) in real money supply leads to a rightward (leftward) shift in the LM curve so the point of intersection of the IS and LM curves now occurs at a **higher** (lower) level if income.

The inverse relationship between the price level (P) and real income (Y) is captured by the **aggregate demand curve**. IS-LM analysis also suggests a positive relationship between the price level and real interest rates.

Slope of the AD Curve

The steepness of the slope of the AD curve depends on the relative sensitivities of investment, saving, and money demand to income and real interest rates. The AD curve will be flatter (small changes in price cause relatively large changes in quantity demanded) if:

- Investment expenditure is highly sensitive to the interest rate
- Saving is insensitive to income
- Money demand is insensitive to interest rates
- Money demand is insensitive to income

Interest Rates and Aggregate Demand

- If the increase in aggregate demand is caused by an increase in money supply, interest rates fall.
- If the increase in aggregate demand is caused by any other factor (with real money supply, M constant) interest rates will rise.

Aggregate Supply

Aggregate supply (AS) represents the quantities of goods and services that domestic producers are willing and able to supply at various price levels.

- The very short run aggregate supply curve is horizontal.
- The short run aggregate supply curve is upward-sloping.
- The long run aggregate supply curve is vertical.

In the long run, wages, prices and expectations can adjust but capital and technology remain fixed. This condition is relaxed in the very long run.

The LRAS curve basically defines the potential output of the economy. The potential output of any economy does not vary with the price level. When an economy operates at its potential output level, all its resources are fully employed and it is said to be working at full employment. At this output level, unemployment is at its natural rate.

- Structural unemployment results from structural changes in the economy, which make some skills obsolete and leave previously employed people jobless.
- Cyclical unemployment is the unemployment generated as an economy goes through the phases of a business cycle.

Short Run versus Long Run Equilibrium

- The point of intersection of the AD curve and the LRAS curve defines the economy's long run equilibrium position. At this point, actual real GDP equals potential GDP.

- The point of intersection of the AD curve and the SRAS curve defines the economy's short run equilibrium position. Short-run fluctuations in equilibrium real GDP may occur due to shifts in either or both the AD and SRAS curves. Short run equilibrium may be established at, below or above potential output. Deviations of short run equilibrium from potential output result in business cycles.
  - In an expansion, real GDP is increasing, the unemployment rate is falling and capacity utilization is rising. Further, inflation tends to rise during an expansion.
  - In a contraction, real GDP is decreasing, the unemployment rate is rising and capacity utilization is falling. Further, inflation tends to fall during a contraction.

Shift in Aggregate Demand

An Increase in the Following Factors	Shifts the AD Curve	Reason
Stock prices	Rightward: Increase in AD	Higher consumption
Housing prices	Rightward: Increase in AD	Higher consumption
Consumer confidence	Rightward: Increase in AD	Higher consumption
Business confidence	Rightward: Increase in AD	Higher investment
Capacity utilization	Rightward: Increase in AD	Higher investment
Government spending	Rightward: Increase in AD	Government spending a component of AD
Taxes	Leftward: Decrease in AD	Lower consumption and investment
Bank reserves	Rightward: Increase in AD	Lower interest rate, higher investment and possibly higher consumption
Exchange rate (foreign currency per unit domestic currency)	Leftward: Decrease in AD	Lower exports and higher imports
Global growth	Rightward: Increase in AD	Higher exports

EC

Shift in Aggregate Supply

An Increase in	Shifts SRAS	Shifts LRAS	Reason
Supply of labor	Rightward	Rightward	Increases resource base
Supply of natural resources	Rightward	Rightward	Increases resource base
Supply of human capital	Rightward	Rightward	Increases resource base
Supply of physical capital	Rightward	Rightward	Increases resource base
Productivity and technology	Rightward	Rightward	Improves efficiency of inputs
Nominal wages	Leftward	No impact	Increases labor cost
Input prices (e.g., energy)	Leftward	No impact	Increases cost of production
Expectation of future prices	Rightward	No impact	Anticipation of higher costs and/or perception of improved pricing power
Business taxes	Leftward	No impact	Increases cost of production
Subsidy	Rightward	No impact	Lowers cost of production
Exchange rate	Rightward	No impact	Lowers cost of production

Business Cycles

Fluctuations in aggregate demand and aggregate supply in the short run explain why short run real GDP deviates from potential GDP. These deviations of actual GDP from full-employment GDP form phases of the business cycle.

Investment Applications of an Increase in AD Resulting in an Inflationary Gap

If economic data suggest that the economy is undergoing an expansion caused by an increase in AD, going forward:

- Corporate profits will be expected to rise.
- Commodity prices will be expected to increase.
- Interest rates will be expected to rise.
- Inflationary pressures will build in the economy.

Therefore, investors should:

- Increase investments in cyclical companies as their earnings would rise significantly in this scenario.
- Increase investments in commodities and/or commodity oriented companies.
- Reduce investments in defensive companies as their profits would not rise as significantly as those of cyclical companies.
- Reduce investments in fixed-income securities (especially those with longer maturities) as their values would fall when interest rates go up.
- Increase investments in junk bonds as default risk (already factored into their prices) should fall in an expansion (and result in an increase in their prices).

Investment Applications of a Decrease in AD Resulting in a Deflationary Gap

If economic data suggest that the economy is undergoing a recession caused by a decrease in AD, going forward:

- Corporate profits will be expected to fall.
- Commodity prices will be expected to decline.
- Interest rates will be expected to fall.
- Demand for credit will decrease.

Therefore, investors should:

- Reduce investments in cyclical companies.
- Reduce investments in commodities and/or commodity oriented companies.
- Increase investments in defensive companies as their profits would decline modestly compared to cyclical companies.
- Increase investments in investment-grade or government-issued fixed-income securities as their values (particularly of those with longer maturities) will rise if interest rates go down.
- Decrease investments in junk bonds as default risk should rise in a recession (and result in a decrease in their prices).

Stagflation

Shifts in the SRAS curve (due to any of the factors discussed earlier in the reading) cause structural fluctuations in real GDP. A decrease in SRAS causes stagflation (high unemployment and higher inflation), while an increase in SRAS brings about economic growth and low inflation.

Investment Applications of a Shift in SRAS

If the SRAS curve shifts to the left (SRAS declines), investors may want to:

- Reduce investments in fixed-income securities because increasing output prices (inflation) may put an upward pressure on nominal interest rates (which would decrease the value of fixed income instruments).

- Reduce exposure to equities in anticipation of a decline in output and profit margins coming under pressure.
- Increase investments in commodities and/or commodity-oriented companies because their prices and profits are likely to rise (due to higher prices).

Conclusions on AD and AS

	Real GDP	Unemployment Rate	Aggregate Level of Prices
An increase in AD	Increases	Falls	Increases
A decrease in AD	Falls	Increases	Falls
An increase in AS	Increases	Falls	Falls
A decrease in AS	Falls	Increases	Increases

Effect of Combined Changes in AS and AD

Change in AS	Change in AD	Effect on Real GDP	Effect on Aggregate Price Level
Increase	Increase	Increase	Uncertain
Decrease	Decrease	Decrease	Uncertain
Increase	Decrease	Uncertain	Decrease
Decrease	Increase	Uncertain	Increase

EC

Economic Growth

Economic growth may be calculated as:

- The annual percentage change in real GDP, which tells us how rapidly the economy is expanding as a whole; or
- The annual change in real per capita GDP. Real GDP per capita is calculated as total real GDP divided by total population. It is a useful indicator of the standard of living in a country.

The Production Function and Potential GDP

The production function asserts that an increase in an economy's potential GDP can be caused by:

- An increase in the quantity of inputs used in the production process (e.g., capital and labor).
- An increase in the productivity of these inputs with the application of better technology. Improving technology enables an economy to produce more output using the same quantity of inputs.

Because of diminishing marginal returns to labor and capital, the only way to "sustain" growth in potential GDP is growth in total factor productivity.

The Growth Accounting Equation

Growth in potential GDP = Growth in technology + W_L(Growth in labor) + W_K(Growth in capital)

Growth in per capital potential GDP = Growth in technology + W_K(Growth in capital-labor ratio)

Takeaway: Advances in technology have a more significant impact on an economy's standard of living compared to capital.

Sources of Economic Growth

- Growth in labor supply
- Improvements in quality of human capital
- Growth in physical capital stock
- Improvements in technology
- Availability of natural resources

EC

Measures of Sustainable Growth

Labor productivity refers to the quantity of goods and services (real GDP) that a worker can produce in one hour of work.

Labor productivity = Real GDP/ Aggregate hours

Labor productivity depends on:

- Physical capital per worker (K/L) or the mix of inputs (which is easily calculated based on input data)
- Total factor productivity or technology (A). This is a scale factor and can be estimated based on output and input data.

Labor productivity is much easier to measure directly than growth in potential GDP. Labor productivity can explain differences in living standards and long term sustainable growth rates across countries.

Measuring Sustainable Growth

Potential GDP is a combination of aggregate hours and productivity of labor:

Potential GDP = Aggregate hours × Labor productivity

Potential GDP growth rate = Long-term growth rate of labor force
+ Long-term labor productivity growth rate

UNDERSTANDING BUSINESS CYCLES
Cross-Reference to CFA Institute Assigned Reading #17

Overview of Business Cycles

- Business cycles usually occur in economies that mainly rely on business enterprises (as opposed to agricultural or centrally planned economies).
- There is a sequence of distinct phases that comprise a business cycle. *See below*
- Almost all sectors of the economy undergo the phases of the business cycle at about the same time. Phases of the business cycle are not restricted to certain sectors.
- Business cycles are recurrent (they occur again and again), but they are not periodic (they do not always have the same intensity and/or duration).
- Business cycles typically last between 1 and 12 years.

Phases of the Business Cycle

- The trough is the lowest point of a business cycle as the economy comes out of a recession towards an expansion.
- An expansion occurs after the trough and before the peak. It is a period during which aggregate economic activity is increasing.
- The peak is the highest point of a business cycle as the expansion slows down and the economy moves towards a recession.
- A contraction (or recession) occurs after the peak. It is a period during which aggregate economic activity is declining. A particularly severe recession is known as a depression.

Describing Phases of the Business Cycle

	Early Expansion (Recovery)	Late Expansion	Peak	Contraction (Recession)
Economic Activity	Gross domestic (GDP), industrial production, and other measures of economic activity stabilize and then begin to increase.	Activity measures show an accelerating rate of growth.	Activity measures show decelerating rate of growth.	Activity measures show outright declines.
Employment	Layoffs slow but new hiring does not yet occur and the unemployment rate remains high. Business turns to overtime and temporary employees to meet rising product demands.	Business begins full time rehiring as overtime hours rise. The unemployment rate falls.	Business slows its rate of hiring. The unemployment rate continues to fall but at a decreasing rate.	Business first cuts hours and freezes hiring, followed by outright layoffs. The unemployment rate rises.
Consumer and Business Spending	Upturn in spending is often most pronounced in housing, durable consumer items, and orders for light producer equipment.	Upturn becomes more broad-based. Business begins to order heavy equipment and engage in construction.	Capital spending expands rapidly, but the growth rate of spending starts to slow down.	Decreased spending is most evident in industrial production, housing, consumer durable items, and orders for new business equipment.
Inflation	Inflation remains moderate and may continue to fall.	Inflation picks up modestly.	Inflation further accelerates.	Inflation decelerates but with a lag.

Fluctuations in Capital Spending over the Business Cycle

Changes in capital spending affect business cycles in three stages or phases:

Stage 1: Spending on equipment falls off abruptly at the onset of an economic slowdown.

Stage 2: In the initial stages of an economic recovery, orders begin to pick up (despite low capacity utilization levels).

Stage 3: Eventually, after an extended expansion, businesses are unable to meet consumer demand with existing capacity and therefore, look to expand.

Fluctuations in Inventory Levels over the Business Cycle

Stage 1: Typically, businesses are slow to cut back on production when the economy starts to slow down. This results in an involuntary build-up of inventories, and combined with a drop in sales, results in a sharp increase in the inventory-sales ratio.

Stage 2: As businesses continue to cut back on production (to get rid of excess inventories), the inventory-sales ratio approaches normal levels. However, businesses soon start to raise production (even though there is no apparent growth in sales) just to arrest the decline in inventory levels.

EC

Stage 3: During the upturn, as sales rise, businesses struggle to keep production on pace with sales growth, which leads to declining inventory levels. The rapidly-falling inventory-sales ratio stimulates businesses to increase production.

Consumer Behavior and the Business Cycle

Spending on Durable Goods

- A decrease in spending on durable goods relative to non-durable goods and services is an early indication of economic weakness.
- An increase in spending on durable goods (to catch up for the delay in spending on them) relative to non-durables and services suggests that a recovery may be on the way.

Permanent Income

Permanent income adjusts for temporary unsustainable sources of income and estimates the income that households can rely on. Spending on durables tends to fluctuate with changes in temporary or unsustainable sources of income, which are excluded from the calculation of permanent income. Basic consumption expenditure is related to permanent income.

The Savings Rate

- Fluctuations in the savings rate capture changes in consumers' willingness to reduce spending out of current income.
- The savings rate is also a good indicator of consumers' expectations regarding future income. A rise in the savings rate may indicate that consumers are uncertain about future income, suggesting that the economy is weakening. Note that a very high savings rate contributes to future spending and therefore, can help revive the economy even before incomes start to rise.

Housing Sector Behavior and the Business Cycle

Although the housing sector forms a relatively small part of the economy, fluctuations in the sector occur so rapidly that it makes a significant contribution to overall economic movements.

- Since most home sales are usually financed by mortgage loans, housing sector activity is particularly sensitive to the level of interest rates. A rise (fall) in interest rates leads to a decline (an increase) in home purchasing and construction.
- Home sales are also affected by income levels relative to housing prices. Low housing prices relative to income, coupled with low costs of supporting an average house (when mortgage rates are low), increase demand for housing units.

External Trade Sector Behaviour and the Business Cycle

- An increase in domestic GDP leads to an increase in demand for imports. Domestic exports usually tend to rise with an increase in GDP of major trading partners even if the domestic economy is weak. Therefore, patterns of external trade balances are not directly linked to domestic economic cycles.
- An appreciation of the domestic currency makes imports cheaper and, at the same time, makes domestic goods more expensive for trading partners, reducing net exports.
- GDP growth differentials have a more immediate and straightforward impact on the external trade balance.
- Currency movements have a more complex and gradual impact on the trade balance.

THEORIES OF THE BUSINESS CYCLE

Neoclassical School of Thought

- The "invisible hand" will lead the market towards general equilibrium. Fluctuations in aggregate economic activity are short-lived as the economy will quickly readjust (e.g., via lower interest rates and lower wages if aggregate demand falls).
- Resources are allocated efficiently when MC equals MR, and there is no voluntary unemployment of labor and capital.

- All that is produced will be sold as supply creates its own demand (Say's Law). When something is produced, factors of production are compensated for their services. This creates purchasing power and stimulates demand.

Austrian School of Thought

- Shares some views with the neoclassical school, but focuses more on money and government.
- Money was not important in the neoclassical school (as barter could be used to achieve equilibrium), while the role of the government was limited to upholding the law and securing borders.
- The Austrian school argues that when governments try to increase employment and GDP through expansionary monetary policies, interest rates fall below their natural rate, which leads to overinvestment (an inflationary gap). Once companies realize that they have gone overboard, they cut back spending drastically, which reduces aggregate demand and causes a recession. The government only causes a "boom-and-bust" cycle. To restore equilibrium, the economy must be left alone and all prices (including wages) must decrease.
- The theory explicitly identifies "misguided government intervention" as the cause of business cycles.

Keynesian School of Thought

- The general price and wage reduction (required under the Austrian and neoclassical schools to bring the economy out of a recession) are hard to attain.
- Even if nominal wages were reduced, lower salary expectations would only result in a further decline in aggregate demand and actually exacerbate a recession (the domino effect).
- Lower interest rates will not necessarily reignite growth due to weak business confidence.
- The economy's self-correcting mechanism may work in the long run, but definitely should not be relied upon in the short run. It is the short run that really matters.
- The government should step in during a recession and stimulate aggregate demand (via larger fiscal deficits) to keep labor and capital employed.
- Note that Keynes did not encourage the government to be ever-present in fine-tuning the economy.

Monetarist School of Thought

- Money supply is supremely important. The government should maintain a steady growth rate of money supply.
- If money supply grows too fast, there will be an unsustainable boom and inflation. If it grows too slow, there will be a recession.
- The government's expansionary fiscal actions may take effect once the recession is over and actually do more harm than good.

- The government should play a very limited role in the economy. Fiscal and monetary policy should be clear and consistent over time.
- Business cycles can be caused by exogenous shocks or government actions. During a recession it would be better to let the economy restore equilibrium on its own than to risk worsening the situation.

The New Classical School (RBC Theory)

- Business cycles have real causes (e.g., changes in technology). Monetary variables (such as inflation) are assumed to have no impact on GDP and unemployment.
- The government should not intervene in the economy (through fiscal or monetary policy).
- Unemployment (apart from frictional unemployment) is only short term. A person would only be unemployed if she is asking for wages that are too high.
- Aggregate supply plays a more prominent role (than in other theories) in bringing about business cycles.

Neo-Keynesian or New Keynesian Theory

- Like the New Classical School, this theory seeks to draw macroeconomic conclusions based on microeconomic (utility-maximizing) reasoning.
- Markets do not self-adjust seamlessly if they find themselves in disequilibrium. This is because:
  - Prices and wages are "downward sticky" (in contrast to the new classical view).
  - It is costly for companies to constantly update prices to clear markets (menu costs).
  - Companies need time to reorganize production in response to economic shocks.
- Therefore, government intervention is useful in eliminating unemployment and restoring macroeconomic equilibrium.

Measuring Unemployment

- Employed: Number of people with a job. This excludes those working in the informal sector (e.g., unlicensed cab drivers, illegal workers, etc.).
- Labor force: Number of people who either have a job, or are actively looking for one. This excludes people who are not employed and are not actively seeking employment (e.g., retirees, children, stay-at-home parents, fulltime students, etc.).
- Unemployed: People who are currently without a job, but are actively looking for one.
  - *Long-term unemployed*: People who have been out of work for a long time (more than 3-4 months) and are still looking for a job.
  - *Frictionally unemployed*: People who have just left a job and are about to start another one i.e., they already have a job waiting for them, which they have not started yet.

EC

- Activity (or participation) ratio: Ratio of the labor force to total working age population (usually those between 16 and 64 years of age).
- Underemployed: People who currently have jobs, but have the qualifications to do significantly higher-paying jobs. They are not considered unemployed.
- Discouraged worker: A person who has stopped looking for a job. These people are excluded from the labor force and therefore, not accounted for in the official unemployment rate.
- Voluntarily unemployed: These are people who choose to remain outside the labor force (e.g., workers who retire early, or those who are unwilling to take up a vacancy because the wage offered is lower than their threshold).

The Unemployment Rate

The unemployment rate equals the ratio of the number of people who are unemployed to the total labor force. Although unemployment measures provide useful insights into the current state of an economy, they are not very useful in predicting an economy's cyclical direction as they are lagging economic indicators. This is because:

- The size of the labor force responds to changes in economic conditions.
- Businesses are reluctant to lay off workers at the first sign of economic weakness and are slow to rehire previously laid-off workers in the early stages of a recovery.

Overall Payroll Employment and Productivity Indicators

- Size of payrolls: This measure is not biased by the number of discouraged workers. Generally speaking, payrolls tend to shrink when the economy slides into a recession, and rise when a recovery is underway.
- The number of hours worked (especially overtime), and the use of temporary workers, tend to increase at the first signs of a recovery, and decrease at the first signs of economic weakness.
- An economy's productivity is measured by dividing total output by the number of hours worked. It measures the intensity of workflow of existing employees. Productivity measures (if available promptly) can identify an economy's cyclical direction even before a change in the number of hours worked is noticed. Productivity increases during an expansion (as output rises) and decreases during a recession (as output falls).

Inflation, Disinflation, and Deflation

Inflation: Generally speaking, inflation is procyclical i.e., it goes up and down with the business cycle, but with a lag of around one year. Inflation is defined as a persistent increase in the overall level of prices (aggregate price level) in an economy over a period of time. The inflation rate measures the speed of overall price movements by calculating the rate of change in a price index. Both investors and policy-makers watch the inflation rate very closely.

Deflation: Deflation is defined as a persistent decrease in the aggregate level of prices in an economy over a period of time. The value of money actually rises in a deflationary environment. Since most debt contracts are written in fixed monetary amounts, the liability (in real terms) of the borrower rises during deflation.

Hyperinflation: Hyperinflation refers to a situation when the inflation rate is extremely high. It typically occurs when, instead of being backed by real tax revenue, large-scale government spending is supported by an increase in money supply.

Disinflation: Disinflation is defined as a fall in the inflation rate (e.g., from 15% to 5%). Disinflation is very different from deflation in the sense that deflation refers to a situation when the inflation rate is negative (aggregate price level is decreasing), while disinflation refers to a situation when the inflation rate falls, but remains positive (the aggregate price level continues to increase, but at a slower rate).

Price Indices

A price index that holds quantities of goods in the consumption basket constant is called a Laspeyres index. Most price indices around the world are Laspeyres indices, and consumption baskets are only updated after a certain number of years (typically 5). Using a fixed basket of goods and services to measure the cost of living gives rise to three biases:

- Substitution bias: Changes in the relative prices of goods motivate consumers to replace expensive goods with cheaper substitutes. Use of a fixed basket results in an upward bias in the computed inflation rate. Use of chained price index formulas (e.g., the Fisher index) can mitigate this bias.
- Quality bias: Improvements in product quality sometimes come at the cost of higher prices. If price indices are not adjusted for quality improvements, there will be an upward bias in the measured inflation rate. Prices can be adjusted for quality improvements through a practice known as hedonic pricing.
- New product bias: Recently introduced products are not included in the price index if the consumption basket is fixed. This usually creates an upward bias in the measured inflation rate. In order to mitigate this bias, new products can be introduced into the basket more regularly.

A Paasche Index is based on the current composition of the basket.

A Fisher Index is calculated as the geometric mean of the Laspeyres index and the Paasche index.

Cost-Push Inflation

Cost-push inflation occurs when rising costs compel businesses to raise prices. Costs of production may rise because of an increase in money wage rates, or an increase in the price of raw materials.

The effect of labor market constraints on wage rates is usually observed relative to the natural rate of unemployment (NARU). It is at the natural rate of unemployment, (not at 0% unemployment) that the economy begins to experience bottlenecks in the labor market and feel wage-push inflationary pressures. It is preferred to combine trends in labor costs with productivity measures to evaluate the state of the labor market.

Labor productivity (output per hour) is important because it determines the number of units across which businesses can spread their labor costs. Unit labor cost (ULC) is calculated as:

$$ULC = W/O$$

- If wage rates grow at a faster rate than labor productivity, business's costs per unit of output (ULC) increase. Businesses then look to increase output prices to protect profit margins so the end result is cost-push inflation.
- If wage rates increase at a slower rate than labor productivity, ULC falls. This eases inflationary pressures.

Demand-Pull Inflation

Demand-pull inflation is caused by increasing demand, which causes higher prices and eventually results in higher wages to compensate for the rise in cost of living. Demand-pull inflation may be analysed based on the economy's capacity utilization levels:

EC

- As the economy's actual GDP approaches its potential GDP (capacity utilization increases), there is an increase in the probability of shortages and bottlenecks occurring, so prices tend to rise.
- The further the economy operates below its potential output, the greater the probability of a slowdown in inflation (or even outright deflation).

Monetarists' Views on Inflation

Monetarists believe that inflation occurs when the growth rate of money supply in the economy outpaces growth in GDP. They explicitly place the blame for demand-pull inflation on excess money growth.

- If money growth exceeds nominal GDP growth, there is a possibility of inflation.
- If money growth is slower than nominal GDP growth, there could be disinflationary or deflationary pressures in the economy.

Inflation Expectations

Inflation expectations also play an important role in policy-making. Once economic agents start expecting prices to continue to rise going forward, they change their actions in line with those expectations. This can lead to higher inflation and cause it to persist in the economy even after its real underlying cause is no longer present.

Economic Indicators

An economic indicator is a variable that provides information on the state of the broader economy.

- Leading economic indicators have turning points that usually **precede** the turning points of the broader economy. Economists use them to predict the economy's **future state**.
- Coincident economic indicators have turning points that usually occur **close to** the turning points of the broader economy. Economists use them to identify the **current state** of the economy.
- Lagging economic indicators have turning points that usually occur **after** the turning points of the broader economy. Economists use them to identify the economy's **past condition**.

More About Economic Indicators

- Practitioners take an aggregate perspective when interpreting various economic indicators. Typically aggregate measures are combined into composites known to lead the cycle, coincide with the cycle or lag the cycle.
- Composites for different countries are usually composed of different indicators based on their own historical experiences.
- The timing record of various composite indices has varied considerably.
- The relationship between an indicator and the business cycle can be quite uncertain.
    - This is why analysts combine different indicators with common factors among them when constructing indicator indices, and why diffusion indices are used.

U.S. Economic Indicators[3]

Indicator and Description

Leading	*Reason*
1. Average weekly hours, manufacturing	Because businesses will cut overtime before laying off workers in a downturn and increase it before rehiring in a cyclical upturn, these measures move up and down before the general economy.
2. Average weekly initial claims for unemployment insurance	This measure offers a very sensitive test of initial layoffs and rehiring.
3. Manufacturers' new orders for consumer goods and materials	Because businesses cannot wait too long to meet demands for consumer goods or materials without ordering, these gauges tend to lead at upturns and downturns. Indirectly, they capture changes in business sentiment as well, which also often leads the cycle.
4. ISM new order index[a]	This index is a diffusion index that reflects the month-to-month change in new orders for final sales. The weakening of demand, which can lead to a recession, is usually first reflected in the decline of new orders.
5. Manufacturers' new orders for non-defense capital goods excluding aircraft	In addition to offering a first signal of movement, up or down, in an important economic sector, movement in this area also indirectly captures business expectations.
6. Building permits for new private housing units	Because most localities require permits before new building can begin, this gauge foretells new construction activity.
7. S&P 500 Index	Because stock prices anticipate economic turning points, both up and down, their movements offer a useful early signal on economic cycles.
8. Leading Credit Index	This index aggregates the information from six leading financial indicators, which reflect the strength of the financial system to endure stress. A vulnerable financial system can amplify and propagate the effects of negative shocks, resulting in a widespread recession for the whole economy.
9. Interest rate spread between 10-year Treasury yields and overnight borrowing rates (federal funds rate)	Because long-term yields express market expectations about the direction of short-term interest rates, and rates ultimately follow the economic cycle up and down, a wider spread, by anticipating short rate increases, also anticipates an economic upswing. Conversely, a narrower spread, by anticipating short rate decreases, also anticipates an economic downturn.
10. Average consumer expectations for business and economic conditions	If consumers are optimistic about future business and economic conditions, they tend to increase spending. Because consumption is about two-thirds of the U.S. economy, its future movements offer early insight into the direction ahead for the whole economy.

(Table continued on next page…)

EC

3 - Exhibit 5, Volume 2, CFA Program Curriculum 2017

(*continued*)

Coincident	*Reason*
1. Employees on non-agricultural payrolls	Once recession or recovery is clear, businesses adjust their full-time payrolls.
2. Aggregate real personal income (less transfer payments)	By measuring the income flow from non-corporate profits and wages, this measure captures the current state of the economy.
3. Industrial Production Index	Measures industrial output, thus capturing the behavior of the most volatile part of the economy. The service sector tends to be more stable.
4. Manufacturing and trade sales	In the same way as aggregate personal income and the industrial production index, this aggregate offers a measure of the current state of business activity.

Lagging	*Reason*
1. Average duration of unemployment	Because businesses wait until downturns look genuine to lay off, and wait until recoveries look secure to rehire, this measure is important because it lags the cycle on both the way down and the way up.
2. Inventory-to-sales ratio	Because inventories accumulate as sales initially decline and then, once a business adjusts its ordering, become depleted as sales pick up, this ratio tends to lag the cycle.
3. Change in unit labor costs	Because businesses are slow to fire workers, these costs tend to rise into the early stages of recession as the existing labor force is used less intensely. Late in the recovery when the labor market gets tight, upward pressure on wages can also raise such costs. In both cases, there is a clear lag at cyclical turns.
4. Average bank prime lending rate	Because this is a bank-administered rate, it tends to lag other rates that move either before cyclical turns or with them.
5. Commercial and industrial loans outstanding	Because these loans frequently support inventory building, they lag the cycle for much the same reason that the inventory–sales ratio does.
6. Ratio of consumer installment debt to income	Because consumers only borrow heavily when confident, this measure lags the cyclical upturn, but debt also overstays cyclical downturns because households have trouble adjusting to income losses, causing it to lag in the downturn.
7. Change in consumer price index for services	Inflation generally adjusts to the cycle late, especially the more stable services area.

[a]A diffusion index usually measures the percentage of components in a series that are rising in the same period. It indicates how widespread a particular movement in the trend is among the individual components.

EC

Study Session 5: Monetary and Fiscal Policy, International Trade, and Currency Exchange Rates

EC

MONETARY AND FISCAL POLICY
Cross-Reference to CFA Institute Assigned Reading #18

Monetary Policy

- Monetary policy refers to the government's or central bank's manipulation of money supply to influence the quantity of money and credit in the economy.

The Functions of Money

- Medium of exchange
- Store of value
- Unit of account

Paper Money and the Money Creation Process

Required reserve ratio = Required reserves / Total deposits

Money multiplier = 1/ (Reserve requirement) = 1/(0.2) = 5

The banking system as a whole that goes through the following cycle and increases the quantity of money:

1. Banks have excess reserves.
2. They lend the excess reserves.
3. Bank deposits increase.
4. Quantity of money increases.
5. Deposits in the banking system increase.
6. These deposits in turn create excess reserves which are loaned out.

Definitions of Money

- Narrow money refers to notes and coins in circulation plus other highly liquid deposits.
- Broad money includes narrow money plus the entire range of liquid assets that can be used to make purchases.

Checking account balances are included in measures of money. Checks make this transfer possible but this does not make the check itself money. Credit cards are not money either.

The Quantity Theory of Money

The quantity theory of money expresses the relationship between money and the price level. The quantity equation of exchange states that:

$$M \times V = P \times Y$$

EC

Money neutrality says that an increase in money supply will not result in an increase in real output (Y). Therefore, an increase in money supply will cause the aggregate price level (P) to rise. The assertions of the quantity theory of money are in line with the consequences of money neutrality (as velocity is assumed constant).

Monetarists use the quantity theory of money to support their belief that inflation can be controlled by manipulating the money supply growth rate.

The Demand for Money

Transactions-related demand for money arises from the need to use money to finance transactions. Generally speaking, transactions-related demand for money is positively related to average transaction size and overall GDP.

Precautionary money balances are held for use in unforeseen circumstances. Precautionary balances are positively related to average transactions size, total volume of transactions and therefore to overall GDP as well.

Speculative or portfolio demand for money is related to perceived opportunities and risks of holding other financial instruments (such as bonds). Speculative demand for money is inversely related to the returns available on other financial assets. At the same time, it is positively related to the perceived risk in these financial assets.

Supply and Demand for Money

Money supply is assumed fixed so it is represented by a vertical line. Money demand is inversely related to interest rates (speculative money demand increases as interest rates fall). Therefore, money demand is represented by a downward-sloping line. The point of intersection between the money demand and supply curves determines short run equilibrium nominal interest rates.

The Fisher Effect

The Fisher effect is directly related to the concept of money neutrality. It states that the nominal interest rate (R_N) reflects the real interest rate (R_R) and the expected rate of inflation (Π^e).

$$R_N = R_R + \Pi^e$$

The Fisher effect does not consider uncertainty. The greater the uncertainty, the higher the required risk premium.

The Roles of the Central Bank

- Monopoly supplier of currency.
- Banker to the government (and to other banks) and lender of last resort.
- Supervise the banking system.
- Oversee, regulate and set the standards for a country's payments system.
- Manage the country's foreign currency and gold reserves.
- Conducting monetary policy.

Objectives of Monetary Policy

- Maximum employment.
- Stable prices (This is the overarching objective of most central banks).
- Moderate long-term interest rates.

Costs of Inflation

Expected inflation is the inflation rate that economic agents expect to see in the economy in the future. Expected inflation gives rise to menu costs and shoe leather costs. Expected or anticipated inflation is reflected in all long-term contracts. People accept this level of inflation, and budget for it.

Unexpected inflation is the level of inflation that comes as a surprise to economic agents. It is arguably more costly than expected inflation. In addition to the costs of expected inflation, unexpected inflation also leads to:

- Inequitable transfers of wealth between borrowers and lenders.
  - If actual inflation is less than expected inflation (which is built into nominal interest rates) lenders benefit and borrowers lose out as the real value of payments on debts rises.
  - If actual inflation is greater than expected inflation borrowers benefit and lenders lose out as the real value of payments on debts falls.
- Higher risk premia in borrowing rates: Higher uncertainty associated with future inflation leads to lenders demanding a higher risk premium, which inflates the nominal interest rate and hurts economic activity.
- A reduction in the information content of market prices: Businesses may attribute an increase in prices of their products to an increase in demand (or decrease in supply) when in fact, the price increase may be in line with the overall level of inflation in the economy. Businesses would increase production only to find that they are struggling to sell their output, and involuntarily build up inventories. As a result, they would cut back production drastically, which would hurt the economy.

Monetary Policy Tools

Required reserve ratio: An increase in the required reserve ratio results in a decrease in money supply.

The central bank's policy rate: Generally speaking, the higher the policy rate, the higher the penalty that banks will have to pay the central bank if they run short of liquidity. This would make them more conservative in lending, reducing broad money supply.

Open market operations: An open-market sale (purchase) directly reduces (increases) banks' reserves.

The Transmission Mechanism

If the central bank increases its official policy rate:

- Banks respond to the increase in the official interest rate by increasing their base rates (the reference rates on which they base lending rates to customers). As a result, individuals and businesses borrow less.
- Asset prices and values of capital projects tend to fall as present values of expected future cash flows decline.
- Economic agents' expectations regarding the economy are dampened as they associate higher interest rates with slower future economic growth and reduced profits.
- The domestic currency appreciates in value (as hot money flows in). This makes domestic goods and services more pricey (less competitive) in the international market, leading to a decline in exports.
- If the increase in interest rates is widely expected to be followed by further rate hikes, economic agents will change their behavior to reflect these revised expectations.
- Overall, the decline in consumption, borrowing and asset prices will reduce aggregate demand.
- Weaker demand will reduce domestic prices. This, along with lower import prices, (due to appreciation of the domestic currency) will put a downward pressure on actual inflation.

Monetary Policy Strategies

Inflation targeting: Under this strategy, the central bank makes a public commitment to achieving an explicit inflation target, and to explaining how its actions will achieve that target. The argument here is that inflationary expectations must be managed, and, when everyone is aware (and believes) that the central bank will move to contain inflation within an acceptable range, spending and investing decisions will be made wisely.

Exchange rate targeting: The central bank supports a target exchange rate by buying and selling the domestic currency in the foreign exchange market. Basically, the aim here is to "import" the inflation experience of an economy with a good track record on inflation, by tying the domestic currency to the currency of that economy.

Qualities of Effective Central Banks

The central bank should be independent and not come under political pressures when formulating policy. There are two aspects of central bank independence:

- Operational independence is when the central bank decides the level of interest rates.
- Target independence is when the central bank determines the inflation rate that is targeted and the horizon over which this target is to be achieved.

The public should have confidence in the central bank i.e., it must have credibility. If economic agents believe that the central bank will hit its inflation target, the belief itself could become self-fulfilling.

There should be transparency in the central bank's decision-making. Transparency comes from the central bank clearly explaining its views on the economy and communicating its views on various economic indicators to economic agents on a regular basis.

Finally, (if the central bank follows an inflation targeting strategy), the central bank must have a realistic, forward-looking inflation target.

Contractionary and Expansionary Monetary Policies

- When the central bank believes that the current growth rate of economic activity will lead to inflation, it will look to reduce money supply and increase interest rates. Such actions are known as contractionary measures as they are meant to rein in an overheating economy.
- When the central bank believes that the current level of economic growth is too slow and inflation is weakening, it will look to increase money supply and reduce interest rates. Such actions are known as expansionary measures as they are meant to stimulate a receding economy.

The Neutral Rate of Interest

The neutral rate is the rate of interest that neither slows down, nor spurs growth in the underlying economy. When the policy rate is below (above) the neutral rate, monetary policy is expansionary (contractionary). However, economists' estimates of the neutral rate for a given economy typically vary. What they do agree on, is that the neutral rate has two components:

- Real trend of growth in the underlying economy: This corresponds to the rate of economic growth that gives rise to stable inflation in the long run.
- Long run expected inflation.

Limitations of Monetary Policy

- Central banks cannot control the amount of money that households and businesses choose to save.
- While central banks can influence the ability of banks to extend loans and create credit, they cannot easily control the willingness of banks to do so.
- If the central bank lacks credibility, there is a lower chance of its "policy message" being successfully transmitted through the economy.

FISCAL POLICY

Roles and Objectives of Fiscal Policy

The main aim of fiscal policy is to regulate the economy's real GDP by influencing aggregate demand.

Fiscal policy is an important tool for economic stabilization through its impact on output.

- In a recession, governments can increase spending and/or reduce taxes (expansionary fiscal policy) to try to raise employment and output.
- In an expansion, governments can reduce spending and/or increase taxes (contractionary fiscal policy) to try to control inflation.

The budget surplus/deficit equals the difference between the government's revenue and expenditure over a period of time. Analysts look at the change in the budgetary position to determine whether fiscal policy is getting tighter or looser:

- An increase (decrease) in a budget surplus is contractionary (expansionary).
- An increase (decrease) in a budget deficit is expansionary (contractionary).

Automatic stabilizers work in the absence of explicit action by the government to bring the economy towards full employment. There are two automatic stabilizers embedded in fiscal policy.

- Induced taxes
- Needs-tested spending

Discretionary fiscal actions are enacted by the government, and involve changing tax rates or the level of government spending. Basically, these actions are up to the government's discretion as opposed to automatic stabilizers, which act on their own to bring the economy towards full employment.

Deficits and National Debt

Reasons to be concerned about national debt relative to GDP:

- High debt levels may lead to high tax rates (to service the debt) going forward. Higher expected future tax rates may serve as a disincentive for labor and entrepreneurial activity.

- If markets lose confidence in the government, the central bank may have to print money to finance the deficit. This would lead to high inflation (e.g., Zimbabwe in 2008-2009).
- Government spending may crowd out private investment. Higher demand for borrowing (to finance the deficit) by the government would raise interest rates, reducing private sector investment.

Reasons not to be concerned about national debt relative to GDP:

- The problem is not really a major issue if debt is owed to the country's own citizens. In this case the government can just print money to retire the debt. However, note that this strategy comes with the risk of high inflation.
- Some of the borrowed funds may have been used for capital investment projects, which would raise the economy's productive capacity (and tax revenues) going forward.
- The private sector may adjust to offset fiscal deficits by increasing savings in anticipation of future tax increases (to finance the deficit). This is known as Ricardian equivalence: the increase in government spending (or reduction in taxes) meant to stimulate aggregate demand will have no impact on economic activity as economic agents will save more because they expect the government to finance the deficit by increasing taxes in the future.
- If there is widespread unemployment in the economy, fiscal deficits will not be diverting any resources away from productive uses so total output will increase.
- Large fiscal deficits require tax changes, which may correct the distortions created by the current tax structure.

Fiscal Policy Tools and the Macroeconomy

Government spending takes the following forms:

- Transfer payments
- Current government spending
- Capital expenditure

Justifications for Government Spending

- The government provides services such as defense that benefit all citizens equally.
- Infrastructure spending helps the country's economic growth.
- Helps redistribute wealth in society.
- Can be used as a tool to control inflation, unemployment and growth.
- Can be used to subsidize the development of innovative and high-risk new products (e.g., alternative energy).

Types of Taxes

- Direct taxes
- Indirect taxes

Taxes can be justified in terms of raising revenue to finance government expenditure and in terms of income and wealth redistribution.

Desirable Properties of Tax Policy

- Simplicity
- Efficiency
- Fairness
- Revenue sufficiency

Advantages and Disadvantages of Different Fiscal Policy Tools

Advantages:

- Indirect taxes can be adjusted very quickly. They are very effective in influencing spending behavior and in generating revenue at little cost to the government.
- Social objectives (e.g., reducing alcohol or cigarette consumption) can easily be met by raising indirect taxes.

Disadvantages:

- Direct taxes, and welfare and other social transfers are difficult to change without significant notice. However, they begin to have an impact on behavior soon after their announcement.
- Capital spending decisions are slow to plan, implement and execute.

EC

In addition to their direct effects on the economy, the above-mentioned fiscal policy tools also have strong expectational effects on the economy.

- Direct government spending has a much bigger impact on aggregate spending and output than income tax cuts or transfer increases.
- However, if transfer increases target the poorest in society (whose marginal propensity to consume is highest), they can have a relatively strong impact on spending.

The Fiscal Multiplier

$$\frac{1}{[1 - MPC(1 - t)]}$$

The Balanced Budget Multiplier

The balanced budget multiplier is positive. An increase in government spending combined with an equivalent dollar increase in taxes leads to a higher real GDP.

Issues in Fiscal Policy Implementation

Deficits and the Fiscal Stance

The size of a fiscal deficit cannot be used to determine whether fiscal policy is expansionary or contractionary.

- Automatic stabilizers for example lead to changes in the budgetary status that are unrelated to fiscal policy changes. Therefore, economists look at the structural or cyclically adjusted budget deficit as an indicator of the government's fiscal stance. The structural deficit is the deficit that would exist were the economy working at full-employment.
- Government expenditure includes the cash amount of payments on debt, which inflates the actual deficit. This is because the real value of outstanding debt falls with inflation.

Difficulties in Executing Fiscal Policy

Recognition lag: This refers to the time that it takes the government to figure out that the economy is not functioning at its potential output.

Action lag: The government might have recognized the need for action, but its implementation may be delayed in obtaining the necessary approvals.

Impact lag: This refers to the time it takes for a fiscal stimulus to flow through the economy and generate the changes in spending patterns that are desired.

The Relationships between Monetary and Fiscal Policy

Easy fiscal policy/tight monetary policy: Results in higher output, higher interest rates and government expenditure would form a larger component of national income.

Tight fiscal policy/easy monetary policy: The private sector's share of overall GDP would rise (as a result of low interest rates), while the public sector's share would fall.

Easy fiscal policy/easy monetary policy: This would lead to a sharp increase in aggregate demand, lowering interest rates and growing private and public sectors.

Tight fiscal policy/tight monetary policy: This would lead to a sharp decrease in aggregate demand, higher interest rates and a decrease in demand from both private and public sectors.

Factors Influencing the Mix of Fiscal and Monetary Policy

- If the government is primarily concerned with growing the economy's potential output, it should aim to keep interest rates low and keep fiscal policy relatively tight to ensure that free resources are available in the growing economy.

- If the government's main concern is to build infrastructure and develop high quality human capital, it should focus on spending in those areas. If monetary policy is kept loose during this time, inflation may result.

INTERNATIONAL TRADE AND CAPITAL FLOWS
Cross-Reference to CFA Institute Assigned Reading #19

Gross Domestic Product (GDP) measures the market value of all **final** goods and services produced by factors of production (e.g., labor, capital, etc.) located **within** a country/economy during a period of time.

- GDP *includes* goods and services produced by foreigners within the country.
- GDP *excludes* goods and services produced by citizens outside the country.

Gross National Product (GNP) measures the market value of all **final** goods and services produced by factors of production (e.g., labor, capital, etc.) supplied by the citizens of the country, regardless of whether production takes place within or outside of the country.

- GNP *includes* goods and services produced by citizens outside the country.
- GNP *excludes* goods and services produced by foreigners within the country.

Terms of trade refer to the ratio of the price of exports to the price of imports.

FDI versus FPI

EC

When a firm in the source country makes an investment in the productive assets of the host country, it is referred to as Foreign Direct Investment (FDI).

Foreign Portfolio Investment (FPI) refers to shorter-term investments in foreign financial instruments (e.g., foreign stocks, foreign government bonds, etc.).

Benefits of International Trade

- Countries gain from exchange and specialization.
- Efficient resource allocation.
- Domestic companies gain access to global markets and customers, which leads to increased exchange of ideas and greater awareness of changing consumer tastes and preferences.
- Capital intensive industries gain access to much larger markets, enabling them to reap the benefits of economies of scale.
- Domestic households are able to choose from a wider variety of goods and services.
- Increased foreign competition reduces monopoly power of domestic firms and forces them to continuously strive to become more efficient.
- Trade liberalization can lead to higher inflation-adjusted GDP as a result of a more efficient allocation of resources, learning by doing, knowledge spillovers and improved productivity.

Costs of International Trade

- Companies that are less efficient than international firms may go out of business if foreign firms are allowed to enter the market. This will lead to higher (structural) unemployment.

- The counter argument is that despite the short and medium term costs and unemployment, these resources will eventually be reemployed in more efficient industries.

Comparative versus Absolute Advantage

Absolute advantage refers to a country's ability to produce a good at a **lower cost** or using fewer resources than its trading partners.

Comparative advantage refers to a country's ability to produce a particular good at a **lower opportunity cost** than its trading partners.

Even if a country does not have an absolute advantage in the production of a good or service, it (and its trading partners) can still gain from trade if it produces and exports goods in which it has a comparative advantage.

Trade Models and Sources of Comparative Advantage

Ricardian Model

- Assumes that labor is the only variable factor of production.
- A country gains a comparative advantage in the production of a good based on differences in labor productivity, which reflect underlying differences in technology.
- Differences in technology are the key source of comparative advantage.
- Even if the country is very small compared to the size of its trading partner, it will continue to produce the good that it holds a comparative advantage in, and trade some of it to obtain other goods.
- Technological gaps between countries can decrease over time, leading to shifts in comparative advantage.

Heckscher-Ohlin Model (also referred to as the factor-proportions theory)

- Assumes that both capital and labor are variable factors of production, so a good can be produced with varying combinations of the two.
- Technology is the same in each industry across countries, but it varies across different industries.
- Differences in factor endowments are the primary source of comparative advantage.
- A country has a comparative advantage in a good whose production requires intensive use of a factor with which it is relatively abundantly endowed.
- Allows for redistribution of income through trade as it assumes that more than one factor of production is variable.
- Theoretically, free trade should eventually result in equal prices of goods and services and equal prices of factors of production across countries.
    - However, in the real world trade only results in a tendency for factor prices to converge in the long run.

EC

Arguments for Trade Restrictions

- Protection of established domestic industries from foreign competition.
- Protection of new (infant) industries from foreign competition until they mature.
- Protection of employment in the country.
- Generation of revenue from tariffs.
- Retaliation against trade restrictions imposed by trading partners.

Tariffs

When the government imposes a tariff on imports, the price effectively rises, domestic demand falls, domestic supply rises and the volume of imports falls.

- The government manages to lower the trade deficit (by decreasing imports) and also manages to earn some revenue for itself (Region C).
- There is an increase in producer surplus (Region A).
- Consumer surplus falls (Regions B, C, and D).
- The overall effect is a net decrease in welfare (Regions B and D).

Quotas

Quotas are restrictions on the quantity of a good that can be imported into a country for a specified period. When a quota is in place, each importing firm receives an import license, which specifies the quantity that it can import.

The main difference between tariffs and quotas is that the government earns direct revenue through tariffs, but this is not the case with quotas. With a quota, foreign producers may raise their prices to earn higher profits than they would in the absence of the quota. These profits are known as quota rents.

- Region C (previously government revenue from the tariff) is now more likely to be captured by foreign producers (quota rents), increasing the welfare loss for the importing country to Regions B+C+D (relative to just Regions B+D under a tariff).
- If the importing country can generate an amount equal to Area C by auctioning import licenses for a fee, then its welfare loss can be limited to just Regions B+D (as is the case with tariffs).
- Quota rents arising from a quota can be captured by the exporting country or the importing country.

Voluntary Export Restraints

Voluntary Export Restraints (VERs) are restrictions on the quantity of a good that can be exported. While quotas are imposed by the importing country, VERs are imposed by the exporting country. Under VERs, the exporting country captures the quota rent (Region C), but the welfare loss to the importing country equals Regions B, C and D.

Export Subsidies

Export subsidies refer to payments made by the government to domestic exporters of certain goods. While they aim to stimulate exports, export subsidies interfere with the free market mechanism and may result in trade patterns that diverge from those dictated by comparative advantage. Further, domestic producers would be more inclined to export their output rather than selling it in the domestic market.

Effects of Alternative Trade Policies

Panel A: Effects of Alternative Trade Policies

	Tariff	Import Quota	Export Subsidy	VER
Impact on	Importing country	Importing country	Exporting country	Importing country
Producer surplus	Increases	Increases	Increases	Increases
Consumer surplus	Decreases	Decreases	Decreases	Decreases
Government revenue	Increases	Mixed (depends on whether the quota rents are captured by the importing country through sale of licenses or by the exporters)	Falls (government spending rises)	No change (rent to foreigners)
National welfare	Decreases in small country Could increase in large country	Decreases in small country Could increase in large country	Decreases	Decreases

Panel B: Effects of Alternative Trade Policies on Price, Production, Consumption, and Trade

	Tariff	Import Quota	Export Subsidy	VER
Impact on	Importing country	Importing country	Exporting country	Importing country
Price	Increases	Increases	Increases	Increases
Domestic consumption	Decreases	Decreases	Decreases	Decreases
Domestic production	Increases	Increases	Increases	Increases
Trade	Imports decrease	Imports decrease	Exports increase	Imports decrease

EC

CAPITAL RESTRICTIONS

Capital restrictions are defined as controls placed on foreigners' ability to own domestic assets and/or domestic citizens' ability to own foreign assets.

Common Objectives

- The government may place restrictions on inward investment by foreigners relating to how much can be invested, and in which industries.
    - The government may impose ownership restrictions on strategic industries such as defense and telecommunications.
    - The government may forbid foreign investment into certain industries to protect domestic companies from foreign competition, and to protect jobs.
- The government may place restrictions on outflow of capital from repatriation of capital, interest, profits, royalty payments, and license fees, and on foreign investments by its citizens in order to conserve scarce foreign exchange reserves.
- Capital restrictions are often used in conjunction with other policy instruments, such as fixed exchange rate targets to achieve policy objectives in times of macroeconomic crises.
    - Capital controls are used to control the economy's external balance, while other, more traditional policy tools are used to pursue other objectives.

Forms of Capital Controls

- Taxes
- Price controls
- Quantity controls
- Outright prohibitions on international trade in assets

Benefits of Free Movement of Financial Capital

- Allows capital to be invested wherever it will earn the highest return.
- The economy's productive capacity can grow at a higher rate than possible based on domestic savings alone.
- Foreign firms may enter domestic industries, bringing competition to local firms, which may:
    - Encourage local firms to improve the quality of their goods and services.
    - Lead to better prices.
    - Bring new technologies into the country.

Effectiveness of Capital Controls

An IMF study found that:

- Effective controls on capital inflows entail significant administrative costs.

- Imposition of controls on capital outflows during times of financial crisis have produced mixed results:
  - They have only provided temporary relief to some countries, but offered others (e.g., Malaysia in 1997) enough time to restructure their economies.
  - If the government is wary of capital leaving the country, capital controls (when combined with fixed exchange rates) afford the central bank a degree of monetary policy independence that would not be possible without capital controls.

Costs of Capital Controls

- Administrative costs.
- Controls may give rise to negative market perceptions and make it more costly for the country to raise foreign funds.
- Protection of domestic financial markets may delay necessary policy adjustments or impede private-sector adaptation to changing international circumstances.

Trade Blocs

Members of a regional trading agreement (RTA) agree to eliminate barriers to trade and movement of factors of production among the members of the bloc.

Members of a **free trade area (FTA)**, for example NAFTA, eliminate almost all barriers to free trade with each other. However, each member still maintains its own policies regarding trade with non-member countries.

A **customs union** (e.g., Benelux) is very similar to an FTA, but all member countries have similar policies regarding trade with non-member countries.

A **common market** (e.g., MERCOSUR) incorporates all the provisions of a customs union, and also allows free movement of factors of production among the member countries.

An **economic union** (e.g., EU) incorporates all the aspects of a common market and also requires common economic institutions and coordination of economic policies among member countries. If the members of the economic union decide to adopt a common currency, it is also referred to as a **monetary union**.

Trade Creation versus Trade Diversion

Only if trade creation is larger than trade diversion, is there a positive net effect on welfare from forming the trade bloc.

- Trade creation occurs when higher-cost domestic production is replaced with lower-cost imports from fellow members of a trade bloc.
- Trade diversion occurs when lower-cost imports from non-member countries are replaced with higher-cost imports from member countries (because tariffs are imposed on imports from non-member countries but not on imports from member countries).

Advantages of Trade Blocs

All the benefits of free trade (greater specialization, reduction in monopoly power due to competition, economies of scale, learning by doing, knowledge spillovers, technology transfers, better quality intermediate inputs, etc.) apply to trade blocs as well. Further, trade blocs:

- Reduce the potential for conflict among members.
- Give members greater bargaining power in the global economy as they form a united front.
- Offer new opportunities for trade and investment.
- Typically, growth in a member country tends to spill over into other members as well.

Challenges in the Formation of an RTA

- Cultural differences and historical conflicts may complicate the process of integration.
- Free trade and mobility of labor limit the extent to which member countries can pursue independent economic and social policies.

The Balance of Payments

The balance of payments (BOP) is a double entry bookkeeping system that summarizes a country's economic transactions with the rest of the world over a period of time.

Balance of Payment Components

The current account can be decomposed into the following sub-accounts:

- Merchandise trade consists of all commodities and manufactured goods bought, sold or given away.
- Services include tourism, transportation, engineering and business services.
- Income receipts include income from ownership of foreign assets (e.g., interest and dividends).
- Unilateral transfers represent one-way transfers of assets (e.g., worker remittances, foreign aid and gifts).

The capital account can be decomposed into the following sub-accounts:

- Capital transfers include debt forgiveness and migrants' transfers. They also include:
    - Transfer of ownership of fixed assets
    - Transfer of funds received for the sale or acquisition of fixed assets
    - Gift and inheritance taxes
    - Death duties
    - Uninsured damage to fixed assets

- Sales and purchases of non-produced, non-financial assets such as rights to natural resources, intangible assets (e.g., patents, copyrights, etc.)

The financial account can be decomposed into the following sub-accounts:

- Financial assets abroad are composed of:
  - Official reserve assets
  - Government assets
  - Private assets
- Foreign owned financial assets in the reporting country are composed of:
  - Official assets
  - Other foreign assets

National Economic Accounts and the Balance of Payments

$Y = C + I + G + X - M$

- A current account deficit must be financed by foreign direct investment, loans by foreign banks, or the sale of domestic debt and equity securities to foreign investors.
- A current account surplus is used to finance the current account deficit of trading partners (through loans and investments in real and financial assets).

$CA = X - M = Y - (C + I + G)$

- A country can have a current account deficit and consume more than it produces (C + I + G greater than Y) if it borrows the shortfall from foreigners.
- A country can have a current account surplus and consume less than it produces (C + I + G less than Y) if it lends the shortfall to foreigners.

$S_P + S_G = I + CA$

- In a closed economy, savings can only be used for domestic investment.
- In an open economy, savings can be used for domestic and foreign investment.

$S_P = I + CA - S_G$

This equation clearly shows that an economy's private savings can be used for:

- Domestic investment.
- Foreign investment (purchasing assets from foreigners).
- Purchasing government debt.

$$CA = S_P + S_G - I$$

A current account deficit results from:

- Low private savings
- A government deficit
- High private investment

If a country running a trade deficit mainly borrows to finance consumption, then eventually it must reduce consumption to repay its debts. If the borrowings are mainly used to finance investment, then future economic growth is likely to provide the means to repay its liabilities.

World Bank Group

The World Bank's main objective is to fight poverty and enhance environmentally sound economic growth. The World Bank and its affiliated entities:

- Provide cheap loans and grants to countries that have limited or no access to international financial markets.
- Provide analysis, advice and information to countries to encourage social and economic development.
- Share knowledge and promote dialogue to increase the capabilities of their partners and members.
- Help members create the basic economic infrastructure that is essential for the development of domestic financial markets.

World Trade Organization (WTO)

The WTO's primary objective is to enhance and liberalize international trade.

- The WTO's important functions include the implementation, administration, and operation of individual agreements, providing a platform for negotiations and settling trade disputes.
- It also provides technical cooperation and training to developing, under developed and poor countries to bring them in compliance with WTO rules.
- It reviews members' trade policies on a regular basis and ensures coherence and transparency of trade policies through surveillance.
- It is a major source of economic research and analysis.
- Its framework of global trade rules provides a major institutional and regulatory base, without which large multinationals would not be able to operate on such a large scale.

International Monetary Fund

The main objective of the IMF is to ensure the stability of the international monetary system, the system of exchange rates and international payments that enables countries to participate in international trade. More specifically, the IMF:

- Provides a forum for cooperation on international monetary problems.
- Facilitates the growth of international trade, thereby promoting job creation, economic growth, and poverty reduction.
- Promotes exchange rate stability and an open system of international payments.
- Lends foreign exchange to member countries when needed, on a temporary basis and under adequate safeguards, to help them address balance of payments problems.

In the aftermath of the global financial crisis of 2007-2009, the IMF has redefined its operations by:

- Enhancing its lending facilities.
- Strengthening the monitoring of global, regional, and country economies.
- Helping resolve global economic imbalances.
- Analysing capital market developments.
- Assessing financial sector vulnerabilities.
- Working to cut poverty.

From an investment perspective the IMF helps to keep country-specific market risk and global systematic risk under control.

CURRENCY EXCHANGE RATES

Cross-Reference to CFA Institute Assigned Reading #20

An exchange rate represents the price of one currency in terms of another currency. It is stated in terms of the number of units of a particular currency (price currency) required to purchase a unit of another currency (base currency). Stated differently, it is the cost of one unit of the base currency in terms of the price currency.

In this reading, we will refer to exchange rates using the convention "A/B," i.e., number of units of Currency A (price currency) required to purchase one unit of Currency B (base currency). For example, suppose that the USD/GBP exchange rate is currently 1.5125. From this exchange rate quote we can infer that:

> Just like the price of any product, an exchange rate reflects the price of the currency in the denominator. For example, a price of $5/bag of chips reflects the price of a bag of chips (base or denominator) in terms of the price currency (USD). Similarly, a price (exchange rate) of $2/GBP is the price of GBP (base currency) in terms of USD (price currency). An increase in the price of chips (e.g., to $6/bag) means that the value of a bag of chips (the item in the denominator) in terms of USD has risen. Similarly, an increase in the exchange rate to $3/GBP implies an increase in the value of GBP (currency in the denominator).

- The GBP is the base currency and USD is the price currency.
- It will take 1.5125 USD to purchase 1 GBP.
- 1 GBP will buy 1.5125 USD or 1 GBP costs 1.5125 USD.
- A decrease in this exchange rate (e.g., to 1.5120) means that 1 GBP will be able to purchase fewer USD.
- Alternatively, less USD will now be required to purchase 1 GBP (the cost of a GBP has fallen).
- This decrease in the exchange rate means that the GBP has depreciated (lost value) against the USD, or equivalently, the USD has appreciated (gained value) against the GBP.
- It would help you to think of exchange rates in the following manner: An increase in the quoted exchange rate (price/base) means an increase (appreciation) in the value of the currency in the denominator (base currency) and a decrease (depreciation) in the value of the currency in the numerator (price currency).
- The numerical value of the exchange rate and the value of the base currency are positively related.
- The numerical value of the exchange rate and the value of the price currency are negatively related.

Nominal versus Real Exchange Rates

- When the value of a currency is stated in terms of units of another currency (as in the example above), it is referred to as a **nominal exchange rate**.
- On the other hand, **real exchange rates** measure changes in the relative purchasing power of one currency compared with another.

Purchasing power parity (PPP) asserts that nominal exchange rates adjust to ensure that identical goods (or baskets of goods) have the same price in different countries.

- The nominal exchange rate and relative purchasing power are **inversely** related.
- The price level in the foreign country (or foreign inflation) and relative purchasing power are **inversely** related.
- The price level in the home country (or domestic inflation) and relative purchasing power are **positively** related.

Determining the Real Exchange Rate

An increase in purchasing power implies a decrease in the real exchange rate (in terms of DC/FC) i.e., purchasing power and the real exchange rate are **inversely** related. Therefore, we can say that the real exchange rate is:

- An increasing function of the nominal exchange rate (in terms of DC/FC).
- An increasing function of the foreign price level.
- A decreasing function of the domestic price level.

The real exchange rate may be calculated as:

$$\text{Real exchange rate}_{DC/FC} = S_{DC/FC} \times (P_{FC} / P_{DC})$$

Spot versus Forward Exchange Rates

Spot exchange rates (S) are quotes for transactions that call for immediate delivery. For most currencies, immediate delivery means "T + 2" delivery i.e., the transaction is actually settled 2 days after the trade is agreed upon by the parties.

Forward exchange rates (F) are quotes for transactions that are contracted (agreed upon) today, but settled at a pre-specified date in the future (settlement occurs after a longer period than the two days for spot transactions).

Types of Contracts Used for Trading Currencies

- Futures contracts
- FX swaps
- FX options

Functions of the Foreign Exchange Market

- Facilitate international trade
- Allow investors to convert between currencies in order to move funds into (or out of) foreign assets.
- Enable market participants who face exchange rate risk to hedge their risks.
- Allow investors to speculate on currency values.

Market Participants

Sell Side

- The very largest dealing banks
- All other regional and local banks

Buy Side

- Corporate accounts
- Real money accounts
- Leveraged accounts
- Retail accounts
- Governments
- Central banks
- Sovereign wealth funds (SWFs)

Market Size and Composition

- Investment pools and professional traders account for a large (and growing) proportion of FX market volumes. Portfolio flows and speculative activities dominate FX market volumes.
- High frequency algorithmic traders are accounting for a growing proportion of FX market volumes.
- Purchases and sales of foreign goods and services by individuals and corporations form a relatively small proportion of FX market volumes.
- London, New York and Tokyo account for the highest FX market volumes.
- The majority of FX market transactions occur in the FX swap market.

Direct versus Indirect Quotes

- In a direct currency quote (DC/FC), the *domestic* currency is stated as the *price* currency and *foreign* currency is stated as the *base* currency.
- In an indirect currency quote (FC/DC), the *foreign* currency is stated as the *price* currency and *domestic* currency is stated as the *base* currency.

Direct and indirect quotes are just the inverse (reciprocal) of each other.

Exchange Rate Quote Conventions

FX Rate Quote Convention	Name Convention	Actual Ratio (Price currency/Base currency)
EUR	Euro	USD/EUR
JPY	Dollar–yen	JPY/USD
GBP	Sterling	USD/GBP
CAD	Dollar–Canada	CAD/USD
AUD	Aussie	USD/AUD
NZD	Kiwi	USD/NZD
CHF	Swiss franc	CHF/USD
EURJPY	Euro–yen	JPY/EUR
EURGBP	Euro–sterling	GBP/EUR
EURCHF	Euro–Swiss	CHF/EUR
GBPJPY	Sterling–yen	JPY/GBP
EURCAD	Euro–Canada	CAD/EUR
CADJPY	Canada–yen	JPY/CAD

Understanding Exchange Rate Quotes

When both currencies are mentioned in the code or the name convention, the first currency is the base currency and the second currency is the price currency. For example, dollar-yen refers to the exchange rate of JPY/USD i.e., USD is the base currency and JPY is the price currency. Note that dollar-yen (quote: JPY) may also be written as USDJPY, USD:JPY or USD-JPY. They all mean the same thing i.e., JPY/USD.

In professional FX markets, an exchange rate is usually quoted as a two-sided price. Dealers usually quote a bid-price (the price at which they are willing to buy), and an ask-price or offer price (the price at which they are willing to sell). Bid-ask prices are always quoted in terms of buying and selling the *base* currency. For example, a EUR:USD (or USD/EUR) quote of 1.3802–1.3806 means that the dealer is willing to buy EUR for 1.3802 USD and is willing to sell EUR for 1.3806 USD. From the client's perspective, she will receive 1.3802 USD for selling 1 EUR, but will have to pay 1.3806 USD to purchase 1 EUR.

Suppose that the JPY/USD exchange rate increases from 77.58 to 78.45. An increase in the JPY/USD exchange rate means that USD has now become more costly in terms of JPY (it now takes more units of JPY to purchase 1 unit of USD). Stated differently, USD has appreciated against JPY, and JPY has depreciated against USD. The unannualized percentage increase in the value of the USD against JPY can be calculated as:

$$(78.45/77.58) - 1 = 1.12\%$$

The percentage increase in the value of the USD against JPY does not equal the percentage decrease in the value of JPY against USD. In order to determine the percentage decrease in the value of JPY against USD, we must make JPY the *base* currency in the exchange rates that we use in the calculation.

Cross Rates

A **cross rate** is an exchange rate between two currencies that is derived from each currency's relationship with a third currency. For example, using the EUR (which represents USD/EUR) and JPY (which represents JPY/USD) exchange rates, we can calculate the cross rate between the Euro and the yen (EURJPY or JPY/EUR) as follows:

$$\frac{\text{JPY}}{\text{EUR}} = \frac{\cancel{\text{USD}}}{\text{EUR}} \times \frac{\text{JPY}}{\cancel{\text{USD}}}$$

The given exchange rates should be multiplied such that the third currency (common currency) disappears (or mathematically cancels out as it forms the numerator of one quote and the denominator of the other).

In order to cancel out the third currency, you might sometimes need to invert one of the exchange rate quotes. For example, consider the EUR (which represents USD/EUR) and GBP (which represents USD/GBP) exchange rates. A trader who wants to calculate the cross rate between the Euro and the British pound cannot do so by simply multiplying these two exchange rates in their presented forms (because the USD will not cancel out). One of the exchange rates must be inverted. The Euro-sterling exchange rate (which represents GBP/EUR) can be calculated as:

$$\frac{\text{GBP}}{\text{EUR}} = \frac{\text{USD}}{\text{EUR}} \times \left(\frac{\text{USD}}{\text{GBP}}\right)^{-1} = \frac{\text{USD}}{\text{EUR}} \times \frac{\text{GBP}}{\text{USD}}$$

Forward Rate Quotes

In professional FX markets, forward exchange rates are quoted in terms of points (pips), which simply represent the difference between the forward rate and the spot rate. Note that these points (pips) are scaled so that they can be related to the last digit in the spot quote (usually the fourth decimal place).

- If the forward rate is higher than the spot rate, the points are positive and the base currency is said to be trading at a **forward premium** because it is expected to appreciate in the future. At the same time, the price currency would be trading at a **forward discount**, which means it is expected to depreciate.
- If the forward rate is lower than the spot rate, the points are negative and the base currency is trading at a forward discount as it is expected to depreciate. At the same time, the price currency would be trading at a forward premium and is expected to appreciate.

EC

For example, assume that a trader is quoted a spot CAD/USD exchange rate of 1.0155 and a one-year forward CAD/USD exchange rate of 1.0183. The forward rate is higher than the spot rate which means that the USD (base currency) is trading at a forward premium and is expected to appreciate. The one-year forward points will be quoted as 28, calculated as follows:

$$\text{Forward points: } (1.0183 - 1.0155) \times 10{,}000 = 28 \text{ points}$$

Dealers typically quote forward rates in terms of the number of forward points. Forward point quotes may be converted into forward rates by dividing the number of points by 10,000 and adding the result to the spot rate quote (assuming that the quote has 4 decimal places). Continuing with our CAD/USD example, the one-year forward rate may be computed based on forward points as:

$$1.0155 + (28/10{,}000) = 1.0155 + 0.0028 = 1.0183$$

Sometimes forward rates or points may be quoted as a percentage of the spot rate rather than in terms of an absolute number of points. Continuing with our CAD/USD example, the one year forward rate for the USD can be quoted as:

$$[(1.0155 + 0.0028)/1.0155] - 1 = (1.0183/1.0155) - 1 = 0.2757\%$$

The base currency (USD) is said to be trading at a forward premium of 0.2757%.

When the forward premium is presented in terms of a percentage, the forward rate may be calculated by multiplying the spot rate by one plus (minus) the percentage premium (discount). Continuing with the CAD/USD example, the forward premium of 0.2757% can be used to calculate the forward rate as:

$$1.0155 \times (1 + 0.002757) = 1.0183$$

If the number of points were -28, (if the base currency were trading at a forward discount), the forward rate would be expressed in terms of a percentage as:

$$[(1.0155 - 0.0028)/1.0155] - 1 = -0.2757\%$$

In this case, the forward exchange rate would be calculated as:

$$1.0155 \times (1 - 0.002757) = 1.0127; \text{ or}$$

$$1.0155 - 0.0028 = 1.0127$$

Forward Rates, Spot Rates and Interest Rates

Forward exchange rates are calculated in a manner that ensures that traders are not able to earn arbitrage profits. This means that a trader with a specific amount of domestic currency should be able to earn the exact same amount from both the following investment options:

Option 1: She invests the funds at the domestic risk-free rate (r_{DC}) for a particular period of time.

Option 2: She converts the funds into a foreign currency (at the current spot rate, $S_{FC/DC}$), invests them at the foreign risk-free rate (r_{FC}) for the same period of time (as in Option 1), and then converts them back to the domestic currency at the forward exchange rate ($F_{DC/FC}$) which she locks in today.

The CFA Program curriculum presents this equation in the following form: $(1+i_d) = S_{f/d}(1+i_f)\frac{1}{F_{f/d}}$

We believe that our approach is easier and more intuitive. Both the formulas will of course give you the same answer.

Both these investment options are risk-free because they require the money to be invested at risk-free interest rates. Further, the exchange rate risk in the second option is eliminated (hedged) by locking in the forward rate at the time of investment. Since these two investments have identical risk characteristics, it follows that they must have the same return (to preclude arbitrage profits), leading to the following equality:

$$(1+r_{DC}) = S_{FC/DC}\ (1+r_{FC})\ F_{DC/FC}$$

The above equality can be used to derive the formula for the forward rate:

$$F_{DC/FC} = \frac{1}{S_{FC/DC}} \times \frac{(1+r_{DC})}{(1+r_{FC})} \text{ or } F_{DC/FC} = S_{DC/FC} \times \frac{(1+r_{DC})}{(1+r_{FC})}$$

This version of the formula is perhaps easiest to remember because it contains the DC term in numerator for all three components: $F_{DC/FC}$, $S_{DC/FC}$ and $(1 + r_{DC})$

Forward rates are sometimes interpreted as expected future spot rates.

$$F_t = S_{t+1}$$

$$\frac{(S_{t+1})}{S} - 1 = \Delta\%S(DC/FC)_{t+1} = \frac{(r_{DC} - r_{FC})}{(1+r_{FC})}$$

Under this interpretation, the expected percentage change in the spot rate is proportional to the interest rate differential ($r_{DC} - r_{FC}$). However, such an interpretation should be used cautiously. Forward rates are unbiased predictors of future spot rates, but this does not make them accurate predictors of future spot rates:

- The direction of the predicted change in spot rates is counterintuitive.
- Historical data show that forward rates are poor predictors of future spot rates. Aside from interest rate differentials, exchange rates are influenced by several other factors.

Important Takeaways

- Given the same interest rate differential, the longer the term to maturity, the higher the absolute number of forward points.
    - However, note that the number of forward points is not exactly proportional to the horizon of the forward contract.
- Given the same term to maturity, the higher the interest rate differential, the higher the absolute number of forward points.
    - The number of forward points is exactly proportional to the interest rate differential.

Exchange Rate Regimes

Desirable Properties

- The exchange rate between any two currencies should be credibly fixed.
- All currencies should be fully convertible to ensure unrestricted flow of capital.
- Each country should be able to undertake fully independent monetary policy.

Generally speaking, the more freely the currency is allowed to float and the more tightly convertibility is controlled, the greater the effectiveness of monetary policy.

Types of Exchange Rate Regimes

Arrangements with No Separate Legal Tender

- Dollarization: A country uses the currency of another nation (usually the U.S. dollar) as its medium of exchange and unit of account.
- Monetary union: Member countries share the same legal tender (e.g., the European Economic and Monetary Union (EMU) whose members use the Euro as their currency).

Currency Board System

- The central bank holds foreign currency reserves to cover, at the fixed parity, the entire monetary base of a country (e.g., Hong Kong).
- Expansion and contraction of the monetary base are directly linked to trade and capital flows.
- The exchange rate is essentially fixed, but it is allowed to fluctuate within a narrow band.
- The central bank cannot act as the lender of last resort, but can provide short term liquidity.
- The monetary authority can earn a profit by paying little or no interest on its liabilities (the monetary base), and earning a market rate on its assets (foreign currency reserves). This profit is referred to as seigniorage. Under dollarization, seigniorage goes to the country whose currency is used.

Fixed Parity

- The exchange rate is either pegged to a single currency or to a basket of currencies of major trading partners. The monetary authority stands ready to buy or sell foreign currency reserves to maintain the exchange rate within a narrow band.
- Although monetary independence is limited, the central bank can act as a lender of last resort.
- The success of this system depends on both the country's willingness as well as its ability to maintain the fixed exchange rate.

Target Zone

- Similar to a fixed-rate system.
- The only difference is that the monetary authority aims to maintain the exchange rate within a slightly broader range.
    - This gives the central bank greater ability to conduct discretionary policy.

Active and Passive Crawling Pegs

- Under a passive crawling peg system, the exchange rate is adjusted frequently in line with the rate of inflation.
- Under an active crawling peg system, the exchange rate is pre-announced for the coming weeks and changes are made in small steps.

Fixed Parity with Crawling Bands

- The country initially fixes its exchange rate to a foreign currency, but gradually moves towards a more flexible system by pre-announcing the widening of bands around the central parity. This allows the country greater flexibility in determining its monetary policy.

Managed Float

- The country does not explicitly state its exchange rate target, but intervenes in the FX markets to meet its policy objectives (regarding balance of trade, price stability or unemployment).
- Such intervention (also called dirty floating) typically also causes the country's trading partners to retaliate in a similar fashion and leads to instability in FX markets as a whole.

Independently Floating Rates

- The central bank rarely intervenes in the determination of its exchange rate, which is left to be determined by market supply and demand factors.
- Enables the central bank to engage in independent monetary policy aimed at achieving price stability and full employment.
- Also allows it to act as a lender of last resort to troubled institutions.

Relating the Trade Balance to Savings

$$(X - M) = (S - I) + (T - G)$$

Trade surplus = Government saving + Private saving – Investment

- A trade surplus means that the economy as whole (government saving and private saving combined) saves enough to fund its investment needs. The excess saving is used to accumulate financial claims against the rest of the world.
- A trade deficit means that the country must borrow from the rest of the word to meet its investment needs.

Exchange Rates and the Trade Balance

The Elasticities Approach

A devaluation or depreciation of the domestic currency makes domestic goods relatively cheaper for foreigners (reduces the price of domestic goods). At the same time it implies an appreciation of foreign currencies, which makes foreign goods relatively more expensive for domestic citizens (increases the price of foreign goods).

The ideal combination for a country that wants to reduce its trade deficit and expects its currency to depreciate is that its imports and exports both be relatively elastic. This is the basic idea behind the Marshall-Lerner condition. Demand for imports and exports must be sufficiently price sensitive such that increasing the price of imports increases the difference between export revenue and import expenditures.

Marshall-Lerner condition: $\omega_X \varepsilon_X + \omega_M(\varepsilon_M - 1) > 0$

Where:
ω_X = Share of exports in total trade
ω_M = Share of imports in total trade
ε_X = Price elasticity of demand for exports
ε_M = Price elasticity of demand for imports

If this condition is satisfied, devaluation/depreciation in the domestic currency will lead the trade balance towards a surplus.

Note that the elasticity of demand for imports becomes more important (and export elasticity less important) as the trade deficit gets larger.

Generally speaking, exchange rates will be more effective in adjusting trade imbalances if the countries' imports and exports are composed of items that have relatively elastic demand.

EC

Finally, note that the impact of exchange rates on the trade balance may not always be immediate due to the fact that there is a time lag between the initial depreciation and the eventual impact on quantities of imports and exports. The increase in import prices will lead to an increase in total expenditure on imports over the short run (leading to a deepening of the deficit). However, as the currency stabilizes at the new (lower) levels, economic agents adapt and eventually the trade balance improves (towards a surplus). Overall, the trade deficits makes a "*J*-like" formation.

The Absorption Approach

Devaluation of the exchange rate can direct the trade balance towards a surplus if it increases:

- National income relative to expenditure; or equivalently
- National saving relative to investment in physical capital

If an economy is operating below full employment, then, by diverting demand towards domestically produced goods, devaluation can increase income/output.

If the economy is operating at full employment, output/income cannot be increased further. As a result, expenditure must decline for there to be an improvement in the trade balance.

Study Session 6: Financial Reporting and Analysis—An Introduction

FRA

FINANCIAL STATEMENT ANALYSIS: AN INTRODUCTION

Cross-Reference to CFA Institute Assigned Reading #21

The **role of financial statement reporting** is to provide information about a company's financial performance, financial position and changes in financial position.

The **role of financial statement analysis** is to assess a company's past performance and evaluate its future prospects using financial reports along with other relevant company information.

- *Liquidity* refers to a company's ability to meet its short term obligations.
- *Solvency* refers to a company's ability to meet its long term obligations.

Footnotes contain important details about accounting methods, estimates and assumptions that have been used by the company in preparing its financial statements. For example, information about the choice of revenue recognition method and assumptions made to calculate depreciation expense are found in the footnotes. The availability of such information allows comparisons between companies that prepare their financial statements in accordance with different accounting standards (IFRS versus U.S. GAAP).

The management discussion and analysis section (required under **U.S. GAAP**) highlights important trends and events that affect a company's liquidity, capital resources and operations. Management also discusses prospects for the upcoming year with respect to inflation, future goals, material events and uncertainties. The section must also discuss critical accounting policies that require management to make subjective judgments and have a material impact on the financial statements. Although it contains important information, analysts should bear in mind that the MD&A section is not audited.

IFRS provides a framework that offers guidance rather than requirements in a standard. According to the framework, "decision-useful" management commentary includes:

- The nature of the business
- Management objectives and strategies
- The company's significant resources, risks and relationships
- Results of operations
- Critical performance measures

FRA

Auditor's Reports

Under International Standards for Auditing, objectives of an auditor are:

1. To obtain reasonable assurance about whether the financial statements as a whole are free from material misstatement, whether due to fraud or error, thereby enabling the auditor to express an opinion on whether the financial statements are prepared, in all material respects, in accordance with an applicable financial reporting framework; and
2. To report on the financial statements, and communicate as required by the ISAs, in accordance with the auditor's findings.

Types of Audit Opinions

- An unqualified opinion states that the financial statements have been fairly presented in accordance with applicable accounting standards.
- A qualified opinion states that the financial statements have been prepared fairly, but do contain exception(s) to the accounting standards. The audit report provides further details and explanations relating to the exception(s).
- An adverse opinion states that the financial statements have not been presented fairly, and significantly deviate from acceptable accounting standards.
- A disclaimer of opinion is issued when the auditor, for whatever reason, is not able to issue an opinion on the financial statements.

Other Sources of Company-Related Information

- **Interim reports** are prepared either semiannually or quarterly. They contain the four financial statements and footnotes but are *not audited.*
- **Proxy statements** are distributed to shareholders to decide on matters that require a shareholder vote. They provide information about management and director compensation, company stock performance and potential conflicts of interest between management, the board of directors and shareholders.
- **Press releases**, in addition to company websites and conference calls, provide current information about companies.
- **External sources** provide information about the economy, the industry that the company operates in, and the company's competitors. Examples of external sources include trade journals and government agencies.

Steps in the Financial Statement Analysis Framework

- Define the context and purpose of analysis.
- Collect data.
- Process data.
- Analyze/interpret the processed data.
- Develop and communicate conclusions.
- Follow up.

FINANCIAL REPORTING MECHANICS

Cross-Reference to CFA Institute Assigned Reading #22

Business activities are classified into three categories for financial reporting purposes:

- Operating activities are related to the day-to-day business activities of a company.
- Investing activities are related to the acquisition and disposal of long-term assets.
- Financing activities are related to raising and retiring capital.

The nature of the firm's operations dictates where certain transactions fall within these classifications. For example, interest received by a music store on a fixed-income investment will be classified as an investing activity, but interest received by a bank will be classified as an operating activity.

Financial Statement Elements

- Assets are a company's economic resources.
  - *Noncurrent assets* are expected to benefit the company over an extended period of time (usually longer than one year).
  - *Current assets* are expected to be used by the company or converted into cash in the short-term (less than one year).
- Liabilities are creditor claims on a company's economic resources.
- Owners' equity represents owners' residual claim on a company's resources.
- Revenues represent the inflow of economic resources.
- Expenses represent outflows of economic resources.

The Accounting Equation

The basic accounting equation is:

$$\text{Assets} = \text{Liabilities} + \text{Owners' equity}$$

It can be expanded into:

$$\text{Assets} = \text{Liabilities} + \text{Contributed capital} + \text{Beginning retained earnings} + \text{Revenue} - \text{Expenses} - \text{Dividends}$$

Accrual Accounting

Accrual accounting is based on the principle that revenues should be recognized when earned, and expenses should be recognized when incurred, irrespective of when the actual exchange of cash occurs. The timing difference between cash movements and recognition of revenues and expenses explains the need for accrual entries. There are four types of accrual entries:

FRA

1. Unearned (or deferred) revenue arises when a company receives the cash payment before it provides a good or a service to the customer. Because the company still has to provide the good/service, unearned revenue is recognized as a *liability.* Unearned revenue is subsequently earned once the good is sold or the service is provided.
2. Unbilled or accrued revenue arises when a company provides a good or service before receiving the cash payment. Because the company is owed money, accrued revenue is recognized as an *asset.*
3. Prepaid expenses arise when a company makes a cash payment before recognizing the expense. Expenses that have been paid for in advance are an *asset.*
4. Accrued expenses arise when a company recognizes an expense in its books before actually making the payment for it. Because the company still owes the payment, the accrued expense is recognized as a *liability.*

Accruals

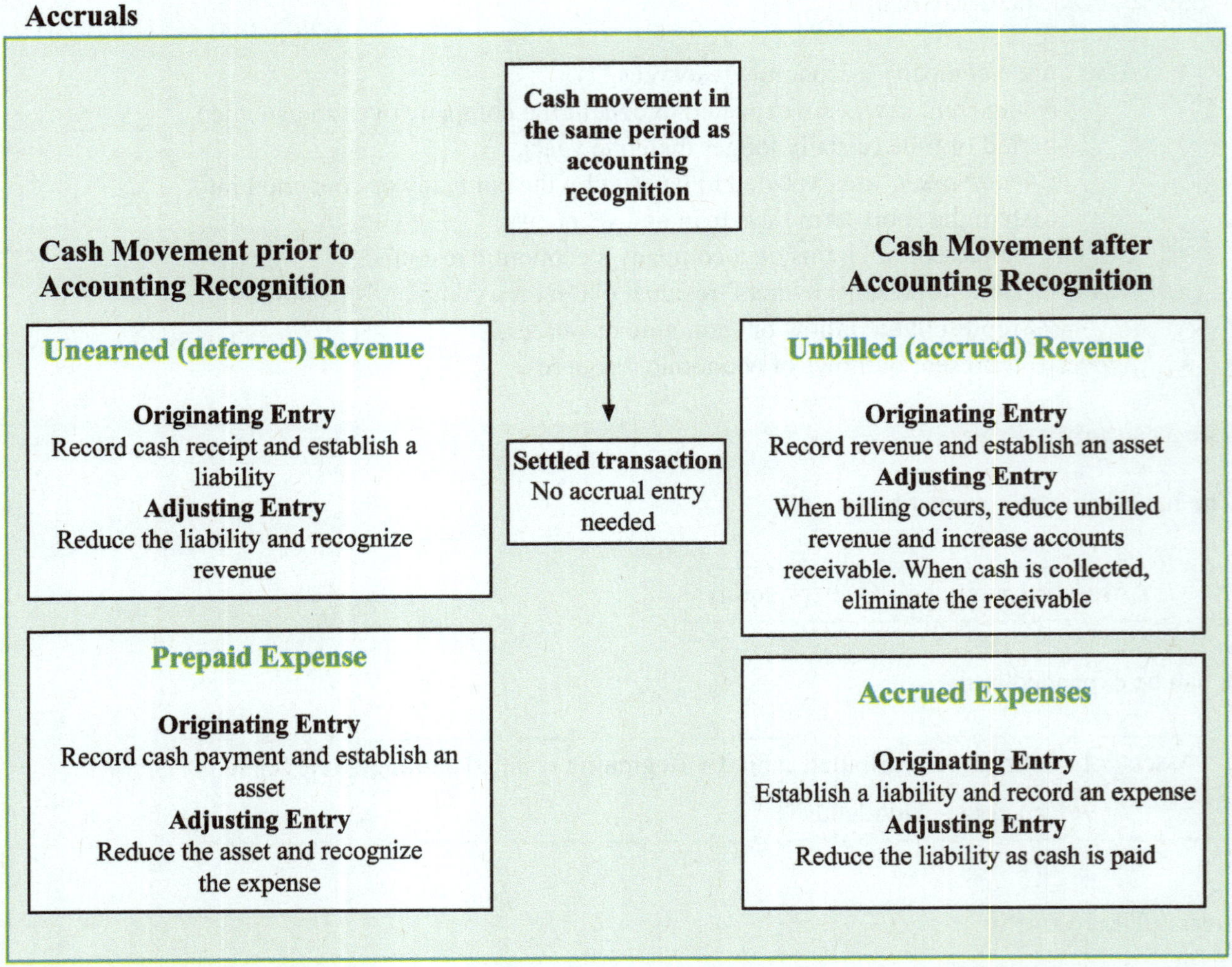

FRA

When cash is transferred in the same period that the related revenue/expense is recognized, there is no need for accrual entries.

Valuation Adjustments

Most assets are recorded on the balance sheet at historical cost. However, accounting standards require certain assets to be shown on the balance sheet at their current market values. The upward or downward adjustments to the values of these assets are known as valuation adjustments.

In an accounting system, information flows through four stages:

- Journal entries.
- General ledger.
- Trial balance.
- Financial statements.

Financial statements provide the basis for analysis of equity and credit instruments. However, analysts may need to make adjustments to reflect items not reported in the statements. Analysts must also evaluate management's assumptions regarding accruals and valuations. Information related to most of these assumptions can be found in the significant accounting policies footnote and in the management discussion and analysis (MD&A) section of the annual report.

Since assumptions within the accounting process are, to an extent, in the hands of management, financial statements can be manipulated to misrepresent a company's financial performance.

FINANCIAL REPORTING STANDARDS

Cross-Reference to CFA Institute Assigned Reading #23

Financial statements are not designed only to facilitate asset valuation; they provide information to a host of users (e.g., creditors, employees and customers). At the same time, they do provide important inputs for the asset valuation process. For analysts, it is extremely important to understand how, and when judgments and subjective estimates affect the financial statements. Such an understanding is important to evaluate the wisdom of business decisions, and to make comparisons between companies.

Standard-Setting Bodies versus Regulatory Bodies

- Standard-setting bodies, such as the International Accounting Standards Board (IASB) and U.S. Financial Accounting Standards Board (FASB), are private sector organizations, of accountants and auditors, who *develop* financial reporting rules, regulations and accounting standards.
- Regulatory authorities like the Securities and Exchange Commission (SEC) in the United States, and FSA in the United Kingdom, have legal authority to *enforce* financial reporting requirements, and can overrule private-sector standard-setting bodies.

Standard-Setting Bodies

The IASB is the independent standard-setting body of the **IFRS** Foundation, which is an independent, not-for-profit private sector organization.

The FASB standards are contained in the FASB Accounting Standard Codification™ (Codification). The Codification is the source of all authoritative U.S. generally accepted accounting principles (U.S. GAAP) for non-governmental entities.

Desirable Attributes of an Accounting Standards Board

FRA

- The responsibilities of all parties involved in the standard-setting process should be clearly defined.
- All parties involved in the standard-setting process should observe high professional and ethical standards, including standards of confidentiality.
- The organization should have adequate authority, resources, and competencies.
- There should be clear and consistent processes to guide the organization and formation of standards.
- There should be a well-articulated framework with a clearly stated objective to guide the board.
- The board should seek and consider input from all stakeholders. However, it should operate independently and make decisions that are in line with the stated objective of the framework.

- The board should not succumb to pressure from external forces.
- Final decisions should be in public interest, and should lead to a set of high-quality standards that will be recognized and adopted by regulatory authorities.

Regulatory Authorities

Regulatory authorities are governmental entities that have the legal authority to enforce the financial reporting requirements set forth by the standard-setting bodies, and to exert control over entities that participate in capital markets within their jurisdiction.

IOSCO (International Organization of Securities Commission) is not a regulatory authority, but its members regulate a large portion of the world's financial capital markets.

Any company issuing securities in the U.S., or otherwise involved in U.S. capital markets is subject to the rules of the **Securities and Exchange Commission (SEC)**. The SEC requires companies to submit numerous forms periodically. These filings, which are available on the SEC website (www.sec.gov), are a key source of information for analysis of listed firms.

Convergence of Global Financial Reporting Standards

The move toward developing one set of universally accepted financial reporting standards is impeded by two factors:

- Standard-setting bodies and regulators have different opinions regarding appropriate accounting treatments due to differences in institutional, regulatory, business and cultural environments.
- Powerful lobbyists and business groups, whose reported financial performance would be affected adversely by changes in reporting standards, exert pressure against the adoption of unfavorable standards.

Objective of Financial Statements

Under the Conceptual Framework, the objective of general purpose financial reporting is to provide financial information that is useful in making decisions about providing resources to the entity to existing and potential providers of resources (e.g., investors, lenders and creditors) to the entity.

FRA

Qualitative Characteristics

Fundamental qualitative characteristics that make financial information useful:

- Relevance
- Faithful representation

Faithful representation requires that the information presented is:

- Complete
- Neutral
- Free from error

Supplementary qualitative characteristics that increase the usefulness of relevant and faithfully represented financial information.

- Comparability
- Verifiability
- Timeliness
- Understandability

Constraints on Financial Statements

While it would be ideal for financial statements to exhibit all the desirable characteristics listed earlier, there are several constraints to achieving this goal:

- There may be a trade-off between certain desirable characteristics.
- There is a cost of providing useful financial information. The benefits from information should exceed the costs of providing it.
- Intangible aspects (e.g., company reputation, brand name, customer loyalty and corporate culture) cannot be quantified and reflected in financial statements.

Reporting Elements

The elements of financial statements that are related to the measurement of financial position are:

- Assets
- Liabilities
- Equity

Elements related to the measurement of financial performance are:

- Income
- Expenses

Underlying Assumptions in Financial Statements

- **Accrual basis** accounting requires that transactions should be recorded on the financial statements (other than on the cash flow statement) when they actually occur, irrespective of when the related exchange of cash occurs.
- **Going concern** refers to the assumption that the company will continue operating for the foreseeable future. If this is not the case, fair representation would require all assets to be written down to their liquidation values.

Recognition and Measurement of Financial Statement Elements

An element should be recognized on the financial statements if the future benefit from the item (flowing into or out of the firm) is probable, and if its value/cost can be estimated with reliability.

Measurement Bases

- Historical cost: For an asset historical cost refers to the amount that it was originally purchased for. For liabilities, it refers to the amount of proceeds that were received initially in exchange for the obligation.
- Amortised cost: Historical cost adjusted for amortisation, depreciation, or depletion and/or impairment.
- Current cost: For an asset, current cost refers to the amount that the asset can be purchased for today. For liabilities, it refers to the total undiscounted amount of cash that would be required to settle the obligation today.
- Realizable (settlement) value: In reference to assets, realizable value refers to the amount that the asset can be sold for in an ordinary disposal today. For liabilities, it refers to the undiscounted amount of cash expected to be paid to settle the liability in the normal course of business.
- Present value: For assets, present value refers to the discounted value of future net cash flows expected from the asset. For liabilities, it refers to the present discounted value of future net cash outflows that are expected to be required to settle the liability.
- Fair value: Fair value is defined in IFRS and U.S. GAAP as an exit price, the price that would be received to sell an asset, or paid to transfer a liability, in an orderly transaction between market participants at the measurement date. This may involve either market measures or present value measures, depending on the availability of information.

Required Financial Statements

- Statement of financial position (balance sheet).
- Statement of comprehensive income (in a single statement or in two separate statements i.e., the income statement + statement of comprehensive income).
- Statement of changes in equity.
- Statement of cash flows.
- Significant accounting policies and explanatory notes to facilitate the understanding of financial statements.
- In certain cases, a statement of financial position from earliest comparative period.

General Features of Financial Statements

- Fair presentation: This requires faithful representation of transactions, in compliance with the definitions and recognition criteria for reporting elements (assets, liabilities, equity, income and expenses) set out in the Conceptual Framework.
- Going concern: Financial statements should be prepared on a going concern basis unless management has plans to liquidate the company.
- Accrual basis: All financial statements, except the cash flow statement, should be prepared on an accrual basis.
- Materiality and aggregation: Financial statements should be free from omissions and misrepresentations that could influence decisions taken by users. Similar items should be grouped and presented as a material class. Dissimilar items, unless immaterial, should be presented separately.
- No offsetting: Assets and liabilities, and income and expenses should not be used to offset each other, unless a standard requires or allows it.
- Frequency of reporting: Financial statements must be prepared at least annually.
- Comparative information: Comparative amounts should be presented for prior periods unless a specific standard permits otherwise.
- Consistency: Items should be presented and classified in the same manner every period.

Structure and Content Requirements

- Classified statement of financial position: Current and noncurrent assets and current and noncurrent liabilities should be shown separately on the balance sheet.
- Minimum information on the face of financial statements: Certain items must be explicitly disclosed on the face of the financial statements.
- Minimum information in the notes (or on the face of financial statements): Disclosures relating to certain items must be in the notes to the financial statements (e.g., measurement bases used).
- Comparative information: Comparative amounts should be presented for prior periods unless a specific standard permits otherwise.

Comparison of Key Concepts of Financial Reporting Standards

- FASB, in addition to the financial performance elements recognized under the IASB Framework (revenues and expenses), also identifies gains, losses and comprehensive income.
- Reporting elements relating to financial position are defined differently. Under FASB, assets are the "future economic benefits" rather than "resources" from which future economic benefits are expected to flow under IASB.

- Under FASB, the word "probable" is not discussed in its revenue recognition criteria, while under IASB it is required that its is probable that a future economic benefit flow to/from the entity. FASB also has a separate recognition criterion of relevance.
- Regarding measurement of financial elements, both frameworks are broadly consistent. However, FASB does not allow upward revaluation of assets except for certain categories of financial instruments that must be reported at fair value.

Characteristics of an Effective Financial Reporting Framework

- Transparency: A transparent reporting framework should reflect the underlying economics of the business. Full disclosure and fair representation create transparency.
- Comprehensiveness: A comprehensive reporting framework is one that is based on universal principles that provide guidance for recording all kinds of financial transactions - those already in existence, and others that emerge with time.
- Consistency: Financial transactions of a similar nature should be measured and reported in a similar manner, irrespective of industry type, geography, and time period.

Barriers to Creating a Single Coherent Framework

- **Valuation:** When choosing a measurement base, it is important to remember the tradeoff between reliability and relevance. Historical cost is a more reliable measure of value but fair value is more relevant over time.
- **Standard-setting approach:** Reporting standards can be based on one of the following approaches:
    - A principles-based approach provides a broad financial reporting framework with limited guidance on how to report specific transactions.
    - A rules-based approach provides strict rules for classifying elements and transactions.
    - An objectives-oriented approach is a combination of a principles-based and rules-based approach.

IFRS has a principles-based approach. FASB has historically followed a rules-based approach, but recently explicitly stated that it is moving towards an objectives-oriented approach.

- **Measurement:** Reporting of financial statement elements can be based on the asset/liability approach (where the elements are properly valued at a point in time) or the revenue/expense approach (where changes in the elements are properly valued over a period of time). In recent years, standard-setters have preferred the asset/liability approach.

Monitoring Developments in Financial Reporting Standards

It is important for analysts to keep track of developments in financial reporting standards and assess their implications for security analysis and valuation. Analysts must pay careful attention to:

- New products and transactions in capital markets.
- Actions of standard-setting bodies.
- Company disclosures including the footnotes and the MD&A section.

FRA

Study Session 7: Financial Reporting and Analysis—Income Statements, Balance Sheets, and Cash Flow Statements

FRA

UNDERSTANDING INCOME STATEMENTS
Cross-Reference to CFA Institute Assigned Reading #24

Under **IFRS**, the income statement may be presented as:

- A section of a single statement of comprehensive income; or
- A separate statement (showing all revenues and expenses) followed by a statement of comprehensive income that begins with net income.

Under **U.S. GAAP**, the income statement may be presented as:

- A section of a single statement of comprehensive income.
- A separate statement followed by a statement of comprehensive income that begins with net income.
- A separate statement with the components of other comprehensive income presented in the statement of changes in shareholders' equity.

Revenues versus Gains

Income includes revenues and gains. Revenues arise from ordinary, core business activities, whereas gains arise from non-core or peripheral activities. For example, for a software development company, the sale of software to customers will be classified as revenue, but profit on the sale of some old office furniture will be classified as a gain.

Income Statement Formats

A company may prepare its income statement using a single-step or multi-step format. When an income statement explicitly calculates gross profit, it uses a multi-step format.

For nonfinancial firms, operating profit refers to earnings *before* financing costs (interest expense) and income taxes. For financial firms, interest expense is usually considered an operating expense. Their operating profit is calculated *after* accounting for interest expense.

If a company has a subsidiary in which it enjoys majority ownership, the subsidiary's accounts are consolidated with its own. Consolidation requires the parent company to combine all the revenues and expenses of the subsidiary with its own and present the combined results on its income statement. If the subsidiary is not wholly-owned, minority interest is deducted from total income as it represents the proportionate share of the subsidiary's minority share holders in the subsidiary's net income.

FRA

The IASB framework defines income as "an increase in economic benefits during the accounting period in the form of inflows or enhancements of assets, or reduction in values of liabilities that result in increases in equity, other than those relating to contributions from equity participants."

Revenue Recognition

Here, we discuss revenue recognition under IFRS and US GAAP prior to the application of the converged standards issued in May 2014.

Under IASB, for a sale of goods, revenue is recognized when:

1. Significant risks and rewards of ownership are transferred to the buyer.
2. There is no managerial involvement or effective control over the goods sold.
3. Revenue can be measured reliably.
4. It is probable that the economic benefits from the transaction will flow to the entity.
5. Costs incurred, or to be incurred for the transaction can be measured reliably.

Under FASB, revenue is recognized on the income statement when it is "realized or realizable" and "earned."

The SEC provides specific guidelines under which these two conditions are met:

1. There is evidence of an arrangement between buyer and seller.
2. The product has been delivered, or the service has been rendered.
3. The price is determined, or determinable.
4. The seller is reasonably sure of collecting money.

Specific Revenue Recognition Applications

There are certain special circumstances in which revenue may be recognized *prior* to the sale of a good/service or even *after* the sale.

1. Long-term contracts

Long-term contracts are contracts that extend over more than one accounting period, such as construction projects. In long-term contracts, questions arise as to how revenues and expenses should be allocated to each accounting period. The treatment of these items depends on how reliably the outcome of the project can be measured.

Under U.S. GAAP, the completed contract method is also appropriate when the contract is not a long-term contract. Note however, that when a contract is started and completed in the same period, there is no difference between the percentage-of-completion and completed contract methods.

- If the outcome of the contract can be measured *reliably*, the percentage of completion revenue recognition method is used under both IFRS and U.S. GAAP. Under this method, revenues, costs and profits are allocated to each accounting period in proportion to the percentage of the contract completed during the given period.
- If the outcome *cannot be measured reliably:*
  - The completed-contract method is used under U.S. GAAP. Under this method, no revenues or costs are recognized on the income statement until the entire project is completed.
  - Under IFRS, revenue is recognized on the income statement to the extent of costs incurred during the period. No profits are recognized until completion of the project.

The percentage of completion method is a more aggressive (less conservative) approach to revenue recognition. It is also more subjective as it depends on management estimates and judgement relating to reliability of estimates.

The percentage of completion method matches revenues with costs over time and provides smoother, less volatile earnings. Remember that cash flows are exactly the same under both the methods.

Under IFRS and U.S. GAAP, if a loss is expected on the contract, it must be recognized immediately, regardless of the revenue recognition method used.

2. Installment Sales

An **installment sale** occurs when a firm finances a customer's purchase of its products. Customers make payments (installments) to the company over an extended period.

Under **IFRS**, installment sales are separated into selling price (discounted present value of installment payments) and an interest component. Revenue attributable to the sale price is recognized at the date of sale, while the interest component is recognized over time.

Under **U.S. GAAP**, a sale of real estate is reported at the time of sale using the normal revenue recognition conditions if the seller:

- Has completed the significant activities in the earnings process; and
- Is either assured of collecting the selling price, or able to estimate amounts that will not be collected.

When these two conditions are not fully met, some of the profit must be deferred and one of the following two methods may be used:

- The installment method is used when collectability of revenues cannot be reasonably estimated. Under this method, profits are recognized as cash is received. The percentage of profit recognized in each period equals the proportion of total cash received in the period.
- The cost-recovery method is used when collectability is highly uncertain. Under this method, profits are only recognized once total cash collections exceed total costs incurred.

FRA

3. Barter Transactions

In barter transactions, goods are exchanged between two parties and there is no exchange of cash. One form of barter transactions is a *round-trip* transaction, in which a good is sold by one party in exchange for the purchase of an identical good. The issue with these transactions is whether revenue should be recognized.

- Under IFRS, revenue from barter transactions can be reported on the income statement based on the fair value of revenues from similar *non-barter* transactions with *unrelated parties.*
- Under U.S. GAAP, revenue from barter transactions can be reported on the income statement at fair value only if the company has a history of making or receiving cash payments for such goods and services and hence, can use its historical experience to determine fair value. Otherwise, revenue should be reported at the carrying amount of the asset surrendered.

4. Gross versus Net Reporting

- Under gross revenue reporting, sales and cost of sales are reported separately.
- Under net reporting, only the difference between sales and costs of sales is reported on the income statement.

Under U.S. GAAP, only if the following conditions are met can the company recognize revenue based on gross reporting:

- The company is the primary obligor under the contract.
- The company bears inventory and credit risk.
- The company can choose its suppliers.
- The company has reasonable latitude to establish price.

Revenue Recognition Accounting Standards Issued in May 2014

FRA

In May 2014, IFRS and FASB issued a set of **converged standards** to make comparisons between companies operating in different jurisdictions easier. Under **IFRS**, these converged standards are effective for reporting periods beginning after January 1, 2018, while under **US GAAP**, they are effective for reporting periods beginning after December 15, 2017. Further, **IFRS** permits early adoption of the standards, while **US GAAP** only allows application as early as the original effective date (December 15, 2016).

The converged standards provide a principles-based approach to revenue recognition that can be applied to different types of revenue-generating activities.

Core Principle

The **core principle** of the converged standards is that revenue should be recognized in order to "depict the transfer of promised goods or services to customers in an amount that reflects the consideration to which the entity expects to be entitled in an exchange for those goods or services." In order to attain this core principle, the standards describe five steps in recognizing revenue:

1. Identify the contract(s) with a customer.
2. Identify the performance obligations in the contract.

3. Determine the transaction price.
4. Allocate the transaction price to the performance obligations in the contract.
5. Recognize revenue when (or as) the entity satisfies a performance obligation.

A **contract** is an agreement and commitment, with commercial substance, between the contacting parties. It establishes each party's obligations and rights, including payment terms. In addition, a contract exists only if collectability is **probable**. While IFRS and US GAAP use the same word (probable), they apply a different threshold for probable collectability. Under **IFRS**, probable means more likely than not, while under **US GAAP**, it means likely to occur. This subtle difference can result in economically similar contracts being treated differently under the two standards.

Performance obligations represent promises to transfer **distinct** good(s) or service(s). A good or service is distinct if (1) the customer can benefit from it on its own or in combination with readily available resources and (2) the promise to transfer it can be separated from other promises in the contract. Each identified performance obligation is accounted for separately.

The **transaction price** is the amount that the seller estimates it will receive in exchange for transferring the good(s) or service(s) identified in the contract to the buyer. The transaction price is then allocated to each identified performance obligation. The amount recognized reflects expectations about collectability and (if applicable) an allocation to multiple obligations within the same contract. Revenue is recognized when the obligation-satisfying transfer is made.

Accounting Treatment

- When revenue is recognized, a **contract asset** is presented on the balance sheet.
- If all performance obligations have been satisfied, but payment has not been received, a **receivable** appears on the seller's balance sheet.
- If payment is received in advance of transferring good(s) or service(s), the seller presents a **contract liability**.

For complex contracts, **variable consideration** may only be recognized as revenue if the company can conclude that it will not have to reverse the cumulative revenue in the future. The converged standards also provide guidance on whether a change in a contract is a **new contract or just a modification** of an existing contract.

- In order to be considered a new contract, the change would need to involve goods and services that are distinct from the goods and services already transferred.
- If the changes do not meet the criteria for a new contract then they are treated as contract modifications. The company must reflect the impact on a **cumulative catch-up basis**, by updating the transaction price and measure of progress.

The converged standards also lay down specific accounting treatments for certain related costs and also require extensive disclosures. The impact of converged standards will be felt more by industries where bundled sales are common, such as telecommunications and software.

Expense Recognition

The IASB framework defines expenses as "decreases in economic benefits during the accounting period in the form of outflows or depletions of assets or incurrence of liabilities that result in decreases in equity, other than those relating to distributions to equity participants."

Expenses also include losses, which result from non-operating activities of the business. The most important principle of expense recognition is the matching principle, which requires that expenses be matched with associated revenues when recognizing them in the income statement. If goods bought in the current year remain unsold at the end of the year, their cost is not included in the cost of goods sold for the current year. Instead, the cost of these goods will be deducted from next period's revenues once they are sold.

Certain expenses, such as administrative costs, cannot be directly linked to the generation of revenues. These expenses are called **period costs** and are expensed in the period in which they are incurred.

Issues in Expense Recognition

- Doubtful accounts.
- Warranties.
- Depreciation and amortization

Operating versus Nonoperating Components of the Income Statement

IFRS does not define operating activities. Therefore, companies that choose to report operating income or the results of operating activities need to ensure that such activities would normally be regarded as operating.

On the other hand, U.S. GAAP defines operating activities as those that generally involve producing and delivering goods and providing services, and include all transactions and other events that are not defined as investing or financing activities.

Discontinued Operations

Under both IFRS and U.S. GAAP, the income statement must report an operation separately as a "discontinued operation" when the company disposes of, or is expected to dispose of a component that is operationally and physically separable from the rest of the firm.

- Discontinued operations are reported *net of tax* as a *separate* line item *after* income from continuing operations (this treatment is permitted under IFRS and U.S. GAAP).
- As the disposed operation will not earn revenue for the company going forward, it will not be taken into account in forecasting the company's future profits.

Extraordinary Items

IFRS does not allow any items to be classified as extraordinary. U.S. GAAP defines extraordinary items as being **both** unusual in nature **and** infrequent in occurrence. A significant degree of judgment is involved in classifying an item as extraordinary. For example, losses caused by Hurricane Katrina in the Unites States were not classified as extraordinary items because natural disasters can reasonably be expected to reoccur.

- Extraordinary items are reported *net of tax* and as a *separate* line item *after* income from continuing operations (below discontinued operations).
- Analysts should eliminate extraordinary items from expectations about a company's future financial performance unless there are indications that these extraordinary items may reoccur.
- For fiscal periods beginning after December 15, 2015, U.S. GAAP will no longer include the concept of extraordinary items. Under the new guidance, items will simply be classified as unusual, infrequent, or unusual and infrequent.

Unusual or Infrequent Items

These items are **either** unusual in nature **or** infrequent in occurrence. Examples of such items include restructuring charges and gains and losses arising from selling an asset for a price other than its carrying value.

- These items are listed as separate line items on the income statement but are *included* in income from continuing operations and hence, reported *before-tax*.
- Analysts should not ignore all unusual or infrequent items. They should assess whether these items are likely to reoccur when forecasting future operations.

Accounting Changes

- A change in accounting principle can occur if it is required by standard setters or because of a management decision (e.g., changing from LIFO to FIFO method of inventory valuation). The change is applied retrospectively, which means that financial data for all periods is presented according to the new principal. This retrospective change facilitates comparisons across reporting periods. A description of, and justification for the change are provided in the footnotes to the financial statements.
- A change in an accounting estimate (e.g., a change in the residual value of an asset) is applied prospectively and only affects financial statements for current and future periods. Significant changes in accounting estimates must be disclosed in the footnotes.
- A correction of prior-period errors is made by restating all prior-period financial statements presented in the financial report. In addition, disclosure about the error is required in the footnotes. Analysts should carefully assess these disclosures as they may point to weaknesses in a company's accounting system or financial controls.

FRA

Earnings Per Share

A firm may have a simple capital structure or a complex capital structure. A company has a **simple capital structure** when it does not have any securities outstanding that can be converted into common stock. Firms with simple capital structures are required to report **basic earnings per share (EPS)** only.

$$\text{Basic EPS} = \frac{\text{Net income} - \text{Preferred dividends}}{\text{Weighted average number of shares outstanding}}$$

If a company declares a stock split or a stock dividend during the year, the calculation of the weighted average number of issued shares outstanding is based on the assumption that the additional (newly issued) shares have been outstanding since the date that the original shares were outstanding from.

A **complex capital structure** includes securities that can be converted into common stock (e.g., convertible bonds, convertible preferred stock, warrants and options). These securities are *potentially dilutive* so companies with complex capital structures are required to report basic and diluted EPS. A dilutive security is one whose conversion into shares of common stock would result in a reduction in EPS. EPS calculated after taking into account all dilutive securities in the capital structure is known as **diluted EPS**.

In determining which potentially dilutive securities should be included in the calculation of diluted EPS, each of the securities must be evaluated individually and independently to determine whether they are dilutive. Any anti-dilutive securities must be ignored from the diluted EPS calculation.

$$\text{Diluted EPS} = \frac{\left[\text{Net income} - \text{Preferred dividends}\right] + \text{Convertible preferred dividends} + \left[\text{Convertible debt interest} \times (1-t)\right]}{\text{Weighted average shares} + \text{Shares from conversion of convertible preferred shares} + \text{Shares from conversion of convertible debt} + \text{Shares issuable from stock options}}$$

IFRS requires the use of a similar method, but does not refer to it as the Treasury stock method. The proceeds of option exercise are assumed to be used to repurchase shares at the average market price and these shares are known as inferred shares. The excess of new issued shares over inferred shares is added to the weighted average number of shares outstanding.

Both U.S. GAAP and IFRS require the presentation of EPS (basic EPS and their diluted EPS) on the face of the income statement.

Treasury Stock Method

In the calculation of diluted EPS, stock options and warrants are accounted for by using the treasury stock method (required under U.S. GAAP). The treasury stock method assumes that all the funds received by the company from the exercise of options and warrants are used by the company to repurchase shares at the average market price. The resulting net increase in the number of shares equals the increase in shares from exercise of options and warrants minus the decrease in the number of outstanding shares from repurchases.

Common-size income statements present each item on the income statement as a percentage of *sales*. They facilitate financial statement analysis as the data can be used to conduct time-series (across time periods) and cross-sectional (across companies) analysis.

Comprehensive Income

IFRS defines total comprehensive income as "the change in equity during a period resulting from transactions and other events, other than those changes resulting from transactions with owners in their capacity as owners."

Under U.S. GAAP, comprehensive income is defined as "the change in equity (net assets) of a business enterprise during a period from transactions and other events and circumstances from nonowner sources. It includes all changes in equity during a period except those resulting from investments by owners and distributions to owners."

Under U.S. GAAP, there are four major types of items that are classified as other comprehensive income:

- Foreign currency translation adjustments.
- Minimum pension liability adjustments.
- Unrealized gains or losses on derivatives contracts, those considered as hedges.
- Unrealized holding gains and losses on available-for-sale securities.

Net income + Other comprehensive income = Comprehensive income

Under IFRS, certain changes in the value of long-lived assets that are measured using the revaluation model (as opposed to the cost model) are also included in other comprehensive income.

Note that the "Available-for-sale" classification no longer appears in IFRS as of 2010, although the relevant standard (IFRS 9: Financial Instruments) is not effective until 2018. However, even though the available-for-sale category will not exist, IFRS will still permit certain equity investments to be measured at fair value with any unrealized holding gains or losses recognized in other comprehensive income if they are classified as "financial assets measured at fair value through other comprehensive income."

UNDERSTANDING BALANCE SHEETS
Cross-Reference to CFA Institute Assigned Reading #25

Limitations of the Balance Sheet

- Under current accounting standards, measurement bases of different assets and liabilities may vary considerably, which can have a significant impact on reported figures.
- The value of items reported on the balance sheet reflects their value at the end of the reporting period, which may not necessarily remain "current" at a later date.
- The balance sheet does not include qualitative factors (e.g., reputation, management skills, etc.) that have an important impact on the company's future cash-generating ability and therefore, its overall value.

Alternative Formats of Balance Sheet Presentation

- Report format: Assets, liabilities and equity are presented in a single column. This format is the most commonly-used balance sheet presentation format.
- Account format: Assets are presented on the left hand side of the balance sheet, with liabilities and equity on the right hand side.
- Classified balance sheet: Different types of assets and liabilities are grouped into subcategories to give a more effective overview of the company's financial position. Classifications typically group assets and liabilities into their current and non-current portions.
- Liquidity-based presentation: **IFRS** allows the preparation of a balance sheet using a liquidity-based presentation format (rather than a current/non-current format), if such a format provides more reliable and relevant information. In a liquidity-based presentation, all assets and liabilities are broadly presented in order of liquidity. This format is typically used by banks.

IFRS and U.S. GAAP Balance Sheet Presentation

Both **IFRS** and **U.S. GAAP** require that assets and liabilities be grouped separately into their current and non-current portions, which makes it easier for analysts to examine the company's liquidity position as of the balance sheet date. However, it is not required that current assets be presented before noncurrent assets, or that current liabilities be presented before noncurrent liabilities. Further, under **IFRS**, the current/non-current classifications are not required if a liquidity-based presentation provides more relevant and reliable information.

Exhibit 1: Measurement Bases of Various Financial Assets

Measured at Fair Value	Measured at Cost or Amortized Cost
Financial Assets Financial assets held for trading (stocks and bonds). Available-for-sale financial assets (stocks and bonds). Derivatives. Non-derivative instruments with face value exposures hedged by derivatives.	**Financial Assets** Unlisted instruments. Held-to-maturity investments. Loans and receivables.

Accounting for Gains and Losses on Marketable Securities

	Held-to-Maturity Securities	Available-for-sale Securities	Trading Securities
Balance Sheet	Reported at cost or amortized cost.	Reported at fair value. Unrealized gains or losses due to changes in market value are reported in other comprehensive income.	Reported at fair value.
Items recognized on the income statement	Interest income Realized gains and losses.	Dividend income. Interest income. Realized gains and losses.	Dividend income. Interest income. Realized gains and losses. Unrealized gains and losses due to changes in market value.

FRA

Measurement Bases of Various Financial Liabilities

Measured at Fair Value	Measured at Cost or Amortized Cost
Financial Liabilities Derivatives. Financial liabilities held for trading. Non-derivative instruments with face value exposures hedged by derivatives.	**Financial Liabilities** All other liabilities (bonds payable and notes payable).

The Components of Shareholders' Equity

- Capital contributed by owners (common stock or issued capital).
    - Authorized shares are the maximum number of shares that can be sold under the company's Articles of Incorporation.
    - Issued shares are the total number of shares that have been sold to shareholders.
    - Outstanding shares equal the number of shares that were issued less the number of shares repurchased (treasury stock).
- Preferred shares
- Treasury shares
- Retained earnings
- Accumulated other comprehensive income
- Noncontrolling interest (minority interest)

Statement of Changes in Owners' Equity

This statement presents the effects of all transactions that increase or decrease company's equity over the period. Under **IFRS**, the following information should be included in the statement of changes in equity:

- Total comprehensive income for the period.
- The effects of any accounting changes that have been retrospectively applied to previous periods.
- Capital transactions with owners and distributions to owners; and
- Reconciliation of the carrying amounts of each component of equity at the beginning and end of the year.

FRA

Under U.S. GAAP, companies are required to provide an analysis of changes in each component of stockholders' equity that is shown in the balance sheet.

Uses and Analysis of Balance Sheets

Analysts can gain information regarding a company's liquidity, solvency, and the economic resources controlled by the company by examining its balance sheet.

- Liquidity refers to a company's ability to meet its short-term financial obligations.
- Solvency refers to a company's ability to meet its long-term financial obligations.

Two of the techniques that may be used to analyze a company's balance sheet are common-size analysis and ratio analysis.

Common-Size Balance Sheets

A vertical common-size balance sheet expresses each balance sheet item as a percentage of total assets. This allows an analyst to perform historical analysis (time-series analysis) and cross-sectional analysis across firms within the same industry.

Balance Sheet Ratios

These are ratios that have balance sheet items in the numerator and the denominator. The two main categories of balance sheet ratios are liquidity ratios, which measure a company's ability to settle short-term obligations and solvency ratios, which evaluate a company's ability to settle long-term obligations.

The *higher* a company's liquidity ratios, the *greater* the likelihood that the company will be able to meet its short-term obligations.

Liquidity ratios

	Numerator	Denominator
Current ratio	Current assets	Current liabilities
Quick ratio (acid test ratio)	Cash + marketable securities + receivables	Current liabilities
Cash ratio	Cash + marketable securities	Current liabilities

FRA

Higher solvency ratios, on the other hand, are *undesirable* and indicate that the company is highly leveraged and risky.

Solvency Ratios

	Numerator	Denominator
Long-term debt-to-equity ratio	Total long-term debt	Total equity
Debt-to-equity ratio	Total debt	Total equity
Total debt ratio	Total debt	Total assets
Financial leverage ratio	Total assets	Total equity

UNDERSTANDING CASH FLOW STATEMENTS

Cross-Reference to CFA Institute Assigned Reading #26

Under both IFRS and U.S. GAAP, cash flows are classified into the following categories:

Cash Flows from Operating Activities (CFO) are inflows and outflows of cash generated from a firm's day-to-day business activities.

Cash Flows from Investing Activities (CFI) are inflows and outflows of cash generated from purchase and disposal of long-term investments. Long-term investments include plant, machinery, equipment, intangible assets, and non-trading debt and equity securities.

All securities that are considered highly liquid (cash equivalents) are not included in investing activities and neither are securities held for trading. Cash flows associated with the purchase and sale of highly liquid cash equivalents, and of securities for trading purposes are classified as cash flows from operating activities.

Cash Flows from Financing Activities (CFF) are cash inflows and outflows generated from issuance and repayment of capital (long-term debt and equity).

Indirect short term borrowings from suppliers that are classified as accounts payable and receivables from customers are not financing activities; they are classified as operating activities.

Cash Flow Classification

CFO

Inflows	Outflows
Cash collected from customers.	Cash paid to employees.
Interest and dividends received.	Cash paid to suppliers.
Proceeds from sale of securities held for trading.	Cash paid for other expenses.
	Cash used to purchase trading securities.
	Interest paid.
	Taxes paid.

CFI

Inflows	Outflows
Sale proceeds from fixed assets.	Purchase of fixed assets.
Sale proceeds from long-term investments.	Cash used to acquire LT investment securities.

CFF

Inflows	Outflows
Proceeds from debt issuance.	Repayment of LT debt.
Proceeds from issuance of equity instruments.	Payments made to repurchase stock.
	Dividends payments.

FRA

Cash Flow Presentation Formats

Under both IFRS and U.S. GAAP, there are two acceptable formats for presenting the cash flow statement—the direct method and the indirect method. These methods differ only in the *presentation* of the *CFO* section of the cash flow statement; calculated values for CFO are the same under both. Further, the presentation of financing and investing activities is exactly the same.

Direct Method versus Indirect Method

- The direct method explicitly lists the actual sources of operating cash inflows and outflows, whereas indirect method only provides net results for these inflows and outflows. The information provided under the direct method is very useful in evaluating past performance and making projections of future cash flows.
- The indirect method provides a list of items that are responsible for the difference between net income and operating cash flows. The differences can then be used to estimate future operating cash flows. The indirect method facilitates forecasting of future cash flows since forecasts of future net income simply have to be adjusted for changes in working capital accounts.

Sources and Uses of Cash

- *Increases* in current assets are *uses* of cash, and *decreases* in current assets are *sources* of cash. Changes in asset balances and cash are *negatively* related.
- *Increases* in current liabilities are *sources* of cash, while *decreases* in current liabilities are *uses* of cash. Changes in liability balances and cash are *positively* related.

The Direct Method

Step 1: Start with sales on the income statement.

Step 2: Go through each income statement account and adjust it for changes in all relevant working capital accounts on the balance sheet. This serves to remove the effects of the timing difference between the recognition of revenues or expenses, and the actual receipt or payment of cash.

Step 3: Check whether changes in these working capital accounts indicate a source or use of cash. Make sure you put the right sign in front of the income statement item. Sales are an inflow item so they have a positive effect on cash flow, while COGS, wages, taxes, and interest expense are all outflow items that have negative effects on cash flow.

Step 4: Ignore all nonoperating items (e.g., gain/loss on sale of plant and equipment) and noncash charges (e.g., depreciation and amortization).

FRA

The Indirect Method

Step 1: Start with net income.

Step 2: Go up the income statement and remove the effect of all noncash expenses and gains from net income. For example, the negative effect of depreciation is removed from net income by adding depreciation back to net income. Cash net income will be higher than accrual-based net income by the amount of noncash expenses.

Step 3: Remove the effects of all nonoperating activities from net income. For example the positive effect of a gain on sale of fixed assets on net income is removed by subtracting the gain from net income.

Step 4: Make adjustments for changes in all working capital accounts. Add all sources of cash (increases in current liabilities and decreases in current assets) and subtract all uses of cash (decreases in current liabilities and increases in current assets).

Cash Flows Statements under IFRS and U.S. GAAP

	IFRS	U.S. GAAP
Classification of Cash Flows		
Interest and dividends received	CFO or CFI	CFO
Interest paid	CFO or CFF	CFO
Dividend paid	CFO or CFF	CFF
Dividends received	CFO or CFI	CFO
Taxes paid	CFO, but part of the tax can be categorized as CFI or CFF if it is clear that the tax arose from investing or financing activities.	CFO
Bank overdrafts	Included as a part of cash equivalents.	Not considered a part of cash equivalents and included in CFF.
Presentation Format		
CFO (No difference in CFI and CFF presentation)	Direct or indirect method. The former is preferred.	Direct or indirect method. The former is preferred. However, if the direct method is used, a reconciliation of net income and CFO must be included.
Disclosures		
	Taxes paid should be presented separately on the cash flow statement.	If taxes and interest paid are not explicitly stated on the cash flow statement, details can be provided in footnotes.

FRA

Cash Flow Analysis

Major sources and uses of cash	Sources and uses of cash depend on the company's stage of growth. • Companies in the early stages of growth may have negative operating cash flows as cash is used to finance inventory and receivables. These negative operating cash flows are supported by financing inflows from issuance of debt or equity. • Inflows of cash from financing activities are not sustainable. Over the long-term, a company must generate positive cash flows from operating activities that exceed capital expenditures and payments to providers of debt and equity capital. • Companies in the mature stage of growth usually have positive cash flows from operating activities. These inflows can be used for debt repayment and stock repurchases. They can also be used by the company to expand its scale of operations (investing activities).
Operating cash flows	Changes in relevant asset and liability accounts should be used to determine whether business operations are a source or use of cash. • Operating cash flow should be compared to net income. If high net income is not being translated into high operating cash flows, the company might be using aggressive revenue recognition policies. • Companies should ideally have operating cash flows that are greater than net income. • The variability of operating cash flows and net income is an important determinant of the overall risk inherent in the company.
Investing cash flows	Changes in long-term asset and investment accounts are used to determine sources and uses of investing cash flows. • Increasing outflows may imply capital expenditures. Analysts should then evaluate how the company plans to finance these investments (i.e., with excess operating cash flows or by undertaking financing activities).
Financing cash flows	Changes in long-term debt and equity are used to determine sources and uses of financing cash flows. • If debt issuance contributes significantly to financing cash flows, the repayment schedule must be considered. • Increasing use of cash to repay debt, repurchase stock and make dividend payments might indicate a lack of lucrative investment opportunities for the company.

FRA

Free Cash Flow

Free cash flow is the excess of a company's operating cash flows over capital expenditure undertaken during the year. Free cash flow to the *firm* and free cash flow to *equity* are more precise measures of free cash flow as they identify specifically whom the cash is available to.

Free cash flow to the firm (FCFF) is cash available to equity and debt holders after the company has met all its operating expenses, and satisfied its capital expenditure and working capital requirements.

$$\text{FCFF} = \text{NI} + \text{NCC} + [\text{Int} \times (1 - \text{tax rate})] - \text{FCInv} - \text{WCInv}$$

$$\text{FCFF} = \text{CFO} + [\text{Int} \times (1 - \text{tax rate})] - \text{FCInv}$$

Free cash flow to equity (FCFE) is the cash that is available only to common shareholders.

$$\text{FCFE} = \text{CFO} - \text{FCInv} + \text{Net borrowing} - \text{Net debt repayment}$$

FRA

FINANCIAL ANALYSIS TECHNIQUES

Cross-Reference to CFA Institute Assigned Reading #27

Limitations of Ratio Analysis

- Companies may have divisions that operate in different industries. This can make it difficult to find relevant industry ratios for comparison purposes.
- There are no set ranges within which particular ratios for a company must lie. An analyst must use her own judgment to evaluate the implications of a given value for a ratio. This usually involves examining the entire operations of a company, the external industry and economic scenario.
- Firms enjoy significant latitude in the choice of accounting methods that are acceptable given the jurisdiction that they operate in. For example, under U.S. GAAP, companies can:
  - Choose from a variety of inventory cost flow assumptions (e.g., FIFO, AVCO or LIFO).
  - Choose from a variety of depreciation methods (e.g., MACRS and straight-line).
- Comparing ratios of firms across international borders is even more difficult, in that several countries use IFRS. Despite the growing convergence between IFRS and U.S. GAAP, significant differences remain.

Common Ratios Used in Financial Analysis

Activity ratios measure how productive a company is in using its assets and how efficiently it performs its everyday operations.

$$\textbf{Inventory turnover} = \frac{\text{Cost of goods sold}}{\text{Average inventory}}$$

$$\textbf{Days of inventory on hand (DOH)} = \frac{365}{\text{Inventory turnover}}$$

$$\textbf{Receivables turnover} = \frac{\text{Revenue}}{\text{Average receivables}}$$

$$\textbf{Days of sales outstanding (DSO)} = \frac{365}{\text{Receivables turnover}}$$

FRA

$$\textbf{Payables turnover} = \frac{\text{Purchases}}{\text{Average trade payables}}$$

$$\textbf{Number of days of payables} = \frac{365}{\text{Payables turnover}}$$

$$\textbf{Working capital turnover} = \frac{\text{Revenue}}{\text{Average working capital}}$$

$$\textbf{Fixed asset turnover} = \frac{\text{Revenue}}{\text{Average fixed assets}}$$

$$\textbf{Total Asset Turnover} = \frac{\text{Revenue}}{\text{Average total assets}}$$

Liquidity ratios measure the company's ability to meet its short-term cash requirements.

$$\textbf{Current ratio} = \frac{\text{Current assets}}{\text{Current liabilities}}$$

$$\textbf{Quick ratio} = \frac{\text{Cash} + \text{Short-term marketable investments} + \text{Receivables}}{\text{Current liabilities}}$$

$$\textbf{Cash ratio} = \frac{\text{Cash} + \text{Short-term marketable investments}}{\text{Current liabilities}}$$

$$\textbf{Defensive interval ratio} = \frac{\text{Cash} + \text{Short-term marketable investments} + \text{Receivables}}{\text{Daily cash expenditures}}$$

$$\textbf{Cash conversion cycle} = \text{DSO} + \text{DOH} - \text{Number of days of payables}$$

Solvency ratios measure a company's ability to meet its long-term obligations.

$$\textbf{Debt-to-assets ratio} = \frac{\text{Total debt}}{\text{Total assets}}$$

$$\textbf{Debt-to-capital ratio} = \frac{\text{Total debt}}{\text{Total debt} + \text{Shareholders' equity}}$$

$$\textbf{Debt-to-equity ratio} = \frac{\text{Total debt}}{\text{Shareholders' equity}}$$

$$\textbf{Financial leverage ratio} = \frac{\text{Average total assets}}{\text{Average total equity}}$$

$$\textbf{Interest coverage ratio} = \frac{\text{EBIT}}{\text{Interest payments}}$$

$$\textbf{Fixed charge coverage ratio} = \frac{\text{EBIT} + \text{Lease payments}}{\text{Interest payments} + \text{Lease payments}}$$

Profitability ratios measure a company's ability to generate an adequate return on invested capital.

$$\textbf{Gross profit margin} = \frac{\text{Gross profit}}{\text{Revenue}}$$

$$\textbf{Operating profit margin} = \frac{\text{Operating profit}}{\text{Revenue}}$$

$$\textbf{Pretax margin} = \frac{\text{EBT (earnings before tax, but after interest)}}{\text{Revenue}}$$

$$\textbf{Net profit margin} = \frac{\text{Net profit}}{\text{Revenue}}$$

$$\textbf{ROA} = \frac{\text{Net income}}{\text{Average total assets}}$$

$$\textbf{Adjusted ROA} = \frac{\text{Net income} + \text{Interest expense } (1 - \text{Tax rate})}{\text{Average total assets}}$$

$$\textbf{Operating ROA} = \frac{\text{Operating income or EBIT}}{\text{Average total assets}}$$

$$\textbf{Return on total capital} = \frac{\text{EBIT}}{\text{Short-term debt} + \text{Long-term debt} + \text{Equity}}$$

$$\textbf{Return on equity} = \frac{\text{Net income}}{\text{Average total equity}}$$

$$\textbf{Return on common equity} = \frac{\text{Net income} - \text{Preferred dividends}}{\text{Average common equity}}$$

Interpretation and Context

- Actual ratios should be compared to the company's stated objectives. This helps in determining whether the company's operations are moving in line with its strategy.
- A company's ratios should be compared with those of others in the industry. When comparing ratios across firms from the same industry, analysts must be careful because:
    - Not all ratios are important to every industry.
    - Companies can have several lines of business, which can cause aggregate financial ratios to be distorted. In such a situation, analysts should evaluate ratios for each segment of the business in relation to the relevant industry average.
    - Companies might be using different accounting methods.
    - Companies could be at different stages of growth, or may have different strategies. This can result in different values for various ratios for firms in the same industry.
- Ratios should be studied in light of the current phase of the business cycle.

DuPont Analysis: The Decomposition of ROE

ROE measures the return a company generates on its equity capital. Decomposing ROE into its components through DuPont analysis has the following uses:

FRA

- It facilitates a meaningful evaluation of the different aspects of the company's performance that affect reported ROE.
- It helps in determining the reasons for changes in ROE over time for a given company. It also helps us understand the reasons for differences in ROE for different companies over a given time period.
- It can direct management to areas that it should focus on to improve ROE.
- It shows the relationship between the various categories of ratios and how they all influence the return that owners realize on their investment.

$$\textbf{ROE} = \frac{\text{Net income}}{\text{Average shareholders' equity}}$$

$$\textbf{ROE} = \frac{\text{Net income}}{\text{Average total assets}} \times \frac{\text{Average total assets}}{\text{Average shareholder's equity}}$$

$$\textbf{ROE} = \frac{\text{Net income}}{\text{Revenue}} \times \frac{\text{Revenue}}{\text{Average total assets}} \times \frac{\text{Average total assets}}{\text{Average shareholders' equity}}$$

$$\textbf{ROE} = \frac{\text{Net income}}{\text{EBT}} \times \frac{\text{EBT}}{\text{EBIT}} \times \frac{\text{EBIT}}{\text{Revenue}} \times \frac{\text{Revenue}}{\text{Average total assets}} \times \frac{\text{Average total assets}}{\text{Avg. shareholders' equity}}$$

Valuation ratios measure the quantity of an asset or flow (for e.g., earnings) associated with ownership of a specific claim (for e.g., common stock).

$$\textbf{P/E} = \frac{\text{Price per share}}{\text{Earnings per share}}$$

$$\textbf{P/CF} = \frac{\text{Price per share}}{\text{Cash flow per share}}$$

$$\textbf{P/S} = \frac{\text{Price per share}}{\text{Sales per share}}$$

$$\textbf{P/BV} = \frac{\text{Price per share}}{\text{Book value per share}}$$

$$\textbf{Cash flow per share} = \frac{\text{Cash flow from operations}}{\text{Average number of shares outstanding}}$$

$$\textbf{EBITDA per share} = \frac{\text{EBITDA}}{\text{Average number of shares outstanding}}$$

$$\textbf{Dividends per share} = \frac{\text{Common dividends declared}}{\text{Weighted average number of ordinary shares}}$$

FRA

$$\textbf{Dividend payout ratio} = \frac{\text{Common share dividends}}{\text{Net income attributable to common shares}}$$

$$\textbf{Retention Rate} = \frac{\text{Net income attributable to common shares} - \text{Common share dividends}}{\text{Net income attributable to common shares}}$$

$$\textbf{Sustainable growth rate} = \text{Retention rate} \times \text{ROE}$$

Credit Analysis

Credit Ratio	Numerator	Denominator
EBIT interest coverage	EBIT	Gross interest
EBITDA interest coverage	EBITDA	Gross interest
Free operating cash flow to total debt	CFO	Total debt
Return on capital	EBIT	Capital = Average Equity
Total debt to total debt plus equity	Total debt	Total debt plus equity

FRA

Industry Specific Ratios

Ratios	Numerator	Denominator
Business Risk		
Coefficient of variation of operating income	Standard deviation of operating income	Average operating income
Coefficient of variation of net income	Standard deviation of net income	Average net income
Coefficient of variation of revenues	Standard deviation of revenues	Average revenue
Financial Sector Ratios		
Capital adequacy—Banks	Various components of capital	Risk weighted assets, market risk exposure, and level of operational risk assumed
Monetary reserve requirement	Reserves held at central bank	Specified deposit liabilities
Liquid asset requirement	Approved "readily marketable securities"	Specified deposit liabilities
Net interest margin	Net interest income	Total interest-earning assets
Retail Ratios		
Same store sales	Average revenue growth year on year for stores open in both periods	Not applicable
Sales per square foot (meter)	Revenue	Total retail space in feet or meters
Service Companies		
Revenue per employee	Revenue	Total number of employees
Net income per employee	Net income	Total number of employees
Hotels		
Average daily rate	Room revenue	Number of rooms sold
Occupancy rate	Number of rooms sold	Number of rooms available

FRA

Segment Analysis

Segment Ratios	Numerator	Denominator	Measures
Segment margin	Segment profit (loss)	Segment revenue	Operating profitability relative to sales.
Segment turnover	Segment revenue	Segment assets	Overall efficiency-how much revenue is generated per dollar of assets.
Segment ROA	Segment profit (loss)	Segment assets	Operating profitability relative to assets.
Segment debt ratio	Segment liabilities	Segment assets	Solvency of the segment.

Model Building and Forecasting

Sensitivity analysis shows the range of possible outcomes as underlying assumptions are altered.

Scenario analysis shows the changes in key financial quantities that result from events such as a loss of supply of raw materials or a reduction in demand for the firm's products.

Simulations are computer generated sensitivity or scenario analyses that are based on probability models for the factors that drive outcomes.

FRA

Study Session 8: Financial Reporting and Analysis—Inventories, Long-Lived Assets, Income Taxes, and Non-Current Liabilities

FRA

INVENTORIES

Cross-Reference to CFA Institute Assigned Reading #28

Cost of Inventories

IFRS and U.S. GAAP suggest a similar treatment of various expenses in the determination of inventory cost. The following items are capitalized inventory costs, which are included in the cost of inventories.

- Costs of purchase.
- Costs of conversion.

Capitalization of these costs results in a build-up of asset balances, and delays recognition of costs until inventory is sold.

The following items are not capitalized as inventory costs; they are expensed on the income statement as incurred:

- Abnormal costs from material wastage.
- Storage costs that are not a part of normal production processes.
- Administrative expenses.
- Selling and marketing costs.

Capitalization of costs that should be expensed results in overstatement of net income due to the delay in recognition of costs, and an overstatement of inventory value on the balance sheet.

Inventory Valuation Methods

FIFO

- Older units are the first ones sold.
- Units that are purchased recently are included in EI.
- COGS is composed of units valued at older prices.
- EI is composed of units valued at recent prices.

LIFO

- Recently acquired units are the first ones to be sold.
- Oldest units are included in EI.
- COGS is composed of units valued at recent prices.
- Ending inventory is composed of units valued at older prices.

AVCO (weighted-average cost)

- COGS is composed of units valued at average prices.
- Ending inventory is also composed of units that are valued at average prices.

FIFO will always give a better reflection of the current economic value of inventory because the units currently in stock are valued at the most *recent* prices.

- If prices are *rising* LIFO and AVCO will *understate* ending inventory value.
- If prices are *falling*, LIFO and AVCO will *overstate* ending inventory value.
- When prices are stable, the three methods will value inventory at the same level.

LIFO will always offer a closer reflection of replacement costs in COGS because it allocates *recent* costs to COGS. LIFO is the most economically accurate method for income statement purposes because it provides a better measure of current income and future profitability.

- If prices are *rising*, FIFO and AVCO will *understate* replacement costs in COGS and *overstate* profits.
- If prices are *falling*, FIFO and AVCO will *overstate* replacements costs in COGS and *understate* profits.
- When prices are stable, the three methods will value COGS at same level.

When prices are *rising* during the year and inventory levels are stable or rising:

- $COGS_{LIFO} > COGS_{AVCO} > COGS_{FIFO}$
- $EI_{FIFO} > EI_{AVCO} > EI_{LIFO}$

When prices are *falling* during the year and inventory levels are stable or rising:

- $COGS_{FIFO} > COGS_{AVCO} > COGS_{LIFO}$
- $EI_{LIFO} > EI_{AVCO} > EI_{FIFO}$

LIFO versus FIFO when Prices Are Rising

	LIFO	FIFO
COGS	Higher	Lower
Income before taxes	Lower	Higher
Income taxes	Lower	Higher
Net income	Lower	Higher
Cash flow	Higher	Lower
EI	Lower	Higher
Working capital	Lower	Higher

FRA

Periodic versus Perpetual Inventory Systems

Periodic inventory system: Under this system, the quantity of inventory on hand is calculated periodically. The cost of goods available for sale during the period is calculated as beginning inventory plus purchases over the period. The ending inventory amount is then deducted from cost of goods available for sale to determine COGS.

Perpetual inventory system: Under this system, changes in the inventory account are updated continuously. Purchases and sales are recorded directly in the inventory account as they occur.

Under the **LIFO** cost flow assumption, in a period of rising prices, use of the periodic system for inventory results in a:

- *Lower* value of ending inventory.
- *Higher* value for COGS.

Therefore, gross profit would be *lower* under the periodic system.

Other important takeaways:

- The value of sales and cost of goods available for sale are the same under the two systems in the first year of operations.
- In subsequent years, the amounts of cost of goods available for sale can be different under the two systems due to different values of opening inventory (previous periods' ending inventory).
- If a company uses FIFO, COGS and EI is the same under the periodic and perpetual inventory systems.
- If a company uses separate identification, COGS and EI is the same under the periodic and perpetual inventory systems.
- If a company uses AVCO:
  - COGS and EI are the same as under FIFO and AVCO under the perpetual inventory system.
  - COGS and EI are different from their value under FIFO under the periodic inventory system.

Generally speaking, analysts do not make adjustments when comparing financial statements of a company that uses AVCO to one that uses FIFO. This is because:

- The perpetual inventory system is more common (the values of COGS and EI are similar under FIFO and AVCO if the perpetual system is used).
- There is a general dearth of relevant disclosures in this area.

Assuming rising prices and stable or increasing inventory quantities, use of the LIFO method generally results in higher COGS, lower EI, lower GP, and lower NP than with the FIFO method, under both periodic and perpetual inventory systems.

LIFO to FIFO Conversion

$$EI_{FIFO} = EI_{LIFO} + \text{LIFO reserve}$$
$$COGS_{FIFO} = COGS - (LR_{Ending} - LR_{Beginning})$$

During a period of rising prices and stable or rising inventory quantities:

- Net income after tax under FIFO will be greater than LIFO net income after tax by:
  - Change in LIFO reserve × (1 – tax rate)
- Equity (retained earnings) under FIFO will be greater by:
  - LIFO reserve × (1– tax rate)
- Liabilities (deferred taxes) under FIFO will be greater by:
  - LIFO reserve × (tax rate)
- Current assets (inventory) under FIFO will be greater by:
  - LIFO reserve

Increase in LIFO Reserve

In every period during which prices are rising and inventory quantities are stable or rising, the LIFO reserve will increase as the excess of FIFO ending inventory over LIFO ending inventory increases.

Decline in LIFO Reserve

There can be two reasons for a decline in LIFO reserve:

1. LIFO liquidation.
2. Declining prices.

LIFO Liquidation

FRA

LIFO liquidation occurs when, during an inflationary period, a firm that uses LIFO sells more units during a given period than it purchases over the period. This causes year-end inventory levels to be lower than beginning-of-year inventory levels.

When a LIFO firm sells more units than it purchases, some of the goods sold are units that were included in beginning inventory. LIFO allocates the oldest prices to inventory, and in some cases these older prices could be outdated by many years. When a company includes older, cheaper stock in its COGS, it severely understates its COGS, and LIFO COGS no longer reflect recent, current prices. Consequently a firm with LIFO liquidation overstates net income. The higher profits are unsustainable because eventually, the firm will run out of cheaper, older stock to liquidate. The higher net income also comes at the cost of higher taxes that reduce operating cash flow. To postpone these taxes on holding gains on old units of inventory, a LIFO firm must always purchase as many as, if not more units, than it sells.

LIFO liquidation can result from strikes, recessions, or a decline in demand for the firm's product. The irony is that when there is LIFO liquidation, the firm reports surprisingly high profits (due to the realization of holding gains) in hard times when production cuts result in the liquidation of lower cost LIFO inventory.

Analysts should be aware that management can inflate their company's reported gross profits and net income by intentionally reducing inventory quantities and liquidating older (cheaper) units of stock. Therefore, it is important to analyse the LIFO reserve footnote disclosures to determine if LIFO liquidation has occurred. If it is found that LIFO liquidation has occurred, analysts must exclude the increase in earnings due to LIFO liquidation from their analysis. COGS must be adjusted upwards for the decline in LIFO reserve, and net income must be lowered.

LIFO liquidations are more likely to occur with firms that break inventory down into numerous categories. When the different types of inventory are pooled into only a few broad categories, decreases in quantities of certain items are usually offset by increases in quantities of others.

Declining Prices

When prices of the firm's products fall over a given period, the firm will see a decline in its LIFO reserve. If the change in LIFO reserve is negative, $COGS_{FIFO}$ will be greater than $COGS_{LIFO}$. FIFO would continue to reflect the latest (and in this case lower) prices in inventory, and will provide the most economically accurate measure of inventory value, while LIFO would continue to reflect current replacement costs in COGS. When the reduction in LIFO reserve is caused by declining prices, no analytical adjustments are necessary.

Inventory Method Changes

Consistency in the inventory costing method used is required under U.S. GAAP and IFRS.

FRA

Under **IFRS**, a change in policy is acceptable only if the change results in the provision of more reliable and relevant information in the financial statements.

- Changes in inventory accounting policy are applied retrospectively.
- Information for all periods presented in the financial report is restated.
- Adjustments for periods prior to the earliest year presented in the financial report are reflected in the beginning balance of retained earnings for the earliest year presented in the report.

U.S. GAAP has a similar requirement for changes in inventory accounting policies.

- However, a company must thoroughly explain how the newly-adopted inventory accounting method is superior and preferable to the old one.
- The company may be required to seek permission from the Internal Revenue Service (IRS) before making any changes.
- If inventory-related accounting policies are modified, changes to the financial statements must be made retrospectively, unless the LIFO method is being adopted (which is applied prospectively).

Inventory Adjustments

Under **IFRS**, inventory must be stated at the **lower of cost or net realizable value (NRV)**. **NRV** is the estimated selling price in the ordinary course of business less the estimated costs necessary to make the sale and estimated costs to get the inventory in condition for sale. If the NRV of inventory falls below the cost recorded on the balance sheet, inventory must be written down, and a loss must be recognized (as a part of COGS or separately) on the income statement. A subsequent increase in NRV would require a reversal of the previous write-down, which would reduce COGS in the period that the increase in value occurs. However, the increase in value that can be recognized is limited to the total write-down that had previously been recorded. Effectively, inventory value can never exceed the amount originally recognized.

U.S. GAAP used to require the application of the lower of cost or market (LCM) principle to value inventory. For fiscal years beginning after December 15, 2016, inventories measured using other than LIFO and retail inventory methods are measured at the lower of cost or net realizable value. This is broadly consistent with IFRS, with one major difference: that U.S. GAAP prohibits the reversal of write-downs.

When the LCM principle must be applied under U.S. GAAP (for inventories measured using LIFO and retail inventory methods), market value is defined as replacement cost, where replacement cost must lie within a range of values from NRV minus normal profit margin to NRV. If replacement cost is higher than NRV, it must be brought down to NRV, and if replacement cost is lower than NRV minus normal profit margin, it must be brought up to NRV minus normal profit margin. This adjusted replacement cost is then compared to carrying value (cost), and the lower of the two is used to value inventory. Any write-down of inventory reduces the value of inventory and increases COGS.

An inventory write-down reduces both profit and the carrying amount of inventory on the balance sheet and thus has a negative effect on profitability, liquidity, and solvency ratios. However, activity ratios such as inventory turnover will be positively affected. Due to overall negative financial impact, some companies may be reluctant to record inventory write-downs unless the decline in value is believed to be permanent. This is especially true under U.S. GAAP where reversal of a write-down is prohibited.

Companies that use separate identification, AVCO, or FIFO inventory methods are more likely to incur inventory write-downs than companies that use LIFO. This is because LIFO values units of inventory at the oldest prices, which, given that prices are generally on the rise, results in lower carrying values for inventory. Since LIFO inventory is based on oldest and lowest costs, there is a lower chance of an inventory write-down, and if there is a write-down, it will likely be of a lesser magnitude.

In certain industries like agriculture, forest products, and mining, both U.S. GAAP and IFRS allow companies to value inventory at NRV even when it exceeds historical cost. If an active market exists for the product, quoted market prices are used as NRV; otherwise the price of the most recent market transaction is used. Unrealized gains and losses on inventory resulting from fluctuating market prices are recognized on the income statement.

The impact of an inventory write-down on a company's reported financial position can be substantial. Therefore, analysts should careful evaluate the potential for any inventory write-downs and gauge their impact on financial ratios, especially if debt covenants entail financial ratio requirements. The potential for inventory write-downs tends to be higher in industries where technological obsolescence of inventories is a significant risk.

Inventory write-downs raise concerns regarding management's ability to anticipate how much and what type of inventory is required. Further, they affect a company's future reported earnings.

Table 3-1: Impact of an Inventory Write-Down on Various Financial Ratios

Type of Ratio	Effect on Numerator	Effect on Denominator	Effect on Ratio
Profitability ratios			
NP and GP margins	COGS increases so profits fall	Sales remain the same	Lower (worsens)
Solvency ratios			
Debt-to-equity and debt ratio	Debt levels remain the same	Equity decreases (due to lower profits) and current assets decrease (due to lower inventory)	Higher (worsens)
Liquidity ratios			
Current ratio	Current assets decrease (due to lower inventory)	Current liabilities remain the same	Lower (worsens)
Activity ratios			
Inventory turnover	COGS increases	Average inventory decreases	Higher (improves)
Total asset turnover	Sales remain the same	Total assets decrease	Higher (improves)

Presentation and Disclosure

IFRS requires companies to make the following disclosures relating to inventory:

1. The accounting policies used to value inventory.
2. The cost formula used for inventory valuation.
3. The total carrying value of inventories, and the carrying value of different classifications (e.g., merchandise, raw materials, work-in-progress, finished goods).
4. The value of inventories carried at fair value less selling costs.
5. Amount of inventory-related expenses for the period (cost of sales).
6. The amount of any write-downs recognized during the period.
7. The amount of reversal recognized on any previous write-down.
8. Description of the circumstances that led to the reversal.
9. The carrying amount of inventories pledged as collateral for liabilities.

U.S. GAAP does not permit the reversal of prior-year inventory write-downs. U.S. GAAP also requires disclosure of significant estimates applicable to inventories and of any material amount of income resulting from the liquidation of LIFO inventory.

Inventory Ratios

$$\text{Inventory turnover} = \frac{\text{COGS}}{\text{Average inventory}}$$

$$\text{No. of days of inventory} = \frac{365}{\text{Inventory turnover}}$$

$$\text{Gross profit margin} = \frac{\text{Gross profit}}{\text{Sales revenue}}$$

If a company has a *higher* inventory turnover ratio and a *lower* number of days of inventory than the industry average, it could mean one of two things:

- It could indicate that the company is more efficient in inventory management as less resources are tied up in inventory at any given point in time.
- It could also suggest that the company does not carry enough inventory at any point in time, which might be hurting sales.

To determine which explanation holds true, analysts should compare the firm's revenue growth with that of the industry. A low sales growth compared to the industry would imply that the company is losing out on sales by holding low inventory quantities. A sales growth rate similar to, or higher than industry sales growth would suggest that the company manages inventory more efficiently than its peers.

A firm whose inventory turnover is *lower* and number of days of inventory is *higher* than industry average could have a problem with slow moving or obsolete inventory.

The gross profit margin indicates the percentage of sales that is contributing to net income as opposed to covering the cost of sales.

- Firms in relatively competitive industries have lower gross profit margins.
- Firms selling luxury products tend to have lower volumes and higher gross profit margins.
- Firms selling luxury products are likely to have lower inventory turnover ratios.

Remember that inventory ratios are directly affected by the cost flow assumption used by the firm. When making comparisons across firms, analysts must understand the differences that arise from the use of different cost flow assumptions.

LIFO versus FIFO Ratio Comparisons when Prices are Rising

Type of Ratio	Effect on Numerator	Effect on Denominator	Effect on Ratio
NP and GP margins	Income is lower under LIFO because COGS is higher	Sales are the same under both	Lower under LIFO
Debt to equity	Same debt levels	Lower equity under LIFO	Higher under LIFO
Current ratio	Current assets are lower under LIFO because EI is lower.	Current liabilities are the same	Lower under LIFO
Quick ratio	Assets are higher as a result of lower taxes paid	Current liabilities are the same	Higher under LIFO
Inventory turnover	COGS is higher under LIFO	Average inventory is lower under LIFO	Higher under LIFO
Total asset turnover	Sales are the same	Lower total assets under LIFO	Higher under LIFO

Financial Statement Analysis Issues

- A significant increase in unit volumes of raw materials and/or WIP inventory may suggest that the company expects an increase in demand for its products.
- An increase in finished goods inventory with declining raw materials and WIP inventory may signal decrease in demand for the company's products.
- If growth in inventories is greater than the growth in sales, it could indicate a decrease in demand.
- To obtain additional information about a company's inventory and its future sales, analysts should examine the MD&A section, industry-related news and publications, and industry data.

Example:

- A superficial comparison between inventory-related ratios of two companies (let's say ABC and XYZ) may show that ABC has a lower percentage of assets ties up in inventory, suggesting that ABC is using its working capital more efficiently. However, if ABC were using LIFO and XYZ were using FIFO in an inflationary environment with stable or rising inventory quantities, ABC's lower ratio could be explained by its use of the LIFO cost flow assumption (inventory is carried at a lower value under LIFO in an inflationary environment), not by relative efficiency in inventory management.
- Further, growth in inventory may exceed growth in sales for both ABC and XYZ, suggesting that both companies may be accumulating excess inventory. A superficial comparison of the ratio of inventory growth to sales growth for the companies may indicate that ABC's growth rate in finished goods compared to growth rate in sales is lower than XYZ's (indicating that XYZ in more danger of being left with too much inventory). However, if ABC were using LIFO and XYZ were using FIFO in an inflationary environment with stable or rising inventory quantities, the analyst would be able to conclude that ABC's growth rate in finished goods to growth rate in sales is relatively lower (at least partially) due to its use of LIFO (which carries ending inventory at a lower value than FIFO in an inflationary environment).

LONG-LIVED ASSETS

Cross-Reference to CFA Institute Assigned Reading #29

Long-lived assets are expected to provide economic benefits to a company over an extended period of time, typically longer than one year. There are three types of long-lived assets:

- **Tangible assets** have physical substance, (e.g., land, plant, and equipment).
- **Intangible assets** do not have physical substance (e.g., patents and trademarks).
- **Financial assets** include securities issued by other companies.

The cost of most long-lived assets is allocated over the period of time that they are expected to provide economic benefits. The two types of long-lived assets whose costs are not expensed over time are **land** and **intangible assets with indefinite useful lives.**

LONG-LIVED TANGIBLE ASSETS: PROPERTY PLANT & EQUIPMENT (PP&E)

Capitalization versus Expensing

Table 1-1: Effects of Capitalization

	Effects on Financial Statements
Initially when the cost is capitalized	• Noncurrent assets *increase.* • Cash flow from investing activities *decreases.*
In future periods when the asset is depreciated or amortized	• Noncurrent assets *decrease.* • Net income *decreases.* • Retained earnings *decrease.* • Equity *decreases.*

Table 1-2: Effects of Expensing

	Effects on Financial Statements
When the item is expensed	• Net income *decreases* by the entire after-tax amount of the cost. • No related asset is recorded on the balance sheet and therefore no depreciation or amortization expense is charged in future periods. • Operating cash flow *decreases.* • Expensed costs have no financial statement impact in future years.

FRA

Impact on Financial Statements and Ratios

Table 1-5: Financial Statement Effects of Capitalizing versus Expensing

	Capitalizing	Expensing
Net income (first year)	Higher	Lower
Net income (future years)	Lower	Higher
Total assets	Higher	Lower
Shareholders' equity	Higher	Lower
Cash flow from operations activities	Higher	Lower
Cash flow from investing activities	Lower	Higher
Income variability	Lower	Higher
Debt-to-equity ratio	Lower	Higher

All other factors remaining the same, the decision to expense an item as opposed to capitalizing it would give the impression of *greater earnings growth*. Further, expensing allows companies to report lower taxable income in the current period and pay out *lower taxes* (conserving cash).

On the other hand, the decision to capitalize an item as opposed to expensing may make it easier for a company to *achieve earnings targets* for a particular period. Further, capitalization allows companies to report *higher operating cash flow*, which is an important valuation metric.

Therefore, when making comparisons across companies, it is important to account for differences in the companies' expenditure capitalizing policies. Analysts should be wary of companies that:

- Inflate reported cash flow from operations by capitalizing expenditures that should be expensed.
- Inflate profits to meet earnings targets by capitalizing costs that should be expensed.
- Depress current period income by expensing costs that should be capitalized, in order to be able to exhibit impressive profitability growth going forward without any real improvement in operating performance.

FRA

If a company continues to purchase comparable or increasing amounts of fixed assets every year, capitalization will result in higher profits over an extended period. This would continue to be the case until the value of fixed assets purchased in a given year (amount expensed by the expensing firm) is lower than depreciation charged on capitalized assets by the capitalizing firm.

Acquisition of Long-Lived Tangible Assets Acquired through an Exchange

- If an asset is acquired in a **nonmonetary exchange**, the amount recognized on the balance sheet typically equals the fair value of the asset acquired.
- In accounting for such exchanges the carrying amount of the asset given up is removed from noncurrent assets on the balance sheet, the fair value of the asset

acquired is added, and any difference between the two values is recognized on the income statement as a gain or a loss.

- If the fair value of the asset acquired is greater (lower) than the value of the asset given up, a gain (loss) is recorded on the income statement.
- In rare cases, if the fair value of the acquired asset cannot be determined, the amount recognized on the balance sheet equals the carrying amount of the asset given up. In this case, no gain or loss is recognized.

Acquisition of Long-Lived Tangible Assets Acquired through a Purchase

When a long-lived asset is purchased, expenses other than the purchase price may be incurred.

- These costs are also capitalized and included in the value of the asset on the balance sheet.
- Subsequent expenses related to the long-lived asset may be capitalized if they are expected to provide economic benefits beyond one year, or expensed if they are not expected to provide economic benefits beyond one year.
- Expenditures that extend an asset's useful life are usually capitalized.

Capitalization of Interest Costs

Companies must capitalize interest costs associated with financing the acquisition or construction of an asset that requires a long period of time to ready for its intended use. For example, if a company constructs a building for its own use, interest expense incurred to finance construction must be capitalized along with the costs of constructing the building. The interest rate used to determine the amount of interest capitalized depends on the company's existing borrowings or, if applicable, on borrowings specifically incurred to finance the cost of the asset.

- Under **IFRS**, but not **U.S. GAAP**, income earned from temporarily investing borrowed funds that were acquired to finance the cost of the asset must be subtracted from interest expense on the borrowed funds to determine the amount that can be capitalized.
- If a company is constructing the asset for its own use, capitalized interest is included in the cost of the asset and appears on the balance sheet as a part of property, plant, and equipment. Once the asset is brought into use, the entire cost of the asset, inclusive of capitalized interest, is depreciated over time, so capitalized interest is then a part of depreciation expense, not interest expense. As a result of this accounting treatment, a company's interest costs can appear on the balance sheet (when capitalized) or on the income statement (when expensed).
- If construction and sale of buildings is the core business activity of the firm, and a building is constructed with the intention of selling it, capitalized interest costs are included along with costs of construction in inventory as a part of current assets. The capitalized interest is expenses as a part of COGS in the period that the building is sold.
- Interest payments made prior to completion of construction that are **capitalized** are classified under cash flow from *investing activities*.
- Interest payments that are **expensed** may be classified as *operating* or *financing* cash outflows under **IFRS**, and are classified as *operating* cash outflows under **U.S. GAAP**.

Analytical Issues Relating to Capitalization of Interest Costs

- Capitalized interest costs reduce investing cash flow, while expensed interest costs reduce operating cash flow. Therefore, analysts may want to examine the impact of classification on reported cash flows.
- To provide a true picture of a company's interest coverage ratio, the entire amount of interest expense for the period, whether capitalized or expensed, should be used in the denominator. If the company is depreciating interest that was capitalized in previous years, net income should be adjusted to remove the effect of depreciation of capitalized interest.

Interest coverage ratio = (EBIT/ Interest expense)

The interest coverage ratio measures the number of times that a company's operating profits (EBIT) cover its interest expense. A higher ratio indicates that the company can comfortably service its debt through operating earnings.

- Any interest costs capitalized in the current period should be treated as interest expense. Net income should be reduced by the amount of interest capitalized in the current period.

INTANGIBLE ASSETS

Intangible assets lack physical substance and include items that involve exclusive rights such as patents, copyrights, and trademarks. Some intangible assets have finite lives, while others have indefinite lives.

- The cost of an intangible assets with a **finite life** (e.g., patent) is **amortized** over its useful life.
- The cost of an intangible asset with an **indefinite life** (e.g., goodwill) is not amortized; instead, the asset is tested (at least annually) for **impairment**. If deemed impaired, the asset's balance sheet value is reduced and a loss is recognized on the income statement.

FRA

Intangible assets can also be classified as **identifiable** or **unidentifiable** intangible assets.

Under **IFRS**, **identifiable intangible assets** must meet three definitional criteria and two recognition criteria.

Definitional criteria:

- They must be identifiable. This means that they should either be separable from the entity or must arise from legal rights.
- They must be under the company's control.
- They must be expected to earn future economic benefits.

Recognition criteria:

- It is probable that their expected future economic benefits will flow to the entity.
- The cost of the asset can be reliably measured.

An **unidentifiable intangible asset** is one that cannot be purchased separately and may have an indefinite life. The best example of such an asset is goodwill, which arises when one company purchases another and the acquisition price exceeds the fair value of the identifiable (tangible and intangible) assets acquired.

Accounting for an intangible asset depends on the manner of its acquisition.

Intangible Assets Acquired in Situations Other than Business Combinations (e.g., Buying a Patent)

These assets are recorded at their **fair value** when acquired, where the fair value is assumed to equal the purchase price. They are recognized on the balance sheet, and costs of acquisition are classified as *investing* activities on the cash flow statement. If several intangible assets are acquired as a group, the purchase price is allocated to each individual asset based on its fair value.

Companies use a significant degree of judgment to determine fair values of individual intangible assets purchased. Therefore, analysts focus more on the types of intangible assets purchased as opposed to the value assigned to each individual asset. Understanding the types of intangible assets the company is acquiring can offer valuable insight into the company's overall strategy and future potential.

Intangible Assets Developed Internally

These are generally expensed when incurred, but may be capitalized in certain situations. Due to the differences in requirements regarding expensing/capitalizing when it comes to intangible assets developed internally versus those acquired, a company's strategy (developing versus acquiring intangible assets) can significantly impact reported financial ratios.

- A company that develops intangible assets internally will expense costs of development and recognize no related assets, while a firm that acquires intangible assets will recognize them as assets.
- A company that develops intangible assets internally will classify development-related cash outflows under *operating* activities on the cash flow statement, while an acquiring firm will classify these costs under *investing* activities.

FRA

Research and Development Costs (R&D)

IFRS requires that expenditures on *research* or during the *research phase* of an internal project be **expensed** rather than capitalized as an intangible asset.

IFRS allows companies to recognize an intangible asset arising from *development* or the *development phase* of an internal project if certain criteria are met, including a demonstration of the technical feasibility of completing the intangible asset and the intent to use or sell the asset.

Generally speaking, **U.S. GAAP** requires that R&D costs be **expensed** when incurred. However, it does require that certain costs related to *software development* be **capitalized**.

- Costs incurred to develop software for sale are expensed until the product's technological feasibility has been established. Once feasibility has been established, associated development costs are capitalized.
- Costs related directly to the development of software for internal use are also expensed until it is probable that the project will be completed and that the software will be used as intended. After that, related development costs are capitalized.

Note the following:

- The probability of "the project being completed" is easier to establish than "technological feasibility."
- The involvement of subjective judgment in determining technological feasibility means that capitalization practices vary to a significant extent across companies.
- Capitalized costs related directly to developing software for sale of internal use include the cost of employees who help build and test the software.
- The treatment of software development costs under **U.S. GAAP** is similar to the treatment of all costs of internally developed intangible assets under **IFRS**.

Expensing rather than capitalizing development costs results in:

- *Lower* net income in the current period.
- *Lower* operating cash flow and higher investing cash flow in the current period.

Note that if current period software development costs exceed amortization of prior periods' capitalized development costs, net income would be *lower* under expensing. If, however, software development expenditures were to slow down such that current year expenses are lower than amortization of prior periods' capitalized costs, net income would be *higher* under expensing.

Intangible Assets Acquired in a Business Combination

FRA

When a company acquires another company, the transaction is accounted for using the **acquisition** method (under both **IFRS** and **US GAAP**). Under this method, if the purchase price paid by the acquirer to buy a company exceeds the fair value of its net assets, the excess is recorded as **goodwill**.

Goodwill is an intangible asset that cannot be identified separately from the business as a whole.

- Only goodwill created in a business acquisition can be recognized on the balance sheet; internally generated goodwill cannot be capitalized.

Under **IFRS**, acquired intangible assets are classified as identifiable intangible assets if they meet the definitional and recognition criteria that we listed earlier. If an item acquired does not meet these criteria and cannot be recognized as a tangible asset, it is recognized as a part of goodwill.

Under **US GAAP**, an intangible asset acquired in a business combination should be recognized separately from goodwill if:

- The asset arises from legal or contractual rights; or
- The item can be separated from the acquired company.

Examples of intangible assets treated separately from goodwill include intangible assets like patents, copyrights, franchises, licenses and internet domain names.

Analyst Adjustments for Variation in Capitalization Practices Across Companies

Adjustments must be made to compare the financial performance of a company that expenses software development costs with that of a peer company that capitalizes these costs. For the company that capitalizes software development costs, an analyst should make the following adjustments:

- The income statement for the current period should include related software development costs as an expense and exclude amortization of development costs capitalized in prior periods.
- The capitalized asset should be removed from the balance sheet (decrease assets and equity).
- Operating cash flow should be reduced and investing cash flow should be increased by the amount of development costs that have been capitalized in the current period.
- Ratios that include income, long-lived assets, or cash flow from operations should be recalculated using adjusted values.

DEPRECIATION METHODS AND CALCULATION OF DEPRECIATION EXPENSE

The Cost Model

The **cost model** is required under **U.S. GAAP** and permitted under **IFRS**. Under this model, the cost of long-lived tangible assets (except land) and intangible assets with finite useful lives is allocated over their useful lives as depreciation and amortization expense. Under the cost model, an asset's carrying value equals its historical cost minus accumulated depreciation/amortization (as long as the asset has not been impaired).

FRA

Straight line depreciation expense

$$\text{Depreciation expense} = \frac{\text{Original cost} - \text{Salvage value}}{\text{Depreciable life}}$$

Double declining balance depreciation

$$\text{DDB depreciation in Year X} = \frac{2}{\text{Depreciable life}} \times \text{BV at the beginning of Year X}$$

Straight Line versus Accelerated Depreciation

All other factors remaining the same, a company that uses the straight-line method to depreciate its assets will report:

- A lower asset turnover ratio during the early years of the asset's use because a lower depreciation charge results in higher net assets.
- Higher operating profit margin in the early years of the asset's use because lower depreciation expense results in higher operating income.
- Higher operating return on assets (ROA) in the early years of the asset's use (due to lower depreciation expense) and lower ROA in later years.

Further, a company that uses an accelerated depreciation method will report an improving asset turnover ratio, operating profit margin, and ROA over time.

Estimates Used for Calculating Depreciation

Assumptions of a *longer* useful life and a *higher* expected residual value result in *lower* annual depreciation expense compared to assumptions of a shorter useful life and a lower salvage value. The subjective nature of these assumptions allows management to manipulate earnings.

Management could significantly write-down the value of long-lived assets and recognize a hefty charge against net income in the current period. While this would depress earnings in the current year, it would allow management to recognize lower annual depreciation expense going forward, inflate profits, and report impressive growth in profitability.

Management could also overstate the useful life and the salvage value of an asset to show impressive profits over the near term, and recognize a significant loss at a later point in time when the asset is eventually retired.

Additional assumptions are required to allocate depreciation expense between cost of goods sold (COGS) and selling, general, and administrative expenses (SG&A). Including a higher proportion of total depreciation expense in COGS lowers the gross profit margin and lowers operation expenses. However, it does not affect the net profit margin.

FRA

There are no significant differences between IFRS and U.S. GAAP regarding the definition of depreciation and acceptable depreciation methods. However, **IFRS** requires companies to use the **component method of depreciation**. Under this method, companies depreciate different components of assets separately (using estimates for each component). Under **U.S. GAAP**, this method is allowed but not widely used.

The Revaluation Model

IFRS allows companies to use the **revaluation model** or the cost model to report the carrying amounts of noncurrent assets on the balance sheet. Revaluation results in the carrying amount of an asset reflecting its fair value (as long as it can be measured reliably). Under **U.S. GAAP**, only use of the cost model is permitted.

A key difference between the revaluation and the cost model is that revaluation allows for the reported value of the asset to be higher than its historical cost. Under the cost model on the other hand, the reported value of an asset can never exceed its historical cost.

IFRS allows the revaluation model to be used for certain classes of assets and for the cost model to be used for others as long as:

1. The company applies the same model to assets in a particular class (e.g., land and buildings, machinery, factory equipment etc.)
2. Whenever a revaluation is performed, all assets in the particular class must be revalued (to avoid selective revaluation).

The revaluation model may also be used to value intangible assets, but only if an active market for the asset exists where its fair value can be determined.

Under the revaluation model, whether a revaluation affects earnings (net income) depends on whether the revaluation initially increases or decreases the carrying amount of the asset class.

- If a revaluation initially *decreases* the carrying amount of an asset:
    - The decrease in value is recognized as a loss on the income statement.
    - Later, if the value of the asset class increases:
        - The increase is recognized as a gain on the income statement to the extent that it reverses a revaluation loss previously recognized on the income statement against the same asset class.
        - Any increase in value beyond the reversal amount will not be recognized on the income statement, but adjusted directly to equity through the revaluation surplus account.
- If a revaluation initially *increases* the carrying amount of an asset:
    - The increase in value bypasses the income statement and goes directly to equity through the revaluation surplus account.
    - Later, if the value of the asset class decreases:
        - The decrease reduces the revaluation surplus to the extent of the gain previously recognized in the revaluation surplus against the same asset class.
        - Any decrease in value beyond the reversal amount will be recognized as a loss on the income statement.

If an asset is sold or disposed of, any associated revaluation surplus recognized in other comprehensive income is transferred directly to retained earnings.

Considerations for Financial Analysis

Asset revaluations require many considerations for financial statement analysis.

- An increase in the carrying value of depreciable long-lived assets increases total assets and shareholders' equity. Hence, revaluation of assets can be used to reduce reported leverage
- Asset revaluations that decrease the value of an asset also decrease net income in the year of revaluation. In the year of revaluation, return on assets and return on equity decline. In future years however, the lower values of assets and equity may result in higher ROA and ROE. Further, reversals of downward revaluations also go through income. Managers can then opportunistically time the reversals to manage earnings and increase income.

- If the carrying value of the asset is increased in a revaluation, assets and equity increase, and annual depreciation expense also increases. As a result, performance measures such as ROA and ROE may decline in the future. This is ironic given that an upward revaluation is usually associated with an improvement in the operating capacity of the asset and is beneficial for the company.
- Analysts should also look into who performs asset value appraisals and how often revaluations are recognized.

AMORTIZATION METHODS AND CALCULATION OF AMORTIZATION EXPENSE

Intangible Assets with Finite Lives

Intangible assets with finite useful lives are amortized over their useful lives. This results in the cost of these assets being "matched" with the benefits that accrue from them. Acceptable amortization methods are the same as acceptable depreciation methods. The estimates required to calculate yearly amortization expense for an intangible fixed asset with a finite life are:

- The original value of the intangible asset.
- The residual value at the end of its useful life.
- The length of its useful life.

IMPAIRMENT OF ASSETS

An **impairment** charge is made to reflect the unexpected decline in the fair value of an asset. Impairment recognition has the following effects on a company's financial statements:

- The carrying value of the asset decreases.
- The impairment charge reduces net income.
- Impairment does not affect cash flows because it is a noncash charge.

FRA

Impairment of Property, Plant, and Equipment

Companies are required to assess whether there are indications of impairment of property, plant, and equipment at the end of each reporting period. If there are no suggestions of impairment, the asset is not tested for impairment. However, if there are indications of impairment, the recoverable amount of the asset must be measured in order to test the asset for impairment. Indications of impairment include evidence of obsolescence, decrease in demand for the asset's output, and technological advancements.

Under **IFRS**, an asset is considered impaired when its carrying amount exceeds its recoverable amount. The recoverable amount equals the higher of "fair value less costs to sell" and "value in use," where value in use refers to the discounted value of future cash flows expected from the asset. The impairment loss that must be recognized equals the carrying amount minus the recoverable amount.

Under **U.S. GAAP**, determining whether an asset is impaired is different from measuring the impairment loss. An asset is considered impaired when its carrying value exceeds the total value of its undiscounted expected future cash flows (recoverable amount). Once the carrying value is determined to be unrecoverable, the impairment loss is measured as the difference between the asset's carrying amount and its fair value (or the discounted value of future cash flows, if fair value is not known).

Impairment of Intangible Assets with a Finite Life

Intangible assets with finite lives are amortized. These assets are not tested for impairment annually (unlike intangible assets with indefinite lives); they are only tested for impairment upon the occurrence of significant adverse events (e.g., a significant decrease in market price or adverse changes in legal and economic factors). Accounting for impairment of these assets is essentially the same as accounting for impairment of property, plant, and equipment.

Impairment of Intangibles with Indefinite Lives

Goodwill and other intangible assets with indefinite lives are not amortized. They are carried on the balance sheet at historical cost and tested at least annually for impairment. Impairment must be recognized when carrying value exceeds fair value.

Impairment of Long-Lived Assets Held for Sale

A long-lived asset is reclassified (from being an asset "held-for-use") to an asset "held-for-sale" when it is no longer in use and management intends to sell it. These assets are tested for impairment when they are categorized as held-for-sale. If it is found that the carrying value exceeds their fair value less selling costs, an impairment loss is recorded and their carrying value is brought down to fair value less selling costs. Once classified as held-for-sale, these assets are no longer depreciated or amortized by the company.

Reversals of Impairments of Long-Lived Assets

Under **U.S. GAAP**, once an impairment loss is recorded for assets held-for-use, it cannot be reversed. However, for assets held-for-sale, if the fair value of the asset increases subsequent to impairment recognition, the loss can be reversed and the asset's value can be revised upward.

IFRS allows reversal of impairment losses if the value of the asset increases regardless of classification of the asset. Reversal of a previously recognized impairment charge increases reported profits. Note that IFRS only allows reversals of impairment losses. It does not allow the value of the asset to be written up to a value greater than the previous carrying amount even if the new recoverable amount is greater than the previous carrying value.

DERECOGNITION

A company **derecognizes** or removes an asset from its financial statements when the asset is disposed of or is not expected to provide any future economic benefits from use or disposal.

Sale of Long-Lived Assets

Gain (loss) on asset disposal = Selling price – Carrying/book value of asset
Carrying/book value = Historical cost – Accumulated depreciation

A gain or loss on the sale of a fixed asset is disclosed on the income statement either as a component of other gains and losses (if the amount is insignificant) or as a separate line item (if the amount is significant). Gains and losses on disposal of fixed assets can also be found on the cash flow statement if prepared using the indirect method. A company may disclose further details about the sale of long-lived assets in the management discussion and analysis (MD&A) section and/or financial statement footnotes.

Long-Lived Assets Disposed of Other than by a Sale

Long-lived assets intended to be disposed of other than by a sale (e.g., abandoned, exchanged for another asset, or distributed to owners in a spin-off) are classified as held for use until disposal. Just like other noncurrent assets held by the company, they continue to be depreciated and tested for impairment until actual disposal.

When an asset is **retired or abandoned**, the company does not receive any cash for it. Assets are reduced by the carrying value of the asset at the time of retirement or abandonment, and a loss equal to the asset's carrying amount is recorded on the income statement.

When an asset is **exchanged** for another asset, the carrying amount of the asset given up is removed from the company's balance sheet, and replaced by the fair value for the asset acquired. Any difference between the carrying amount and the fair value is recognized as a gain or loss on the income statement. Note that the fair value used is the fair value of the asset given up unless the fair value of the asset acquired is more clearly evident. If no reliable measure of fair value exists, the acquired asset is measured at the carrying amount of the asset given up.

FRA

In a **spin-off** an entire cash-generating unit of a company is separated into a new entity, with shareholders of the parent company receiving a proportional number of shares in the new company. All the assets of the new entity are removed from the balance sheet of the parent at the time of the spin-off.

PRESENTATION AND DISCLOSURES

Disclosures: Tangible Assets

IFRS

- The measurement bases used.
- The depreciation method used.
- Useful lives (or depreciation rate).
- Accumulated depreciation at the beginning and end of the period.
- Restrictions on title.
- Pledges of property as security.
- Contractual agreements to acquire PP&E.
- If the revaluation model is used, the company must disclose:
  - The date of revaluation.
  - Details of fair value determination.
  - The carrying amount under the cost model.
  - Amount of revaluation surplus.

U.S. GAAP

- Depreciation expense for the period.
- The balances of major classes of depreciable assets.
- Accumulated depreciation by major classes or in total.
- General description of depreciation methods used for major classes of depreciable assets.

Disclosures: Intangible Assets

IFRS

- For each class of intangible assets whether they have a finite or indefinite life.
  - If finite, for each class disclose:
    - The useful life (or amortization rate).
    - The amortization methods used.
    - The gross carrying amount.
    - Accumulated amortization at the beginning and end of the period.
    - Where amortization is included on the income statement.
    - Reconciliation of carrying amounts at the beginning and end of the period.
  - If indefinite:
    - Carrying amount of the asset.
    - Why it is considered to have an indefinite life.
- Restrictions on title.
- Pledges as security.
- Contractual agreement to purchase any intangible assets.
- If the revaluation model is used, the company must disclose:
  - The date of revaluation.
  - Details of fair value determination.
  - The carrying amount under the cost model.
  - Amount of revaluation surplus.

U.S. GAAP

- Gross carrying amounts in total and by major classes of intangible assets.
- Accumulated amortization in total and by major classes of intangible assets.
- Aggregate amortization expense for the period.
- Estimated amortization expense for the next 5 fiscal years.

FRA

Disclosures: Impairment

IFRS

- The amounts of impairment losses and reversal of impairment losses recognized in the period.
- Where these impairment losses and reversals are recognized on the financial statements.
- Main classes of assets affected by impairment losses and reversals.
- Events and circumstances that led to these impairment losses and reversals.

U.S. GAAP

- Description of the impaired asset.
- Circumstances that led to impairment.
- The method of fair value determination.
- The amount of impairment loss.
- Where the loss is recognized on the financial statements.

Disclosures about long-lived assets appear throughout the financial statements:

- The balance sheet reports the carrying value of the asset.
- On the income statement, depreciation expense may or may not appear as a separate line item.
- On the cash flow statement:
    - Acquisitions and disposals of fixed assets are found in the investing section.
    - Further, if prepared using the indirect method, depreciation and amortization are shown as separate line item adjustments to net income in the computation of cash flow from operating activities.
- The notes to the financial statements describe the company's accounting methods, estimated useful lives, historical cost by categories of fixed asset, accumulated depreciation, and annual depreciation expense.

Evaluating a Company's Fixed Assets

The higher the **fixed asset turnover ratio**, the higher the amount of sales a company is able to generate with a given amount of investment in fixed assets, suggesting that the company is operating more efficiently.

Estimated useful life = Gross investment in fixed assets / Annual depreciation expense

Average age of asset = Accumulated depreciation / Annual depreciation expense

Remaining useful life = Net investment in fixed assets / Annual depreciation expense

Asset age ratios help identify older, obsolete assets that might make the firm's operations less efficient. Further, they help forecast future cash flows from investing activities and identify major capital expenditures that the company might need to raise cash for in the future. If the calculated average depreciable life of a company's assets is in line with that of other firms in the industry that use similar equipment, we can conclude that management is not tweaking useful life and salvage value assumptions to manipulate reported profits.

Another popular method for making comparisons across companies is calculating **annual capital expenditure as a percentage of depreciation expense**.

- A company for whom this ratio is significantly lower than 100% is currently replacing its fixed assets at a rate that is slower than the rate at which they are being depreciated. This might indicate the need for hefty capital expenditure in the future and that further examination of the company's capital expenditure policies is required.
- A company for whom this ratio is close to 100% is replacing its fixed assets at a rate similar to that of their use.

INVESTMENT PROPERTY

IFRS defines **investment property** as property that is owned (or leased under a finance lease) for the purpose of earning rentals or capital appreciation or both. Investment property differs from long-lived tangible assets (e.g., PP&E) in that investment property is not owner occupied, nor is used for producing the company's products and services.

Under IFRS, investment property may be valued using either the cost model or the fair value model.

Cost model: This is identical to the cost model used for property, plant, and equipment.

Fair value model: This differs from the revaluation model used for PP&E in the way net income is affected.

- Under the revaluation model, the impact of the revaluation on net income depends on a previously recognized increase or decrease in the carrying amount of the asset.
- Under the fair value model, all changes in the fair value of an asset have an impact on net income.

Further, note that:

- A company is required to use one model (either cost or fair value) for all its investment properties.
- The fair value model may be used only if the company is able to reliably estimate the property's fair value on a continuing basis.
- If a company chooses the fair value model, it must continue to do so until it disposes of the property or changes its use such that it is no longer classified as investment property.

Valuation Issues

FRA

- If investment property is valued using the cost model, a move to owner-occupied property or inventory will not lead to a change in the carrying amount of the property.
- If investment property is valued using the fair value model, a move to owner-occupied property or inventory will be made at fair value. The property's fair value will become its new cost for the purpose of ongoing accounting for the property.
- If owner-occupied property is reclassified as investment property (and the owner prefers to use the fair value model), the change in the value from depreciated cost to fair value at the time of transfer is treated like a revaluation.
- If inventory is reclassified as investment property (and the owner prefers to use the fair value model), the difference between the carrying amount and fair value at the time of transfer is recognized as a profit or loss.

Investment property is reported as a separate line item on the balance sheet. Further, companies must disclose which model they have used (cost or fair value) to value the property.

U.S. GAAP does not specifically define investment property. U.S. companies that hold investment property use the historical cost model.

LEASING

A lease is a contract between the owner of the asset (lessor) and another party that wants to use the asset (lessee). The lessee gains the right to use the asset for a period of time in return for periodic lease payments.

Leasing an asset holds the following advantages over purchasing the asset:

- Leases often have fixed interest rates.
- They require no down payment so they conserve cash.
- At the end of the lease the asset can be returned to the lessor so the lessee escapes the risk of obsolescence and is not burdened with having to find a buyer for the asset.
- Operating leases do not require recognition of an asset or a liability on the balance sheet so they improve reported performance and leverage ratios.
- In the U.S., leases can be structured as synthetic leases where the company can gain tax benefits of ownership, while not reflecting the asset on its financial statements.

U.S. GAAP requires classification as a finance (capital) lease if any of the following hold:

1. The lease transfers ownership of the asset to the lessee at the end of the term.
2. A bargain purchase option exists.
3. The lease term is greater than 75% of the asset's useful economic life.
4. The present value of the lease payments exceeds 90% of the fair value of the leased asset.

Under **IFRS**, classification of a lease depends on the economic substance of the transaction and managerial judgment.

LESSEE'S PERSPECTIVE

Operating Lease

The accounting treatment for an operating lease is similar to that of renting an asset for a period of time. The asset is not purchased; instead annual payments are made for using it. Under an operating lease, no lease-related entries are made on the balance sheet. The firm has not purchased the asset so there is no addition to fixed assets, and it has not borrowed any money to finance the purchase, so there is no related liability.

Accounting entries at inception

Balance sheet: None because no asset or liability is recognized.

Income statement: None because the asset has not been used yet.

Statement of cash flows: None because there has been no cash transaction.

Accounting entries every year during the lease term

Balance sheet: None because there are no lease-related assets and liabilities.

Income statement: Leasehold (rental) expense is charged every year.

Statement of cash flows: The lease-related expense is classified as a cash outflow from operating activities.

Capital or Finance Lease

A finance lease requires the company to recognize a lease-related asset and liability at inception. The accounting treatment for a finance lease is similar to that of purchasing an asset and financing the purchase with a long-term loan.

Accounting entries at inception

Balance sheet: The present value of lease payments is recognized as a long-lived asset. The same amount is also recognized as a long-term liability.

Income statement: None because the asset has not been used yet.

Statement of cash flows: None because no cash transaction has occurred. Disclosure of lease inception is reported as a "significant noncash financing and investing activity."

Accounting entries every year during the term of the lease

Balance sheet: The value of the asset falls every year as it is depreciated. Interest is charged on the liability (discount rate multiplied by the beginning-of-period liability). The excess of the lease payment over the year's interest expense reduces the liability.

Income statement: Depreciation expense (against the asset) and interest expense (on the liability) are charged every year.

Statement of cash flows: The portion of the lease payment attributable to interest expense is deducted from CFO, while the remainder that serves to reduce the liability is subtracted from CFF.

Finance versus Operating Lease: Lessee's Perspective

Income Statement Item	Finance Lease	Operating Lease
Operating expenses	Lower	Higher
Non-operating expenses	Higher	Lower
EBIT (operating income)	Higher	Lower
Total expenses—early years	Higher	Lower
Total expenses—later years	Lower	Higher
Net income—early years	Lower	Higher
Net income—later years	Higher	Lower

Balance Sheet Item	Capital Lease	Operating Lease
Assets	Higher	Lower
Current liabilities	Higher	Lower
Long term liabilities	Higher	Lower
Total cash	Same	Same

CF Item	Capital Lease	Operating Lease
CFO	Higher	Lower
CFF	Lower	Higher
Total cash flow	Same	Same

Ratio	Numerator under Finance Lease	Denominator under Finance Lease	Effect on Ratio	Ratio Better or Worse under Finance Lease
Asset turnover	Sales—same	Assets—higher	Lower	Worse
Return on assets*	Net income—lower	Assets—higher	Lower	Worse
Current ratio	Current assets—same	Current liabilities—higher	Lower	Worse
Leverage ratios (D/E and D/A**)	Debt—higher	Equity—same Assets—higher	Higher	Worse
Return on equity*	Net income—lower	Equity—same	Lower	Worse

*In early years of the lease agreement.

Note: Lower ROE under a finance lease is due to lower net income (numerator effect), while lower ROA is primarily due to higher assets (denominator effect).

LESSOR'S PERSPECTIVE

Lessors are required to recognize finance leases when any one of the four previously defined criteria for recognizing finance leases by lessees hold, and the following two criteria also hold:

1. Collectability of the lease payments is predictable.
2. There are no significant uncertainties regarding the amount of costs still to be incurred by the lessor under the provisions of the lease agreement.

Leases not meeting the above criteria must be classified as operating leases because the earnings process is not complete, or the risks and benefits of the leased assets have not been transferred.

- If the lessor classifies the lease as an operating lease, it records lease revenue when earned, continues to list the asset on its balance sheet, and depreciates it every year on its income statement. In this case, the lessee does not record a lease-related long-lived asset on its balance sheet.
- If the lessor classifies the lease as a finance lease, it records a receivable equal to the present value of lease payments on its balance sheet, and removes the asset from long-lived assets in its books. In this case, the lessee records a lease-related long-lived asset.

Direct Financing Leases

Financial institutions and leasing companies offer financial leases that generate interest income only. These are known as direct financing leases, where the present value of lease payments equals the carrying value of the asset. In direct financing leases, no gross profits are recognized.

Direct Financing versus Operating Leases: Lessor's Perspective

	Financing Lease	Operating Lease
Total net income	Same	Same
Taxes (early years)	Higher	Lower
Total CFO	Lower	Higher
Total CFI	Higher	Lower

Sales Type Leases

Some manufacturers offer their customers financing options to purchase their products. These sales-type leases include a gross profit (the normal selling price of the product minus the carrying value), which is recognized at inception of the lease, and interest income as payments are received over a period of time. In a sales-type lease, the present value of lease payments equals the selling price of the asset, which is higher than the cost or carrying value of asset.

Disclosures

Under **U.S. GAAP**, lease disclosures require a company to list the lease obligations of the firm for the next five years under all operating and finance leases. These disclosures allow analysts to evaluate the extent of off-balance sheet financing used by the company. They can also be used to determine the effects on the financial statements if all the operating leases were capitalized and brought "on to" the balance sheet.

Under **IFRS**, companies are required to:

- Present finance lease obligations as a part of debt on the balance sheet.
- Disclose the amount of total debt attributable to obligations under finance leases.
- Present information about all lease obligations (operating and finance leases).

Summary of Financial Statement Impact of Leases on the Lessee and Lessor

Lessee	Balance Sheet	Income Statement	Statement of Cash Flows
Operating Lease	No effect	Reports rent expense	Rent payment is an operating cash outflow
Finance Lease under IFRS (capital lease under U.S. GAAP)	Recognizes leased asset and lease liability	Reports depreciation expense on leased asset	Reduction of leased liability is a financing cash outflow
Lessor			
Operating Lease	Retains asset on balance sheet	Reports rent income	Rent payments received are an operating cash inflow
Finance Lease*			
When present value of lease payments equals the carrying amount of the leased asset (called a direct financing lease in U.S. GAAP)	Removes asset from balance sheet. Recognizes lease receivable.	Reports interest revenue on lease receivable	Interest position of lease payment received is either an operating or investing cash inflow under IFRS and an operating cash inflow under U.S. GAAP. Receipt of lease principal is an investing cash inflow**.
When present value of lease payments exceeds the carrying amount of the leased asset (called a sales-type lease in U.S. GAAP)	Removes asset. Recognizes lease receivable.	Reports profit on sale. Reports interest revenue on lease receivable.	Interest position of lease payment received is either an operating or investing cash inflow under IFRS and an operating cash inflow under U.S. GAAP. Receipt of lease principal is an investing cash inflow**.

** U.S GAAP distinguishes between a direct finance lease and a sales-type lease, but IFRS does not. The accounting is the same for IFRS and U.S. GAAP despite this additional classification under U.S. GAAP.*
*** If providing leases is part of a company's normal business activity, the cash flows related to the leases are classified as operating cash.*

FRA

INCOME TAXES

Cross-Reference to CFA Institute Assigned Reading #30

The tax return is prepared to calculate taxes payable to the authorities. Taxes payable result in an outflow of cash from the firm, so firms try to minimize taxes payable and retain cash. This objective is achieved by recognizing *higher* expenses on the tax return, which leads to *lower* taxable income and consequently, *lower* taxes payable.

Financial statements are prepared to report the company's operating performance over the year to shareholders, financial institutions and other stakeholders. For financial reporting purposes, companies try to show healthy performance and profitability. This objective is achieved by recognizing *lower* expenses on the income statement, which leads to *higher* pretax income, and (despite *higher* income tax expense) *higher* net income than on the tax return.

- The **tax base** of an asset or liability is the amount that is recognized on the balance sheet for tax purposes.
- The **carrying value** is the amount recognized on the balance sheet for financial reporting.

Determining the Tax Base of an Asset

An asset's tax base is the amount that will be expensed on the income statement in the future as the economic benefits are realized from the asset. For example, if the historical cost of the asset is \$10,000, and \$4,000 worth of accumulated depreciation has already been charged against it on *tax returns* over previous years, the asset's tax base equals \$6,000. This amount will be depreciated in future periods (expensed on the tax return) as the asset is utilized over its remaining life (economic benefits of the asset are realized).

The carrying value of the asset is simply the historical cost of the asset minus the accumulated depreciation charged against over previous years on the company's *financial statements.*

FRA

Determining the Tax Base of a Liability

Two types of liabilities can result from accrual accounting; unearned revenues and accrued expenses. The *carrying value* of these liabilities is the amount recognized on the balance sheet in the financial statements. The rules for calculating the *tax base* of liabilities are given below:

1. Tax base of accrued *expense* liability = Carrying amount of the liability on the balance sheet (financial reporting) minus amounts that have **not** been expensed for tax purposes yet; but **can** be expensed (are tax-deductible) in the future.
2. The tax base of unearned *revenue* liability = Carrying value of the liability minus the amount of revenue that **has already been taxed**, and therefore, will **not** be taxed in the future.

Deferred Tax Liabilities

A deferred tax liability usually arises when:

- *Higher* expenses are charged on the tax return as compared to the financial statements.
- Taxable income is *lower* than pretax or accounting profit.
- Taxes payable are *lower* than income tax expense.
- An asset's tax base is *lower* than its carrying value.

Accounting Entries for an Increase in Deferred Tax Liabilities

- Any *increase* in deferred tax liabilities **increases total liabilities** on the balance sheet.
- The increase in deferred tax liabilities is added to taxes payable in the calculation of income tax expense, so it decreases net income, retained earnings and **reduces owners' equity**.

Deferred Tax Assets

A deferred tax asset usually arises when:

- *Higher* expenses are charged on the financial statements than on the tax return.
- Taxable income is *higher* than pretax or accounting profit.
- Taxes payable are *higher* than income tax expense.
- A liability's tax base is *lower* than its carrying value.

Accounting Entries for an Increase in Deferred Tax Assets

- Any *increase* in deferred tax assets **increases total assets** on the balance sheet.
- The increase in deferred tax assets is subtracted from taxes payable in the calculation of income tax expense, so it **increases net income, retained earnings and equity**.

Effects of Changes in Tax Rates

FRA

When tax rates *rise*, the balances of both deferred tax assets and liabilities *rise*. When tax rates *fall*, the balances of both deferred tax assets and liabilities *fall*.

$$\text{Income tax expense} = \text{Taxes payable} + \text{Change in DTL} - \text{Change in DTA}$$

- If a company has a net DTL (excess of DTL over DTA), a reduction in tax rates would *reduce* liabilities, *reduce* income tax expense, and *increase* equity.
- If the company has a net DTA (excess of DTA over DTL), a reduction in tax rates will *reduce* assets, *increase* income tax expense, and *decrease* equity.
- If a company has a net DTL, an increase in tax rates would *increase* liabilities, *increase* income tax expense, and *reduce* equity.
- If the company has a net DTA, an increase in tax rates will *increase* assets, *decrease* income tax expense, and *increase* equity.

Temporary versus Permanent Differences

- Temporary differences arise because of differences between the tax base and carrying amounts of assets and liabilities.
- Permanent differences are differences between tax and financial reporting of revenues and expenses that *will not* reverse at any point in the future. Examples of the items that give rise to permanent differences include:

1. Revenue items that are not taxable.
2. Expense items that are not tax deductible.
3. Tax credits for some expenses that directly reduce taxes.

The important thing to remember is that permanent differences do not result in deferred taxes. They result in a difference between effective and statutory tax rates and should be considered in the analysis of effective tax rates. A firm's reported effective tax rate is given by:

$$\text{Effective tax rate} = \frac{\text{Income tax expense}}{\text{Pretax income}}$$

Temporary differences can be divided into two categories:

Taxable temporary differences

Taxable temporary differences result in deferred tax liabilities. They are expected to result in future taxable income. Deferred tax liabilities arise when:

- The carrying amount of an asset *exceeds* its tax base; or
- The carrying amount of a liability is *less* than its tax base.

Deductible temporary differences

Deductible temporary differences result in deferred tax assets. They are expected to provide tax deductions in the future. Deferred tax assets arise when:

- The tax base of an asset *exceeds* its carrying amount; or
- The tax base of a liability is *less* than its carrying amount.

FRA

Treatment of Temporary Differences

Balance Sheet Item	Carrying Value vs. Tax Base	Results in...
Asset	Carrying amount is greater.	DTL
Asset	Tax base is greater.	DTA
Liability	Carrying amount is greater.	DTA
Liability	Tax base is greater.	DTL

Temporary Differences at Initial Recognition of Assets and Liabilities

In some situations, the carrying value and tax base of certain assets and liabilities may not be equal at initial recognition. In such circumstances (even though the tax base and the carrying amount of the item are different) a company cannot recognize deferred tax assets or liabilities.

In a business combination, if the fair value of acquired intangible assets (including goodwill) is different from their carrying amounts, deferred taxes can be recognized.

With regards to investments in subsidiaries, branches, associates and interests in joint ventures, deferred tax liabilities can be recognized unless:

- The parent is in a position to control the timing of the future reversal of the temporary difference, and
- It is probable that the temporary difference will not reverse in the future.

While deferred tax assets will only be recognized if:

- The temporary difference will reverse in the future, and
- Sufficient taxable profits exist against which the temporary difference can be used.

Unused Losses and Tax Credits

Under IFRS, unused tax losses and credits may only be recognized to the extent of probable future taxable income against which these can be applied. On the other hand, under U.S. GAAP, deferred tax assets are recognized in full and then reduced through a valuation allowance if they are unlikely to be realized. A company that has a history of tax losses may be unlikely to earn taxable profits in the future against which it can apply deferred tax assets.

Recognition and Measurement of Current and Deferred Tax

Current taxes are based on the tax rates applicable at the balance sheet date. Deferred taxes on the other hand, are measured at the rate that is expected to apply when they are realized (when the temporary differences that gave rise to them reverse).

Even though deferred tax assets and liabilities arise from temporary differences that are expected to reverse at some point in the future, present values are not used in determining the amounts to be recognized. Deferred taxes should always be recognized unless they pertain to:

- Taxes or deferred taxes charged directly to equity.
- A possible provision for deferred taxes relates to a business combination.

Even if there has been no change in temporary differences during the current period, the carrying amount of DTA and DTL may change due to:

- Changes in tax rates.
- Reassessments of recoverability of DTA.
- Change in expectations as to how the DTA or DTL will be realized.

Valuation Allowance

Deferred tax assets must be evaluated at each balance sheet date to ensure that they will be recovered. If there are any doubts regarding their realization, their carrying value should be reduced to the expected recoverable amount. Doubts regarding realization of deferred tax assets may stem from the expectation of insufficient future taxable income to recover the tax assets (prepaid taxes).

DTA are reduced by creating a contra-asset account known as the **valuation allowance**. An increase in the valuation allowance reduces deferred tax assets. The negative change in deferred tax assets causes an increase in income tax expense. Higher income tax expense translates into lower net income, retained earnings and equity. Subsequently, if the likelihood of realizing deferred tax assets increases, the previous reduction in DTA is reversed by reducing the valuation allowance.

Recognition of Current and Deferred Tax Charged Directly to Equity

Under both IFRS and U.S. GAAP, deferred tax assets and liabilities should generally have the same accounting treatment as the assets and liabilities that give rise to them. If the item that gave rise to the deferred tax asset/liability be taken directly to equity, the resulting deferred tax item should also be taken directly to equity.

A deferred tax liability should be reduced if it is not expected to reverse. The amount by which it is reduced should be taken directly to equity.

Comparison of IFRS and U.S. GAAP

	IFRS	U.S. GAAP
ISSUE SPECIFIC TREATMENTS		
Revaluation of fixed assets and intangible assets.	Recognized in equity as deferred taxes.	Revaluation is prohibited.
Treatment of undistributed profit from investment in subsidiaries.	Recognized as deferred taxes except when the parent company is able to control the distribution of profits and it is probable that temporary differences will not reverse in future.	No recognition of deferred taxes for foreign subsidiaries that fulfill indefinite reversal criteria. No recognition of deferred taxes for domestic subsidiaries when amounts are tax-free.
Treatment of undistributed profit from investments in joint ventures.	Recognized as deferred taxes except when the investor controls the sharing of profits and it is probable that there will be no reversal of temporary differences in future.	No recognition of deferred taxes for foreign corporate joint ventures that fulfill indefinite reversal criteria.
Treatment of undistributed profit from investments in associates.	Recognized as deferred taxes except when the investor controls the sharing of profits and it is probable that there will be no reversal of temporary differences in future.	Deferred taxes are recognized from temporary differences.
DEFERRED TAX MEASUREMENT		
Tax rates.	Tax rates and tax laws enacted or substantively enacted.	Only enacted tax rates and tax laws are used.
Deferred tax asset recognition.	Recognized if it is probable that sufficient taxable profit will be available in the future.	Deferred tax assets are recognized in full and then reduced by a valuation allowance if it is likely that they will not be realized.
DEFERRED TAX PRESENTATION		
Offsetting of deferred tax assets and liabilities.	Offsetting allowed only if the entity has right to legally enforce it and the balance is related to a tax levied by the same authority.	Same as in IFRS.
Balance sheet classification.	Classified on balance sheet as net noncurrent with supplementary disclosures.	Classified as either current or noncurrent based on classification of underlying asset and liability.

FRA

NON-CURRENT (LONG-TERM) LIABILITIES

Cross-Reference to CFA Institute Assigned Reading #31

A bond is a contract between a borrower and a lender that obligates the borrower to make payments to the lender over the term of the bond. Two types of payments are usually involved-periodic interest payments and principal repayments.

Accounting for Financing Liabilities

The effective interest method results in a constant rate of interest over the life of the bond. It is required under IFRS and preferred under U.S. GAAP. Under this method, the market interest rate at issuance is applied to the carrying amount of the bonds to determine periodic interest expense. Further, the difference between interest expense and the actual coupon payment equals the amount of discount/premium amortized over the period.

The straight-line method, which is also permitted under U.S. GAAP, evenly amortizes the premium or discount over the life of the bond (similar to straight-line depreciation).

The par or face value is the amount that the borrower has to pay back at the maturity of the bond. It does not necessarily equal the amount that the issuer receives upon issuing debt.

The coupon rate is multiplied by the par value of the bond to compute the periodic coupon payment.

Market interest rates are used to value bonds. These rates incorporate various types of risks inherent in the bond, and must not be confused with coupon rates. Market interest rates change frequently.

- To value a company's debt obligations at a particular point in time, we discount the remaining payments at current market interest rates.
- For accounting purposes, under the effective interest method, the book value of the liability recognized on a firm's balance sheet upon debt issuance equals the present value of its obligations discounted at *market interest rates at issuance.*
- Market interest rates at issuance determine how much the company receives in bond proceeds.
  - If market interest rates equal the bond's coupon rate, the bond will be issued at par.
  - If the market interest rate is *greater* than the coupon rate, the bond will be issued at a *discount.*
  - If the market interest rate is *lower* than the coupon rate, the bond will be issued at *a premium.*

FRA

Interest Expense versus Coupon Payment

- Interest expense (under the effective interest method) for a given period is calculated as the book value of the liability at the beginning of the period multiplied by market interest rates at issuance. Interest expense is charged every year on the *income statement.*
- Coupon payments are calculated as the coupon rate times the par value of the bonds. Coupon payments are classified as outflows from operating activities on the *cash flow statement.*

Effects of Issuing a Par Bond on Financial Statements

Balance sheet: The year end value of the liability is listed on the balance sheet. For bonds issued at par, the liability balance remains at par throughout the life of the bond.

Income statement: Interest expense is deducted from operating profits. For bonds issued at par, interest expense equals the coupon payment, and is constant over the life of the bond.

Statement of cash flows:

- At issuance, the bond proceeds are reported as inflows from financing activities.
- During the term of the bond, coupon payments (not interest expense) are deducted from CFO.
- At maturity, cash used to repay the principal amount (par value) is deducted from CFF.

For bonds issued at par the inflows recorded at issuance under CFF equal the outflows at maturity from CFF. Coupon payments are deducted from CFO every year.

Effects of Issuing a Discount Bond on Financial Statements

Balance sheet: The liability increases over the life of the bond as the discount is amortized over the term of the bond. The value of the liability at bond maturity equals par.

Income statement: Interest expense rises each year in line with the increasing balance of the liability.

Statement of cash flows: Inflows recorded at issuance under CFF are lower than outflows at maturity from CFF. Coupon payments are deducted from CFO every year.

Effect of Issuing a Premium Bond on Financial Statements

Balance sheet: The liability decreases over the life of the bond as the premium is amortized over the term of the bond. The value of the liability at maturity equals par.

Income statement: Interest expense declines every year in line with the decreasing balance of the liability.

Statement of cash flows: Inflows recorded at issuance under CFF are greater than the outflows at maturity from CFF. Coupon payments are deducted from CFO every year.

Important Shortcuts

- Interest expense over the term of the bond can also be calculated as all the issuer's outflows over the life of the bond (coupon payments plus principal repayment) minus the inflows received at issuance (bond proceeds).
- To determine the book value of the liability at any point in time simply compute the present value of the bond's remaining cash flows discounting them at market interest rates at issuance.

IFRS versus U.S. GAAP

- The **effective interest** method is *required* under IFRS and *preferred* under U.S. GAAP because it accurately reflects the economics of the transaction. U.S. GAAP also permits use of the **straight-line method** of amortization, which evenly amortizes the premium or discount over the life of the bond.
- Printing costs, legal fees and other charges are incurred when debt is issued. Under IFRS, these costs are included in the measurement of the liability. Under U.S. GAAP, companies used to capitalize these costs and write them off over the bond's term on a straight-line basis. For fiscal years beginning after December 15, 2015, under U.S. GAAP, these costs should be deducted from the related debt liability. Companies reporting under U.S. GAAP may still report as asset because the SEC indicated that it would not object to this treatment.
- U.S. GAAP requires interest payments on bonds to be classified under cash flows from operations. IFRS allows more flexibility in that classification of interest payments as CFO or CFF is permitted.
- Amortization of the bond discount/premium is a non-cash item so it has no effect on cash flows (aside from the effect on taxable income). In the reconciliation of net income to operating cash flow, amortization of a discount (premium) is added back to (deducted from) net income.

Fair Value Reporting Option

When a company uses the effective interest method to amortize bond discounts and premiums, the book value of debt is based on market interest rates at issuance. Over the life of the bonds, as market interest rates fluctuate, the actual value of the firm's debt deviates from its reported book value. For example, if interest rates rise, the current market value of debt would fall. The reported book value of debt (based on the market interest rates at issuance) would be *higher* than the true economic value of the firm's obligations. In this case, using the book value will *overstate* leverage levels as the firm is actually better off than its financial statements indicate.

Recently, companies have been allowed to report financing liabilities at fair value. Companies that choose to report their financing liabilities at fair value report gains (losses) when market interest rates increase (decrease) as the carrying value of their obligations (liabilities) falls (rises).

If fair values are not explicitly reported on the financial statements, IFRS and U.S. GAAP both require companies to disclose the fair value of their financing liabilities. An analysis of a company could be materially affected if the company's reported carrying amount of debt (based on amortized cost) is significantly different from the fair value of its liabilities.

Derecognition of Debt

A company may leave the bonds that it issues outstanding until maturity or retire them prior to maturity by either purchasing them from the open market or calling them (if a call provision exists). If the company leaves the bonds outstanding until maturity, it pays investors the par value of the bonds at maturity.

However, if the company decides to retire the bonds prior to maturity, the book value of the liability is reduced to zero and a gain or loss on extinguishment is computed by subtracting the amount paid to retire the bonds from their book value.

- Under **U.S. GAAP**, because issuance costs are capitalized, any unamortized issuance costs must also be subtracted from gains on extinguishment.
- Under **IFRS**, issuance costs are included in the book value of the liability so there is no need to adjust the gain on extinguishment for these expenses.

Financial Statement Presentation of and Disclosures Relating to Debt

On the balance sheet, long-term liabilities are listed as one aggregate figure for all liabilities due after one year. Liabilities due within one year are included in short-term liabilities (current liabilities). Financial statement footnotes usually include:

- Stated and effective interest rates.
- Maturity dates.
- Restrictions imposed by creditors (covenants).
- Pledged collateral.
- Scheduled repayments over the next five years.

More information regarding a firm's debt and off balance-sheet financing sources can be found in the MD&A section.

Leases

A lease is a contract between the owner of the asset (lessor) and another party that wants to use the asset (lessee). The lessee gains the right to use the asset for a period of time in return for periodic lease payments.

Leasing an asset holds the following advantages over purchasing the asset:

- Leases often have fixed interest rates.
- They require no down payment so they conserve cash.
- At the end of the lease the asset can be returned to the lessor so the lessee escapes the risk of obsolescence and is not burdened with having to find a buyer for the asset.
- Operating leases do not require recognition of an asset or a liability on the balance sheet so they improve reported performance and leverage ratios.
- In the U.S., leases can be structured as synthetic leases where the company can gain tax benefits of ownership, while not reflecting the asset on its financial statements.

U.S. GAAP requires classification as a finance (capital) lease if any of the following hold:

1. The lease transfers ownership of the asset to the lessee at the end of the term.
2. A bargain purchase option exists.
3. The lease term is greater than 75% of the asset's useful economic life.
4. The present value of the lease payments exceeds 90% of the fair value of the leased asset.

Under IFRS, classification of a lease depends on the economic substance of the transaction and managerial judgement.

LESSEE'S PERSPECTIVE

Operating Lease

The accounting treatment for an operating lease is similar to that of renting an asset for a period of time. The asset is not purchased; instead annual payments are made for using it.

Under an operating lease, no lease-related entries are made on the balance sheet. The firm has not purchased the asset so there is no addition to fixed assets, and it has not borrowed any money to finance the purchase, so there is no related liability.

Accounting entries at inception

FRA

Balance sheet: None because no asset or liability is recognized.

Income statement: None because the asset has not been used yet.

Statement of cash flows: None because there has been no cash transaction.

Accounting entries every year during the lease term

Balance sheet: None because there are no lease-related assets and liabilities.

Income statement: Leasehold (rental) expense is charged every year.

Statement of cash flows: The lease-related expense is classified as a cash outflow from operating activities.

Capital or Finance Lease

A finance lease requires the company to recognize a lease-related asset and liability at inception. The accounting treatment for a finance lease is similar to that of purchasing an asset and financing the purchase with a long-term loan.

Accounting entries at inception

Balance sheet: The present value of lease payments is recognized as a long-lived asset. The same amount is also recognized as a long-term liability.

Income statement: None because the asset has not been used yet.

Statement of cash flows: None because no cash transaction has occurred. Disclosure of lease inception is reported as a "significant noncash financing and investing activity."

Accounting entries every year during the term of the lease

Balance sheet: The value of the asset falls every year as it is depreciated. Interest is charged on the liability (discount rate multiplied by the beginning-of-period liability). The excess of the lease payment over the year's interest expense reduces the liability.

Income statement: Depreciation expense (against the asset) and interest expense (on the liability) are charged every year.

Statement of cash flows: The portion of the lease payment attributable to interest expense is deducted from CFO, while the remainder that serves to reduce the liability is subtracted from CFF.

Finance versus Operating Lease: Lessee's Perspective

Income Statement Item	Finance Lease	Operating Lease
Operating expenses	Lower	Higher
Nonoperating expenses	Higher	Lower
EBIT (operating income)	Higher	Lower
Total expenses—early years	Higher	Lower
Total expenses—later years	Lower	Higher
Net income—early years	Lower	Higher
Net income—later years	Higher	Lower

Balance Sheet Item	Capital Lease	Operating Lease
Assets	Higher	Lower
Current liabilities	Higher	Lower
Long term liabilities	Higher	Lower
Total cash	Same	Same

FRA

CF Item	Capital Lease	Operating Lease
CFO	Higher	Lower
CFF	Lower	Higher
Total cash flow	Same	Same

Ratio	Numerator under Finance Lease	Denominator under Finance Lease	Effect on Ratio	Ratio Better or Worse under Finance Lease
Asset turnover	Sales—same	Assets—higher	Lower	Worse
Return on assets*	Net income lower in early years	Assets—higher	Lower	Worse
Current ratio	Current assets-same	Current Liabilities-higher	Lower	Worse
Leverage ratios (D/E and D/A)	Debt—higher	Equity same Assets higher	Higher	Worse
Return on equity*	Net income lower in early years	Equity same	Lower	Worse

* In early years of the lease agreement.

LESSOR'S PERSPECTIVE

Lessors are required to recognize finance leases when any one of the four previously defined criteria for recognizing finance leases by lessees hold, and the following two criteria also hold:

1. Collectability of the lease payments is predictable.
2. There are no significant uncertainties regarding the amount of costs still to be incurred by the lessor under the provisions of the lease agreement.

Leases not meeting the above criteria must be classified as operating leases because the earnings process is not complete, or the risks and benefits of the leased assets have not been transferred.

- If the lessor classifies the lease as an operating lease, it records lease revenue when earned, continues to list the asset on its balance sheet, and depreciates it every year on its income statement. In this case, the lessee does not record a lease-related long-lived asset on its balance sheet.
- If the lessor classifies the lease as a finance lease, it records a receivable equal to the present value of lease payments on its balance sheet, and removes the asset from long-lived assets in its books. In this case, the lessee records a lease-related long-lived asset.

Direct Financing Leases

Financial institutions and leasing companies offer financial leases that generate interest income only. These are known as *direct financing leases*, where the present value of lease payments equals the *carrying value* of the asset. In direct financing leases no gross profits are recognized.

Direct Financing versus Operating Leases: Lessor's Perspective

	Direct Financing Lease	Operating Lease
Total net income	Same	Same
Taxes (early years)	Higher	Lower
Total CFO	Lower	Higher
Total CFI	Higher	Lower

Sales Type Leases

Some manufacturers offer their customers financing options to purchase their products. These *sales-type* leases include a gross profit (the normal selling price of the product minus the carrying value), which is recognized at inception of the lease, and interest income as payments are received over a period of time. In a sales-type lease the present value of lease payments equals the *selling price* of the asset, which is *higher* than the cost or carrying value of asset.

Disclosures

Under **U.S. GAAP**, lease disclosures require a company to list the lease obligations of the firm for the next five years under all operating and finance leases. These disclosures allow analysts to evaluate the extent of off-balance sheet financing used by the company. They can also be used to determine the effects on the financial statements if all the operating leases were capitalized and brought "on to" the balance sheet.

FRA

Under **IFRS**, companies are required to:

- Present finance lease obligations as a part of debt on the balance sheet.
- Disclose the amount of total debt attributable to obligations under finance leases.
- Present information about all lease obligations (operating and finance leases).

Table: Summary of Financial Statement Impact of Leases on the Lessee and Lessor

Lessee	Balance Sheet	Income Statement	Statement of Cash Flows
Operating Lease	No effect	Reports rent expense	Rent payment is an operating cash outflow
Finance Lease under IFRS (capital lease under U.S. GAAP)	Recognizes leased asset and lease liability	Reports depreciation expense on leased asset	Reduction of lease liability is a financing cash outflow
		Reports interest expense on lease liability	Interest portion of lease payment is either an operating, or financing cash outflow under IFRS and an operating cash outflow under U.S. GAAP.
Lessor			
Operating Lease	Retains asset on balance sheet	Reports rent income	Rent payments received are an operating cash inflow.
		Reports depreciation expense on leased asset	
Finance Lease[a]			
When present value of lease payments equals the carrying amount of the leased asset (called a direct financing lease in U.S. GAAP)	Removes asset from balance sheet Recognizes lease receivable	Reports interest revenue on lease receivable	Interest portion of lease payment received is either an operating or investing cash inflow under IFRS and an operating cash inflow under U.S. GAAP. Receipt of lease principal is an investing cash inflow[b].
When present value of lease payments exceeds the carrying amount of the leased asset (called a sales-type lease in U.S. GAAP)	Removes asset Recognizes lease receivable	Reports profit on sale Reports interest revenue on lease receivable	Interest portion of lease payment received is either an operating, or investing cash inflow under IFRS and an operating cash inflow under U.S. GAAP. Receipt of lease principal is an investing cash inflow[b].

[a] U.S. GAAP distinguishes between a direct financing lease and a sales-type lease, but IFRS does not. The accounting is the same for IFRS and U.S. GAAP despite this additional classification under U.S. GAAP.

[b] If providing leases is part of a company's normal business activity, the cash flows related to the leases are classified as operating cash.

FRA

Pensions

Defined contribution plans are pension plans in which the company contributes a certain amount of funds into the plan. Accounting for defined contribution plans is quite straightforward.

- On the income statement, the company recognizes the amount it is required to contribute into the plan as pension expense for the period.
- On the balance sheet, the company records a decrease in cash. If the agreed upon amount is not deposited into the plan during a particular period, the outstanding amount is recognized as a liability.
- On the cash flow statement, the outflow is treated as an operating cash flow.

Under a **defined benefit plan**, the company promises to make future payments to the employee during retirement. For example, a company could promise an employee annual pension payments equal to 60% of her final salary at retirement until death. A number of assumptions are made to determine the total amount that must be paid to the employee during retirement, including:

- Expected salary at date of retirement
- Number of years of retirement

The company estimates the amount of benefits it will pay out to an employee during retirement and then allocates the present value of these payments (known as pension obligation) over the employment term of the employee as a part of pension expense.

1. The service cost for an employee over a period refers to the present value of the increase in pension benefits earned by the employee over the year (as a result of her service to the company).
2. Interest costs are added to pension expense because the company does not pay out service costs earned by the employee over the year until her retirement. The company owes these benefits to the employee so interest accrues on the amount of benefits outstanding.
3. Companies make pension payments into a pension trust fund. The assets in this fund are invested until funds are required to make payments. The expected return on these investments is subtracted from other pension costs to determine pension expense for a particular period. In order to reduce the volatility in reported pension expense, companies are allowed to use the expected return on plan assets instead of the actual return on plan assets in the calculation of pension expense for the period. However, if the difference between expected return and actual return is significant, companies are required to amortize a portion of the difference into pension expense.
4. Actuarial gains and losses arise due to changes in the assumptions used for calculating pension expense (e.g., employee turnover, mortality rates, and compensation increases).
5. Prior service costs arise due to changes in promised benefits.

Evaluating Solvency Ratios

Solvency refers to the ability of a company to satisfy its long term debt obligation (both principal and interest payments). Ratio analysis is frequently used to evaluate a company's solvency levels relative to its competitors. The two main types of solvency ratios used are leverage ratios and coverage ratios.

Leverage ratios are derived from balance sheet numbers and measure the extent to which a company uses debt rather than equity to finance its assets. Higher leverage ratios indicate weaker solvency.

Coverage ratios focus more on income statement and cash flow numbers to measure the company's ability to service its debt. Higher coverage ratios indicate stronger solvency.

Solvency Ratios	Description	Numerator	Denominator
Leverage Ratios			
Debt-to-assets ratio	Expresses the percentage of total assets financed by debt	Total debt	Total assets
Debt-to-capital ratio	Measures the percentage of a company's total capital (debt + equity) financed by debt	Total debt	Total debt + Total shareholders' equity
Debt-to-equity ratio	Measures the amount of debt financing relative to equity financing	Total debt	Total shareholders' equity
Financial leverage ratio	Measures the amount of total assets supported by one money unit of equity	Average total assets	Average shareholders' equity
Coverage Ratios			
Interest coverage ratio	Measures the number of times a company's EBIT could cover its interest payments	EBIT	Interest payments
Fixed charge coverage ratio	Measures the number of times a company's earnings (before interest, taxes and lease payments) can cover the company's interest and lease payments	EBIT + Lease payments	Interest payments + Lease payments

FRA

Study Session 9: Financial Reporting and Analysis—Financial Reporting Quality and Financial Statement Analysis

FRA

FINANCIAL REPORTING QUALITY
Cross-Reference to CFA Institute Assigned Reading #32

Financial reporting quality refers to the usefulness of information contained in the financial reports, including disclosures in notes.

- High-quality reporting provides information that is useful in investment decision-making in that it is relevant and faithfully represents the company's performance and position.

Earnings quality (or quality of reported results) pertains to the earnings and cash generated by the company's core economic activities and its resulting financial condition.

- High-quality earnings (1) come from activities that the company will be able to sustain in the future and (2) provide an adequate return on the company's investment.
- Note that the term, **earnings quality**, encompasses quality of earnings, cash flow, and balance sheet items.

Relationship between Financial Reporting Quality and Earnings Quality

<table>
<tr><th></th><th></th><th colspan="2">Financial Reporting Quality</th></tr>
<tr><th></th><th></th><th>Low</th><th>High</th></tr>
<tr><td rowspan="2">Earnings (Results) Quality</td><td>High</td><td rowspan="2">LOW financial reporting quality impedes assessment of earnings quality and impedes valuation.</td><td>HIGH financial reporting quality enables assessment. HIGH earnings quality increases company value.</td></tr>
<tr><td>Low</td><td>HIGH financial reporting quality enables assessment. LOW earnings quality decreases company value.</td></tr>
</table>

QUALITY SPECTRUM OF FINANCIAL REPORTS

FRA

GAAP, decision-useful, sustainable, and adequate returns: These are high-quality reports that provide useful information about high-quality earnings.

GAAP, decision-useful, but sustainable? This level refers to a situation where reporting is of high quality, but earnings are either inadequate or unsustainable.

Within GAAP, but biased accounting choices: Biased choices result in financial reports that do not faithfully represent the company's true economic situation.

- Management can make aggressive or conservative accounting choices, both of which go against the concept of neutrality as **unbiased** financial reporting is the ideal.

- Earnings smoothing results from employing conservative assumptions to understate performance when the company is actually doing well and then using aggressive assumptions when the company is not doing as well.
- Biases can also creep into the way information is presented. A company may choose to present information in a manner that obscures unfavorable information and/or highlights favorable information.

Within GAAP, but "earnings management": Earnings can be managed by taking real actions or through accounting choices. Note that it is typically very difficult to determine intent so there is a very fine line between earnings management and biased accounting choices.

Departures from GAAP Non-Compliant Accounting: Financial information that deviates from GAAP is obviously of low quality. Further, such financial information cannot be used to assess earnings quality as comparisons with other entities or earlier periods cannot be made.

Departures from GAAP Fictitious Transactions: Companies may use fictitious transactions to (1) fraudulently obtain investments by inflating company performance, or (2) to obscure fraudulent misappropriation of company assets.

Conservative versus Aggressive Accounting

When it comes to financial reporting, the ideal situation would be if financial reporting were **unbiased,** i.e., neither conservative nor aggressive.

- Aggressive choices can (1) increase reported revenues, (2) increase reported earnings, (3) increase reported operating cash flow, (4) decrease reported expenses, and/or (5) decrease reported debt in the current period.
  - Aggressive accounting choices in the current period may create a sustainability issue.
- Conservative choices can (1) decrease reported revenues, (2) decrease reported earnings, (3) decrease reported operating cash flow, (4) increase reported expenses, and/or (5) increase reported debt in the current period.
  - Conservative accounting choices do not give rise to a sustainability issue.

FRA

Conservatism in Accounting Standards

Despite efforts to encourage neutrality in financial reporting, some conservatively biased standards remain. Further, different sets of accounting standards may have different degrees of conservatism embedded in them.

Bias in the Application of Accounting Standards

In order to characterize the application of an accounting standard as conservative or aggressive, we must look at *intent* (rather than at a definition). Intent can be inferred from a careful analysis of disclosures, facts, and circumstances. Examples of biased accounting disguised as conservatism include:

- Big bath behavior: This refers to the strategy of manipulating a company's income statement to make poor results look even worse. The big bath is often implemented in a bad year with a view to inflating subsequent period earnings. New management teams sometime use the big bath so that poor current performance can be blamed on previous management, while they take credit for the impressive growth that follows in subsequent periods.

- Cookie jar reserve accounting: This refers to the practice of creating a liability when a company incurs an expense that cannot be directly linked to a specific accounting period. Companies may recognize such expenses in periods during which profits are high as they can afford to take the hit to income, with a view to reducing the liability (the reserve) in future periods during which the company may struggle. The practice results in smoothing of income over time.

CONTEXT FOR ASSESSING FINANCIAL REPORTING QUALITY

In assessing financial reporting quality, it is important to consider (1) whether a company's management may be motivated to issue financial reports that are not of high quality, and (2) whether the reporting environment is conducive to misreporting.

Motivations for Issuing Low-Quality Financial Reports

- To mask poor performance.
- To meet or beat analyst's forecasts or management's own forecasts.
    - Equity market effects refer to management trying to build credibility with market participants and to positively impact the company's stock price.
    - Trade effects refer to management trying to improve the company's reputation with customers and suppliers.
- To address managers' concerns regarding their careers.
- To avoid debt covenant violations.

Conditions Conducive to Issuing Low-Quality Financial Reports

- Opportunity: Poor internal controls, an ineffective board of directors, or accounting standards that allow divergent choices and/or provide minimal consequences for inappropriate choices can give rise to opportunities for management to issue low-quality financial reports.
- Motivation: Motivation to issue low-quality financial reports can come from personal reasons (e.g., increasing bonus payments) or corporate reasons (e.g., alleviating concerns about being able to raise funds in the future).
- Rationalization: This is important because individuals need to justify their choices to themselves.

FRA

MECHANISMS THAT DISCIPLINE FINANCIAL REPORTING QUALITY

- Markets
- Regulatory authorities
- Registration requirements
    - Disclosure requirements
    - Auditing requirements

- Management commentaries
- Responsibility statements
- Regulatory review of filings
- Enforcement mechanisms

- Auditors
- Private contracting

DETECTION OF FINANCIAL REPORTING QUALITY ISSUES

Presentation Choices

- Under the pretext of assisting investors in evaluating operating performance, struggling companies may (conveniently) exclude restructuringcharges in pro forma measures of financial performance.
- Due to investors' focus on EBITDA, companies may come up with their own definitions of EBITDA (sometimes referring to it as adjusted EBITDA) which may exclude certain expenses.
- Companies may use non-GAAP measures to distract users from GAAP measures. US GAAP and IFRS have both moved to pacify these concerns.

Accounting Choices and Estimates

Revenue Recognition

- Sometimes management may be pushing shipments out the door (channel stuffing) under FOB shipping point arrangements in order to maximize revenue recognized in the current accounting period.
    - If the ratio of accounts receivable to revenues is abnormally high relative to the company's history or its peers, there is a chance that channel stuffing has occurred.
- At other times, for shipments towards the end of the reporting period, management may set shipping terms as FOB destination. Management may engage in this practice if there was an overabundance of orders during the current period, and it does not want investors/analysts to get too optimistic.
- A company can reduce its allowance for sales returns as a proportion of sales to reduce expenses and increase profits.
    - Analysts should examine whether the company's actual collection experience has tended to be different from historical provisioning in order to assess the accuracy of the company's provisioning policies.
- If a company participates in "bill-and-hold" transactions, it is possible that it is recognizing fictitious sales by reclassifying end-of-period inventory as "sold but held" through minimal effort and fake documentation.
- If the company uses rebates as part of its marketing approach, changes in estimates of rebate fulfillment can be used to manipulate reported revenues and profitability (similar to allowance for sales returns).
- Companies can use changes in depreciation estimates (useful life and salvage value) and depreciation methods to manipulate reported earnings and profits.

    - If the company has recorded significant asset write-downs in the recent past, it may suggest that the company's policies relating to asset lives need to be examined.
- Management may try to capitalize costs that ought to be recorded as expenses to increase reported income.
    - Management may use low fair value estimates for assets acquired in an acquisition in order to depress future depreciation expense and inflate future profitability.
    - In order to determine the fair value of goodwill, forecasts of future financial performance must be made, and these projections may be biased upward to avoid a goodwill write-down.
    - Analysts should also examine how the company's capitalization policies compare with the competition, and determine whether its amortization policies are reasonable.
- Analysts should determine how a company's inventory methods compare with others in its industry.
    - If the company uses reserves for obsolescence in its inventory valuation, unusual fluctuations in this reserve might suggest that the company is manipulating them to attain a desired level of earnings.
    - If a company uses LIFO in an inflationary environment, it can temporarily increase reported profits through LIFO liquidation.
- Analysts must evaluate whether the company's estimate of the valuation allowance (against deferred tax assets) is reasonable given its current operating environment and future prospects. Specifically they should:
    - Determine whether there are contradictions between the management commentary and the allowance level, or the tax note and the allowance level.
    - Look for changes in the tax asset valuation account.
- Analysts should examine whether warranty reserves have been manipulated to meet earnings targets. Further, the trend in actual costs relative to amounts allocated to reserves should be assessed as it can offer insight into the quality of products sold.
- If the company engages in extensive dealings with related parties, those entities could be used to absorb losses (e.g., through supply arrangements that are unfavorable to the non-public company) in order to improve the public company's reported performance.

FRA

Choices that Affect the Cash Flow Statement

- Management may try to delay payments to creditors (stretch out payables) until after the balance sheet date, so that the increase in accounts payable over the period (source of cash) results in an increase in cash generated from operations. In order to detect this issue, analysts could:
    - Examine changes in working capital to look for unusual patterns that may indicate manipulation of cash provided from operations.
    - Compare the company's cash generation with the cash operating performance of its competitors.

    - Compare the relationship between cash generated from operations and net income. Analysts should be concerned if cash generated from operations is less than net income, as it may suggest that accounting estimates are being used to inflate net income.
- A company may misclassify uses of operating cash flow into the investing or financing section of the cash flow statement to inflate cash generated from operating activities.
- In certain areas where investors may not even be aware that choices exist (e.g., amortization of discount/premium on capitalized interest), accounting standards offer companies the flexibility to manage cash generated from operations to a certain extent.

ACCOUNTING WARNING SIGNS

Warning Signs Related to Revenue

Analysts should:

- Determine whether company policies make it easy to prematurely recognize revenue by allowing use of FOB shipping point shipping terms and bill-and-hold arrangements.
- Determine whether a significant portion of revenues come from barter transactions (which are difficult to value properly).
- Evaluate the impact of estimates relating to the company's rebate programs on revenue recognition.
- Look for sufficient clarity regarding revenue recognition practices relating to each item or service delivered under multiple-deliverable arrangements of goods and services.
- Determine whether the company's revenue growth is in line with its competitors, the industry, and the overall economy.
- Determine whether receivables are increasing as a percentage of sales. This may suggest channel-stuffing activities or even recognition of fictitious sales.
- Determine whether there are any unusual changes in the trend in receivables turnover and seek an explanation for any changes.
- Compare the company's receivables turnover (or DSO) with competitors and look out for suggestions that revenues have been recognized prematurely, or that the provision for doubtful accounts is insufficient.
- Examine asset turnover.
    - If post-acquisition revenue generation is weak, management may try to play with estimates to increase reported revenue in order to be able to justify their strategic choices.
    - If asset turnover is trending lower, or if it lags the asset turnover of competitors, it may signal future asset write-downs by the company.

Warning Signs Related to Inventories

Analysts should:

- Compare growth in inventories with competitors and industry benchmarks. If inventory levels are increasing with no accompanying increase in sales, it could suggest (1) poor inventory management or (2) inventory obsolescence. In case of the latter, current profitability and inventory value would be overstated.
- Compute the inventory turnover ratio. Declining inventory turnover could also suggest inventory obsolescence.
- Check for inflated profits through LIFO liquidations (only applicable for firms using LIFO).

Warning Signs Related to Capitalization Policies and Deferred Costs

- Analysts should examine the company's accounting policy notes for its capitalization policy for long-term assets (including interest costs) and for its handling of other deferred costs and compare those policies with industry practice.

Warning Signs Related to the Relationship between Cash Flow and Income

If a company's net income is persistently higher than cash provided by operations, it raises the possibility that aggressive accrual accounting policies have been used to shift current expenses to later periods.

- Analysts may consider constructing a time series of cash generated by operations divided by net income. If the ratio is consistently below 1.0, or has declined consistently, there may be problems in the company's accrual accounts.

Other Potential Warning Signs

- Depreciation methods and useful life estimates that are inconsistent with peer companies.
- Fourth-quarter surprises.
- Presence of related-party transactions.
- Non-operating income and one-time sales included in revenue.
- Classification of an expense as non-recurring.
- Gross/operating margins out of line with competitors or industry.
- Younger companies with an unblemished record of meeting growth projections.
- Management has adopted a minimalist approach to disclosure.
- Management fixation on earnings reports.
- Significant restructuring and/or impairment charges.
- Management has a merger and acquisition orientation.

FRA

FINANCIAL STATEMENT ANALYSIS: APPLICATIONS
Cross-Reference to CFA Institute Assigned Reading #33

Evaluating Past Financial Performance

Analysts should focus on:

- Important changes that have occurred in corporate measures of profitability, efficiency, liquidity and solvency and the reasons behind these changes.
- Comparisons of ratios with firms from the same industry, and the reasons behind any differences.
- Examination of performance aspects that are critical for a company to successfully compete in the industry, and a comparison of the company's performance on these fronts with that of competitors.
- The company's business model and strategy, and how it influences operating performance.

Projecting Performance

The **top-down approach** that is typically used to forecast sales involves the following steps:

- Attain forecasts for the economy's expected GDP growth rate.
- Use regression models to determine the historical relationship between the economy's growth rate and the industry's growth rate.
- Undertake market share analysis to evaluate whether the firm being analyzed is expected to gain, lose or retain its market share over the forecasting horizon.

Once a forecast for sales has been established, earnings and cash flows can be estimated.

- Estimate gross profit margins over the forecasting horizon. Net profit margins are affected by leverage ratios and tax rates, so historical data provides a more reliable measure for gross profit margins. This model tends to be simpler and works well for mature companies that operate in non-volatile markets.
- Make separate forecasts for individual expense items, aggregate them, and subtract the total from sales to calculate net income. This is a very subjective exercise as each expense item must be projected based on a relationship with sales or some other relevant variable.

FRA

The most important things that an analyst needs to consider when forecasting cash flows are:

- Required increases in working capital.
- Capital expenditures on new fixed assets.
- Repayment and issuance of debt.
- Repurchase and issuance of stock (equity).

Assessing Credit Risk

Credit analysis involves evaluation of the 4 "C's" of a company.

- Character refers to the quality of management.
- Capacity deals with the ability of the issuer to fulfill its obligations.
- Collateral refers to the assets pledged to secure a loan.
- Covenants are limitations and restrictions on the activities of issuers.

The four general categories of items considered in credit analysis are:

- Scale and diversification of the business.
- Operational efficiency.
- Stability and sustainability of profit margins.
- Degree of financial leverage.

Screening is the process of filtering a set of potential investments into a smaller set by applying a set of criteria. Ratios computed from the information in financial statements and market data are used to screen potential equity investments.

Growth versus Value Investors

Growth investors invest in those companies that are expected to see higher earnings growth in the future. A growth investor would set screens like high price-to-cash flow ratios, and sales growth exceeding 20% over the last three years.

Value investors try to pay a low price relative to a company's net asset value or earning prowess. A value investor might set screens like a higher-than-average ROE, and a lower-than-average P/E ratio to shortlist equity investments that suit her style.

Back-Testing

Analysts evaluate how a portfolio based on particular screens would have performed historically through the process of *back-testing.* This method applies the portfolio selection rules to historical data and calculates returns that would have been realized had particular screens been used. Back-testing has its limitations in that it suffers from:

- Survivorship bias.
- Look-ahead bias.
- Data-snooping bias.

Analyst Adjustments to Reported Financials

Adjustments related to investments: Investments in securities issued by other companies can be classified under different categories. Unrealized gains and losses on securities classified as "available-for-sale" are not recorded on the income statement. Changes in their values are reflected in "other comprehensive income" as a part of equity on the balance sheet. Changes in the value of "trading" securities are recorded on the income statement and have an impact on reported profits. If an analyst is comparing two firms with significant differences in the classification of investments, adjustments for the different financial statement impact of the classifications will be necessary.

Adjustments related to inventory: A LIFO company's financial statements need to be adjusted before comparisons with FIFO firms can be undertaken. Important accounts affected by conversion from LIFO to FIFO are net income, retained earnings, inventory, COGS and deferred taxes.

FIFO to LIFO Conversions

$$EI_{FIFO} = EI_{LIFO} + \text{LIFO reserve}$$

$$COGS_{FIFO} = COGS_{LIFO} - (LR_{ending} - LR_{beginning})$$

During a period of rising prices:

- Net income after tax under FIFO will be greater than LIFO net income after tax by: Change in LIFO reserve × (1 − tax rate)

- Equity (retained earnings) under FIFO will greater by: LIFO reserve × (1 − tax rate)

- Liabilities (deferred taxes) under FIFO will be greater by: LIFO reserve × (tax rate)

- Current assets (inventory) under FIFO will be greater by: LIFO reserve

FRA

The calculations of estimated useful life, average age, and remaining useful life are important because:

- They help identify older, obsolete assets that might make the firm's operations less efficient.
- They help forecast future cash flows from investing activities and identify major capital expenditures that the company might need to raise cash for in the future.

Adjustments related to property, plant and equipment: A company that uses accelerated depreciation methods and shorter estimated life assumptions for long-lived assets will report lower net income than a firm that employs longer useful life assumptions and uses straight-line depreciation. Depreciation and net fixed asset values must be assessed and necessary adjustments must be made to bring sets of financial statements on the same footing before making comparisons.

$$\text{Estimated useful life} = \frac{\text{Gross investment in fixed assets}}{\text{Annual depreciation expense}}$$

$$\text{Average age of asset} = \frac{\text{Accumulated depreciation}}{\text{Annual depreciation expense}}$$

$$\text{Remaining useful life} = \frac{\text{Net investment in fixed assets}}{\text{Annual depreciation expense}}$$

Adjustments related to goodwill: Goodwill is recognized when the price paid for an acquisition exceeds the fair value of its net assets. A company that grows via acquisitions will have higher reported assets and a greater book value than a company that grows internally. Analysts must remove the inflating effect of goodwill on book values and rely on the price-to-tangible book value ratio to make comparisons.

Adjustments related to off-balance sheet financing: Bringing off-balance sheet items "on to" the balance sheet decreases return on assets and increases leverage ratios.

FRA

Study Session 10: Corporate Finance—Corporate Governance, Capital Budgeting, and Cost of Capital

CF

CORPORATE GOVERNANCE AND ESG: AN INTRODUCTION

Cross-Reference to CFA Institute Assigned Reading #34

Corporate governance is defined as the system of internal controls and procedures through which individual companies are managed. It aims to minimize and manage conflicts of interest between those within the company and stakeholders. A **stakeholder** is any person or group that has an interest in the company. Not all stakeholders' interests are aligned in the same manner, and they often conflict with each other.

Key Stakeholders

- **Shareholders** own shares of stock in a corporation and are entitled to certain rights, such as the right to receive dividends and the right to vote on certain corporate issues. They are typically focused on those efforts that support growing the profitability of the company and maximizing its value.
- **Creditors** have little influence on the company, other than covenants and restrictions they can put in place as its banks or bondholders.
- **Employees** have a significant stake in the company's operation, as they are paid salaries and wages as well as other incentives and perquisites for their work.
- The **board of directors** acts in the best interests of the shareholders who elect them.
- **Customers** would like a product that is a good value for the price and is safe to operate.
- Company **suppliers** have a goal of being paid for their services and materials.
- The **government and regulators** wish to protect the economy and the interests of the general public.

Key Relationships in Corporate Governance

Shareholder and manager/director relationships. Although they are agents of shareholders, managers and directors may take advantage of information asymmetries to take more risk than warranted to maximize personal benefit.

Controlling and minority shareholders. Controlling groups may behave in a manner that does not maximize value for minority shareholders (e.g., during voting on takeover offers, and related-party transactions).

Manager and board relationships. If management provides only limited information to the directors, the board's ability to effectively monitor the business is reduced.

Shareholder versus creditor interests. Shareholders may look for additional risk for greater return, while creditors look for stability and lower risk.

Other stakeholder conflicts. Conflicts may arise between customers and shareholders (e.g., product safety), between customers and suppliers (e.g., when the company extends lenient terms of credit to customers), and between the government and shareholders (e.g., if the government raises company taxes).

CF

Stakeholder Management

The foundations of stakeholder management frameworks are constructed from the various legal, contractual, organizational, and governmental components that define the rights, responsibilities, and powers of each group.

- The **legal** infrastructure lays out the framework of rights established by law as well as the ease or availability of legal recourse.
- The **contractual** infrastructure is the means used to secure the rights of both parties through contractual agreements between the company and its stakeholders.
- The way the company manages its stakeholder relationships through its governance procedures, internal systems, and practices is the **organizational** infrastructure.
- The regulations imposed on the company are considered the **governmental** infrastructure.

Mechanisms to Manage Stakeholder Relationships and Mitigate Associated Risks

- General meetings
- Board of directors
- Audit function
- Reporting and transparency
- Remuneration policies
- Say on pay
- Contractual agreements with creditors
- Employee laws and contracts
- Contractual agreements with customers and suppliers
- Laws and regulations

The Board of Directors

The board of directors monitors management and the strategic direction of the company while reporting to shareholders.

The board plays an active role in managing the company through managers, who are given the responsibility for day-to-day operations of the company. The board establishes milestones for the company based on the strategic direction it oversees. In monitoring progress, the board selects, appoints, and terminates the employment of senior management.

The board also establishes committees to aid in the oversight of key functions. Common committees are the following:

- Audit committee
- Governance committee
- Remuneration committee
- Nomination committee
- Risk committee
- Investment committee

Factors That Affect the Stakeholder Relationship and Corporate Governance

Market Factors

- Shareholder engagement. The transparency and information sharing from frequent engagement with shareholders tend to increase support for management and to reduce the potential for efforts by shareholders to more actively pursue other means to influence outcomes.
- Shareholder activism. Activism by shareholders involves more forceful paths to increase shareholder value. Examples include lawsuits, raising public awareness, and proxy battles.
- Competition and takeovers. Corporate takeovers can take the form of proxy contests, tender offers, or hostile takeovers.

Non-Market Factors

- The legal environment. Generally speaking, around the world, creditors enjoy better-protected positions compared to shareholders.
- Media. Increasingly, the media (especially social media) can influence stakeholder relationships.
- The corporate governance industry. External corporate governance services increasingly exert significant influence. Thus, corporations pay attention to their ratings and change their behavior if necessary.

Risks of Poor Corporate Governance and Stakeholder Management

- Weak control systems
- Ineffective decision-making
- Legal, regulatory, and reputational risks
- Default and bankruptcy risks

Benefits of Effective Governance

- Operational efficiency
- Improved control
- Better operating and financial performance
- Lower default risk and cost of debt

Analysis of Corporate Governance and Stakeholder Management

Key areas of interest are:

- Economic ownership and voting control. Dual-class companies tend to trade at a discount to their peers.
- Board of directors representation. Generally speaking, well-diversified, diverse, and skilled boards are desirable.
- Remuneration and company performance. It is important that compensation programs align with shareholders.

- Investors in the company. Concentrated holdings can dictate how the company is run. Further, a significant number of activist investors may force the company to focus on the short term.
- Strength of shareholders' rights. Ideally, shareholders would like the power to remove board members and convene special stockholder meetings.
- Managing long-term risks. It is desirable for the company to have healthy stakeholder relations and for management to be able to deal effectively with long-term risks.

Environmental and Social Considerations in Investment Analysis

Environmental, social, and governance (ESG) integration refers to the use of environmental and social factors alongside corporate governance in the investment process. Both sustainable investing (SI) and responsible investing (RI) utilize ESG in their investment processes.

Socially responsible investing (SRI) limits investments in companies whose products are contrary to the ethical and moral values of an investor, such as weapons and tobacco. Impact investing seeks to meet specific social and environmental goals with identifiable financial returns.

ESG Factors in Investment Analysis

Environmental issues have various financial risks for companies. Stranded assets (also referred to as carbon assets) face the risk of no longer being economically viable because of changes in regulations or investor sentiment. Material events that impact the environment can be costly in terms of legal and regulatory issues, such as fines and litigation. They very well may include clean-up costs as well as reputational costs.

Societal issues can be very broad, including issues within the workplace, human rights, and welfare. They can also include the impact on the community.

Implementation of ESG Mandates

Negative screening is used to exclude certain sectors as defined by the investor, such as fossil fuels, companies with human rights or environmental issues, or companies that do not align with religious or personal beliefs.

Positive screening and best-in-class approaches focus on including investments with favorable ESG aspects.

Thematic investing is utilized when a strategy is implemented using only one factor to evaluate companies relative to ESG criteria.

CAPITAL BUDGETING

Cross-Reference to CFA Institute Assigned Reading #35

Capital budgeting is used to determine whether long-term investments such as acquiring new machinery, replacing current machinery, launching new products, and spending on research and development, are worth pursuing.

Steps in Capital Budgeting

- Generating ideas.
- Analyzing individual proposals.
- Planning the capital budgeting.
- Monitoring and post-auditing.

Categories of Capital Projects

- Replacement projects.
- Expansion projects.
- New products and services.
- Regulatory/safety and environmental projects.
- Other projects.

Important Definitions

Sunk costs are those costs that cannot be recovered once they have been incurred. Capital budgeting ignores sunk costs as it is based only on current and future cash flows. Example of sunk costs are the market research costs incurred by the company to evaluate whether a new product should be launched.

Opportunity cost is the value of the next best alternative that is *foregone* in making the decision to pursue a particular project. Opportunity costs should be *included* in project costs.

An incremental cash flow is the additional cash flow realized as a result of a decision. Incremental cash flow equals cash flow with a decision minus cash flow without the decision.

An externality is the effect of an investment decision on things other than the investment itself. Externalities can be positive or negative and, if possible, externalities should be considered in investment decision-making. An example of a negative externality is *cannibalization* as new products reduce sales of existing products of the company.

A conventional cash flow stream is a cash flow stream that consists of an initial outflow followed by a series of inflows. The sign of the cash flows changes only once. For a nonconventional cash flow pattern, the initial outflow is not followed by inflows only, but the direction of the cash flows can change from positive to negative again.

Basic Principles of Capital Budgeting

1. **Decisions are based on actual cash flows:** Only incremental cash flows are relevant to the capital budgeting process, while sunk costs are completely ignored. Analysts must also attempt to incorporate the effects of both positive and negative externalities into their analysis.
2. **Timing of cash flows is crucial:** Analysts try to predict exactly when cash flows will occur, as cash flows received earlier in the life of the project are worth more than cash flows received later.
3. **Cash flows are based on opportunity costs:** Projects are evaluated on the incremental cash flows they bring in over and above the amount that they would generate in their next best alternative use (opportunity cost).
4. **Cash flows are analyzed on an after-tax basis.**
5. **Financing costs are ignored from calculations of operating cash flows.** Financing costs are reflected in the required rate of return from an investment project, so cash flows are not adjusted for these costs.
6. **Accounting net income is not used as cash flows for capital budgeting** because accounting net income is subject to noncash charges (e.g., depreciation) and financing charges (e.g., interest expense).

Interactions between Projects

- **Independent versus mutually exclusive projects:** Independent projects are those whose cash flows are unrelated. Mutually exclusive projects compete directly with each other for acceptance.
- **Project sequencing:** Sometimes projects may only be undertaken in a certain order, so investing in one project creates the opportunity to invest in other projects in the future.
- **Unlimited funds versus capital rationing:** If the capital required to invest in all profitable projects exceeds resources available, the company must allocate funds to only the most lucrative projects to ensure that shareholder wealth is maximized.

INVESTMENT DECISION CRITERIA

Net Present Value (NPV)

A project's NPV equals the present value of all expected inflows minus the present value of all expect outflows. The rate used to discount each cash flow is the project's cost of capital.

- A project should be undertaken if its NPV is greater than zero. Positive NPV projects increase shareholder wealth.
- Projects with a negative NPV decrease shareholder wealth and should not be undertaken.
- A project with an NPV of zero has no impact on shareholder wealth.

Internal Rate of Return (IRR)

For an investment project that requires only one investment outlay that is made at inception, IRR is the discount rate that equates the sum of the present values of future after-tax cash flows to the initial investment outlay. Alternatively, IRR is the discount rate that equates the sum of present values of all after-tax cash flows for a project (inflows and outflows) to zero. Therefore, IRR is the discount rate at which NPV equals zero.

- A company should invest in a project if its IRR is *greater* than the required rate of return. When the IRR is greater than the required return, NPV is positive.
- A company should not invest in a project if its IRR is *less* than the required rate of return. When the IRR is lower than the required return, NPV is negative.

Payback Period

A project's payback period equals the time it takes for the initial investment for the project to be recovered through after-tax cash flows from the project. All other things being equal, the best investment is the one with the shortest payback period.

Advantages

- It is simple to calculate and explain.
- It can also be used as an indicator of *liquidity.* A project with a shorter payback period may be more liquid than one that has a longer payback period.

Drawbacks

- It ignores the time value of money and the risk of the project. Cash flows are *not* discounted at the project's required rate of return.
- It ignores cash flows that occur after the payback period is reached.
- It is not a measure of profitability so it cannot be used in isolation to evaluate capital investment projects. The payback period should be used along with the NPV or IRR to ensure that decisions reflect the overall profitability of the project being considered.

Discounted Payback Period

The discounted payback period equals the number of years it takes for cumulative *discounted* cash flows from the project to equal the initial outlay. A project's discounted payback period will always be *greater* than its payback period because the payback period does not discount the cash flows.

Advantage

- It accounts for the time value of money and risks associated with the project's cash flows.

Drawback

- It ignores cash flows that occur after the payback period is reached. Therefore, it does not consider the overall profitability of the project.

Average Accounting Rate of Return (AAR)

The AAR is the ratio of the project's average net income to its average book value.

Advantage

- It is easy to understand and easy to calculate.

Drawbacks

- It is based on accounting numbers and not cash flows. Accounting numbers are more susceptible to manipulation than cash flows.
- It does not account for time value of money.
- It does not differentiate between profitable and unprofitable investments accurately as there are no benchmarks for acceptable AARs.

Profitability Index

The profitability index (PI) of an investment equals the present value (PV) of a project's future cash flows divided by the initial investment. Therefore, the PI is the *ratio* of future discounted cash flows to the initial investment. NPV is the *difference* between future discounted cash flows and the initial investment. The PI indicates the value that a company receives in exchange for one unit of currency invested. It is also known as the "benefit-cost" ratio.

- A company should invest in a project if its PI is *greater* than 1. The PI is greater than 1 when NPV is positive.
- A company should not invest in a project if its PI is *less* than 1. The PI is less than 1 when NPV is negative.

NPV Profiles

An NPV profile is a graphical illustration of a project's NPV at different discount rates. NPV profiles are downward-sloping because as the cost of capital increases, the NPV of an investment falls.

- The discount rate at which the NPVs of two projects are the same (their NPV profiles intersect) is called the *crossover* rate.
- A project's NPV profile intersects the x-axis at its IRR.

NPV versus IRR

For independent projects, the NPV and IRR criteria for acceptance lead to the same result:

- Accept the project if NPV is greater than zero.
- Accept the project if IRR is greater than the cost of capital.

For mutually exclusive projects, NPV and IRR may offer different recommendations. In such a situation, a company should select the project with the *higher NPV.* NPV is a better criterion because of its more realistic reinvestment rate assumption.

- IRR assumes that interim cash flows received during the project are reinvested at the IRR. This assumption is sometimes rather inappropriate—especially for projects with high IRRs.
- NPV makes a more realistic assumption that interim cash flows are reinvested at the required rate of return.

NPV and IRR may give conflicting project rankings because of *differences in project size* and *cash flow timing differences.*

Problems with the IRR

It is possible for a project's cash flow stream to have no IRR or even multiple IRRs. This may occur even though the project has a positive NPV.

Popularity of Capital Budgeting Techniques

- The payback method is very popular in European countries.
- Larger companies prefer the NPV and IRR methods over the payback method.
- Private corporations use the payback period more often than the public companies.
- Companies headed by MBAs have a preference for discounted cash flow techniques.

NPV, Company Value, and Stock Price

If a company invests in a positive NPV project, the expected addition to shareholder wealth should lead to an increase in the company's stock price.

However, the effect of a project's NPV on share prices is not so simple. The value of a company is determined by valuing its existing investments and adding the expected NPV of its future investments. The impact of the decision to undertake a particular project on a company's stock price depends on how the actual profitability of the investment differs from its expected profitability. Expected profitability is usually already factored into current market prices.

If the profitability of a positive NPV project that the company is about to undertake is below expectations, stock prices may fall. On the other hand, certain capital projects undertaken by the company may signal that there are other potentially lucrative projects to follow. Taking on a project that brings with it the expectation of even greater future profits from subsequent opportunities may increase stock prices beyond the actual addition to the company value from the said project alone.

Capital budgeting processes tell us two things about company management:

- The extent to which management pursues the goal of shareholder wealth maximization.
- Management's effectiveness in pursuit of this goal.

COST OF CAPITAL

Cross-Reference to CFA Institute Assigned Reading #36

The weighted average cost of capital (WACC) is the expected rate of return that investors demand for financing an average risk investment of a company.

$$WACC = (w_d)(r_d)(1 - t) + (w_p)(r_p) + (w_e)(r_e)$$

- Interest payments result in tax savings for the company. Therefore, the after-tax cost of debt is used in the WACC formula.
- Payments to holders of preferred and common stock do not result in tax savings.

Methods of Determining Weights of Components of Capital

- Use the weights of each component in the *target capital structure* that the company aims to maintain.
- Use the weights of each component in the company's *current capital structure* based on *market* values.
- Examine trends in the company's capital structure over time and statements made by management regarding the company's capital structure policy to estimate the target capital structure.
- Use average weights of components in comparable companies' capital structures to estimate the target capital structure for the company.

The Optimal Capital Budget

A company's marginal cost of capital (MCC) *increases* as it raises additional capital. This is because most firms are required to pay a higher cost to obtain increasing amounts of capital.

The profitability of a company's investment opportunities *decreases* as the company makes additional investments. The company prioritizes investments in projects with the highest IRRs. As more resources are invested in the most rewarding projects, remaining opportunities offer lower and lower IRRs. This fact is represented by an investment opportunity schedule (IOS), that is downward-sloping.

The optimal capital budget occurs at the point where the marginal cost of capital intersects the investment opportunity schedule.

The WACC and Capital Budgeting

The WACC is the discount rate that reflects the average risk of the company. When we choose the WACC to evaluate a particular investment project, we assume that:

- The project under consideration is an average-risk project.
- The project will have a constant capital structure throughout its life, which will be the same as the company's target capital structure.

If the project being evaluated has *a higher* risk than the average risk of the firm's existing projects, the WACC is adjusted *upwards.* If the project has *less* risk than the average risk of the firm's existing projects, the WACC is adjusted *downwards.*

Estimating Cost of Debt

Yield-to-Maturity Approach

The bond's yield to maturity (YTM) is the IRR of an investment in the bond, assuming that it is purchased at the current market price and held till maturity. It is the yield that equates the present value of a bond's expected future cash flows to its current market price.

Debt Rating Approach

When a reliable current market price for the company's debt is not available, the before-tax cost of debt can be estimated by using the yield on similarly-rated bonds that have terms to maturity that are similar to the company's existing debt.

Issues in Estimating Cost of Debt

- *Fixed-rate versus floating-rate debt:* The cost of floating-rate debt is reset periodically based on a reference rate (usually LIBOR) and is therefore, more difficult to estimate than the cost of fixed-rate debt.
- *Debt with option like features:* If option-like features are expected to be removed from future debt issues, an analyst must adjust the yield to maturity on existing bonds for their option features, and use the adjusted rate as the company's cost of debt.
- *Nonrated debt:* If a company does not have any debt outstanding (to be rated) or yields on existing debt are not available (due to lack of current price information), an analyst may not be able to use the yield on similarly-rated bonds or the yield to maturity approach to estimate the company's cost of debt.
- *Leases:* If a company uses leases as a source of finance, the cost of these leases should be included in its cost of capital.

Estimating Cost of Preferred Stock

$$r_p = D_p / V_p$$

Estimating Cost of Equity

1. Capital Asset Pricing Model (CAPM)

The capital asset pricing model (CAPM) states that the expected rate of return from a stock equals the risk-free interest rate plus a premium for bearing risk.

$$r_e = R_F + B_i[E(R_M) - R_F]$$

CF

2. Dividend Discount Model (DDM)

The dividend discount model asserts that the value of a stock equals the present value of its expected future dividends.

$$r_e = \frac{D_1}{P_0} + g$$

3. Bond Yield plus Risk Premium Approach

The bond yield plus risk premium approach is based on the basic assumption that the cost of capital for riskier cash flows is higher than that of less risky cash flows. Therefore, we calculate the return on equity by adding a risk premium to the before-tax cost of debt.

$$r_e = r_d + \text{risk premium}$$

Estimating Betas

- Beta can be calculated by regressing the company's stock returns against market returns over a given period of time.
- Analysts use the **pure-play** method to estimate the beta of a particular project or of a company that is not publicly traded. This method involves the adjustment of a comparable publicly-listed company's beta for differences in financial leverage.
  - First find a comparable company that faces similar business risks as the company or project under study and estimate the equity beta of that company.
  - To remove all elements of financial risk from the comparable's beta "unlever" the beta. The unlevered beta reflects only the business risk of the comparable and is known as *asset beta.*
  - Finally, adjust the unlevered beta of the comparable for the level of financial risk (leverage) in the project or company under study.

Business Risk versus Financial Risk

Business risk comprises of sales risk and operating risk. Sales risk refers to the unpredictability of revenues and operating risk refers to the company's operating cost structure.

Financial risk refers to the uncertainty of profits and cash flows because of the use of fixed-cost financing sources such as debt and leases. The greater the use of debt financing, the greater the financial risk of the firm.

Country Risk Premium

Studies have shown that a stock's beta captures the country risk of a stock accurately only in developed markets. Beta does not effectively capture country risk in developing nations. To deal with this problem, the CAPM equation for stocks in developing countries is modified to add a country spread, or the country equity premium (CRP) to the market risk premium.

$$k_e = R_F + \beta\ [E(R_M) - R_F + CRP]$$

$$\text{Country risk premium} = \text{Sovereign yield spread} \times \frac{\text{Annualized standard deviation of equity index of developing country}}{\text{Annualized standard deviation of sovereign bond market in terms of the developed market currency}}$$

MCC Schedules and Break Points

A company's marginal cost of capital (MCC) increases as additional capital is raised. This is because of the following reasons:

- The company may have existing *debt covenants* that restrict the company from issuing debt with similar seniority. Subsequent rounds of debt will be subordinated to the senior issue so they will obviously carry more risk, and therefore, entail a higher cost.
- Due to economies of scale in raising significant amounts of a component (debt or equity) of capital in one go, a company may deviate from its target (optimal) capital structure over the short-term. These deviations may cause the marginal cost of capital to rise.

The amount of capital at which the WACC changes is referred to as a **break point**.

$$\text{Break point} = \frac{\text{Amount of capital at which the component's cost of capital changes}}{\text{Proportion of new capital raised from the component}}$$

CF

Flotation Costs

Flotation costs refer to the fee charged by investment bankers to assist a company in raising new capital. In the case of debt and preferred stock, we do not usually incorporate flotation costs in the estimated cost of capital because the amount of these costs is quite small. However, for equity issues, flotation costs are usually quite significant.

Accounting for Flotation Costs in Capital Budgeting

- Incorporate flotation costs into the cost of capital. This approach is theoretically incorrect.
- Adjust the cash flows used in the valuation by adding the estimated dollar amount of flotation costs to the initial cost of the project.

Study Session 11:
Corporate Finance—Leverage and Working Capital Management

CF

CF

MEASURES OF LEVERAGE

Cross-Reference to CFA Institute Assigned Reading #37

Leverage refers to a company's use of fixed costs in conducting business. Fixed costs include:

- Operating costs (e.g., rent and depreciation)
- Financial costs (e.g., interest expense)

Importance of Leverage

- Leverage increases the volatility of a company's earnings and cash flows, thereby increasing the risk borne by investors in the company.
- The more significant the use of leverage by the company, the more risky it is and therefore, the higher the discount rate that must be used to value the company.
- A company that is highly leveraged risks significant losses during economic downturns.

Leverage is affected by a company's cost structure. Generally companies incur two types of costs.

- Variable costs vary with the level of production and sales (e.g., raw materials costs and sales commissions).
- Fixed costs remain the same irrespective of the level of production and sales (e.g., depreciation and interest expense).

The higher the proportion of fixed costs (both operating and financial) in a company's cost structure (higher leverage) the greater the company's earnings volatility.
The greater the degree of leverage for a company, the steeper the slope of the line representing net income.

Business Risk

Business risk refers to the risk associated with a company's operating earnings. Operating earnings are risky because total revenues and costs of sales are both uncertain. Therefore, business risk can be broken down into sales risk and operating risk.

Sales risk: The uncertainty associated with total revenue is referred to as sales risk. Revenue is affected by economic conditions, industry dynamics, government regulation and demographics.

The higher the standard deviation of price and units sold, the wider the distribution of operating profit.

Operating risk: The risk associated with a company's operating cost structure is referred to as operating risk. A company that has a greater proportion of fixed costs in its cost structure has greater operating risk.

In order to examine a company's sensitivity of operating income to changes in unit sales, we use the **degree of operating leverage (DOL)**. DOL is the ratio of the percentage change in operating income to the percentage change in units sold.

$$\text{DOL} = \frac{\text{Percentage change in operating income}}{\text{Percentage change in units sold}}$$

$$\text{DOL} = \frac{Q \times (P - V)}{Q \times (P - V) - F}$$

DOL is different at different levels of sales. If the company is making operating profits, the sensitivity of operating income to changes in units sold decreases at higher sales volumes (in units).

- DOL is negative when operating income (the denominator in the DOL equation) is negative, and is positive when the company earns operating profits.
- Operating income is most sensitive to changes in sales around the point where the company makes zero operating income.
- DOL is undefined when operating income is zero.
- The lower the proportion of fixed costs in a company's cost structure, the less sensitive its operating income is to changes in units sold and therefore, lower is the company's operating risk.

Business risk is composed of operating and sales risk, both of which are largely determined by the industry in which the company operates.
A company has more control over operating risk than sales risk.

Financial Risk

Financial risk refers to the risk associated with how a company chooses to finance its operations. The higher the amount of fixed financial costs taken on by a company, the greater is its financial risk.

Financial risk can be measured as the sensitivity of cash flows available to owners to changes in operating income. This measure is known as the **degree of financial leverage (DFL)**.

$$\text{DFL} = \frac{\text{Percentage change in net income}}{\text{Percentage change in operating income}}$$

$$\text{DFL} = \frac{[Q(P - V) - F](1 - t)}{[Q(P - V) - F - C](1 - t)} = \frac{[Q(P - V) - F]}{[Q(P - V) - F - C]}$$

CF

The higher the use of fixed financing sources by a company, the greater the sensitivity of net income to changes in operating income and therefore, the higher the financial risk of the company.

The degree of financial leverage is also different at different levels of operating income. The degree of financial leverage is usually determined by the company's management. Companies with relatively high ratios of tangible assets to total assets or those with revenues that have below-average business cycle sensitivity are able to use more financial leverage.

Total Leverage

The degree of total leverage (DTL) looks at the combined effect of operating and financial leverage i.e., it measures the sensitivity of net income to changes in units produced and sold.

$$\text{DTL} = \frac{\text{Percentage change in net income}}{\text{Percentage change in the number of units sold}}$$

$$\text{DTL} = \text{DOL} \times \text{DFL}$$

$$\text{DTL} = \frac{Q \times (P - V)}{[Q(P - V) - F - C]}$$

DTL is also different at different numbers of units produced and sold. This is because DOL is different at different levels of units produced and sold, while DFL is different at different levels of operating earnings. DTL combines the effects of DOL and DFL.

Breakeven Points and Operating Breakeven Points

A company's breakeven point occurs at the number of units produced and sold at which its net income equals zero. It is the point at which a company's revenues equal its total costs and the company goes from making losses to making profits.

The breakeven point for a company occurs when:

$$PQ = VQ + F + C$$

The breakeven number of units can be calculated as:

$$Q_{BE} = \frac{F + C}{P - V}$$

While greater leverage entails higher risk, it also raises the company's potential for profit.

CF

A breakeven point can also be specified in terms of operating profit, in which case it is known as the operating breakeven point. At this point, revenues equal operating costs. The expression for operating breakeven point is given as:

$$PQ_{OBE} = VQ_{OBE} + F$$

$$Q_{OBE} = \frac{F}{P - V}$$

The farther unit sales are from the breakeven point for high-leverage companies, the greater the magnifying effect of leverage.

The Risks of Creditors and Owners

Creditor claims on the assets of the company are senior to those of equity holders. In return for lending money to the company, creditors demand timely interest and principal payments. Payments to creditors must be made irrespective of whether the company is profitable. Inability to make these payments may lead to the company having to declare bankruptcy. Returns for creditors are predefined; even if the company does very well, they do not see any of the upside.

Owners only have a claim on what is left over after all the financial obligations of the company have been met. In return for the lower priority in claims, equity holders enjoy decision-making power in the company, and participate in the upside if the company does well.

Legal codes in most countries are provided for companies to file for bankruptcy protection. There are two main types of bankruptcy protection.

- Reorganization (Chapter 11), which provides the company temporary protection from creditors so that it can reorganize its capital structure and emerge from bankruptcy as a going concern.
- Liquidation (Chapter 7), which allows for an orderly settlement of the creditors' claims. In this category of bankruptcy, the original business ceases to exist.

Companies with high operating leverage have less flexibility in making changes to their operating structures so bankruptcy protection does little to help reduce operating costs. On the other hand, companies with high financial leverage can use Chapter 11 protection to change their capital structure and, once the restructuring is complete, emerge as ongoing concerns.

Under both Chapter 7 and Chapter 11, providers of equity capital generally lose out. On the other hand, debt holders typically receive at least a portion of their capital, but only after the period of bankruptcy protection ends.

WORKING CAPITAL MANAGEMENT
Cross-Reference to CFA Institute Assigned Reading #38

Working capital management deals with the short-term aspects of corporate finance activities. Effective working capital management ensures that a company has adequate ready access to funds that are needed for day-to-day expenses, and at the same time invests its assets in the most productive manner.

Sources of Liquidity

- Primary sources are readily available resources such as cash balances and short-term funds.
- Secondary sources provide liquidity at a higher cost than primary sources. They include negotiating debt contracts, liquidating assets or filing for bankruptcy protection.

Drags versus Pulls on Liquidity

A **drag on liquidity** occurs when there is a delay in cash coming into the company. Major drags on liquidity include:

- Uncollected receivables.
- Obsolete inventory.
- Tight credit.

Drags on liquidity can be dealt with by enforcing strict credit and collection policies.

A **pull on liquidity** occurs when cash leaves the company too quickly. Major pulls on payments include:

- Making payments early.
- Reduced credit limits.
- Limits on short terms lines of credit.
- Low existing levels of liquidity.

Evaluation of Liquidity Management

Current ratio

- A higher current ratio means that a company is better positioned to meet its short term obligations.
- A current ratio of less than one indicates negative working capital, which might imply that the company faces a liquidity crisis.

In order to gauge whether a given quick or current ratio is good or bad, we must look at the trend in ratios, how they compare with ratios of competitors, and available opportunities to invest in more profitable, longer-term investments.

Accounts receivable turnover ratio

- It is desirable to have an accounts receivable turnover ratio close to the industry average.

Number of days of receivables

- A collection period that is too high might imply that customers are too slow in making payments and too much of the company's capital is tied up in accounts receivable.
- A collection period that is too low might suggest that the company's credit policy is too strict, which might hurt sales.

The number of days of receivables must be evaluated in light of the credit terms offered to customers, and the relation between sales and extension of credit.

Inventory turnover ratio

- An inventory TO ratio that is too high might indicate that the company has too little stock on hand at any given point in time, which might hurt sales.
- A low inventory TO ratio might suggest that the company has too much liquidity tied up in inventory, perhaps because the units held are obsolete.

Payables' turnover

- A high payables' turnover ratio might indicate that the company is not making full use of available credit facilities.
- A low ratio could suggest that the company has trouble making payments on time.

The **operating cycle** is a measure of the time needed to convert raw materials into cash from sales.

Operating cycle = Number of days of inventory + Number of days of receivables

The **cash conversion cycle** or the **net operating cycle** equals the time period between paying suppliers for materials and collecting cash from sales to customers.

Net operating cycle = Number of days of inventory + Number of days of receivables – Number of days of payables

Examples of Cash Inflows and Outflows

Inflows	Outflows
• Receipts from operations.	• Payables and payroll disbursements.
• Funds transfers from subsidiaries, joint ventures and third parties.	• Funds transfers to subsidiaries.
• Maturing investments.	• Investments made.
• Debt proceeds (short and long term).	• Debt repayments.
• Other income items (interest, etc.).	• Tax payments.
• Tax refunds.	• Interest and dividend payments.

CF

Components of a Cash Forecast

	Short Term	Medium Term	Long Term
Data Frequency	Daily/weekly for 4-6 weeks	Monthly for one year	Annually for 3-5 years
Format	Receipts and disbursements	Receipts and disbursements	Projected financial statements
Techniques	Simple projections	Projection models and averages	Statistical models
Accuracy	Very high	Moderate	Lowest
Reliability	Very high	Fairly high	Not as high
Uses	Daily cash management	Planning financial transactions	Long-range financial position

Predicting sales peaks caused by seasonality is very important if the company will have to borrow funds to cover its needs.

- If a company sets aside too much money, it will lose out in terms of investment income forgone (opportunity cost).
- If a company sets aside too little, it will incur higher costs to raise funds very quickly.

A company maintains a daily cash position to make sure that it has the necessary funds (the target balance) to carry on its day-to-day activities. If it keeps too much cash on hand, it loses out in terms of interest foregone. *Short-term investments* represent a temporary store for funds that are not needed for financing daily operations. Typical short-term investments that businesses invest their excess cash in are highly liquid and have low risk.

Yields on Short-Term Investments

$$\text{Money market yield} = \left(\frac{\text{Face value} - \text{price}}{\text{Price}}\right) \times \left(\frac{360}{\text{Days}}\right) = \text{Holding period yield} \times \left(\frac{360}{\text{Days}}\right)$$

$$\text{Bond equivalent yield} = \left(\frac{\text{Face value} - \text{price}}{\text{Price}}\right) \times \left(\frac{365}{\text{Days}}\right) = \text{Holding period yield} \times \left(\frac{365}{\text{Days}}\right)$$

$$\text{Discount basis yield} = \left(\frac{\text{Face value} - \text{price}}{\text{Face value}}\right) \times \left(\frac{360}{\text{Days}}\right) = \%\,\text{discount} \times \left(\frac{360}{\text{Days}}\right)$$

CF

Cash Management Investment Strategies

- A passive strategy involves a limited number of transactions, and is based on very few rules for making daily investments. The focus is simply on reinvesting funds as they mature with little attention paid to yields.
- An active strategy involves constant monitoring to exploit profitable opportunities in a wider array of investments. Active strategies call for more involvement, more thorough study, evaluation, forecasts, and a flexible investment policy.

Cash Management Investment Policy

- The *purpose* of the investment policy states reasons for the existence of the portfolio and describes its general attributes, such as the investment strategy to be followed.
- It identifies the *authorities* who supervise the portfolio managers and details actions that must be undertaken if the policy is not followed.
- It describes the types of investments that should be considered for inclusion in the portfolio. The policy also contains *restrictions* on the maximum proportion of each type of security in the portfolio and the minimum credit rating of portfolio securities.

Evaluating Management of Accounts Receivable

- An *aging schedule* classifies accounts receivable according to the length of time that they have been outstanding.
- The *weighted average collection period* measures how long it takes to collect cash from the company's customers irrespective of the level of sales or changes in sales.

Evaluating Inventory Management

The main goal of inventory management is to maintain a level of inventory that ensures smooth delivery of sales without having more than necessary invested in stock.

- A high level of inventory is undesirable as it inflates storage costs, can result in losses from obsolescence or damage, and can squeeze liquidity from the firm.
- A shortage of inventory can hurt sales as the company loses out on potential customers.

Evaluating Management of Accounts Payable

Managing accounts payable is an important part of working capital management as accounts payable can be a source of working capital for the firm.

- If it pays too early, a company loses out on interest income.
- If it pays late, the company risks ruining its reputation and relationships with suppliers. Further, penalties and interest charges for late payment can be very significant.

Evaluating Trade Discounts

A company should review its evaluation of trade discounts periodically. An early payment discount must be availed if the savings from paying suppliers early are *greater* than the returns that could have been earned by investing the funds instead. The rate implicit in the discount must be compared to the return on the alternative short-term investment.

$$\text{Implicit rate} = \text{Cost of trade credit} = \left(1+\frac{\text{Discount}}{1-\text{Discount}}\right)^{\left(365 \big/ \text{Number of days beyond discount period}\right)} - 1$$

Terms of "2/10 net 30" mean that a 2% discount is available if the amount owed is paid within 10 days; otherwise, the full amount is due by the 30th day.

Bank Sources of Finance

- *Uncommitted lines of credit* are the weakest and least reliable form of borrowing. Their advantage is that they do not require any compensation other than interest.
- *Regular lines of credit (committed lines of credit)* are stronger than uncommitted lines of credit as they require a formal commitment from the bank.
- *Revolving credit agreements* are the strongest form of short term borrowing.

Computing the Cost of Borrowing

$$\text{Line of credit cost} = \frac{\text{Interest} + \text{Commitment fee}}{\text{Loan amount}}$$

Cost of banker's acceptance and other sources whose costs are stated as "all inclusive":

$$= \frac{\text{Interest}}{\text{Net proceeds}} = \frac{\text{Interest}}{\text{Loan amount} - \text{Interest}}$$

Cost of sources with dealer's fees and backup fees that are quoted as "all inclusive":

$$= \frac{\text{Interest} + \text{Dealer's comission} + \text{Backup costs}}{\text{Loan amount} - \text{Interest}}$$

CF

Study Session 12: Portfolio Management

PM

PORTFOLIO MANAGEMENT: AN OVERVIEW

Cross-Reference to CFA Institute Assigned Reading #39

Importance of the Portfolio Perspective

- Portfolios of securities may offer equivalent expected returns with lower volatility of returns (lower risk) compared to individual securities.
- A simple measure of the value of diversification is the diversification ratio. It is the ratio of the standard deviation of an equal-weighted portfolio to the standard deviation of a randomly selected component of the portfolio. The lower the diversification ratio, the greater the risk reduction benefits of diversification, and the greater the portfolio effect.
- The composition of the portfolio (weight of each security held in the portfolio) is an important determinant of the overall level of risk inherent in the portfolio. By varying the weights of the individual securities, investors can arrive at a portfolio that offers the same return as an equally weighted portfolio, but with a lower standard deviation (risk).

Types of Investment Management Clients

Table 1: Summary of Investment Needs by Client Type:

Client	Time Horizon	Risk Tolerance	Income Needs	Liquidity Needs
Individual investors	Varies by individual	Varies by individual	Varies by individual	Varies by individual
Defined benefit pension plans	Typically long-term	Typically quite high	High for mature funds; low for growing funds	Typically quite low
Endowments and foundations	Very long-term	Typically high	To meet spending commitments	Typically quite low
Banks	Short-term	Quite low	To pay interest on deposits and operations expenses	High to meet repayment of deposits

(Table continued on next page...)

Table 1: Continued

Client	Time Horizon	Risk Tolerance	Income Needs	Liquidity Needs
Insurance companies	Short-term for property and casualty; long-term for life insurance companies	Typically quite low	Typically low	High to meet claims
Investment companies	Varies by fund	Varies by fund	Varies by fund	High to meet redemptions

Steps in the Portfolio Management Process

Planning

The planning step involves understanding the client's needs and constraints and developing an investment policy statement (IPS). The IPS is a written document that describes the objectives and constraints of the investor.

Execution

Asset Allocation: The asset allocation of a portfolio refers to the distribution of investable funds between various asset classes (e.g., equities, fixed-income securities, alternative investments, etc.).

Security analysis: Analysts use their knowledge of various companies and the industry to identify investments that offer the most attractive risk return characteristics from within each asset class.

Portfolio construction: After determining the target asset allocation and conducting security analysis, the portfolio manager will construct the portfolio in line with the objectives outlined in the IPS.

Feedback

Portfolio monitoring and rebalancing: The portfolio must be regularly monitored. Changes in fundamental factors and client circumstances may require changes in the portfolio's composition. Rebalancing may be required when changes in security prices cause a significant change in weights of assets in the portfolio.

Performance measurement and reporting: This step involves measuring the performance of the portfolio relative to the benchmark stated in the IPS and reporting portfolio performance to the client.

Pooled Investments

Pooled investments are investments in securities issued by entities that represent ownership in the underlying assets held by those entities. These include:

- Mutual funds and exchange traded funds, in which investors can participate with a relatively small initial investment.
- Hedge funds and private equity funds, which may require a minimum investment of US$1 million or more.

Mutual Funds

Mutual funds pool money from several investors and invest these funds in a portfolio of securities.

- *Open-end funds* accept new investment funds and issue new shares at a value equal to the fund's net asset value per share at the time of investment. These funds also allow investors to redeem their investment in the fund at the prevailing net asset value per share.
- *Closed-end funds* accept no new investment money into fund. Shares in the fund are traded in the secondary market so new investors invest in the fund by purchasing shares in the market, and investors liquidate their holdings by selling the shares in the market. Unlike open-end funds, shares of closed-end funds can trade at a discount or premium to the net asset value per share, depending on the demand and supply of shares in the market.

The structure of open-end funds makes it easy for them to grow in size, but it does pose the following problems:

- The portfolio manager needs to manage cash inflows and outflows.
- An inflow of new investment requires the manager to find new investments.
- Funds need to keep cash for redemptions.

Closed-end funds do not face these problems, but as mentioned earlier, they cannot accept new investments.

Mutual funds may also be classified into:

- *Load funds* that charge a percentage fee for investing in the fund and/or for redemptions from the fund on top of an annual fee.
- *No-load funds* that only charge an annual fee based on a percentage of the fund's NAV.

Types of Mutual Funds

- *Money market funds:* These invest in high-quality, short-term debt instruments. Money-market mutual funds can be divided into tax-free and taxable funds.
- *Bond funds:* These invest in individual bonds and sometimes preference shares as well. Unlike money-market mutual funds, they usually invest in longer term instruments.
- *Stock funds:* These invest in equities and equity indices. Stock mutual funds can be actively or passively managed.
- *Hybrid or balanced funds:* These invest in both bonds and equities.

Other Investment Products Compared with Mutual Funds

Exchange Traded Funds (ETFs)

- Investors in index mutual funds purchase shares directly from the fund, while investors in an ETF purchase shares from other investors (just like buying or selling shares of stock). Investors are allowed to short ETF shares and even purchase them on margin.
- ETFs have lower costs, but unlike index mutual funds, investors do incur brokerage costs when trading ETFs.
- ETFs are constantly traded throughout the business day. Each trade occurs at the prevailing market price at that time. All purchases and redemptions for a mutual fund for a given day occur at the end of a trading day, at the same price.
- ETFs pay out dividends, while index mutual funds usually reinvest dividends.
- The minimum required investment is usually smaller for an ETF.
- ETFs are generally considered to have a tax advantage over index mutual funds.

Separately Managed Accounts (SMAs)

- Unlike investors in mutual funds, investors in SMAs directly own the shares and therefore, have control over which assets are bought and sold, and over the timing of transactions.
- Unlike mutual funds, in which no consideration is given to the tax position of the investor, transactions in SMAs take into account the specific tax needs of the investor.
- The required minimum investment for an SMA is usually much higher than for a mutual fund.

Hedge Funds

- Hedge funds differ from mutual funds in that most hedge funds are exempt from many of the reporting requirements for a typical public investment company.
- They require a minimum investment that is typically US$250,000 for new funds and US$1 million or more for well-established funds.
- They usually place restrictions on investors' ability to make withdrawals from the fund.
- Total management fee also has a performance-based component.

Buyout and Venture Capital Funds

- They take equity positions in companies and play a very active role in managing those companies.
- The eventual exit strategy is an important consideration when funds evaluate potential investments.

RISK MANAGEMENT: AN INTRODUCTION

Cross-Reference to CFA Institute Assigned Reading #40

Risk encompasses all of the uncertain environmental variables that lead unpredictability of outcomes. Taking risk is an integral part of conducting business and managing investment portfolios. While risk is generally seen in an unfavorable light, the challenge for companies/investment managers lies in carefully choosing, understanding, and managing the risks entailed by their decisions.

RISK MANAGEMENT FRAMEWORK

A **risk management framework** refers to the infrastructure, process, and analytics required to support the risk management function in an organization.

Risk governance comes from the board. It is the top-down process and guidance, which directs risk management activities to align with the organization's goals and risk appetite.

Risk identification and measurement is an ongoing process that requires entails analyzing the business or portfolio to identify risk exposures, tracking changes in those risk exposures, calculating risk metrics to gauge the significance of those risks under various scenarios, as well as keeping an eye on the business environment for potential risk drivers.

- A **risk driver** refers to any fundamental underlying factor that gives rise to a risk that is relevant to the entity.

Risk infrastructure refers to the people, systems and technology required to track risk exposures and conduct quantitative risk analysis. It includes the process (known as **risk capture**) through which risk exposures are populated in the risk management system, as well as the databases, models, and skilled personnel needed to develop and maintain the risk framework.

Policies and processes translate risk governance into the organization's day-to-day operations and decision-making processes in order to ensure that risky activities kept in line with the entity's risk tolerance levels.

Risk monitoring, mitigation, and management requires pulling together risk governance, identification and measurement, infrastructure, and policies and processes and continually reviewing and reevaluating in the face of changing risk exposures and risk drivers. Further, it requires recognizing when the entity's risk exposure is not aligned with its predetermined risk tolerance, and then taking action to bring them back into alignment.

Communication of critical risk issues must happen continuously across all levels of the organization.

Note that:

- Risk management is not about minimizing risk. It is about actively understanding and embracing those risks that offer the best chance of achieving organization's goals with an acceptable chance of failure.
- Risk management is not even about predicting risks. It is about being prepared for (positive or negative) unpredictable events such that their impact would have already been quantified and considered in advance.

RISK GOVERNANCE

An Enterprise View of Risk

The governing body, or board, plays the following roles within the risk management framework:

- It determines the organization's goals and priorities, which form the basis of enterprise risk management.
- It determines the organization's risk appetite/tolerance i.e., defines which risks are acceptable, which risks must be mitigated and to what extent, and which risks are unacceptable.
- It is responsible for overseeing risk management to continually ensure that it is functioning properly, and is consistent with the goal of maximizing value.

Desirable Properties of Good Risk Governance

- Good risk governance should provide a sense of the worst loss that the organization can manage in various scenarios.
- It should provide clear guidance, but at the same time leave enough flexibility for management to execute strategy.
- The focus should be on enterprise risk management (that focuses on the objectives, health and value of the organization as a whole).
- It should provide a regular forum (e.g., a **risk management committee**) where the risk framework and key risk issues are discussed at management level.
- It should provide for the appointment of a **chief risk officer (CRO)** who is responsible for building and implementing the risk framework for the enterprise and managing all related activities. Further, the CRO's insight should be used in making key strategic decisions.

Risk Tolerance

Risk tolerance identifies the extent to which the entity is willing to experience losses or opportunity costs and to fail meeting its objectives. At the governance level, the idea is not really to select activities that will maximize value or produce the highest returns given an acceptable level of risk (this duty falls on management), but to define the entity's risk appetite.

PM

Defining an organization's risk tolerance calls for answering the following questions:

- What shortfalls within the organization would cause it to fail to achieve critical goals? This questions looks to address **internal** risk factors.
- What uncertain forces is the organization exposed to? This question focusses on **outside** risk factors.

Factors that Affect a Company's Risk Tolerance

- The more dynamic a company in its ability to respond to adverse events, the higher its risk tolerance.
- The greater the loss a company can bear without impairing its status as a going concern, the higher its risk tolerance.
- The stronger the company's competitive position, the higher its risk tolerance.
- The overall competitive landscape in the industry and the regulatory landscape also influence a company's risk tolerance.

Risk Budgeting

Risk budgeting focuses on how risk is taken by quantifying and allocating tolerable risk to various activities/investments based on their characteristics.
Risk budgets can be complex/multi-dimensional or simple/one-dimensional.

- **Single-dimension risk measures** include standard deviation, beta, value at risk (VaR) and scenario loss.
- **Multi-dimension risk approaches** include one where portfolio risk is evaluated based on the risk profiles of underlying asset classes (equity, fixed income, etc.), and another risk-factor approach where exposure to various risk factors is used to capture associated risk premiums (value stocks versus growth stocks).

The benefit of risk budgeting lies in the fact that it forces the organization into thinking about risk trade-offs and fosters a culture where risk is an important consideration in all key decisions.

IDENTIFICATION OF RISKS

Financial Risks

- **Market risk** arises from changes in interest rates, stock prices, exchange rates and commodity prices.
    - Generally speaking, the underlying risk drivers of market risk are fundamental economic conditions or events in the overall economy, industry or the company itself.
- **Credit risk** (**default risk** or **counterparty risk**) is the risk of loss if one party fails to pay an amount owed on an obligation (e.g., bond or derivative).
    - Generally speaking, the underlying risk drivers of credit risk tend to be fundamental weakness in the economy, industry or in demand for a company's products.

- **Liquidity risk** (or **transaction cost risk**) is the risk of a substantial downward valuation adjustment when trying to sell an asset.
    - In several transactions, there is a bid-ask spread that is known at the time of purchase. This spread is simply a **transaction cost**. Liquidity risk would arise if this spread would widen when it the asset is being sold.
    - Generally speaking, the primary drivers of liquidity risk are (1) changes in market conditions or the market for the individual asset and (2) the size of the position i.e., large positions are typically more difficult and costly to offload.

Non-Financial Risks

- **Settlement risk** (also known as **Herstatt risk**) is related to default risk, but has more to do with settlement of payments just before a default.
- **Legal risk** is of two types. First, there is the risk of being sued for something the entity does or fails to do. Second, there is the risk of the terms of a contract not being upheld by the legal system.
- **Compliance risk** encompasses **regulatory risk**, **accounting risk** and **tax risk**. It refers to the risk of the organization incurring significant unexpected costs, back taxes, financial restatements and penalties.
- **Model risk** is the risk of a valuation error resulting from using an incorrectly specified model or improperly using a valid model.
    - **Tail risk** is related to model risk, and can even be viewed as a form of model risk. It refers to the risk of events captured by the tail of a distribution occurring more frequently than expected by the model.
- **Operational risk** is used to describe all internal risks that arise from the people and processes that work together in an organization to produce its output. Examples include the risk of hackers breaking into the company's computer systems, its computers becoming infected with a virus, and programming errors and bugs.
- **Solvency risk** is the risk that the entity runs out cash, and is therefore unable to survive or succeed, even if it is otherwise solvent.

Interactions between Risks

It is very important for organizations to recognize that risks interact, and that the interaction is more 'toxic' in stressed market conditions. When different sources of risk come together, the combined risk is almost always non-linear in that the total risk faced is much greater than the simple sum of the individual risks, and this makes the situation even worse. Unfortunately, most risk models and systems do not directly account for risk interactions.

PM

MEASURING AND MODIFYING RISKS

Value at Risk (VaR)

Value at risk or **VaR** is a measure of the size of the tail of the distribution of profits on a portfolio or for an entity. A VaR measure is composed of (1) a currency amount, (2) a time period, and (3) a probability. If a bank states that its VaR is $4 million at 3% for one day, it means that bank expects to lose a minimum of $4 million in one day 3% of the time.

- VaR is a **minimum** extreme loss metric.
  - There is no ultimate maximum loss that is stated in the measure. However, the statistics used to compute VaR can be used to estimate average extreme losses.
    - **Conditional VaR** or **CVaR** is calculated as the weighted average of all loss outcomes in a statistical distribution that exceed the VaR loss.
    - **Expected loss given default** (which is used to measure credit risk) measures the average expected loss if the underlying company defaults.
- VaR can be measured in several different ways, which results in highly diverse estimates.
- VaR is subject to model risk as well.
  - VaR is based on a particular assumption about the probability distribution of returns or profits. If that assumption is incorrect, the VaR estimate will be incorrect.
  - VaR also requires certain inputs. If those inputs are incorrect, the VaR estimate will be incorrect.
- VaR can understate actual risk. Under the normal distribution, extreme negative returns are accounted for, but they are offset by extreme positive returns. However, actual historical returns have exhibited a tendency for more extreme negative returns than assumed by the normal distribution (tail risk). In response, statisticians have developed **extreme value theory** to help them gauge the likelihood of outcomes that exceed those that would normally be expected.

Due to its shortcomings, critics have argued that naive users of VaR can be lulled into a false sense of security. A presumably tolerable VaR can give the illusion that risk is under control, even when it is actually not. Nonetheless, VaR is accepted as a risk measure by most banking regulators and is approved for disclosure purposes in accounting standards.

Two measures in particular that are often used to complement VaR are **scenario analysis** and **stress testing**. Although scenario analysis and stress testing can provide useful information (and banks are required to perform them) they are also subject to model risk.

METHODS OF RISK MODIFICATION

Risk Prevention and Avoidance

In organizations, the board typically decides which business or investment activities are not worth pursuing based on the organization's goals and the perceived risk-return trade-off. Areas where the board believes management has a better chance of adding value are the ones whose risks are taken, but they are still managed via (1) self-insurance, (2) risk transfer, or (3) risk shifting.

Risk Acceptance: Self-Insurance and Diversification

- **Self-insurance** refers to retaining exposure to a risk that is considered undesirable but is too costly to eliminate by external means.
- **Diversification** is another form of accepting risk, but it does so in the most efficient manner possible. When it comes to portfolio risk management, diversification is the key to eliminating non-systematic risk, but other forms of risk management may be needed to mitigate other risks.

Risk Transfer is the process of passing on a risk to another party, usually in the form of an insurance policy.

Risk shifting refers to actions that change the distribution of risk outcomes. Risk shifting is associated with derivative contracts and risk modification vehicles. Risk shifting mechanism are used when the organization wants to modify the probability distribution of returns, or adjust the payoff diagram of its risk exposures.

How to Choose a Method for Modifying Risk

Generally speaking:

- For risks that lie outside the core competencies of the organization, management should try to avoid those risks. If the potential value added is too great to ignore, then management must at least take adequate precautions.
- Organizations that have large amounts of free cash flow should self-insure as much as possible because self-insurance reduces costs and enables the company to retain flexibility. At the same time, organizations should aim to diversify as much as possible.
- Insurance works best when risks can be pooled, but this is not the case for many types of risks, particularly those that can affect a large number of parties at the same time as premiums can be prohibitively high.
- For financial risks that exceed risk appetite, risk shifting is a very common choice. However, risk shifting tools such as derivatives may not be available for all types of risks.

PM

PORTFOLIO RISK AND RETURN: PART I

Cross-Reference to CFA Institute Assigned Reading #41

Measures of Return

Holding period return is simply the return earned on an investment over a single specified period of time.

$$R = \frac{P_T + D_T}{P_0} - 1$$

Holding period returns may also be calculated for more than one period by compounding single period returns:

$$R = [(1+R_1)\times(1+R_2)\times....\times(1+R_n)] - 1$$

The arithmetic or mean return is a simple average of all holding period returns.

- Arithmetic return is easy to calculate and has known statistical properties such as standard deviation, which is used to evaluate the dispersion of observed returns.
- The arithmetic mean return is biased upwards as it assumes that the amount invested at the beginning of each period is the same. This bias is particularly severe if holding period returns are a mix of both positive and negative returns.

$$R = \frac{R_{i1} + R_{i2} + ... + R_{iT}}{T} = \frac{1}{T}\sum_{t=1}^{T} R_{iT}$$

The geometric mean return accounts for compounding of returns, and does not assume that the amount invested in each period is the same.

- The geometric mean is lower than the arithmetic mean (due to the effects of compounding) unless there is no variation in returns, in which case they are equal.

$$R = \{[(1+R_1)\times(1+R_2)\times....\times(1+R_n)]^{1/n}\} - 1$$

The money-weighted return accounts for the amount of money invested in each period and provides information on the return earned on the actual amount invested.

- The money-weighted return equals the internal rate of return of an investment.
- A drawback of the money-weighted return is that it does not allow for return comparisons between different individuals or different investment opportunities.

Annualized returns are calculated to make comparisons across investment instruments with different maturities.

- It is assumed that returns earned over short investment horizons can be replicated over the year.

$$r_{annual} = (1 + r_{period})^n - 1$$

The return on a portfolio is simply the weighted average of the returns on individual assets. For example, the return of a two-asset portfolio can be calculated as:

$$R_p = w_1R_1 + w_2R_2$$

Other Return Measures and Their Applications

Gross versus Net Returns

- Gross returns are calculated before deductions for management expenses, custodial fees, taxes and other expenses that are not directly linked to the generation of returns.
- Net returns deduct all managerial and administrative expenses that reduce an investor's return. Investors are primarily concerned with net returns.

Pre-Tax versus After-Tax Nominal Returns

- Pre-tax nominal returns do not adjust for taxes or inflation.
- After-tax nominal returns account for taxes. Most investors are concerned with returns on an after-tax basis.

Real versus Nominal Returns

- Nominal returns consist of the real risk-free rate of return, a premium for risk, and a premium for inflation.
- Investors calculate the real return because:
  - It is useful in comparing returns across time periods as inflation rates may vary over time.
  - It is useful in comparing returns among countries when returns are expressed in local currencies in which inflation rates vary between countries.
  - The after-tax real return is what an investor receives as compensation for postponing consumption and assuming risk after paying taxes on investment returns.

Leveraged Return

The leveraged return is computed when an investor uses leverage (by either borrowing money or using derivative contracts) to invest in a security. Leverage enhances returns, but also magnifies losses.

PM

Variance and Covariance of Returns

The risk of an asset or a portfolio of assets can be measured by its standard deviation, which is the positive square root of variance.

Variance of a Single Asset

Variance equals the average squared deviation of observed values from their mean.

- A higher variance indicates higher volatility or dispersion of returns.

Standard Deviation of an Asset

The population and sample standard deviations are calculated as:

$$\sigma = \sqrt{\frac{\sum_{t=1}^{T}(R_t - \mu)^2}{T}}$$

$$s = \sqrt{\frac{\sum_{t=1}^{T}(R_t - \bar{R})^2}{T-1}}$$

Variance of a Portfolio of Assets

The formula for the variance of a portfolio is:

$$\sigma_P^2 = \sum_{i,j=1}^{N} w_i w_j \mathrm{Cov}(R_i, R_j)$$

$$\sigma_P^2 = \sum_{i=1}^{N} w_i^2 \mathrm{Var}(R_i) + \sum_{i,j=1,\, i \neq j}^{N} w_i w_j \mathrm{Cov}\left(R_i, R_j\right)$$

The standard deviation of a portfolio of two risky assets is calculated as:

$$\sigma_p = \sqrt{w_1^2\sigma_1^2 + w_2^2\sigma_2^2 + 2w_1w_2\sigma_1\sigma_2\rho_{1,2}} \text{ or } \sqrt{w_1^2\sigma_1^2 + w_2^2\sigma_2^2 + 2w_1w_2\mathrm{Cov}_{1,2}}$$

Other Investment Characteristics

Distributional Characteristics

- *Skewness* refers to the asymmetry of a returns distribution.
  - When most of the distribution is concentrated on the left, it is referred to as right skewed or positively skewed.
  - When most of the distribution is concentrated to the right, it is referred to as left skewed or negatively skewed.

- *Kurtosis* refers to fat tails or higher than normal probabilities for extreme returns. This leads to an increase in an asset's risk that is not captured by the mean-variance framework.

Market Characteristics

Markets are not always *operationally efficient*. One limitation on operational efficiency in markets is liquidity. Liquidity has an impact on the bid-ask spread (illiquid stocks have a wider spread) and on the price impact of a trade (illiquid stocks suffer a greater price impact).

Informational efficiency is discussed in later readings on market efficiency.

The Concept of Risk Aversion

Risk-averse investors aim to maximize returns for a given level of risk, and minimize risk for a given level or return.

Risk-seeking investors get extra utility or satisfaction from the uncertainty associated with their investments.

Risk-neutral investors seek higher returns irrespective of the level of risk inherent in an investment.

Risk tolerance refers to the level of risk that an investor is willing to accept to achieve her investment goals.

- The lower the risk tolerance, the lower the level of risk acceptable to the investor.
- The lower the risk tolerance, the higher the risk aversion.

Utility Theory

In order to quantify the preferences for investment choices using risk and return, utility functions are used. An example of a utility function is:

$$U = E(R) - \frac{1}{2}A\sigma^2$$

"A" is a measure of risk aversion. It is higher for investors who are more risk averse as they require larger compensation for accepting more risk.

The utility function assumes the following:

- Investors are generally risk averse, but prefer more return to less return.
- Investors are able to rank different portfolios based on their preferences and these preferences are internally consistent.

We can draw the following conclusions from the utility function:

- Utility is unbounded on both sides- it can be highly negative or highly positive.
- Higher return results in higher utility.
- Higher risk results in lower utility.
- The higher the value of "A" the higher the negative effect of risk on utility.

Important Notes Regarding the Risk Aversion Coefficient, "A":

- "A" is positive for a risk-averse investor. Additional risk reduces total utility.
- It is negative for a risk seeking investor. Additional risk enhances total utility.
- It equals zero for a risk neutral investor. Additional risk has no impact on total utility.

Indifference Curves

The risk-return trade-off that an investor is willing to bear can be illustrated by an indifference curve. An investor realizes the same total utility or satisfaction from every point on a given indifference curve. Since each investor can have an infinite number of risk-return combinations that generate the same utility, indifference curves are continuous at all points.

1. They are *upward sloping*. This means that an investor will be indifferent between two investments with different expected returns only if the investment with the lower expected return entails a lower level of risk as well.
2. They are *curved*, and their slope becomes steeper as more risk is taken. The increase in return required for every unit of additional risk increases at an increasing rate because of the diminishing marginal utility of wealth.

The slope of an indifference curve represents the extra return required by the investor to accept an additional unit of risk.

- A risk-averse investor would have a relatively steep indifference curve (significant extra return required to take on more risk).
- A less risk-averse investor would have a flatter indifference curve (lower extra return required to take on more risk).
- A risk-seeking investor would have an indifference curve with a negative slope. Her utility increases with higher return and higher risk.
- A risk-neutral investor would have a perfectly horizontal indifference curve. Her utility does not vary with risk.

Application of Utility Theory to Portfolio Selection

Capital Allocation Line

$$E(R_p) = RFR + \sigma_{port}\frac{[E(R_i) - RFR]}{\sigma_i}$$

- The CAL has an intercept of RFR.
- The expression for the slope of the CAL is the extra return required for each additional unit of risk and is also known as the market price of risk.

The point of tangency between the CAL and an investor's indifference curve indicates the optimal risky asset portfolio that the investor should invest in.

Portfolio Risk

The formula for the standard deviation of a portfolio consisting of 2 risky assets is:

$$\sigma_p = \sqrt{w_1^2\sigma_1^2 + w_2^2\sigma_2^2 + 2w_1w_2\sigma_1\sigma_2\rho_{1,2}} \text{ or } \sqrt{w_1^2\sigma_1^2 + w_2^2\sigma_2^2 + 2w_1w_2\text{Cov}_{1,2}}$$

The first part of the formula for the 2-asset portfolio standard deviation $(w_1^2\sigma_1^2 + w_2^2\sigma_2^2)$ tells us that portfolio standard deviation is a *positive* function of the standard deviation and weights of the individual assets held in the portfolio. The second part $(2w_1w_2\text{Cov}_{1,2})$ shows us that portfolio standard deviation is also dependent on how the two assets move in relation to each other (covariance or correlation).

From the 2-asset portfolio standard deviation formula it is also important to understand that:

- The maximum value for portfolio standard deviation will be obtained when the correlation coefficient equals +1.
- Portfolio standard deviation will be minimized when the correlation coefficient equals –1.
- If the correlation coefficient equals zero, the second part of the formula will equal zero and portfolio standard deviation will lie somewhere in between.

Implications

- When asset returns are *negatively* correlated, the final term in the standard deviation formula is negative and serves to *reduce* portfolio standard deviation.
- If the correlation between assets equals zero, portfolio standard deviation is *greater* than when correlation is negative.
- When asset returns are positively correlated, the second part of the formula for portfolio standard deviation is also positive, and portfolio standard deviation is higher than when the correlation coefficient equals zero. With a correlation coefficient of +1 (perfect positive correlation) there are no diversification benefits.
- The risk (standard deviation) of a portfolio of risky assets depends on the asset weights and standard deviations, *and most importantly on the correlation of asset returns.* The *higher* the correlation between the individual assets, the *higher* the portfolio's standard deviation.
- A conservative investor can experience both a higher return and a lower risk by diversifying into a higher-risk, higher-return asset if the correlation between the assets is fairly low.
- When correlation equals +1, the risk-return combinations that result from altering the weights lie along a straight line between the two assets' risk-return profiles.
- As correlation falls, the curvature of this line increases.
- When correlation equals –1, the curve is represented by two straight lines that meet at the vertical axis. This point represents a zero-risk portfolio where portfolio return must equal the risk-free rate to prevent arbitrage.

Avenues for Diversification

- Investing in a variety of asset classes that are not highly correlated.
- Using index funds that minimize the costs of diversification and grant exposure to specific asset classes.
- Investing among countries that focus on different industries, are undergoing different stages of the business cycle and have different currencies.
- Choosing not to invest a significant portion of their wealth in employee stock plans as their human capital is already entirely invested in their employing companies.
- Only adding a security to the portfolio if its Sharpe ratio is greater than the Sharpe ratio of the portfolio times the correlation coefficient.
- Only adding a security to the portfolio if the benefit (additional expected return, reduced portfolio risk) is greater than the associated costs (trading costs and costs of tracking a larger portfolio).
- Adding insurance to the portfolio by purchasing put options or adding an asset class that has a negative correlation with the assets in the portfolio (e.g., commodities).

The Minimum-Variance and Efficient Frontiers, and the Global Minimum-Variance Portfolio

- Combining risky assets may result in a portfolio that has lower risk than any of the individual assets in the portfolio.
- As the number of assets available increases, they can be combined into a large number of different portfolios (each with different assets and weights), and we can create an opportunity set of investments.
- Combinations of these assets can be formed into portfolios that entail the lowest level of risk for each level of expected return. An envelope curve that plots the risk-return characteristics of the lowest risk portfolios is known as the minimum variance frontier.
    - No risk-averse investor would invest in any portfolio that lies to the right of the MVF as it would entail a higher level of risk than a portfolio that lies on the MVF for a given level of return.
- The global minimum-variance portfolio is the portfolio of risky securities that entails the lowest level of risk among all the risky asset portfolios on the minimum variance frontier.
- All portfolios on the MVF that lie above and to the right of the global minimum-variance portfolio dominate all portfolios on the MVF that lie below and to the right of the global minimum variance portfolio.
    - This dominant portion of the MVF (the one above and to the right of the global minimum variance portfolio) is known as the Markowitz efficient frontier. It contains all the possible portfolios that rational, risk-averse investors will consider investing in.

A Risk-Free Asset and Many Risky Assets

- The risk-free asset has zero risk (so it plots on the y-axis), an expected return of RFR, and zero correlation with risky assets.
- The risk-return characteristics of portfolios that combine the risk-free asset with a risky asset or a portfolio of risky assets lie along a straight line.

As the investor combines the risk-free asset with portfolios further up the efficient frontier, she keeps attaining better portfolio combinations. Each successive portfolio on the efficient frontier has a steeper line (higher slope) joining it to the risk-free asset. The slope of this line represents the additional return per unit of extra risk. The steeper the slope of the line, the better the risk-return trade-off the portfolio offers. The line with the steepest slope is the one that is drawn from the risk-free asset to Portfolio M (which occurs at the point of tangency between the efficient frontier and a straight line drawn from the risk-free rate). This particular line offers the best risk-return trade-off to the investor. Any combination of the risk-free asset and Portfolio M dominates all portfolios below **CAL_M**.

The Two-Fund Separation Theorem

The two-fund separation theorem states that regardless of risk and return preferences, all investors hold some combination of the risk-free asset and an optimal portfolio of risky assets. Therefore, the investment problem can be broken down into two steps:

1. The investing decision, where an investor identifies her optimal risky portfolio.
2. The financing decision, where she determines where exactly on the optimal CAL, she wants her portfolio to lie. Her risk preferences (as delineated by her indifference curves) determine whether her desired portfolio requires borrowing or lending at the risk-free rate.

Optimal Investor Portfolio

- The line CAL_M represents the best portfolios available to an investor. The portfolios along this line contain the risk-free asset and the optimal portfolio, Portfolio M, with varying weights.
- An individual's optimal portfolio depends on her risk-return preferences, which are incorporated into her indifference curves. The point where her indifference curve is tangent to CAL_M indicates her optimal investor portfolio.

PM

PORTFOLIO RISK AND RETURN: PART II

Cross-Reference to CFA Institute Assigned Reading #42

Review

- Risky assets can be combined into portfolios that may have a lower risk than each of the individual assets in the portfolio if assets are not perfectly positively correlated.
- An investor's investment opportunity set includes all the individual risky assets and risky asset portfolios that she can invest in.
- The minimum variance frontier reduces the investment opportunity set to a curve that contains only those portfolios that entail the lowest level of risk for each level of expected return.
- The global minimum variance portfolio is the portfolio of risky assets that entails the lowest level of risk among all portfolios on the minimum variance frontier.
- Investors aim to maximize return for every level of risk. Therefore, all portfolios above and to the right of the global minimum variance portfolio dominate those that lie below and to the right of the global minimum variance portfolio.
- The section of the minimum variance frontier that lies above and to the right of the global minimum variance portfolio is referred to as the Markowitz efficient frontier.

A risk-free asset has an expected return of RFR, a standard deviation (risk) of zero, and a correlation with any risky asset of zero. Once the risk-free asset is introduced into the mix:

- Any portfolio that combines a risky asset portfolio that lies on the Markowitz efficient frontier and the risk-free asset has a risk return trade-off that is linear (CAL is represented by a straight line).
- The point at which a line drawn from the risk-free rate is tangent to the Markowitz efficient frontier defines the optimal risky asset portfolio. This line is known as the optimal CAL.
- Each investor will choose a portfolio (optimal investor portfolio) that contains some combination of the risk-free asset and the optimal risky portfolio. The weights of the risk free asset and the optimal risky portfolio in the optimal investor portfolio depend on the investor's risk tolerance (indifference curve).
- The optimal investor portfolio is defined by the point where the investor's indifference curve is tangent to the optimal CAL.

The CAL and the CML

A capital allocation line (CAL) includes all combinations of the risk-free asset and **any risky asset portfolio**.

The capital market line (CML) is a special case of the capital allocation line where the risky asset portfolio that is combined with the risk-free asset is the **market portfolio**.

Graphically, the market portfolio occurs at the point where a line from the risk-free asset is tangent to the Markowitz efficient frontier. The market portfolio is the optimal risky asset portfolio given homogenous expectations. All portfolios that lie below the CML offer a lower return than portfolios that plot on the CML for each level of risk.

Equation of CML:

$$E(R_p) = R_f + \frac{E(R_m) - R_f}{\sigma_m} \times \sigma$$

Figure 1 illustrates the CML.

Figure 1: Capital Market Line

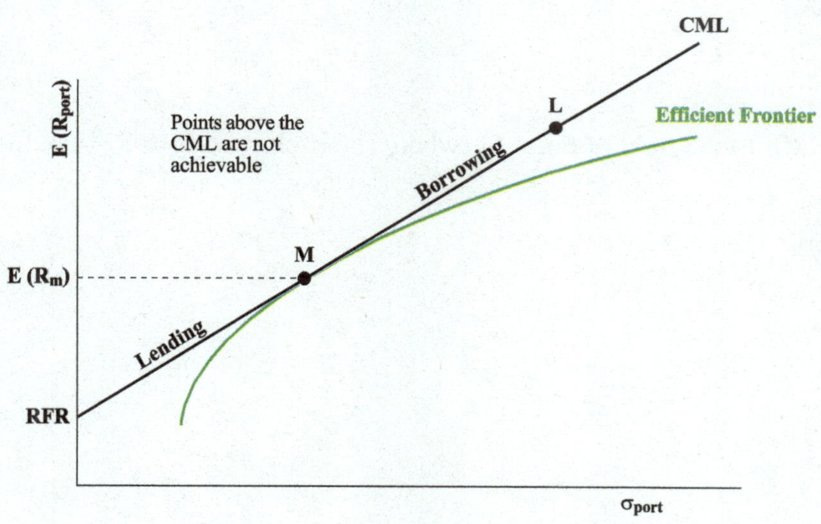

- At Point RFR, an investor has all her funds invested in the risk-free asset.
- At Point M, she has all of her funds invested in the market portfolio (which only contains risky securities).
- At any point between RFR and M, she holds both the market portfolio and the risk-free asset (i.e., she is lending some of her funds at the risk-free rate).

However, an investor may want to attain a higher expected return than available at Point M, where all her funds are invested in the market portfolio. Adding leverage to the portfolio by borrowing money at the RFR and investing it in the market portfolio will allow her to attain a risk-return profile beyond (to the right of, or above) Point M on the CML (e.g., Point L).

The particular point that an investor chooses on the CML depends on her utility function, which in turn is determined by her risk and return preferences.

Leveraged Positions with Different Lending and Borrowing Rates

Practically speaking, an investor's ability to repay is not as certain as that of the U.S. government, so the rate at which she would be able to borrow would be higher than the rate at which she would be able to lend. Given the disparity in borrowing and lending rates, the CML would no longer be a straight line.

- The slope of the CML to the left of Point M (when she invests a portion of her portfolio in the risk-free asset at R_f) would be:

$$\frac{E(R_m) - R_f}{\sigma_m}$$

- The slope CML to the right of Point M (where she is borrowing at R_b) would be:

$$\frac{E(R_m) - R_b}{\sigma_m}$$

Systematic and Nonsystematic Risk

When investors diversify across assets that are not perfectly positively correlated, the portfolio's risk is lower than the weighted average of the individual assets' risks. In the market portfolio, all the risk unique to individual assets comprising the portfolio has been diversified away.

- The risk that disappears due to diversification in the portfolio construction process is known as unsystematic risk (also known as unique, diversifiable or firm-specific risk).
- The risk inherent in all risky assets (caused by macro-economic variables) that cannot be eliminated by diversification is known as systematic risk (also known as non-diversifiable or market risk).

$$\text{Total Risk} = \text{Systematic risk} + \text{Unsystematic risk}$$

Complete diversification of a portfolio requires the elimination of all unsystematic or diversifiable risk. Once unsystematic risk has been eliminated and only systematic risk remains, a completely diversified portfolio would correlate perfectly with the market.

By adding assets to a portfolio that are not perfectly correlated with the assets already in the portfolio, we can reduce the overall standard deviation of the portfolio. However, we cannot eliminate the variability and uncertainty of macroeconomic factors that affect returns on all risky assets. We do not have to include all the assets in the market portfolio to diversify away unsystematic risk. Studies have shown that a portfolio consisting of 12-30 different stocks can diversify away 90% of unsystematic risk.

In capital market theory, taking on a higher degree of unsystematic risk will not be compensated with a higher return because unsystematic risk can be eliminated, without additional cost, through diversification. Only if an investor takes on a higher level of risk that cannot be easily diversified away (systematic risk) should she expect to be rewarded in the form of a higher return. Systematic risk is measured as the contribution of a security to the risk of a well diversified portfolio.

Return-Generating Models

A return generating model is a model that is used to forecast the return on a security given certain parameters. A multi-factor model uses more than one variable to estimate returns.

- Macroeconomic factor models use economic factors (e.g., economic growth rates, interest rates and inflation rates) that correlate with security returns to estimate returns.
- Fundamental factor models use relationships between security returns and underlying fundamentals (e.g., earnings, earnings growth and cash flow growth) to estimate returns.
- Statistical factor models use historical and cross-sectional returns data to identify factors that explain returns and use an asset's sensitivity to those factors to project future returns.

PM

The Market Model

The market model is an example of a single-index return generation model. It is used to estimate beta risk and to compute abnormal returns. The market model is given as:

$$R_i = \alpha_i + \beta_i R_m + e_i$$

First, the intercept α_i and slope coefficient β_i are estimated using historical asset and market returns. These estimates are then used to predict returns in the future.

Calculation and Interpretation of Beta

Beta is a measure of the sensitivity of an asset's return to the market's return. It is computed as the covariance of the return on the asset and the return on the market divided by the variance of the market.

$$\beta_i = \frac{\text{Cov}(R_i, R_m)}{\sigma_m^2} = \frac{\rho_{i,m}\sigma_i\sigma_m}{\sigma_m^2} = \frac{\rho_{i,m}\sigma_i}{\sigma_m}$$

Important Points Regarding Beta

- Beta captures an asset's systematic or non-diversifiable risk.
- A positive beta suggests that the return on the asset follows the overall trend in the market.
- A negative beta indicates that the return on the asset generally follows a trend that is opposite to that of the current market trend.
- A beta of zero means that the return on the asset is uncorrelated with market movements.
- The market has a beta of 1. Therefore, the average beta of stocks in the market also equals 1.

The market model described previously can also be used to compute beta.

The Capital Asset Pricing Model

The capital asset pricing model (CAPM) is a single-index model that is widely used to estimate returns given security betas. The CAPM is expressed as:

$$E(R_i) = R_f + \beta_i[E(R_m) - R_f]$$

Assumptions of the CAPM

- Investors are utility maximizing, risk-averse, rational individuals.
- Markets are frictionless, and there are no transaction costs and taxes.
- All investors have the same single period investment horizon.
- Investors have homogenous expectations and therefore, arrive at the same valuation for any given asset.
- All investments are infinitely divisible.
- Investors are price-takers. No investor is large enough to influence security prices.

The Security Market Line

The SML illustrates the CAPM equation. Its y-intercept equals the risk-free rate and its slope equals the market risk premium, $(R_m - R_f)$.

Recall that the CAL and the CML only applied to efficient portfolios; not to individual assets or inefficient portfolios. They used total risk on the x-axis, and since only systematic risk is priced, they could only be used for efficient portfolios (those with no unsystematic risk and whose total risk therefore was the same as their systematic risk).

The SML and the CAPM on the other hand, apply to any security or portfolio, regardless of whether it is efficient. This is because they are based only on a security's systematic risk, not total risk.

The CAPM equation tells us that the expected (required) rate of return for a risky asset is determined by the risk-free rate plus a risk premium. The risk premium for an asset is determined by the systematic risk of the asset (β_i), and the prevailing market risk premium, $(R_m - R_f)$.

Portfolio Beta

The CAPM can also be applied to portfolios of assets.

- The beta of a portfolio equals the weighted average of the betas of the securities in the portfolio.
- The portfolio's expected return can be computed using the CAPM:

$$E(R_p) = R_f + \beta_p[E(R_m) - R_f]$$

Applications of the CAPM

Estimate of expected return: The expected rate of return computed from the CAPM is used by investors to value stocks, bonds, real estate and other assets. In capital budgeting, where the NPV is used to make investing decisions, the CAPM is used to compute the required rate of return, which is then used to discount expected future cash flows.

Portfolio Performance Evaluation

The *Sharpe ratio* is used to compute excess returns per unit of total risk. It is calculated as:

$$\text{Sharpe ratio} = \frac{R_p - R_f}{\sigma_p}$$

Notice that the Sharpe ratio basically equals the slope of the CAL. A portfolio with a higher Sharpe ratio is preferred to one with a lower Sharpe ratio given that the numerator of the portfolios being compared is positive. If the numerator is negative, the ratio will be closer to zero (less negative) for riskier portfolios, resulting in distorted rankings. Two drawbacks of the Sharpe ratio are that it uses total risk as a measure of risk even though only systematic risk is priced, and that the ratio itself is not informative.

The *Treynor ratio* basically replaces total risk in the Sharpe ratio with systematic risk (beta). It is calculated as:

$$\text{Treynor ratio} = \frac{R_p - R_f}{\beta_p}$$

For the Treynor ratio to offer meaningful results, both the numerator and the denominator must be positive. Neither the Sharpe nor the Treynor ratio offer any information about the significance of the differences between the ratios for portfolios.

M-squared (M^2) is also based on total risk, not beta risk. It is calculated as:

$$M^2 = (R_p - R_f)\frac{\sigma_m}{\sigma_p} - (R_m - R_f)$$

M^2 offers rankings that are identical to those provided by the Sharpe ratio. However, these rankings are easier to interpret as they are in percentage terms. A portfolio that matches the market's performance will have an M^2 of zero, while one that outperforms the market will have a positive M^2. The M^2 also enables us to tell which portfolios beat the market on a risk-adjusted basis.

Jensen's alpha is based on systematic risk (like the Treynor ratio). It first estimates a portfolio's beta risk using the market model, and then uses the CAPM to determine the required return from the investment (given its beta risk). The difference between the portfolio's actual return and the required return (as predicted by the CAPM) is called Jensen's alpha. Jensen's alpha is calculated as:

$$\alpha_p = R_p - [R_f + \beta_p(R_m - R_f)]$$

Jensen's alpha for the market equals zero. The higher the Jensen's alpha for a portfolio, the better its risk adjusted performance.

Security Characteristic Line

The security characteristic line (SCL) plots the excess returns of a security against the excess returns on the market. The equation of the SCL is given as:

$$R_i - R_f = \alpha_i + \beta_i(R_m - R_f)$$

Note that Jensen's alpha is the y-intercept, and beta is the slope of the SCL.

Security Selection

- If the expected return using price and dividend forecasts is higher than the investor's required return given the systematic risk in the security, the security is undervalued and the investor should buy it.
- If the expected return using price and dividend forecasts is lower than the investor's required return given the systematic risk in the security, the security is overvalued and the investor should sell it.

Constructing a Portfolio

The CAPM tells us that investors should hold a portfolio that combines the risk-free asset with the market portfolio. Let's assume that we begin with the S&P 500 as our risky asset portfolio. The S&P 500 index only contains large-cap U.S. stocks, but does not encompass the entire global market. Therefore, we might want to consider a security not included in the S&P 500 for inclusion in the portfolio. The decision regarding whether the particular security should be included in our portfolio depends on the α_i of the security (based on the CAPM and the S&P 500 as the market portfolio). Positive α_i securities (even if they are correctly priced) should be added to the portfolio.

PM

The information ratio $\left(\frac{\alpha_i}{\sigma_{ei}}\right)$ measures the abnormal return per unit of risk added by the security to a well-diversified portfolio. The larger the information ratio is, the more valuable the security.

Further, within the set of securities included in the S&P 500, some may be undervalued (expected to generate positive alpha) and others may be overvalued (expected to generate negative alpha) based on investor expectations. The weight of undervalued securities should be increased and that of overvalued securities should be reduced.

The weight of each nonmarket security in the portfolio should be proportional to:

$$\frac{\alpha_i}{\sigma_{ei}^2}$$

where:

α_i = Jensen's alpha

σ_{ei}^2 = Nonsystematic variance of the security

Beyond the CAPM

Limitations of the CAPM

Theoretical limitations

- The CAPM is a single-factor model; only systematic risk is priced in the CAPM.
- It is only a single period model.

Practical limitations

- A true market portfolio is unobservable as it would also include assets that are not investable (e.g., human capital).
- In the absence of a true market portfolio, the proxy for the market portfolio used varies across analysts, which leads to different return estimates for the same asset (not permissible in the CAPM world).

Extensions of the CAPM

Theoretical models like the arbitrage pricing theory (APT) expand the number of risk factors.

Practical models use extensive research to uncover risk factors that explain returns.

BASICS OF PORTFOLIO PLANNING AND CONSTRUCTION

Cross-Reference to CFA Institute Assigned Reading #43

The Investment Policy Statement

An investment policy statement is an invaluable planning tool that adds discipline to the investment process. Before developing an IPS, an investment manager must conduct a fact finding discussion with the client to learn about the client's risk tolerance and other specific circumstances.

The IPS can be thought of as a roadmap which serves the following purposes:

- It helps the investor decide on realistic investment goals after learning about financial markets and associated risks.
- It creates a standard according to which the portfolio manager's performance can be judged.
- It guides the actions of portfolio managers, who should refer to it from time to time to assess the suitability of particular investments for their clients.

Major Components of an IPS

- An introduction that describes the client.
- A statement of purpose.
- A statement of duties and responsibilities, which describes the duties and responsibilities of the client, the custodian of the client's assets, and the investment manager.
- Procedures that outline the steps required to keep the IPS updated and steps required to respond to various contingencies.
- The client's investment objectives.
- The client's investment constraints.
- Investment guidelines regarding how the policy should be executed (e.g., whether use of leverage and derivatives is permitted) and specific types of assets that must be excluded.
- Evaluation and review guidelines on obtaining feedback on investment results.
- Appendices that describe the strategic asset allocation and the rebalancing policy.

Risk Objectives

- An example of an absolute risk objective would be that the client does not want to lose more than 5% of her capital over a particular period.
- Relative risk objectives relate risk to a certain benchmark that represents an appropriate level of risk.

Risk tolerance is a function of both, a client's ability to take risk as well as her willingness to take risk. The ability to take risk is a function of several factors including time horizon, expected income, and net worth. Generally speaking, a client with a longer time horizon, high expected income and greater net worth has a greater ability to bear risk. A client's willingness to bear risk, on the other hand, is based on more subjective factors including her psychological makeup, and level of understanding of financial markets.

- When the client's ability to take risk is below average and her willingness to take risk is also below average, the investor's overall risk tolerance is below average.
- When the client's ability to take risk is above average and her willingness to take risk is also above average, the investor's overall risk tolerance is above average.
- When the client's ability to take risk is below average and her willingness to take risk is above average, the investor's overall risk tolerance is below average.
- When the client's ability to take risk is above average and her willingness to take risk is below average, the investment manager should explain the conflict and implications to the client.

When there is a mismatch between a client's ability and willingness to take risk, the prudent approach is to conclude that the client's tolerance for risk is the lower of the two factors. Further, any decisions made must be documented.

Return Objectives

- Absolute return objectives state the percentage return desired by the client. The return may be expressed on a real or nominal basis.
- Relative return objectives express the required return relative to a stated benchmark. A good benchmark should be investable i.e., an investor should be able to replicate it.

The return objective may be stated before or after fees and on a pre- or post-tax basis. Further, it could also be expressed in terms of a required return i.e., the amount an investor needs to earn over the investment horizon to meet a specified future goal.

The portfolio manager must ensure that the client's return objective is realistic in light of her tolerance for risk.

Investment Constraints

Liquidity refers to the ability to readily convert investments into cash at a price close to fair market value. Investors may require ready cash to meet unexpected needs and could be forced to sell their assets at unfavorable terms if the investment plan does not consider their liquidity needs.

Time Horizon refers to the time period between putting funds into an investment and requiring them for use. A close relationship exists between an investor's time horizon, liquidity needs and ability to take risk. The shorter the time horizon, the harder it would be for an investor to overcome losses.

Tax Concerns play a very important role in investment planning because, unlike tax-exempt investors, taxable investors are really only concerned with after-tax returns on their portfolios.

Legal and Regulatory Factors: Investors also need to be aware of legal and regulatory factors. For example, some countries impose a limit on the proportion of equity securities in a pension fund's portfolio.

Unique Circumstances: There may be a number of individual and unusual considerations that affect investors. For example, many investors may want to exclude certain investments from their portfolios based on personal or socially conscious reasons.

Portfolio Construction

Once the IPS has been compiled, the investment manager begins constructing the portfolio. How the portfolio funds are allocated across different asset classes is referred to as the portfolio's strategic asset allocation (SAA). A portfolio's SAA is important because it is a portfolio's allocation across various asset classes (not its allocation across securities within those asset classes) that is the primary determinant of portfolio returns.

Capital Market Expectations

Capital market expectations refer to a portfolio manager's expectations regarding the risk and return prospects of various asset classes. Capital market expectations are quantified in terms of expected returns, standard deviation of returns, and correlations among asset classes.

The Strategic Asset Allocation

The strategic asset allocation defines how the investor's funds are divided across different asset classes. Traditionally, cash, equities, bonds, and real estate were defined as the major asset classes. Recently, hedge funds, private equity and commodities have been added to the list. Further, each asset class can be subdivided into several sub-classes.

The risk return characteristics of the strategic asset allocation depend on the expected returns and risk of the individual asset classes, and on the correlations between the asset classes. Typically, risk-averse investors will place a higher weight on government bonds and cash in their SAA's, while those with a higher risk tolerance will have a higher weight invested in equities.

Steps Toward an Actual Portfolio

1. Risk budgeting: This is the process of subdividing the desired level of portfolio risk (which has been determined in the IPS) across the different sources of investment returns i.e., the strategic asset allocation, tactical asset allocation and security selection.
2. Tactical asset allocation: This refers to an allocation where the manager deliberately deviates from the strategic asset allocation for the short term.
3. Security selection: A manager may be able to outperform the asset class benchmark by investing in particular securities within the asset class that she expects to do well (better than the benchmark).
4. Portfolio rebalancing: Changes in security prices will lead to changes in the weights of different asset classes in the portfolio and cause them to deviate or "drift" from policy weights. Therefore, the portfolio should be rebalanced periodically and brought in line with policy weights.

Additional Portfolio Organizing Principles

The top-down investment framework has two drawbacks:

- If several managers are hired to manage different subclasses within the same asset class it may result in underutilization of the risk budget.
- Each manager would trade within the portfolio under her management so the portfolio overall may not be efficient from a capital gains tax point of view.

In order to avoid this, managers invest most of their funds in passive investments and trade a minority of assets actively. This approach is known as the "core-satellite" approach.

Study Session 13: Equity—Market Organization, Market Indices, and Market Efficiency

EQ

MARKET ORGANIZATION AND STRUCTURE

Cross-Reference to CFA Institute Assigned Reading #44

Functions of a Financial System

1. Help people achieve their purposes in using the financial system.
2. To facilitate the discovery of the rate of return where aggregate savings equal aggregate borrowings.
3. Allocating capital to its most efficient uses.

Classifications of Assets and Markets

Assets may be classified as financial or physical assets:

- Financial assets include securities, currencies and contracts.
- Physical assets include commodities and real assets.

Markets may be classified on the basis of:

- The timing of delivery.
- Who the seller is.
- The maturity of instruments that are traded.
- The types of securities.

Securities

Securities include bonds, notes, commercial paper, mortgages, common stock, preferred stock, warrants, mutual fund shares, unit trusts and depository receipts. They may be classified as:

- **Public securities** that trade in public markets (e.g., exchanges). Issuers of public securities are usually required to comply with strict rules and regulatory standards.
- **Private securities** that can typically only be purchased by qualified investors. Private securities are relatively illiquid.

Fixed Income Securities

Fixed income instruments are promises to repay borrowed money. Payments (which include interest and principal amounts) may be pre-specified or may vary according to a fixed formula based on a reference rate. Fixed income instruments may be classified as:

- *Notes:* Fixed income securities with maturities of 10 years or less.
- *Bonds:* Fixed income securities with maturities greater than 10 years.
- *Bills:* These are issued by governments and have maturities of one year or less.
- *Certificates of deposit:* These are issued by banks and usually mature within a year.
- *Commercial paper:* These are issued by corporations and usually mature within a year.
- *Repurchase agreements:* These are short-term lending instruments.
- *Money market instruments:* These are traded in the money market and have maturities of one year or less.

Equities

Equity owners have ownership rights in a company. Equity securities include:

- *Common shares:* Holders of common shares can participate in the company's decision-making process. They are entitled to receive dividends declared by the company, and if the company goes bankrupt, they have a claim on the company's assets after all other claims have been satisfied.
- *Preferred shares:* Preferred shareholders have a higher priority in claims on dividends and on the company's assets in case of liquidation. They are entitled to receive fixed dividends on a regular basis.
- *Warrants:* Holders of warrants have the right to purchase an entity's common stock at a pre-specified price at, or before the warrants' expiration date.

Pooled Investments

Pooled investment vehicles (e.g., mutual funds, depositories, and hedge funds) issue securities that represent shared ownership in the assets held by them. People invest in these vehicles to benefit from their investment management expertise and to diversify their portfolios.

- *Asset-backed securities:* Companies often use pools of loans or receivables (e.g., auto loans and leases, consumer loans, credit cards, etc.) as underlying assets to issue securities known as asset-backed securities. These securities then transfer any interest and principal payments from the underlying assets to their holders on a monthly basis.

Currencies

These are monies issued by national monetary authorities and primarily trade in the foreign currency market. Retail currency trades occur through ATM machines, credit cards and debit cards when transactions are executed in currencies different from the currency held in customers' accounts.

Contracts

Contracts are agreements between two or more parties to do something in the future. A contract's value depends on the value of its underlying, which may be a commodity, a security, an index, an interest rate or even another contract. Contracts may be settled in cash or may require physical delivery, and may be classified on the basis of:

- The nature of the underlying asset
- The timing of delivery

Forward Contracts

A forward is a contract between two parties, where one (the long position) has the obligation to buy, and the other (the short position) has an obligation to sell an underlying asset at a fixed price (established at the inception of the contract) at a future date. Market participants usually enter a forward contract to hedge a pre-existing risk.

Futures Contracts

Futures contracts are similar to forward contracts in that they may also be deliverable or cash-settled, but there are also significant differences between the two. Unlike forward contracts:

- Futures contracts are standardized and trade on organized exchanges.
- A clearinghouse is the counterparty to all futures contracts.

Swap Contracts

A swap is an agreement between two parties to exchange a series of cash flows at periodic settlement dates over a certain period of time. A swap may also be looked upon as a series of forward contracts.

Option Contracts

Option contracts give their holders the right to buy or sell a security at a predetermined price (exercise price) some time in the future.

- **Call options** give their holders the right to purchase the underlying asset at some future date at the option's exercise price. Holders are likely to exercise their call options when the price of the underlying asset is greater than the exercise price.
- **Put options** give their holders the right to sell the underlying asset at some future date at the option's exercise price. Holders are likely to exercise their put options when the price of the underlying asset is lower than the exercise price.

Options that can only be exercised at their expiration dates are known as European options, while options that can be exercised anytime until, or at their expiration dates are known as American options.

Other Contracts

People often enter into insurance contracts to protect themselves from unexpected losses. Insurance contracts include credit default swaps (CDSs) that promise to pay their holders the amount of principal in case a company defaults on its bonds.

Commodities

Commodities include precious metals, energy products, industrial metals, agricultural products, and carbon credits. Commodities may trade in the spot market (for immediate delivery) or in the forward or futures market (for delivery in the future).

Real Assets

Real assets include tangible properties such as real estate, airplanes, machinery and lumber stands. Institutional investors are increasingly adding them to their portfolios either directly (through direct ownership of the asset), or indirectly (through investments in securities of companies that invest in these assets). Real assets are attractive because:

- They may have low correlations with other assets in the investor's portfolio, thus providing diversification benefits.
- They offer income and tax benefits to investors.

Real asset valuation is very difficult due to the heterogeneous nature of each investment. Further, real assets tend to be relatively illiquid and entail high management costs.

FINANCIAL INTERMEDIARIES

Brokers, Exchanges, and Alternative Trading Systems

Brokers are agents who fulfill orders for their clients. They reduce costs of trading for their clients by finding counterparties for their trades.

- *Block brokers* provide brokerage services to large traders.
- *Investment banks* provide a variety of services to companies, including:
  - Arranging initial and seasoned security offerings.
  - Issuing securities to finance their business.
  - Identifying and acquiring other companies.

Exchanges provide a platform where traders can carry out their trades.

Alternative Trading Systems (ATSs) (also known as electronic communications networks, ECNs, and multilateral trading facilities, MTFs) are trading venues just like exchanges. However, they differ from exchanges in that they do not exercise regulatory authority over their members except with respect to the conduct of their trading in their trading networks. Many ATSs are known as "dark pools" because they do not display orders sent to them.

Dealers

Unlike brokers, dealers fulfil orders for their clients by actually taking positions as counterparties for their trades. Essentially, they indirectly connect two traders who arrive in the market at different points in time. By acting as counterparties to trades, dealers create liquidity in the market.

Dealers may also often act as brokers and vice-versa, so practitioners often use the term **broker-dealer** to refer to brokers and dealers.

Securitizers

Securitization is the process of buying assets, placing them in a pool, and issuing securities that represent ownership of the assets in the pool. Entities that undertake this process are known as securitizers. They create and sell securitized instruments and act as financial intermediaries by connecting borrowers and lenders.

Depository Institutions and Other Financial Corporations

Depository institutions include commercial banks, savings and loan banks, credit unions, and other institutions that gather funds from depositors and lend them to borrowers. Brokers also act as financial intermediaries when they lend funds deposited by their clients to other clients who wish to buy securities on margin. Such brokers are known as **prime brokers**.

Insurance Companies

Insurance companies create and sell contracts that protect buyers of these contracts from risks that they seek protection from. Insurance companies are financial intermediaries as they connect the buyers of insurance contracts with investors, creditors and reinsurers who are willing to bear the insured risks. Insurance buyers benefit as they are able to transfer risks to entities that are willing to assume them, while owners, creditors and reinsurers of the insurance company (who assume these risks) benefit from being able to sell their tolerance to risk without having to manage the contracts. Managing insurance contracts requires the insurance company to manage fraud, moral hazard and adverse selection.

- Fraud occurs when people deliberately report fake losses.
- Moral hazard occurs when people are less careful about avoiding losses as they are covered by insurance.
- Adverse selection occurs as only those who are most at risk usually buy insurance.

Arbitrageurs

Arbitrageurs, who buy and sell the same security in two different markets (at different prices), act as financial intermediaries as they effectively connect sellers in one market with buyers in another market. They also bring liquidity to markets.

Settlement and Custodial Services

Clearinghouses arrange for the final settlement of trades. They also serve as guarantors of performance in futures markets and as escrow agents in other markets. Banks and broker-dealers may offer custodial services for holding securities on behalf of their clients. This helps prevent the loss of securities through fraud or oversight.

A **position** in an asset refers to the quantity of the asset that an entity owns or owes.

- A person with a long position owns an assets or a contract. She benefits when there is an increase in the price of the asset or contract.
- A person with a short position has sold an asset that she does not own, or has written or sold a contract. She benefits when there is a decrease in the price of the asset or contract.

Positions on Forwards and Futures

The long position in a forward or a futures contract is the side that is obligated to take physical delivery of the asset or its cash equivalent at contract expiration. She will benefit from an increase in the price of the underlying asset.

The short position in a forward or a futures contract is the side that is obligated to make physical delivery of the asset or its cash equivalent at contract expiration. She will benefit from a decrease in the price of the underlying asset.

Positions on Options

The long position on an options contract is the party that holds the right to exercise the option. The short side refers to the writer of the option, who must satisfy any obligations arising from the contract.

- The long position on a call option will benefit when the underlying rises in value.
- The short position on a call option will benefit when the underlying falls in value.
- The long position on a put option will benefit when the underlying falls in value.
- The short position on a put option will benefit when the underlying rises in value.

Swap Contracts

The two parties in a swap contract simply agree to exchange contractually determined cash flows. There is no real buyer or seller, which makes it difficult to determine the long and short side of the contract. Usually, the party that benefits from an increase in the quoted price is referred to as the long.

Currency Contracts

A party that purchases one currency simultaneously sells another currency (the other currency in the price quote or exchange rate). Therefore, whenever we mention a long or a short position in a currency contract, we must mention the other currency as well. For example, we may state that a party is long on the dollar against the yen.

Short Positions

Short positions in contracts are created by selling contracts that the short seller does not own. The short seller is basically the issuer of the contract.

Short positions in securities are created by selling securities that the short seller does not own. In order to sell the securities, the short seller borrows the securities from long holders to deliver them to buyers. To unwind the position, the short seller then repurchases the security (hopefully at a lower price) from the market and returns it to the long holder.

The maximum profit for the holder of a long position on an asset is unlimited, while her losses are limited to the price she purchased the asset for. In contrast, the maximum profit for a short seller of an asset is limited to her selling price, while her losses are unlimited.

Levered Positions

Many markets allow investors to borrow funds from brokers to purchase securities. The investor borrows a portion of the price of the stock, contributes the rest of the funds herself and puts up the stock as collateral. The borrowed money is known as the margin loan and the interest rate paid on it is the call money rate.

Traders who purchase securities on margin face minimum margin requirements. The initial margin requirement refers to the proportion of the total cost of the asset that an investor must invest with her own equity. This requirement may be determined by the government, the exchange or the clearinghouse.

When traders borrow money to purchase securities, they are said to be leveraging their positions. The leverage ratio is the ratio of the value of the position to the value of the equity investment in it. The maximum leverage ratio for a position financed by a margin loan equals one divided by the minimum margin requirement.

Leverage enhances a trader's returns, but also magnifies losses.

In addition to the initial margin requirement, traders who invest on margin must also adhere to maintenance margin requirements. If the proportion of the value of the security financed by the investor's own equity (after adjusting for the price change) falls below the maintenance margin, the investor will receive a margin call, and she would have to deposit enough funds into her account to at least meet the maintenance margin level. If she fails to do so, her broker can sell the stock to pay off the margin loan.

The price at which an investor who goes long on a stock receives a margin call is calculated as:

$$P_0 \times \frac{(1 - \text{Initial margin})}{(1 - \text{Maintenance margin})}$$

Traders who sell securities short are also subject to margin requirements as they have borrowed securities to take their positions.

Execution, Validity, and Clearing Instructions

The prices at which dealers and other proprietary traders are willing to buy securities are called bid prices and those at which they are willing to sell are called ask (or offer) prices. The quantities that market participants are willing to trade at the bid and ask prices are called bid sizes and ask sizes respectively.

The highest bid in the market is the highest price that a dealer is willing to pay for the security and is known as the best bid. On the other hand, the lowest ask price is the best offer. The difference between the best bid and the best offer is the market bid-ask spread. Liquid markets with low transaction costs generally have small bid-ask spreads.

Execution Instructions

Execution instructions indicate how an order should be filled. They include:

- Market orders, which instruct brokers or the exchange to fill an order immediately at the best available price. Market orders generally execute immediately as long as there are traders willing to take the other side of the trade. However, they may be expensive to execute, especially when the order size is large relative to the normal trading activity in the market.
- Limit orders, which instruct the broker or the exchange to fill an order at a specified price or better. These specified prices (maximum price for a limit buy order and minimum price for a limit sell order) are referred to as limit prices. Limit orders prevent trades from executing at unacceptable prices. However, this also means that they may not execute at all if the limit price on a buy order is too low or the limit price on a sell order is too high.
    - A limit buy order is aggressively priced when the limit price is high relative to the market "bid" and "ask" prices.
    - A limit buy order placed above the best offer is likely to be at least partially executed immediately and is called a marketable limit order.
    - A limit buy order placed above the best bid but below the best offer is said to have created a new market by establishing the new best bid.
    - A limit buy order placed at the best bid is said to make market. This order will have to wait for all buy orders (that were placed earlier) at that price to execute first.
    - A limit buy order placed below the best bid is referred to as behind the market and will not execute unless market prices drop. These orders are known as standing limit orders.

Exposure Instructions

Exposure instructions specify whether, how and to whom orders may be exposed.

Hidden orders are exposed only to the brokers or exchanges that receive them. Other traders can discover hidden size only after submitting orders that will trade with that size. However, hidden orders may not execute at all as other traders do not know about them. Therefore, traders may sometimes indicate a specific display size (which is lower than the actual order size) with their orders to signal to other traders that someone is willing to trade at the displayed price. As most of the order size is hidden, these orders are also referred to as iceberg orders.

Validity Instructions

Validity instructions indicate when an order may be filled. They include:

- Day orders, which are only valid for the day on which they are submitted. These orders expire if not filled at the close of business.
- Good till-cancelled orders, which are valid until cancelled by the broker.
- Immediate or cancel orders, which may only be filled, completely or in part, immediately and are otherwise cancelled. These are also known as fill or kill orders.
- Good-on-close orders, which only execute at the close of trading and are also called market-on-close orders.
- Stop orders (often referred to as stop-loss orders), which are placed by investors to protect themselves from adverse price movements.

Clearing Instructions

Clearing instructions indicate how the final settlement of trades should be arranged. They include details of the entities responsible for clearing and settling the trade. Further, security sale orders must also indicate whether the sale is a long sale or a short sale.

Primary Markets

Primary markets are markets where issuers first sell their securities to investors. When a security is issued to the public for the first time, it is referred to as an initial public offering (IPO). On the other hand, when additional units of a previously issued security are sold, it is referred to as a seasoned offering (or a secondary offering) and the issue is called a seasoned issue.

Public Offerings

Companies generally issue securities to the public through an investment bank. The investment bank performs the following functions:

- Through a process called book building, it lines up subscribers who wish to purchase the security.
- It provides investment information about the issuer to its clients and to the public.

The issuer's arrangement with the investment bank may take one of the following forms:

- In an underwriting offer, the investment bank guarantees the sale of the issue at an offering price negotiated with the issuer. If the issue is not fully subscribed, the investment bank commits to purchasing the leftover securities at the offer price.
- In a best efforts offering, the investment bank merely acts as a broker. It tries its best to sell the securities at the negotiated price, but does not promise to purchase unsold securities.

Private Placements

In a private placement securities are not offered to the public. Companies sell securities directly to a group of qualified investors, usually through an investment bank. Qualified investors are generally those who understand associated risks and have sufficient wealth to withstand significant losses. Privately placements are typically cheaper than public offerings as they do not require as much public disclosure. However, since privately placed securities do not trade on organized secondary markets, investors require a higher rate of return from them.

Other Primary Market Transactions

- Companies that issue securities via a *shelf registration* make all the public disclosures that are required in a regular offering, but they do not need to issue all the shares at once. They can sell them directly in the secondary market over time, which offers them flexibility as they can raise capital when they need it.
- Companies that issue securities through *dividend reinvestment plans (DRPs)* allow shareholders to reinvest their dividends by purchasing shares of the company. These shares may be newly issued or purchased from the open market.
- Companies sometimes offer *rights* to existing shareholders to purchase additional shares of the company in proportion to their current holdings at a fixed price.

Secondary Markets

The secondary market is that part of the financial market where previously issued securities and financial instruments are traded. Secondary markets play a very important role in that they provide liquidity to investors who purchased their securities in the primary market. Investors will hesitate to participate in the primary market if they cannot subsequently sell their holdings in the secondary market.

Secondary markets are also important for seasoned security issuers as the prices of their new offerings are derived from the secondary market prices of currently outstanding securities that trade on the secondary market.

Trading Sessions

In a call market, all bid and ask prices for an asset are gathered to determine one price where the quantity offered for sale is close to the quantity demanded. All transactions take place at this single price. Call markets are popular in smaller markets. However, they are also used on larger exchanges to determine the opening price of a trading session.

In a continuous market, transactions can take place whenever the market is open. Prices are set either through an auction process or by dealer bid-ask quotes. Most global stock exchanges are continuous markets.

The advantage of a call market is that it makes it easier for buyers and sellers to find each other by gathering all traders at the same place at the same time. In a continuous market, if a buyer and seller (or their orders) are not present at the same time, they cannot trade. The advantage of a continuous market is that a willing buyer and seller can trade anytime the market is open. In a call market they would only be able to trade when the market is called.

Execution Mechanisms

A pure auction market (order-driven) is one where participants submit their bid and ask prices to a central location. Matching bids and offers are paired together and orders are executed. Order-driven matching mechanisms are characterized by two sets of rules:

- Order matching rules match buy orders to sell orders. They rank buy and sell orders based on:
  - Price precedence: Highest priced buy orders and lowest priced sell orders are ranked first.
  - Display precedence: Displayed quantities have precedence over undisplayed quantities at the same price.
  - Time precedence: Orders that arrived first have precedence over orders that arrived later with the same price and with the same display status.

- Trade pricing rules determine the prices at which matched trades take place. Prices may be determined based on any of the following:
    - Under a uniform pricing rule, the same price is used for all trades. This rule is used by call markets where the market chooses the price that maximizes total quantity traded.
    - Under a discriminatory pricing rule, the limit price of the order or quote that arrived first (the standing order) determines the trade price. Continuous trading markets use this rule.
    - A derivative pricing rule uses the mid-point of the best bid and ask quotes from another market. Crossing networks (which may themselves be organized as call or continuous trading markets) use this pricing rule.

A dealer market (quote driven market or price-driven market) consists of individual dealers who are assigned specific securities. These dealers create liquidity by purchasing and selling against their own inventory of securities. Competition between dealers ensures that competitive prices are available.

In a brokered market, brokers arrange trades among their clients. Brokers organize markets for unique items (e.g., real estate properties and fine art masterpieces) that only interest a limited number of people.

Market Information Systems

Markets may be structured based on the type and quantity of information they disseminate to the public.

- Pre-trade transparent markets publish real time data about quotes and orders.
- Post-trade transparent markets publish data about trade prices soon after trades occur.

Characteristics of a Well-Functioning Financial System

- Timely and accurate information on the price and volume of recent transactions. If timely information is not available, a seller may not get the best possible price, and a buyer may end up paying too high a price.
- Liquidity, which refers to the ability to buy or sell the asset quickly, at a price close to that of a recent market transaction, assuming no new information has been received. To achieve price continuity, the market must be significantly deep.
- Internal efficiency in that there are low transaction costs, which include the costs of reaching the market and brokerage costs.
- External or informational efficiency, which is achieved when market prices reflect all external available information about an asset. Prices should rapidly adjust to reflect any new information.

Objectives of Market Regulation

- Control fraud or deception of uninformed market participants.
- Control agency problems by setting minimum standards of competence for agents and by defining and enforcing minimum standards of practice.
- Promote fairness by creating a level playing field for market participants.
- Set mutually beneficial standards for financial reporting.
- Prevent undercapitalized financial firms from exploiting their investors by making excessively risky investments; and
- Ensure that long-term liabilities are funded.

SECURITY MARKET INDEXES

Cross-Reference to CFA Institute Assigned Reading #45

EQ

A **security market index** consists of individual securities (also called constituent securities) that represent a given security market, market segment, or asset class. Each security market index may have two versions depending on how returns are calculated:

- A price return index only reflects the prices of constituent securities.
- A total return index not only reflects prices, but also assumes reinvestment of all income received since inception.

The values of both versions of an index are the same at inception. However, as time passes, the total return index will be greater in value than the price return index by an increasing amount.

Index Construction

Constructing and managing a security market index involves:

- Target market selection
- Security selection
- Index weighting
- Rebalancing
- Reconstitution

Target Market and Security Selection

The target market may be based on:

- Asset class (e.g., equities, fixed income, or real estate)
- Geographic region (e.g., Japan, South Africa or Europe)
- The exchange on which the securities are traded (e.g., New York, London or Tokyo)
- Other characteristics (e.g., economic sector, company size and investment style)

An index may consist of all the securities in the target market or just a representative sample of the target market.

Index Weighting

Price Weighting

In a price-weighted index the weight of each constituent security is determined by dividing its price by the sum of the prices of all constituent securities:

$$w_i^P = \frac{P_i}{\sum_{i=1}^{N} P_i}$$

The value of a price-weighted index is computed by dividing the sum of the security prices by the divisor. At inception, the divisor is typically set to the number of securities in the index.

The advantage of a price-weighted index is its simplicity. One of the issues with a price-weighted index is that a stock split or stock dividend by one of the constituent securities changes the weights of all securities in the index. To prevent stock splits and stock dividends from changing the value of the index, the divisor of a price-weighted index must be adjusted.

Equal Weighting

In an equal-weighted index, each constituent security is given an identical weight in the index at inception. The weights are calculated as:

$$w_i^E = \frac{1}{N}$$

The number of shares of each security included in the index is calculated as the value allotted to each constituent security divided by the price of the security. Unlike a price-weighted index, where the weights are arbitrarily determined by market prices, the weights in an equal-weighted index are effectively determined by the index provider (in choosing the particular weighting mechanism).

Equal-weighted indices are also preferred because of their simplicity. However, they have a few disadvantages:

- Assigning an equal weight to all securities under-represents (over-represents) those securities that constitute a relatively large (small) fraction of the target market.
- The index does not remain equally weighted once the prices of the constituent securities change. Frequent adjustments must be made to maintain equal weighting.

Market-Capitalization Weighting

A market-capitalization weighted (value weighted) index is based on the total market value (current stock price times the total number of shares outstanding) of all stocks in the index. The proportion of each constituent security is determined by dividing its market capitalization by the total market capitalization of all the securities in the index:

$$w_i^M = \frac{Q_i P_i}{\sum_{j=1}^{N} Q_j P_j}$$

The initial market value is assigned a base number (e.g., 100) and a new market value is computed periodically. The change in the index is measured by comparing the new market value to the base market value.

Value-weighted indices automatically adjust for stock splits and stock dividends.

Float-Adjusted Market-Capitalization Weighting

In a float-adjusted market-capitalization weighted index, the proportion of each constituent security is determined by adjusting its market capitalization for its market float.

Market float generally refers to the number of shares of the constituent security that are available to the investing public. Shares held by controlling shareholders, other corporations and governments are subtracted from the total number of outstanding shares to determine the market float.

EQ

The float-adjusted market-capitalization weight of each constituent security is calculated as:

$$w_i^M = \frac{f_i Q_i P_i}{\sum_{j=1}^{N} f_j Q_j P_j}$$

The primary advantage of market capitalization weighting (and float-adjusted market capitalization weighting) is that securities are held in proportion to their value in the target market. A disadvantage is that stocks with larger market values have a larger impact on the index. Stocks that have seen their prices rise (fall) will see their relative weight in the index increase (decline). The effect of market value weighting is therefore similar to that of a momentum trading strategy.

Fundamental Weighting

Instead of using prices of constituent securities, a fundamental weighted index uses other measures of a company's size (that are independent of the stock price) such as book value, cash flow, revenues and earnings to determine weights of securities in the index. Some fundamental indices use a single measure to weight the constituent securities, while others combine weights from several measures to form a composite value that is used for weighting.

The fundamental weight on security i can be calculated as:

$$w_i^F = \frac{F_i}{\sum_{j=1}^{N} F_j}$$

In contrast to market-capitalization weighted indices, in which the weight of a stock in the index moves in the same direction as its price, fundamental weighted indices have a "contrarian" effect in that the portfolio weights move away from securities whose prices have risen.

Rebalancing

In order to keep the weights of constituent securities consistent with the index's weighting method security weights must be adjusted or rebalanced.

- In equal-weighted indices, the weights of securities that have witnessed price appreciation increase over time, and weights of securities that have underperformed decrease over time. Rebalancing an equal-weighted index would require reducing the weight of securities that have outperformed and increasing the weight of securities that have underperformed.
- Price-weighted indices do not need to be rebalanced as the weight of each constituent security is determined by its price.
- Market-capitalization weighted indices rebalance themselves to reflect changes in the market-capitalization of constituent securities. They only need to be rebalanced to reflect mergers, acquisitions, liquidations, etc.

Reconstitution

Constituent securities need to be examined on a regular basis to evaluate whether they still meet the criteria for inclusion in the index. If they no longer meet the criteria, they must be replaced with securities that do meet the criteria. Index reconstitution is performed in order to:

- Reflect changes in the target market as a result of bankruptcies, de-listings, mergers, etc.
- Reflect the judgement of the selection committee.

Uses of Security Market Indices

- To gauge market sentiment.
- As proxies for measuring and modeling returns, systematic risk, and risk-adjusted performance.
- As proxies for asset classes in asset allocation models.
- As benchmarks for actively managed portfolios.
- As the basis for the creation of numerous investment products.

Types of Equity Indices

Broad market indices: A broad equity market index contains securities representing more than 90% of the selected market.

Multi-market indices: Multi-market indices consist of security market indices from different countries and may represent multiple national markets, geographic regions, economic development groups or even the entire world.

Sector indices: Sector indices only include securities representing a particular economic sector (e.g., finance, health care, technology, etc.) where the economic sector may be classified on a national, regional or global basis.

Style indices: Financial firms like Dow Jones and Standard & Poor's have developed different indices based on specific investment strategies used by portfolio managers. These indices include those based on size (e.g., small-cap versus large-cap equities) and others based on style (e.g., growth versus value stocks). Style indices generally have much higher turnover than broad market indices.

Fixed-Income Indices

Creating bond-market indices presents the following challenges:

- There is a broader universe of bonds than of stocks.
- The universe of bonds is constantly changing as a result of new issues, calls, and maturities.
- The price volatility of a bond (as measured by duration) is constantly changing. Duration changes with a bond's maturity and market yields.
- Current and continuous transaction prices are not available for bonds.

Types of Fixed-Income Indices

Fixed-income securities can be classified along the following dimensions:

- Type of issuer (government, government agency, corporation).
- Type of financing (general obligation, collateralized).
- Currency of payments.
- Maturity.
- Credit quality (investment grade, high yield, credit agency ratings).
- Absence or presence of inflation protection.

Fixed-income indices can be categorized as follows:

- Aggregate or broad market indices.
- Market sector indices.
- Style indices.
- Economic sector indices.
- Specialized indices such as high-yield, inflation-linked, and emerging market indices.

Indices Representing Alternative Investments

Commodity indices: Commodity indices consist of futures contracts on one or more commodities and have the following characteristics:

- They do not have an obvious weighting method so index providers create their own weighting methods.
- Different weighting methods lead to different exposures to specific commodities, which result in very different risk and return profiles of commodity indices.
- The performance of commodity indices may differ from that of the underlying commodities because indices consist of futures contracts on commodities rather than the actual commodities.

Real estate investment trust indices: Real estate indices represent the market for real estate and real estate securities. They can be categorized as:

- Appraisal indices
- Repeat sales indices
- Real estate investment trust (REIT) indices

REIT indices consist of shares of publicly traded REITs (public or private organizations that combine individual investors' funds and provide them access to real estate investments). Shares issued by REITs trade on various exchanges around the world and are priced continuously.

Hedge fund indices: Hedge fund indices are designed to represent the performance of hedge funds (private investment vehicles that typically use leverage and long and short investment strategies) on a very broad, global level or the strategy level. Hedge fund indices have the following characteristics:

- They rely on voluntary disclosures from funds as it is not mandatory for hedge funds to disclose performance to any party other than investors.
- If they do decide to disclose performance, hedge funds have a choice regarding which index or indices they report their performance to. Therefore, rather than index providers determining the constituents, the constituents determine the index. Further, different hedge fund indices may reflect very different performance for the hedge fund industry over the same period of time based on the hedge funds represented in those indices.
- Poorly performing hedge funds may stop reporting their performance to hedge fund indices or may cease to exist altogether. This leads to survivorship bias and an upward bias in hedge fund performance as represented by these indices.

MARKET EFFICIENCY

Cross-Reference to CFA Institute Assigned Reading #46

An informationally efficient market (an efficient market) is one where security prices adjust rapidly to reflect any new information. It is a market where asset prices reflect all past and present information.

Investment managers and analysts are interested in market efficiency because it dictates how many profitable trading opportunities may abound in the market.

- In an efficient market, it is difficult to find inaccurately priced securities. Therefore, superior risk-adjusted returns cannot be attained in an efficient market, and it would be wise to pursue a passive investment strategy which entails lower costs.
- In an inefficient market, securities may be mispriced and trading in these securities can offer positive risk-adjusted returns. In such a market, an active investment strategy may outperform a passive strategy on a risk-adjusted basis.

In an efficient market, the time frame required for security prices to reflect any new information is very short. Further, prices only adjust to new or unexpected information (surprises).

Market Value versus Intrinsic Value

The market value or market price of the asset is the price at which the asset can currently be bought or sold. It is determined by the interaction of demand and supply for the security in the market. Intrinsic value or fundamental value is the value of the asset that reflects all its investment characteristics accurately. Intrinsic values are estimated in light of all the available information regarding the asset; they are not known for certain.

In an efficient market, investors widely believe that the market price reflects a security's intrinsic value. On the other hand, in an inefficient market, investors may try to develop their own estimates of intrinsic value in order to profit from any mispricing (difference between the market price and intrinsic value).

Factors Contributing to and Impeding a Market's Efficiency

Market participants: Generally speaking, the greater the number of active market participants (investors and financial analysts) that analyze an asset or security, the greater the degree of efficiency in the market.

Information availability and financial disclosure: The availability of accurate and timely information regarding trading activities and traded companies contributes to market efficiency.

Limits to trading: The activities of arbitrageurs, who seek opportunities to trade on mispricings in the market to earn arbitrage (riskless) profits, contribute to market efficiency.

Transactions costs and information acquisition costs: Investors should consider transaction costs and information-acquisition costs in evaluating the efficiency of a market.

Two securities that should trade for the exact same price in an efficient market may trade at different prices if the costs of trading on the mispricing (to make a profit) for the lowest cost traders are greater than the potential profit. In such cases, these prices are still "efficient" within the bounds of arbitrage. The bounds of arbitrage are relatively narrow in highly liquid markets (e.g., U.S. T-bills), but wider in relatively illiquid markets.

Further, there are always costs associated with gathering and analyzing information. Net of information acquisition costs, the return offered on a security should be commensurate with the security's level of risk. If superior returns can be earned after deducting information-acquisition costs, the market is relatively inefficient.

EFFICIENT MARKET HYPOTHESES

Weak-Form Efficient Market Hypothesis

Weak-form EMH assumes that current stock prices reflect *all security market information* including historical trends in prices, returns, volumes and other market-generated information such as block trades and trading by specialists. Under this hypothesis, because current stock market prices have essentially factored in all historical data, future returns on a stock should be independent of past returns or patterns.

Proponents of weak-form EMH assert that abnormal risk-adjusted returns cannot be earned by using trading rules and technical analysis, which make investing decisions based on historical security market data.

On the whole, various tests for weak-form EMH have backed the theory that current market prices reflect all available security market information and lead to the conclusion that the markets tend to be weak-form efficient. However, there is evidence that in countries with developing markets (e.g., China, Bangladesh and Turkey) opportunities to profit from technical analysis do exist.

Semi-Strong Form Efficient Market Hypothesis

Semi-strong form EMH assumes that current security prices fully reflect *all security market information* and other public information. It encompasses weak-form EMH and also includes non-market public information such as dividend announcements, various financial ratios, and economic and political news in the set of information that is already factored into market values.

Proponents of the hypothesis assert that investors cannot earn abnormal risk-adjusted returns if their investment decisions are based on important material information after it has been made public. They stress that security prices rapidly adjust to reflect all public information.

Overall, semi-strong form EMH has received considerable support from studies in developed markets. In these markets, it has been found that abnormal risk-adjusted returns cannot be earned based on public information because security prices adjust for the information very quickly. However, there is some evidence that developing countries may not have semi-strong form efficient markets.

Strong-Form Efficient Market Hypothesis

Strong form EMH contends that stock prices reflect *all public and private information*. It implies that no group of investors has sole access to any information that is relevant in price formation. Basically, there is no information out there that has not already been accounted for in current market prices.

Strong-form EMH encompasses weak-form and semi-strong form EMH and assumes perfect markets where information is cost free and available to all. Under strong-form EMH, no one can consistently achieve abnormal risk-adjusted returns, not even company insiders.

Studies have found that securities markets are not strong form efficient. Abnormal risk-adjusted returns can be earned if material non-public information is used.

Implications of Efficient Market Hypothesis

- Securities markets are weak-form efficient. Therefore, past trends in prices cannot be used to earn superior risk-adjusted returns.
- Securities markets are also semi-strong form efficient. Therefore, investors who analyze information should consider what information is already factored into a security's price, and how any new information may affect its value.
- Securities markets are not strong-form efficient. This is because insider trading is illegal.

Efficient Markets and Technical Analysis

Technical analysts utilize charts to identify price patterns, which are used to make investment decisions. If the market is weak-form efficient, prices already reflect all available security market public information, and technical trading systems that depend only on past trading and price data cannot hold much value. Since tests have predominantly confirmed weak-form efficiency of markets, technical trading rules should not generate abnormal risk adjusted-profits after accounting for risks and transaction costs.

Efficient Markets and Fundamental Analysis

Fundamental analysts are concerned with the company that underlies the stock. They evaluate a company's past performance and examine its financial statements. They compute many performance ratios that aid them in assessing the validity of the stock's current price. They believe that a company's stock price can differ from its true intrinsic value, and investors who recognize the discrepancy can profit from it.

Fundamental analysis is necessary in a well-functioning securities market as it helps market participants understand the implications of any new information. Further, fundamental analysis can help generate abnormal risk-adjusted returns if an analyst is superior to her peers in valuing securities.

Efficient Markets and Portfolio Management

If markets and weak and semi-strong form efficient, active management is not likely to earn superior risk-adjusted returns on a consistent basis. Therefore, passive portfolio management would outperform active management. Studies have shown that on a risk-adjusted basis, mutual funds perform as well as the market before considering fees and expenses, but underperform the market after considering these costs.

The implication here is that the role of the portfolio manager is not necessarily to beat the market, but to manage the portfolio in light on the investor's risk and return objectives.

Pricing Anomalies

An anomaly occurs when a change in the price of an asset cannot be explained by the release of new information into the market.

- If markets are efficient, trading strategies designed to exploit market anomalies will not generate superior risk-adjusted returns on a consistent basis.
- An exception to the notion of market efficiency (an anomaly) would occur if a mispricing can be used to earn superior risk adjusted returns consistently.

Observed anomalies can be placed into three categories.

1. Time-Series Anomalies

Calendar Anomalies

January effect: Studies have shown that since the 1980s, investors have earned significantly higher returns in the equity market during January compared to other months of the year. Recent evidence has suggested that the January effect is not persistent and does not produce superior returns on a risk-adjusted basis. Therefore, it is not a pricing anomaly.

Momentum and Overreaction Anomalies

Investors tend to inflate (depress) stock prices of companies that have released good (bad) news. Studies have shown that "losers" (stocks that have witnessed a recent price decline due to the release of bad news) have outperformed the market in subsequent periods, while winners have underperformed in subsequent periods. Other studies have also shown that securities that have outperformed in the short term continue to generate high returns in subsequent periods (carrying on price momentum).

The overreaction and momentum anomalies go against the assertions of weak-form efficiency in markets.

2. Cross-Sectional Anomalies

Size Effect

Studies conducted in the past showed that shares of smaller companies outperformed shares of larger companies on a risk-adjusted basis. However, recent studies have failed to reach the same conclusion.

Value Effect

Studies have found that low P/E stocks have experienced higher risk-adjusted returns than high P/E stocks. These results go against semi-strong form market efficiency. However, when the Fama and French three-factor model is used instead of the CAPM to predict stock returns, the value stock anomaly disappears.

Other Anomalies

Closed-End Investment Fund Discounts

Several studies have shown that closed-end funds tend to trade at a discount (sometimes exceeding 50%) to their per share NAVs. Theoretically, investors could purchase all the shares in the fund, liquidate the fund, and make a profit by selling the constituent securities at their market prices. However, after accounting for management fees, unrealized capital gains taxes, liquidity and transaction costs, any profit potential is eliminated.

Earnings Surprises

Several studies have shown that although earnings surprises are quickly reflected in stock prices most of the time, this is not always the case. Investors may be able to earn abnormal returns using publicly available earnings information by purchasing stocks of companies that have announced positive earnings surprises. However, recent evidence has suggested that abnormal returns observed after earnings surprises do not control for transaction costs and risk.

Initial Public Offerings (IPOs)

Evidence suggests that investors who are able to acquire the shares of a company in an IPO at the offer price may be able to earn abnormal profits. However, this has not always proven to be the case. Further, over the long run, performance of IPOs has generally been below average.

Predictability of Returns based on prior Information

Considerable research has suggested that equity returns are based on factors such as interest rates, inflation rates, stock volatility, etc. However, the fact that equity returns are related to economic fundamentals is not evidence of market inefficiency.

Implications for Investment Strategies

Although there is some evidence to support the existence of valid anomalies, it is difficult to consistently earn abnormal returns by trading on them. On average, markets are efficient. Further, it is possible that identified anomalies may not be violations of market efficiency, but the result of the statistical methodologies used to detect them.

BEHAVIORAL FINANCE

Behavioral finance looks at investor behavior to explain why individuals make the decisions that they do, whether these decisions are rational or irrational. It is based on the premise that individuals do not always make 'efficient' investment decisions, nor do they always act 'rationally' due to the presence of **behavioral biases**.

> Most asset-pricing models assume that markets are rational and that the intrinsic value of a security reflects the rationality. But market efficiency and asset-pricing models do not require that each individual is rational–rather, only that the market is rational.

Behavioral Biases

Loss Aversion

Behavioral finance asserts that investors exhibit **loss aversion** i.e., they dislike losses more than they like comparable gains, which results in a strong preference for avoiding losses as opposed to achieving gains. Advocates of this bias argue that loss aversion is more important to investors than risk aversion, which is why the 'overreaction' anomaly is observed. While loss aversion can explain the overreaction anomaly, studies have shown that under reactions are just as common as overreactions, which counters the assertions of this bias.

Herding

Herding behavior is a behavioral bias that explains both under reactions and overreactions in financial markets. Herding occurs when investors ignore their own analysis, and instead make investment decisions in line with the direction of the market.

Overconfidence

Overconfidence bias asserts investors have an inflated view of their ability to process new information appropriately. Overconfident investors are inaccurate when it comes to valuing securities given new information, and therefore stocks will be mispriced if there is an adequate number of such investors in the market.

Evidence has suggested that overconfidence has led to mispricing in most major markets around the world, but the bias has been observed predominantly in higher-growth companies, whose prices are slow to factor in any new information.

Another aspect of this bias is that overconfident investors tend to maintain portfolios that are less-than-optimally diversified because they tend to overestimate their stock-picking abilities.

Information Cascades

An information cascade refers to the transfer of information from market participants who are the first to take investment action upon the release of new information, and whose decisions influence the decisions of others.

Information cascades can be rational. If informed traders act first and uninformed traders follow their lead, there will be an improvement in market efficiency as the cascade is helping the market correctly incorporate relevant information. Information cascades can also result in serial correlation in stock returns and to overreactions to information. Studies have shown that information cascades tend to be greater for stocks when reliable and relevant information about the underlying company is not easily available. They can actually improve the quality of information available to investors.

Other Behavioral Biases

- **Representativeness**, where investors assess probabilities of future outcomes based on how similar they are to the current state.
- **Mental accounting**, where investors keep track of gains and losses from different investments in separate mental accounts.
- **Conservatism**, where investors are slow to react to changes and continue to maintain their initial views.
- **Narrow framing**, where investors focus on issues in isolation.

Concluding Remarks

Whether investor behavior can explain market anomalies is a subject open to debate.

- If investors must be rational for the market to be efficient, then markets cannot be efficient.
- If markets are defined as being efficient, investors cannot earn superior risk-adjusted profits consistently, available evidence suggests that markets are efficient even though investors do exhibit irrational behavior, such as herding.

STUDY SESSION 14: EQUITY ANALYSIS AND VALUATION

OVERVIEW OF EQUITY SECURITIES

Cross-Reference to CFA Institute Assigned Reading #47

Importance of Equities in Global Financial Markets

- In 2008, on a global level, the equity market capitalization to GDP ratio was close to 100% (more than twice the long run average of 50%).
- Studies have shown that during 1900-2008, government bonds and bills earned annualized real returns of 1% to 2% on average, which is in line with the inflation rate. On the other hand, equity markets earned real returns in excess of 4% per year in most markets.
- In most developed countries, equity ownership as a percentage of the population was between 20% and 50%.

Types of Equity Securities

Common Shares

Investors in common shares have an ownership interest in the company. They share the operating performance of the company, participate in the governance process through voting rights, and have a residual claim on the company's net assets in case of liquidation.

- **Callable** common shares give the issuing company the right, but not the obligation, to buy back shares from investors at a later date at the call price (which is specified when the shares are originally issued). Companies are likely to buy back shares when their market price is higher than the call price. This is beneficial for the company as it is able to:
  - Buy shares at a lower price and resell them at the higher market price.
  - Save on dividend payments and preserve its capital.

Callable common shares are also beneficial for the investors as they get a guaranteed return on their investments when the shares are called.

- **Putable** common shares give investors the right, but not the obligation, to sell their shares back to the issuing company at the put price (which is specified when the shares are originally issued). Investors are likely to exercise this right when the market price of shares is lower than the put price. Putable common shares limit investor losses. As far as the company is concerned, they make it easier to raise capital as the put feature makes the shares more appealing to investors.

Preference Shares

Preference shares (also known as preferred stock) have the following characteristics:

- They do not give holders the right to participate in the operating performance of the company and they do not carry voting rights unless explicitly allowed for at issuance.
- They receive dividends before ordinary shareholders. Further, preferred dividends are fixed and are usually higher than dividends on common shares. However, the company is still not contractually obligated to make regular payments to holders of preferred stock.
- In case of liquidation, they have a higher priority in claims on the company's net assets than common shares. However, they still have a lower priority than bondholders.
- They can be perpetual (i.e., have no fixed maturity date), can pay dividends indefinitely, and can be callable or putable.

Preference shares can be classified into the following categories:

- **Cumulative:** Unpaid dividends on cumulative preference shares accrue over time and must be paid in full before dividends on common shares can be paid.
- **Non-cumulative:** Unpaid dividends for one or more periods are forfeited permanently and are not accrued over time to be paid at a later date.
- **Participating:** These are entitled to preferred dividends plus additional dividends if the company's profits exceed a pre-specified level. Further, investors in participating preferred shares might be entitled to an additional distribution of the company's assets upon liquidation above the par value of the preference shares. Participating preference shares are more common in smaller, riskier companies in which investors are concerned about the company's possible future liquidation.
- **Non-participating:** These are only entitled to a fixed preferred dividend and the par value of shares in the event of liquidation.
- **Convertible:** These are convertible into a specified number of common shares based on a conversion ratio that is determined at issuance. They have the following advantages:
    - They allow investors to earn a higher dividend than if they had invested in the company's common shares.
    - They offer investors the opportunity to share the profits of the company.
    - They allow investors to benefit from a rise in the price of common shares through the conversion option.
    - Their price is less volatile than the underlying common shares because their dividend payments are known and more stable.

Convertible preference shares are becoming increasingly common in venture capital and private equity transactions.

Private Equity Securities

Private securities are issued primarily to institutional investors via non-public offerings, such as private placements, and have the following characteristics:

- There is no active secondary market for them as they are not listed on public exchanges. Therefore, they do not have market-determined quoted prices.
- They are highly illiquid, and require negotiations between investors in order to be traded.
- The issuing companies are not required by regulatory authorities to publish financial statements and other important information regarding the company, which makes it difficult to determine fair values.

Types of Private Equity Investments

- Venture capital
- Leveraged Buyout (LBO)
- Private Investment in Public Equity

Advantages of Private Companies

- The longer investment horizons allow investors to focus on long-term value creation and to address any underlying operational issues facing the company. Publicly-traded companies feel pressured to focus on short term performance (e.g., to meet market expectations regarding earnings, growth, etc.).
- Certain costs that public companies must bear, such as those incurred to meet regulatory and stock exchange filing requirements, are avoided by private companies.

Advantages of Public Companies

- Public equity markets are much larger than private equity networks. Therefore, they provide more opportunities to companies for raising capital cheaply.
- Publicly traded companies are encouraged to be open about their policies, which ensures that they act in shareholder interest.

Non-Domestic Equity Securities

- An increasing number of companies have issued shares in markets outside of their home country.
- The number of companies whose shares are traded in markets outside of their home country has increased.
- An increasing number of companies are dual-listed i.e., their shares are simultaneously issued and traded in two or more markets.

Listing a company on an international exchange has the following benefits:

- It improves awareness about the company's products and services.
- It enhances the liquidity of the company's shares.
- It increases corporate transparency due to the additional market exposure and the need to meet a greater number of filing requirements.

Methods for Investing in Non-Domestic Equity Securities

Direct Investing

The most obvious way to invest in equity securities of foreign companies is to buy and sell securities directly in foreign markets. However, direct investing has the following implications:

- All transactions are in the company's, not the investor's domestic currency. Therefore, investors are also exposed to exchange rate risk.
- Investors must be familiar with the trading, clearing, and settlement regulations and procedures of the foreign market.
- Investing directly may lead to less transparency (due to the unavailability of audited financial statements on a regular basis) and increased volatility (due to limited liquidity).

Depository Receipts

A depository receipt (DR) is a security that trades like an ordinary share on a local exchange and represents an economic interest in a foreign company. It is created when a foreign company deposits its shares with a bank (the depository) in the country on whose exchange the shares will trade. The bank then issues a specific number of receipts representing the deposited shares based on a pre-determined ratio. Hence, one DR might represent one share, a number of shares or a fractional share of the underlying stock.

A DR can be sponsored or unsponsored.

- A sponsored DR is when the foreign company that deposits its shares with the depository has a direct involvement in the issuance of receipts.
- In an unsponsored DR, the foreign company that deposits its shares with the depository has no involvement in the issuance of receipts.

There are two types of depository receipts:

- *Global Depository Receipts (GDRs):* GDRs are issued by the depository bank outside of the company's home country and outside of the U.S.
- *American Depository Receipts (ADRs):* ADRs are denominated in U.S. dollars and trade like a common share on U.S. exchanges. They are basically GDRs that can be publicly traded in the U.S.

Global Registered Shares (GRS)

A GRS is an ordinary share that is quoted and traded in different currencies on different stock exchanges around the world. GRSs offer more flexibility than DRs as the shares represent actual ownership in the issuing company, they can be traded anywhere and currency conversions are not required to trade them.

Basket of Listed Depository Receipts (BLDR)

This is an exchange-traded fund (ETF) that represents a portfolio of DRs. Like all other ETFs, it trades throughout the day and can be bought, sold, or sold short just like an individual share. Further, it can be purchased on margin and used in hedging and arbitrage strategies.

Return Characteristics of Equity Securities

The two main sources of an equity security's total return are:

- Capital gains from price appreciation.
- Dividend income.

The total return on non-dividend paying stocks only consists of capital gains.

Investors in depository receipts and foreign shares also incur foreign exchange gains (or losses).

Another source of return arises from the compounding effects of reinvested dividends.

Risks of Equity Securities

- Preference shares are less risky than common shares.
- Putable common shares are less risky than callable or non-callable common shares.
- Callable common and preference shares are more risky than their non-callable counterparts.
- Cumulative preference shares are less risky than non-cumulative preference shares as they accrue unpaid dividends.

Equity Securities and Company Value

The primary aim of management is to increase the book value and market value of the company. Book value (shareholders' equity on the company's balance sheet) is calculated as total assets less total liabilities. It reflects the historical operating and financing decisions made by the company. Management can directly influence book value (e.g., by retaining net income).

However, management can only indirectly influence a company's market value as it is primarily determined by investors' expectations about the amount, timing and uncertainty of the company's future cash flows. A company may increase its book value by retaining net income, but it will only have a positive effect on the company's market value if investors expect the company to invest its retained earnings in profitable growth opportunities. If investors believe that the company has a significant number of cash flow generating investment opportunities coming through, the market value of the company's equity will exceed its book value.

A useful ratio to evaluate investor's expectations about a company is the price-to-book ratio (also known as the market-to-book) ratio.

- If a company has a price-to-book ratio that is greater than industry average, it suggests that investors believe that the company has more significant future growth opportunities than its industry peers.
- It may not be appropriate to compare price-to-book ratios of companies in different industries because the ratio also reflects investors' growth outlook for the industry itself.

An important measure used by investors to evaluate the effectiveness of management in increasing the company's book value is accounting return on equity.

Accounting Return on Equity

The accounting return on equity (ROE) measures the rate of return earned by a company on its equity capital. It indicates how efficient a firm is in generating profits from every dollar of net assets. The ROE is computed as net income available to ordinary shareholders (after preference dividends have been paid) divided by the average total book value of equity.

$$\mathrm{ROE_t} = \frac{\mathrm{NI_t}}{\text{Average } \mathrm{BVE_t}} = \frac{\mathrm{NI_t}}{(\mathrm{BVE_t} + \mathrm{BVE_{t-1}})/2}$$

An increase in ROE might not always be a positive sign for the company.

- The increase in ROE may be the result of net income decreasing at a slower rate than shareholders' equity. A declining net income is a source of concern for investors.
- The increase in ROE may be the result of debt issuance proceeds being used to repurchase shares. This would increase the company's financial leverage (risk).

Book values and ROE do help analysts evaluate companies, but they cannot be used as the primary means to determine a company's intrinsic value. Intrinsic value refers to the present value of the company's expected future cash flows, and can only be estimated as it is impossible to accurately predict the amount and timing of a company's future cash flows. Astute investors aim to profit from differences between market prices and intrinsic values.

The Cost of Equity and Investors' Required Rates of Return

A company may raise capital by issuing debt or equity, both of which have associated costs.

- A company's cost of debt is easy to estimate as it is reflected in the interest payments that the company is contractually obligated to make to debt holders.
- Estimating cost of equity is difficult because the company is not contractually obligated to make any payments to common shareholders.

Investors' minimum required rates of return refer to the return they require for providing funds to the company.

- For investors who provide debt capital to the company, their minimum required rate of return is the periodic interest rate they charge the company for using their funds. Further, all providers of debt capital receive the same interest rate. Therefore, the company's cost of debt and investors' minimum required rate of return on debt are the same.
- For investors who provide equity capital to the company, the future cash flows that they expect to receive are uncertain (in both timing and amount) so their minimum required rate of return must be estimated. Further, each investor may have different expectations regarding future cash flows. Therefore, the company's cost of equity may be different from investors' minimum required rate of return on equity.

You should think about the cost of equity as the minimum expected rate of return that a company must offer investors to purchase its shares in the primary market and to maintain its share price in the secondary market. If the required rate of return is not maintained, the price of the security in the secondary market will adjust to reflect the minimum rate of return required by investors.

- If investors require a higher return than the company's cost of equity, they will sell the company's shares and invest elsewhere, which would bring down the company's stock price. This decline in the stock price will lead to an increase in the expected return on equity and bring it in line with the (higher) required rate of return.

Note:

- The company's cost of equity can be estimated using the dividend discount model (DDM) and capital asset pricing model (CAPM) which are discussed in other readings.
- The costs of debt and equity are used to estimate a company's weighted average cost of capital (WACC), which represents the minimum required rate of return that the company must earn on its average investment.

INTRODUCTION TO INDUSTRY AND COMPANY ANALYSIS
Cross-Reference to CFA Institute Assigned Reading #48

Industry analysis has the following uses:

- To understand a company's business and business environment.
- To identify active equity investment opportunities.
- To attribute portfolio performance.

APPROACHES TO INDUSTRY CLASSIFICATION

Products and/or Services Supplied

This classification scheme groups companies that make similar products and/or services. Companies are placed in industries based on their principal business activity i.e., the source from which the company derives most of its revenues and/or earnings. Industries that are related to each other are grouped together to form a sector.

Business-Cycle Sensitivities

This approach groups companies based on their relative sensitivity to business cycles.

A cyclical company is one whose performance is positively correlated with the performance of the overall economy. Cyclical companies perform very well when the economy is booming, but perform relatively poorly during recessions. Cyclical companies typically have high operating leverage, which may be accompanied by high financial risk. Examples of cyclical industries include autos, industrials and technology.

A non-cyclical company is one whose performance is relatively independent of the business cycle. Demand for products made by non-cyclical companies remains relatively stable. Examples of non-cyclical industries include healthcare and utilities.

Analysts also often classify industries as defensive or growth industries. Defensive or stable industries are those whose profits are least affected by fluctuations in overall economic activity. Growth industries are industries whose specific demand dynamics override economic factors in determining their performance. These industries generate growth irrespective of overall economic conditions, though their growth rates may decline in recessions.

Limitations of these Classifications:

- The classification of companies as cyclical or non-cyclical is somewhat arbitrary. Economic downturns affect all companies so cyclical and non-cyclical industries are better understood on a relative basis.
- At a given point in time different countries and regions may be undergoing different stages of the business cycle. Comparing companies in the same industry that are currently operating in very different economic conditions may help identify investment opportunities, but establishing industry benchmark values with the data would be misleading.

Statistical Similarities

Statistical approaches group companies on the basis of correlations of historical returns. This approach has the following limitations:

- The composition of industry groups may vary significantly over time and across geographical regions.
- There is no guarantee that past correlations will continue to hold going forward.
- A relationship may arise by chance.
- A relationship that is actually economically significant may be excluded.

Industry Classification Systems

Commercial Industry Classification Systems

- Global Industry Classification Standard (GICS)
- Russell Global Sectors (RGS)
- Industry Classification Benchmark (ICB)

Governmental Industry Classification Systems

- International Standard Industrial Classification of All Economic Activities (ISIC)
- Statistical Classification of Economic Activities in the European Community (NACE)
- Australian and New Zealand Standard Industrial Classification (ANZSIC)
- North American Industry Classification System (NAICS)

Strengths and Weaknesses of Current Systems

Commercial classification systems generally have an advantage over government systems because of the following reasons:

- Most government systems do not disclose information about specific businesses or companies, so an analyst does not have access to the constituents of a particular category.
- Commercial classification systems are reviewed and updated more frequently than government classification systems.
- Government classification systems do not distinguish between small and large businesses, between for-profit and not-for-profit organizations, or between public and private companies. Commercial classification systems make distinctions between small and large companies automatically by virtue of the companies' association with a particular equity index. Further, commercial classification systems only include for-profit and publicly traded organizations.

Peer Groups

A **peer group** is a group of companies engaged in similar business activities whose economics and valuation are influenced by closely-related factors. Comparing a company to a well-defined peer group is very useful in evaluating company performance and in relative valuation.

Steps in constructing a preliminary list of peer companies:

- Examine commercial classification systems to identify companies operating in the same industry.
- Review the subject company's annual report to identify any mention of competitors.
- Review competitors' annual reports to identify other potential comparable companies.
- Review industry trade publications to identify comparable companies.
- Confirm that comparable companies have primary business activities that are similar to those of the subject company.

Strategic Analysis

Analysis of the industry with a view to examining the implications of the industrial environment on corporate strategy is known as strategic analysis.

Porter's Five Forces Framework

- Threat of substitute product
- Bargaining power of customers
- Bargaining power of suppliers
- Threat of new entrants
- Intensity of rivalry

Barriers to Entry

Generally speaking:

- Low barriers to entry mean that new competitors can easily enter the industry, which makes the industry highly competitive. Companies in relatively competitive industries typically have little pricing power.
- High barriers to entry mean that existing companies are able to enjoy economic profits for a long period of time. These companies have greater pricing power.

However, bear in mind that the above mentioned characteristics of high and low barrier industries are not always observed. Further, it is important to note that:

- Barriers to entry should not be confused with barriers to success.
- Barriers to entry can change over time.

Industry Concentration

Generally speaking:

- If an industry is relatively concentrated i.e., a few large firms dominate the industry, there is relatively less price competition. This is because:
  - It is relatively easy for a few firms to coordinate their activities.
  - Larger firms have more to lose from destructive price behavior.
  - The fortunes of large firms are more tied to those of the industry as a whole so they are more likely to be wary of the long run impact of a price war on industry economics.
- If an industry is relatively fragmented i.e., there is a large number of small firms in the industry, there is relatively high price competition. This is because of the following reasons:
  - Firms are unable to monitor their competitors' actions, which makes coordination difficult.
  - Each firm only has a small share of the market, so a small market share gain (through aggressive pricing) can make a large difference to each firm.
  - Each firm is small relative to the overall market so it tends to think of itself individualistically, rather than as a member of a larger group.

Bear in mind that there are important exceptions to the rules defined above. For example, Boeing and Airbus dominate the aircraft manufacturing industry, but competition between the two remains fierce.

Industry Capacity

Generally speaking:

- Limited capacity gives companies more pricing power as demand exceeds supply.
- Excess capacity results in weak pricing power as excess supply chases demand.

In evaluating the future competitive environment in an industry, analysts should examine current capacity levels as well as how capacity levels are expected to change in the future. Further, it is important to keep in mind that:

- If new capacity is physical (e.g., manufacturing facilities) it will take longer for the new capacity to come online so tight supply conditions may linger on for an extended period. Usually however, once physical capacity is added, supply may overshoot, outstrip demand, and result in weak pricing power for an extended period.
- If new capacity requires financial and human capital, companies can respond to tight supply conditions fairly quickly.

Market Share Stability

Generally speaking:

- Stable market shares indicate less competitive industries.
- Unstable market shares often indicate highly competitive industries with little pricing power.

Market shares are affected by the following factors:

- Barriers to entry
- New products
- Product differentiation

Industry Life-Cycle Analysis

Embryonic: Industries in this stage are just beginning to develop. They are characterized by:

- Slow growth as customers are still unfamiliar with the product.
- High prices as volumes are too low to achieve significant economies of scale.
- Significant initial investment.
- High risk of failure.

Companies focus on raising product awareness and developing distribution channels during this stage.

Growth: Once the new product starts gaining acceptance in the market, the industry experiences rapid growth. The growth stage is characterized by:

- New customers entering the market, which increases demand.
- Improved profitability as sales grow rapidly.
- Lower prices as economies of scale are achieved.
- Relatively low competition among companies in the industry as the overall market size is growing rapidly. Firms do not need to wrestle market share away from competitors to grow.
- High threat of new competitors entering the market due to low barriers to entry.

During this stage, companies focus on building customer loyalty and reinvest heavily in the business.

Shakeout: The period of rapid growth is followed by a period of slower growth. The shakeout stage is characterized by:

- Slower demand growth as fewer new customers are left to enter the industry.
- Intense competition as growth becomes dependent on market share growth.
- Excess industry capacity, which leads to price reductions and declining profitability.

During this stage, companies focus on reducing their costs and building brand loyalty. Some firms may fail or merge with others.

Mature: Eventually demand stops growing and the industry matures. Characteristics of this stage are:

- Little or no growth in demand as the market is completely saturated.
- Companies move towards consolidation. They recognize that they are interdependent so they stay away from price wars. However, price wars may occur during downturns.
- High barriers to entry in the form of brand loyalty and relatively efficient cost structures.

During this stage, companies are likely to be pursuing replacement demand rather than new buyers and should focus on extending successful product lines rather than introducing revolutionary new products. Companies have limited opportunities to reinvest and often have strong cash flows. As a result, they are more likely to pay dividends.

Decline: Technological substitution, social changes or global competition may eventually cause an industry to decline. The decline stage is characterized by:

- Negative growth.
- Excess capacity due to diminishing demand.
- Price competition due to excess capacity.
- Weaker firms leaving the industry.

Limitations of Industry Life-Cycle Analysis

- The following factors may change the shape of the industry life cycle, cause some stages to be longer or shorter than expected, or even result in certain stages being skipped altogether.
  - Technological changes
  - Regulatory changes
  - Social changes
  - Demographics
- Industry life-cycle analysis is most useful in analyzing industries during periods of relative stability. It is not as useful in analyzing industries experiencing rapid change.
- Not all companies in an industry display similar performance.

EQ

Price Competition

Generally speaking:

- Industries in which price is the most significant consideration in customers' purchase decisions tend to be highly competitive. A slight increase in price may cause customers to switch to substitute products if they are widely available.
- Price is not as important if companies in an industry are able to effectively differentiate their products in terms of quality and performance. Customers may not focus on price as much if product reliability is more important to them.

Factors Affecting Industry Growth, Profitability, and Risk

- Macroeconomic influences
- Technological influences
- Demographic influences
- Governmental influences
- Social influences

Competitive Strategies

Cost Leadership

Companies pursuing this strategy strive to cut down their costs to become the lowest cost producers in an industry so that they can gain market share by charging lower prices. Pricing may be defensive (to protect market positions when competition is low) or aggressive (to increase market share when competition is intense).

Product/Service Differentiation

Companies pursuing this strategy strive to differentiate their products from those of competitors in terms of quality, type, or means of distribution. These companies are then able to charge a premium price for their products. This strategy is successful only if the price premium is greater than the cost of differentiation and the source of differentiation appeals to customers and is sustainable over time.

Elements that should be Considered in a Company Analysis

A thorough company analysis should:

- Provide an overview of the company.
- Explain relevant industry characteristics.
- Analyze the demand for the company's products and services.
- Analyze the supply of products and services including an analysis of costs.
- Explain the company's pricing environment.
- Present and interpret relevant financial ratios, including comparisons over time and comparisons with competitors.

EQUITY VALUATION: CONCEPTS AND BASIC TOOLS

Cross-Reference to CFA Institute Assigned Reading #49

The aim of equity analysis is to identify mispriced securities. Securities are mispriced or incorrectly priced by the market when their market prices are different from their intrinsic values. Intrinsic or fundamental value refers to a security's true value and is estimated by analysts using a variety of models/techniques.

- If the estimate for a security's intrinsic value is lower than the market price, the security is overvalued by market.
- If the estimate for a security's intrinsic value is greater than the market price, the security is undervalued by the market.
- If the estimate for a security's intrinsic value equals the market price, the security is fairly valued.

EQUITY VALUATION MODELS

Present Value Models

Generally speaking, there are two sources of return from investing in a stock: (1) cash dividends received during the holding period and (2) the change in the stock price over the holding period.

- A **cash dividend** is a cash distribution made to a company's shareholders. Cash dividends are typically paid out regularly at known intervals, and these are known as **regular cash dividends**.
- An **extra dividend** or **special dividend** refers to a dividend payment by a company that does not usually pay dividends, or a dividend payment on top of the company's regular dividend.
- A **stock dividend** or a **bonus issue** occurs when a company issues additional common shares in the company (instead of cash) to shareholders.

  It basically divides the market value of shareholders' equity into smaller pieces without affecting (1) the total value of the pie or (2) shareholders' proportional ownership in the company. Thus, stock dividends are not relevant for valuation.
- **Stock splits** and **reverse stock splits** also have no economic effect on the company or shareholders.
  - A stock split results in an increase in the number of shares outstanding and a consequent decrease in share price.
  - A reverse stock split increases the share price and reduces the number of shares outstanding.
- **Share repurchases** refer to a company buying back its own shares.
  - Shares that are repurchased by the company are known as treasury shares and, once repurchased, are not considered for dividends, voting, or calculating earnings per share.
  - All other things remaining the same, share repurchases can be viewed as equivalent to cash dividends in terms of their impact on shareholder wealth.

Arguments for Share Repurchases

- Share repurchases send out a signal to the market that management believes that the company's stock is undervalued, or that management will support the stock price.
- They offer the company flexibility in its cash distributions. A share repurchase does not set the expectation of continued distributions in the future as cash dividends might.
- There is a tax advantage to distributing cash through stock repurchases in markets where capital gains are taxed at a lower rate than dividends.
- They can be used to limit the increase in the number of shares outstanding when a significant number of employee stock options have been exercised.

Dividend Payment Chronology

- Declaration date is the date on which a company announces a particular dividend.
- The company also announces the holder-of-record date and the payment date on the declaration date.
- Ex-dividend date or ex-date is the first day that the share trades without the dividend.
- Any investor who holds the stock on the ex-dividend date or who purchased it the day before the ex-dividend date is entitled to receive the dividend.
- On the ex-dividend date, the share price is adjusted for the amount of the dividend.
- Holder-of-record date, also known as the owner-of-record date, shareholder-of-record date, record date, date of record, or date of book closure, is the date at which a shareholder listed in the company's records will be entitled to receive the upcoming dividend.
- Payment date or payable date is the date on which the company actually mails out or transfers the dividend payment to shareholders.

Dividend Discount Model

The dividend discount model (DDM) values a share of common stock as the present value of its expected future cash flows (dividends).

$$\text{Value} = \frac{D_1}{(1+k_e)^1} + \frac{D_2}{(1+k_e)^2} + \ldots + \frac{D_\infty}{(1+k_e)^\infty}$$

$$\text{Value} = \sum_{t=1}^{n} \frac{D_t}{(1+k_e)^t}$$

- When an investor sells a share of common stock, the value that the purchaser will pay equals the present value of the future stream of cash flows (i.e., the remaining dividend stream). Therefore, the value of the stock at any point in time is still determined by its expected future dividends. When this value is discounted to the present, we are back at the original dividend discount model.

- If a company pays no dividends currently, it does not mean that its stock will be worthless. There is an expectation that after a certain period of time the firm will start making dividend payments. Currently, the company is reinvesting all its earnings in its business with the expectation that its earnings and dividends will be larger and will grow faster in the future. If the company does not make positive earnings going forward, there will still be an expectation of a liquidating dividend. The amount of this dividend will be discounted at the required rate of return to compute the stock's current price.
- The required rate of return on equity (k_e) is usually estimated using the CAPM. Another approach for calculating the required return on equity simply adds a risk premium to the before-tax cost of debt of the company.

One year holding period: If our holding period is just one year, the value that we will place on the stock today is the present value of the dividends that we will receive over the year plus the present value of the price that we expect to sell the stock for at the end of the holding period.

$$\text{Value} = \frac{\text{dividend to be received}}{(1+k_e)^1} + \frac{\text{year-end price}}{(1+k_e)^1}$$

Multiple-Year Holding Period DDM

We apply the same discounting principles for valuing common stock over multiple holding periods. In order to estimate the intrinsic value of the stock, we first estimate the dividends that will be received every year that the stock is held and the price that the stock will sell for at the end of the holding period. Then we simply discount these expected cash flows at the cost of equity (required return).

$$V = \frac{D_1}{(1+k_e)^1} + \frac{D_2}{(1+k_e)^2} + \ldots + \frac{P_n}{(1+k_e)^n}$$

where:

P_n = Price at the end of n years.

Infinite Period DDM (Gordon Growth Model)

The infinite period dividend discount model assumes that a company will continue to pay dividends for an infinite number of periods. It also assumes that the dividend stream will grow at a constant rate (g_c) over the infinite period. In this case, the intrinsic value of the stock is calculated as:

$$PV_0 = \frac{D_0(1+g_c)^1}{(1+k_e)^1} + \frac{D_0(1+g_c)^2}{(1+k_e)^2} + \frac{D_0(1+g_c)^3}{(1+k_e)^3} + \ldots + \frac{D_0(1+g_c)^\infty}{(1+k_e)^\infty}$$

This equation simplifies to:

$$PV = \frac{D_0(1+g_c)^1}{(k_e - g_c)^1} = \frac{D_1}{k_e - g_c}$$

The relation between k_e and g_c is critical:

- As the difference between k_e and g_c *increases,* the intrinsic value of the stock *falls.*
- As the difference *narrows,* the intrinsic value of the stock *rises.*
- Small changes in either k_e or g_c can cause *large* changes in the value of the stock.

For the infinite-period DDM model to work, the following assumptions must hold:

- Dividends grow at a rate, g_c, which is not expected to change.
- k_e must be greater than g_c; otherwise, the model breaks down because of the denominator being negative.

Notice that the DDM formula on the previous page can be rearranged to make the required return, k_e, the subject:

$$k_e = \frac{D_1}{PV_0} + g_c$$

This expression for the cost of equity tells us that the return on an equity investment has two components:

- The dividend yield (D_1/P_0).
- Growth over time (g_c).

Applying Present Value Models

The Gordon growth model is highly appropriate for valuing dividend-paying stocks that are relatively immune to the business cycle and are relatively mature (e.g., utilities). It is also useful for valuing companies that have historically been raising their dividend at a stable rate.

Applying the DDM is relatively difficult if the company is not currently paying out a dividend. A company may not pay out a dividend because:

- It has a lot of lucrative investment opportunities available and it wants to retain profits to reinvest them in the business.
- It does not have sufficient excess cash flow to pay out a dividend.

Even though the Gordon growth model can be used for valuing such companies, the forecasts used are generally quite uncertain. Therefore, analysts use one of the other valuation models to value such companies and may use the DDM model as a supplement. The DDM can be extended to numerous stages. For example:

- A three-stage DDM is used to value fairly young companies that are just entering the growth phase. Their development falls into three stages- growth (with very high growth rates), transition (with decent growth rates) and maturity (with a lower growth into perpetuity).
- A two-stage DDM can be used to value a company currently undergoing moderate growth, but whose growth rate is expected to improve (rise) to its long term growth rate.

Valuation of Common Stock with Temporary Supernormal Growth

The correct valuation model to value such "supernormal growth" companies is the **multi-stage dividend discount model** that combines the multi-period and infinite-period dividend discount models.

$$\text{Value} = \frac{D_1}{(1+k_e)^1} + \frac{D_2}{(1+k_e)^2} + \ldots + \frac{D_n}{(1+k_e)^n} + \frac{P_n}{(1+k_e)^n}$$

where:

$$P_n = \frac{D_{n+1}}{k_e - g_c}$$

D_n = Last dividend of the supernormal growth period

D_{n+1} = First dividend of the constant growth period

The Free-Cash-Flow-to-Equity (FCFE) Model

Many analysts assert that a company's dividend-paying capacity should be reflected in its cash flow estimates instead of estimated future dividends. FCFE is a measure of dividend paying capacity and can also be used to value companies that currently do not make any dividend payments. FCFE can be calculated as:

$$\text{FCFE} = \text{CFO} - \text{FC Inv} + \text{Net borrowing}$$

Analysts may calculate the intrinsic value of the company's stock by discounting their projections of future FCFE at the required rate of return on equity.

$$V_0 = \sum_{t=1}^{\infty} \frac{FCFE_t}{(1+k_e)^t}$$

Intrinsic Value of Preferred Stock

When preferred stock is non-callable, non-convertible, has no maturity date and pays dividends at a fixed rate, the value of the preferred stock can be calculated using the perpetuity formula:

$$V_0 = \frac{D_0}{r}$$

For a non-callable, non-convertible preferred stock with maturity at time, n, the value of the stock can be calculated using the following formula:

$$V_0 = \sum_{t=1}^{n} \frac{D_t}{(1+r)^t} + \frac{F}{(1+r)^n}$$

Price Multiples - Relative Valuation

Price multiples are ratios that compare the price of a stock to some sort of value. Price multiples allow an analyst to evaluate the relative worth of a company's stock. Popular multiples used in relative valuation include price-to-earnings, price-to-sales, price-to-book and price-to-cash flow.

Multiples based on Fundamentals

A price multiple may be related to fundamentals through a dividend discount model such as the Gordon growth model. The expressions developed in such an exercise are interpreted as the justified (or based on fundamental) values for a multiple.

The Justified P/E Ratio:

$$\frac{P_0}{E_1} = \frac{D_1/E_1}{r - g}$$

- The P/E ratio is inversely related to the required rate of return.
- The P/E ratio is positively related to the growth rate.
- The P/E ratio appears to be positively related to the dividend payout ratio. However, this relationship may not always hold because a higher dividend payout ratio implies that the company's earnings retention ratio is lower. A lower earnings retention ratio translates into a lower growth rate. This is known as the "dividend displacement" of earnings.

Multiples based on Comparables

This method compares relative values estimated using multiples to determine whether an asset is undervalued, overvalued or fairly valued. The benchmark multiple can be any of:

- A multiple of a closely matched individual stock.
- The average or median multiple of a peer group or the firm's industry.
- The average multiple derived from trend or time-series analysis.

Analysts should be careful to select only those companies that have similar size, product lines, and growth prospects to the company being valued as comparables.

$$\text{Price to cash flow ratio} = \frac{\text{Market price of share}}{\text{Cash flow per share}}$$

$$\text{Price to sales ratio} = \frac{\text{Market price per share}}{\text{Net sales per share}}$$

$$\text{Price to sales ratio} = \frac{\text{Market value of equity}}{\text{Total net sales}}$$

$$\text{P/BV} = \frac{\text{Current market price of share}}{\text{Book value per share}}$$

$$\text{P/BV} = \frac{\text{Market value of common shareholders' equity}}{\text{Book value of common shareholders' equity}}$$

where:
Book value of common shareholders' equity = (Total assets - Total liabilities) - Preferred stock

EQ

Enterprise Value Multiples

Enterprise value (EV) is calculated as the market value of the company's common stock plus the market value of outstanding preferred stock if any, plus the market value of debt, less cash and short term investments (cash equivalents). It can be thought of as the cost of taking over a company.

The most widely used EV multiple is the EV/EBITDA multiple. EBITDA measures a company's income before payments to any providers of capital are made.

- The EV/EBITDA multiple is often used when comparing two companies with different capital structures.
- Loss-making companies usually have a positive EBITDA, which allows analysts to use the EV/EBITDA multiple to value them. The P/E ratio is meaningless (negative) for a loss-making company as its earnings are negative.

Asset-Based Valuation

Asset-based valuation uses market values of a company's assets and liabilities to determine the value of the company as a whole.

Asset based valuation works well for:

- Companies that do not have a significant number of intangible or "off-the-book" assets, and have a higher proportion of current assets and liabilities.
- Private companies, especially if applied together with multiplier models.
- Financial companies, natural resource companies and companies that are being liquidated.

Asset-based valuation may not be appropriate when:

- Market values of assets and liabilities cannot be easily determined.
- The company has a significant amount of intangible assets.
- Asset values are difficult to determine (e.g., in periods of very high inflation).
- Market values of assets and liabilities significantly differ from their carrying values.

Study Session 15: Fixed Income—Basic Concepts

FI

FIXED-INCOME SECURITIES: DEFINING ELEMENTS

Cross-Reference to CFA Institute Assigned Reading #50

IMPORTANT RELATIONSHIPS

- The higher (lower) the coupon rate on a bond, the higher (lower) its price.
- An increase (decrease) in interest rates or the required yield on a bond will lead to a decrease (increase) in price, i.e., bond prices and yields are inversely related.
- The more risky the bond, the higher the yield required by investors to purchase the bond, and the lower the bond's price.

OVERVIEW OF A FIXED-INCOME SECURITY

Issuers

- Supranational organizations.
- Sovereign (national) governments.
- Non-sovereign (local) governments.
- Quasi-government entities.

Bond issuers can also be classified based on their credit-worthiness as judged by credit rating agencies. Bonds can broadly be categorized as investment-grade or non-investment grade (or high-yield or speculative) bonds.

Maturity

- Fixed-income securities which, at the time of issuance, are expected to mature in one year or less are known as money market securities.
- Fixed-income securities which, at the time of issuance, are expected to mature in more than one year are referred to as capital market securities.
- Fixed-income securities which have no stated maturity are known as perpetual bonds.

Par Value

The par value (also known as face value, nominal value, redemption value and maturity value) of a bond refers to the principal amount that the issuer promises to repay bondholders on the maturity date. Bond prices are usually quoted as a percentage of the par value.

- When a bond's price is above 100% of par, it is said to be trading at a premium.
- When a bond's price is at 100% of par, it is said to be trading at par.
- When a bond's price is below 100% of par, it is said to be trading at a discount.

Coupon Rate and Frequency

The coupon rate (also known as the nominal rate) of a bond refers to the annual interest rate that the issuer promises to pay bondholders until the bond matures. The amount of interest paid each year by the issuer is known as the coupon, and is calculated by multiplying the coupon rate by the bond's par value.

Zero-coupon (or pure discount) bonds are issued at a discount to par value and redeemed at par (the issuer pays the entire par amount to investors at the maturity date). The difference between the (discounted) purchase price and the par value is effectively the interest on the loan.

Currency Denomination

- Dual-currency bonds make coupon payments in one currency and the principal payment at maturity in another currency.
- Currency option bonds give bondholders a choice regarding which of the two currencies they would like to receive interest and principal payments in.

Yield Measures

- The current yield or running yield equals the bond's annual coupon amount divided by its current price (not par value), expressed as a percentage.
- The yield-to-maturity (YTM) is also known as the yield-to-redemption or the redemption yield. It is calculated as the discount rate that equates the present value of a bond's expected future cash flows until maturity to its current price.
    - Given a set of expected future cash flows, the lower (higher) the YTM or discount rate, the higher (lower) the bond's current price.

THE BOND INDENTURE

A bond is a contractual agreement between the issuer and the bondholder. The **trust deed** is the legal contract that describes the form of the bond, obligations of the issuer and the rights of bondholders, and it is commonly referred to as the **bond indenture**. The indenture captures the following information:

- The name of the issuer.
- The principal value of the bond.
- The coupon rate.
- Dates when the interest payments will be made.
- The maturity date.
- Funding sources for the interest payments and principal repayments.
- Collaterals (i.e., assets or financial guarantees underlying the debt obligation above and beyond the issuer's promise to pay).
- Covenants (i.e., actions that the issuer is obligated to perform or prohibited from performing).
- Credit enhancements (i.e., provisions designed to reduce the bond's credit risk).

AREAS THAT INVESTORS SHOULD REVIEW BEFORE PURCHASING A BOND

Legal Identity of the Bond Issuer and its Legal Form

- For sovereign bonds, the legal issuer is typically the institution responsible for managing the national budget.
- Corporate bonds are typically issued by the corporate legal entity.
    - Note that bonds may be issued by the parent company or a subsidiary.
        - If issued by a subsidiary, investors must focus on the creditworthiness of the subsidiary, unless the bond is guaranteed by the parent. Oftentimes, subsidiaries carry a lower credit rating than the parent.
        - If issued by the parent company, it becomes important to analyze the assets actually held by the parent, as investors may not have recourse to assets held by subsidiaries or operating companies.
- In case of securitized bonds, the relationship between the sponsor and the SPE must be evaluated. Investors must ensure that the SPE is structured as a bankruptcy-remote vehicle.

Sources of Repayment Proceeds

- Bonds issued by supranational organizations are usually repaid through (1) proceeds from repayments of previous loans made by the organization or (2) paid-in capital from its members.
- Sovereign bonds are backed by the "full faith and credit" of the national government.
    - Sovereign bonds issued in local currency are usually considered safer than those issued in a foreign currency.
- Non-sovereign government debt can usually be repaid through the following sources:
    - The general taxing authority of the issuer.
    - Cash flows from the project that the bonds were issued to finance.
    - Special taxes or fees specifically set up to make interest and principal payments.
- Corporate bond issuers typically rely on their cash flow-generating ability to repay bonds, which in turn depends on their financial strength and integrity.
- For securitized bonds, repayment depends on the cash flow generated by the underlying pool of financial assets.

Asset or Collateral Backing

- **Seniority ranking:** Secured bonds are backed by assets or financial guarantees to ensure debt repayment in case of default, while unsecured bonds are not protected by a pledge of any specific assets (i.e., they only have a general claim on the issuer's assets and cash flows).

- In the event of default, unsecured bonds are repaid after secured bonds have been paid off.
  - Senior secured debt is paid off before subordinated or junior secured debt.
- Investors should review the indenture to identify whether a particular debenture is actually secured or unsecured.

- **Types of collateral backing**:
  - Collateral trust bonds are secured by securities such as common stock, other bonds, or other financial assets.
  - Equipment trust certificates are secured by specific types of equipment or physical assets (e.g., aircraft, railroad cars, or oil rigs).
  - Mortgage-backed securities (MBS) are backed by a pool of mortgage loans. Cash flows generated by the pool are used to make payments on MBS.
  - Covered bonds are backed by a segregated pool of assets (known as the cover pool).

Credit Enhancements

Credit enhancements are provisions that serve to reduce the credit risk of a bond issue, resulting in a lower yield.

- Internal credit enhancement focuses on the structure of the issue regarding priority of payment or the value of collateral. It includes:
  - Subordination: This refers to the allocation of cash flows among the various bond classes or tranches based on their seniority.
  - Overcollateralization: This occurs when the value of the collateral posted to secure an issue exceeds the par value of the securities issued.
  - Excess spread (or excess interest cash flow): A transaction can be structured in a manner such that the cash flows generated from the collateral pool exceed the amount of interest payable to bondholders so that there is a cushion for making interest payments.
- External credit enhancement refers to guarantees received from a third-party guarantor. Types of external credit enhancement include:
  - Surety bonds (issued by an insurance company) and bank guarantees: In the event of default, both these forms of enhancement reimburse investors for losses (up to a pre-specified maximum amount known as the penal sum).
  - Letters of credit: These are lines of credit provided by a financial institution to the issuer to reimburse any shortfalls in the cash flow generated from the collateral pool.

Note that surety bonds, bank guarantees, and letters of credit all expose investors to third party credit risk (i.e., the risk that the gurantor will not be able to fulfil its obligations). This risk can be mitigated by setting up a cash collateral account.

Covenants

Covenants are legally enforceable rules agreed upon by the borrower/issuer and lenders/investors at the time of bond issuance.

- Affirmative covenants are **requirements** placed on the issuer. They are typically administrative in nature so they do not lead to additional costs for the issuer, nor do they significantly restrict the issuer's ability to make business decisions.
- Negative covenants are **restrictions** placed on the issuer. While they entail more costs than affirmative covenants and can constrain the issuer in operating the business, they protect bondholders from dilution of their claims, asset withdrawals or substitutions, and inefficient investments by the issuer.

Legal and Regulatory Considerations

The differences between domestic bonds, foreign bonds, Eurobonds, and global bonds are important to investors as these different types of bonds are subject to different legal, regulatory, and tax requirements. There are also differences in terms of frequency of interest payments and how interest payments are calculated, both of which influence the bond's cash flows and price. Bear in mind however, that the currency denomination has a bigger influence on a bond's price than where it is issued or traded.

National Bond Markets versus Eurobond Market

A national bond market includes all the bonds that are issued and traded in a particular country, and denominated in that country's local currency.

- Bonds issued by entities that are incorporated in that country are known as domestic bonds.
- Bonds issued by entities that are incorporated in another country are known as foreign bonds.

Eurobonds refer to bonds that are denominated in a currency other than the local currency where they are issued. They may be issued in any country and in any currency (including the issuer's domestic currency), and are named based on the currency in which they are denominated.

- Generally speaking, Eurobonds are less regulated than domestic and foreign bonds as they do not fall under the jurisdiction of any single country.

Global bonds are bonds that are issued simultaneously (1) in the Eurobond market and (2) in at least one domestic bond market.

Tax Considerations

- Interest income is generally taxed at the ordinary income tax rate, which is the same rate that an individual pays tax on her wage or salary.
- Municipal bonds in the U.S. are often tax-exempt, in that interest income is often exempt from federal income tax and state income tax in the state of issue.
- In most jurisdictions, capital gains are taxed at a lower rate than interest income.
- In some countries, a prorated portion of any **original issue discount** must be included in interest income each year for tax purposes.
- In other jurisdictions, investors who have purchased bonds at a premium can either (1) deduct a prorated portion of the premium paid from taxable income each year until the bond matures, or (2) declare a capital loss when the bond is eventually redeemed at maturity.

PRINCIPAL REPAYMENT STRUCTURES

Credit risk is reduced if there are any provisions that call for periodic retirement of some of the principal amount outstanding during the term of the loan.

- A **bullet bond** is one that only makes periodic interest payments, with the entire principal amount paid back at maturity.
- An **amortizing bond** is one that makes periodic interest **and** principal payments over the term of the bond.
  - A fully amortized bond is one whose outstanding principal amount at maturity is reduced to zero through a fixed periodic payment schedule.
  - A partially amortized bond also makes fixed periodic principal repayments, but the principal is not fully repaid by the maturity date. Therefore, a balloon payment is required at maturity to repay the outstanding principal amount.

FI

Sinking Fund Arrangements

A sinking fund arrangement requires the issuer to repay a specified portion of the principal amount every year throughout the bond's life or after a specified date.

Sometimes a call provision may also be added to the bond issue. This call provision usually gives the issuer the option to repurchase bonds before maturity at the lowest of (1) market price (2) par, and (3) a specified sinking fund price.

From the bondholders' perspective, the advantage of a sinking fund arrangement is that it reduces credit risk. However, it entails two disadvantages. First, it results in reinvestment risk, and second, if the issue has an embedded call option, the issuer may be able to repurchase bonds at a price lower than the current market price.

COUPON PAYMENT STRUCTURES

Floating-Rate Notes (FRN)

- The coupon rate of a FRN has two components: a reference rate (such as LIBOR) plus a spread (also known as margin).
- FRNs have less interest rate risk (i.e., the risk of bond price volatility resulting from changes in market interest rates) than fixed-rate bonds, but still entail credit risk.
- FRNs may be structured to include a floor and/or a cap on the periodic coupon rate.
- Reverse FRNs or inverse floaters are structured such that the periodic coupon rate is inversely related to the reference rate.

Step-Up Coupon Bonds

A step-up coupon bond (which can be fixed or floating) is one where the periodic coupon rate increases by specified margins at specified dates. Typically, the step-up coupon structure is offered with callable bonds to protect bondholders in a rising interest rate environment. However, note that despite the step-up in coupons (and the consequent increase in interest expense), the issuer may not call the bond if refinancing is less advantageous.

Credit-Linked Coupon Bonds

The coupon rate on credit-linked coupon bonds changes when the bond's credit rating changes. Credit-linked coupon bonds protect investors against a decline in the credit quality, and are therefore attractive to investors who are concerned about the future creditworthiness of the issuer. They also provide some protection against poor economic conditions as credit ratings tend to decline during recessions. A problem with credit-linked coupon bonds is that since a rating downgrade results in higher interest payments for the issuer, it can contribute to further downgrades or even an eventual default.

Payment-in-Kind (PIK) Coupon Bonds

PIK coupon bonds allow the issuer to pay interest in the form of additional bonds instead of cash. They are preferred by issuers that are financially distressed and fear liquidity and solvency problems in the future. Investors usually demand a higher yield on these bonds to compensate them for the higher credit risk and high leverage of the issuer.

Deferred Coupon Bonds (or Split Coupon Bonds)

Deferred Coupon Bonds do not pay any coupon for the first few years after issuance, but then pay a higher coupon than they normally would for the remainder of their terms. Deferred coupon bonds are usually preferred by issuers who want to conserve cash in the short run, or for project financing where cash-generation will commence after an initial development phase.

Investors are attracted to deferred coupon bonds as they are usually priced significantly below par. Further, the deferred coupon structure may help investors manage their tax liability by delaying taxes due on interest income (in certain jurisdictions).

Index-Linked Bonds

These are bonds whose coupon payments and/or principal repayments are linked to a specified index (such as a commodity or equity index). An example of index-linked bonds are inflation-linked bonds (also known as linkers) whose coupon and/or principal payments are linked to an index of consumer prices (e.g., Treasury Inflation Protection Securities or TIPS issued by the U.S. Government are linked to the Consumer Price Index, CPI, in the U.S.). Investors are attracted to inflation-linked bonds because they offer a long-term asset with a fixed **real** return that is protected against inflation risk.

- Zero-coupon-indexed bonds do not pay any coupon so only the principal repayment is linked to a specified index.
- For interest-indexed bonds, only coupon payments are adjusted to changes in the specified index. They repay the fixed nominal principal at maturity.
- Capital-indexed bonds pay a fixed coupon rate, but this rate is applied to a principal amount that is adjusted to reflect changes in the specified index. As a result, both interest payments as well as the principal repayment are adjusted for inflation.
- Indexed-annuity bonds are fully amortized bonds. The annual payment on these bonds is linked to the specified index so effectively that both interest and principal payments reflect changes in the index.

An equity-linked note (ELN) is a fixed-income security whose final payment is linked to the return on an equity index.

- ELNs are generally principal-protected.
- If the underlying index increases in value, investors receive an amount greater than par upon maturity.
- Note that the principal payment is still subject to credit risk of the issuer.

BONDS WITH CONTINGENCY PROVISIONS

Callable Bonds

Callable bonds give the **issuer** the right to redeem (or call) all or part of the bond before maturity. This embedded option offers the issuer the ability to take advantage of (1) a decline in market interest rates and/or (2) an improvement in its creditworthiness.

From the perspective of the bondholder, she would pay less for a callable bond than for an otherwise identical non-callable bond. The difference in the value of a non-callable bond and an otherwise identical callable bond is the value of the embedded call option.

Value of callable bond = Value of non-callable bond – Value of embedded call option

Value of embedded call option = Value of non-callable bond – Value of callable bond

From the perspective of the issuer, it would have to pay more (in the form of a higher coupon or higher yield) to get investors to purchase a callable bond than an otherwise identical non-callable bond. The difference between the yield on a callable bond and the yield on a non-callable bond is the cost of the embedded option to the issuer.

Yield on callable bond = Yield on non-callable bond + Embedded call option cost in terms of yield

Embedded call option cost in terms of yield = Yield on callable bond – Yield on non-callable bond

- The more heavily the embedded call option favors the issuer, the lower the value of the callable bond to the investor and the higher the yield that must be offered by the issuer.
- Some callable bonds are issued with an initial call protection period (also known as lockout period, cushion or deferment period), during which the issuer is prohibited from calling the bond. The bond can only be called at or after the specified call date.
- A make-whole provision in a callable bond usually requires the issuer to pay a relatively high lump-sum amount to call the bonds.

Putable Bonds

Putable bonds give **bondholders** the right to sell (or put) the bond back to the issuer at a pre-determined price on specified dates. The embedded put option offers bondholders protection against an increase in interest rates, i.e., if interest rates increase (decreasing the value of the bond), they can sell the bond back to the issuer at a pre-specified price and then reinvest the principal at (higher) newer interest rates.

FI

From the perspective of the bondholder, she would pay more for a putable bond than for an otherwise identical non-putable bond. The difference in the value between a putable bond and an otherwise identical non-putable bond is the value of the embedded put option (which the bond holder has effectively purchased from the issuer):

Value of putable bond = Value of non-putable bond + Value of embedded put option

Value of embedded put option = Value of putable bond – Value of non-putable bond

From the perspective of the issuer, it would pay out less (in the form of a lower coupon or lower yield) on a putable bond than it would on an otherwise identical non-putable bond. The difference between the yield on a non-putable bond and the yield on a putable bond is the cost of the embedded option borne by the investor.

Yield on putable bond = Yield on non-putable bond – Embedded put option cost in terms of yield

Embedded put option cost in terms of yield = Yield on non-putable bond – Yield on putable bond

Note that the more heavily the embedded put option favors the investor, the higher the value of the putable bond to the investor and the lower the yield that must be offered by the issuer.

Convertible Bonds

A **convertible bond** gives the bondholder the right to convert the bond into a pre-specified number of common shares of the issuer.

Convertible bonds are attractive to investors as the conversion (to equity) option allows them to benefit from price appreciation of the issuer's stock. On the other hand, if there is a decline in the issuer's share price (which causes a decline in the value of the embedded equity conversion/call option), the price of the convertible bond cannot fall below the price of an otherwise identical straight bond. Because of these attractive features, convertible bonds offer a lower yield and sell at higher prices than similar bonds without the conversion option. Note however, that the coupon rate offered on convertible bonds is usually higher than the dividend yield on the underlying equity.

FI

- The conversion price is the price per share at which the convertible bond can be converted into shares.
- The conversion ratio refers to the number of common shares that each bond can be converted into. It is calculated as the par value divided by the conversion price.
- The conversion value is calculated as current share price multiplied by the conversion ratio.
- The conversion premium equals the difference between the convertible bond's price and the conversion value.
- Conversion parity occurs if the conversion value equals the convertible bond's price.

Although it is common for convertible bonds to reach conversion parity before they mature, bondholders rarely exercise the conversion option, choosing to retain their bonds and receive (higher) coupon payments instead of (lower) dividend payments. As a result, issuers often embed a call option alongside the conversion option in the convertible bond, making them **callable convertible bonds**.

Warrants

A **warrant** is somewhat similar to a conversion option, but it is not embedded in the bond's structure. It offers the holder the right to purchase the issuer's stock at a fixed exercise price until the expiration date. Warrants are attached to bond issues as sweeteners, allowing investors to participate in the upside from an increase in share prices.

Contingent Convertible Bonds ("CoCos")

CoCos are bonds with contingent write-down provisions. They differ from traditional convertible bonds in two ways:

- Unlike traditional convertible bonds, which are convertible at the **option** of the bondholder, CoCos convert **automatically** upon the occurrence of a pre-specified event.
- Unlike traditional convertible bonds, in which conversion occurs if the issuer's share price **increases** (i.e., on the upside), contingent write-down provisions are convertible on the **downside**.

FI

FIXED-INCOME MARKETS: ISSUANCE, TRADING, AND FUNDING
Cross-Reference to CFA Institute Assigned Reading #51

OVERVIEW OF GLOBAL FIXED-INCOME MARKETS

Classification of Fixed-Income Markets

Type of Issuer

Bond markets can be classified based on the following three types of issuers:

- The government and government-related sector.
- The corporate sector.
- The structured finance (or securitized) sector.

Credit Quality

- Bonds with a credit rating of Baa3 or above by Moody's, or BBB- or above by S&P and Fitch are classified as investment-grade bonds.
- Bonds with ratings below these levels are classified as non-investment grade (or high-yield, speculative or junk) bonds.

Maturity

FI

- Money market securities are fixed-income securities that have a maturity of one year or less at the time of issuance.
- Capital market securities are fixed-income securities that have a maturity of more than one year at the time of issuance.

Currency Denomination

- The currency in which a bond is issued determines which country's interest rates affect its price.

Geography

- Bonds that are issued in a specific country, denominated in the currency of that country and sold in that country are classified as:
    - Domestic bonds, if they are issued by entities incorporated in that country.
    - Foreign bonds, if the issuer is domiciled in another country.
- A Eurobond is issued internationally i.e., outside the jurisdiction of the country whose currency it is denominated in.

Other Classifications of Fixed-Income Markets

- Inflation-linked bonds offer investors protection against inflation by linking the coupon payment and/or the principal repayment to a consumer price index.

- Tax-exempt bonds, such as municipal bonds (or munis) in the U.S. are attractive for investors who are subject to income tax because interest income from these bonds is usually exempt from federal income tax and from state income tax (subject to some restrictions).

Type of Coupon

- The coupon rate for a bond may (1) be fixed throughout its term, or (2) may change periodically based on some reference rate.

Reference Rates

The reference rate used for a particular floating-rate bond issue depends on where the bonds are issued and the currency denomination. For example, a FRN denominated in GBP that pays coupon semi-annually, would typically calculate the coupon as 6-month Libor (or LIBOR-180) plus a spread.

Fixed-Income Indices

Fixed-income indices are generally used by investors (1) to describe a bond market or sector, and (2) to evaluate investment performance.

Investors in Fixed-Income Securities

- Central banks.
- Institutional investors.
- Retail investors.

FI

Primary Markets

In a public offering (or public offer), any member of the public may purchase the bonds.

- In an underwritten offerings (or firm commitment offering), the investment bank guarantees the sale of the issue at that price. The risk associated with selling the bonds is therefore borne by the investment bank (also known as the underwriter).
- In a best efforts offering, the investment bank only acts as a broker and tries its best to sell the bond at the negotiated offering price for a commission.
- In an auction, bonds are sold to investors through a bidding process, which helps in price discovery and allocation of securities.

Shelf Registration allows certain (authorized) issuers to offer additional bonds to the general public without having to prepare a new and separate prospectus for each bond issue. Since shelf issuances are subject to lower levels of scrutiny than standard public offerings, only well-established issuers with proven financial strength can make use of this facility. Further, in some jurisdictions, shelf registrations can only be purchased by qualified investors.

In a private placement, only a selected group of qualified investors (typically large institutional investors) are allowed to invest in the issue.

- The bonds are neither underwritten nor registered, and can be relatively illiquid as there is usually no secondary market to trade them.
- Investors are usually able to influence the terms of the issue, so privately placed bonds typically have more customized and restrictive covenants compared to publicly issued bonds.

Secondary Markets

Secondary markets (or **aftermarkets**) are those in which existing bonds are traded among investors.

- Organized exchanges are places where buyers and sellers can meet to arrange their trades. Buyers and sellers may come from anywhere, but transactions must be executed at the exchange in accordance with the rules and regulations of the exchange.
- In over-the-counter (OTC) markets, buyers and sellers submit their orders from various locations through electronic trading platforms. Orders are then matched and executed through a communications network.

The vast majority of bond trading occurs in OTC markets.

Sovereign Bonds

Sovereign bonds are bonds that are issued by a country's central government (or their treasuries). They are issued primarily to cover expenditures when tax revenues are insufficient.

- Sovereign bonds are backed by the taxing authority of the national government.
- Sovereign bonds can be issued in the sovereign's local (domestic) currency or in a foreign currency.

Secondary market trading of sovereign bonds is primarily in securities that were most recently issued (known as on-the-run securities or benchmark issues). Generally speaking, as a sovereign issue ages (or becomes more seasoned), it tends to trade less frequently.

Non-Sovereign Government Bonds

Non-sovereign bonds are those issued by levels of government that lie below the national level (e.g., provinces, regions, states, and cities). These bonds can be serviced through the following sources of income:

- The taxing authority of the local government.
- The cash flows from the project that is being financed with bond proceeds.
- Special taxes and fees established specifically for making interest payments and principal repayments.

Generally speaking, non-sovereign bonds are of high credit quality, but they still trade at higher yields (lower prices) than sovereign bonds.

Quasi-Government Bonds

Quasi-government or agency bonds are issued by organizations that perform various functions for the national government, but are not actual governmental entities. These bonds are issued to fund specific financing needs.

- Quasi-government bonds guaranteed by the national government trade at lower yields than similar bonds not carrying the government guarantee.
- Generally speaking, quasi-government entities do not have direct taxing authority, so bonds are serviced with cash flows generated by the entity or from the project that is being financed by the issue.
- In some cases, quasi-government bonds may be backed by collateral.
- Historical default rates on quasi-government bonds have been extremely low.

Supranational Bonds

These bonds are issued by **supranational** (or **multilateral**) **agencies** such as the World Bank (WB) and the International Monetary Fund (IMF). Generally speaking, supranational bonds are issued as plain vanilla bonds. They are typically highly-rated and issued in large sizes (so they tend to be very liquid).

CORPORATE DEBT

Bank Loans and Syndicated Loans

- Most bank loans are floating-rate loans, with Libor, a sovereign rate (e.g., the T-bill rate), or the prime rate serving as the reference rate.
- Bank loans can be customized (with respect to maturity and payment structure) to borrower requirements.
- Access to bank loans depends on (1) the company's financial position and (2) market conditions and capital availability.

Commercial Paper

- Commercial paper is an unsecured debt instrument that is popular among issuers because it is a source of flexible, readily-available, and relatively low-cost financing.
- It can be used to meet seasonal demands for cash and is also commonly used to provide **bridge financing**.
- Commercial paper is usually "rolled over" by issuers, which is why they tend to retain access to backup bank lines of credit.
- Terms to maturity can range from overnight to one year.
- Historically, defaults on commercial paper have been relatively rare because commercial paper has a short maturity and tends to be rolled over.

- Most investors hold on to commercial paper until maturity, which results in very little secondary market trading in these instruments.
- Yields on commercial paper are higher than yields on short-term sovereign bonds of the same maturity.

Corporate Notes and Bonds

- Corporate bonds can differ based on:
    - Coupon payment structures.
    - Principal payment structures.
        - Bonds with a serial maturity structure have maturity dates that are spread out over the bond's life.
        - Bonds with a term maturity structure are paid off in one lump sum payment at maturity.
    - Terms to maturity.
    - Asset or collateral backing.
    - Contingency provisions.

Medium-Term Notes (MTNs)

- The MTN market can be broken down into three segments:
    - Short-term securities that may be fixed- or floating-rate.
    - Medium- to long-term securities that generally tend to be fixed-rate.
    - Structured notes, which are essentially notes combined with derivative instruments to create special features desired by certain institutional investors.
- MTNs are unique in that they are offered continuously to investors by the agent of the issuer.
- MTNs can be customized/structured to meet investor requirements. While their customized features result in limited liquidity, MTNs offer higher yields than otherwise identical publicly-traded bonds.

STRUCTURED FINANCIAL INSTRUMENTS

Generally speaking, structured financial instruments have customized structures that often combine a bond and at least one derivative. The use of derivatives gives the holder of the instrument exposure to one or more underlying assets, such as equities, bonds, or commodities. The redemption value and often the coupons of structured financial instruments are tied to the performance of the underlying asset(s), as opposed to being tied to the issuer's cash flows (as is the case with traditional bonds).

Capital-Protected Instruments

Capital-protected instruments may offer different levels of capital protection. A guarantee certificate offers full capital protection, but other structured financial instruments may offer only partial capital protection. It is important to note that the capital protection is only as good as the creditworthiness of the issuer of the instrument. Should the issuer of guarantee certificates go bankrupt, investors may lose their entire capital.

Yield Enhancement Instruments

Yield enhancement aims to improve the expected return on an investment by increasing risk exposure. An example of such an instrument is a credit-linked note (CLN), which is basically a bond that pays regular coupons but whose redemption value depends on the occurrence of a well-defined credit event (e.g., a rating downgrade or the default of a reference asset).

- If the specified credit event does not occur, the investor receives the par value of the CLN at maturity.
- However, if the specified credit event occurs, the investor receives the par value of the CLN minus the nominal value of the reference asset to which the CLN is linked.

A CLN allows the issuer to effectively transfer the effect of a particular credit event to investors. The issuer is the protection buyer (as it benefits from having to redeem a lower amount if the credit event occurs), whereas the investor is the protection seller. In return for taking on credit risk, investors are offered higher coupons on CLNs than on otherwise identical bonds. Additionally, CLNs are usually issued at a discount, which further improves the potential return for investors.

Participation Instruments

Participation instruments allow investors to participate in the return of an underlying asset. Floating-rate bonds (whose coupon rates are reset periodically and brought in line with market interest rates) are examples of such instruments, as they offer investors the opportunity to participate in movements of interest rates.

FI

Most participation instruments are designed to give investors indirect exposure to a particular index or asset price that they are precluded from investing in directly. While both may offer equity exposure, it is important to note that participation instruments differ from capital-protected instruments in that they do not offer capital protection.

Leveraged Instruments

Leveraged instruments are structured financial instruments that aim to magnify returns. An inverse floater is an example of a leveraged instrument, where cash flows move in the opposite direction from changes in the reference rate.

An inverse floater's periodic coupon rate is determined as:

$$\text{Inverse floater coupon rate} = C - (L \times R)$$

- Inverse floaters with a coupon leverage greater than zero but lower than 1.0 are called **deleveraged inverse floaters**.
- Those with a coupon leverage greater than 1.0 are called **leveraged inverse floaters**.
- Inverse floaters often have a floor that specifies a minimum coupon rate (e.g., a floor may be set at zero to avoid the possibility of a negative coupon).

SHORT-TERM FUNDING ALTERNATIVES AVAILABLE TO BANKS

Retail deposits: These include funds deposited at the bank by individual and commercial depositors into their accounts.

Short-term wholesale funds: These include:

- Central bank funds.
- Interbank funds.
- Certificates of deposit (CDs).

Repurchase and Reverse Repurchase Agreements

A repurchase agreement is an arrangement between two parties, where one party sells a security to the other with a commitment to buy it back at a later date for a predetermined higher price. The difference between the (lower) selling price and the (higher) repurchase price is the interest cost of the loan. Effectively, what is happening is that the seller is borrowing funds from the buyer and putting up the security as collateral.

- The annualized interest cost of the loan is called the repo rate.
- A repurchase agreement for one day is known as an overnight repo, and an agreement for a longer period is known as a term repo.
- Repo rates are usually lower than the rates that a broker or bank would charge on a margin loan.
- The percentage difference between the market value of the security and the amount of the loan is known as the repo margin or haircut.
- Any coupon income received from the bond during the repo term belongs to the seller (borrower).
- Both parties in the repo face counterparty credit risk.
- When looking at things from the perspective of the seller or borrower, the transaction is referred to as a repo.
- When looking at things from the perspective of the buyer or lender, the transaction is referred to as a reverse repo.
  - Reverse repos are used to borrow securities to cover short positions.
- Standard practice is to define the transaction based on the perspective of the dealer.

Factors that Affect the Repo Rate

- Repo rates increase with the level of credit risk in the collateral.
- A longer term typically entails higher repo rates.
- Repo rates are lower when the collateral must be delivered to the lender.
- The more scarce a particular piece of collateral, the lower the repo rate.
- If rates for borrowing from other sources are higher, repo rates will also tend to be higher.

FI

Factors that Affect the Repo Margin

- The longer the term, the higher the repo margin.
- The higher the quality of the collateral, the lower the repo margin.
- The higher the creditworthiness of the counterparty, the lower the repo margin.
- The higher the demand or the lower the supply of the collateral, the lower the repo margin.

FI

INTRODUCTION TO FIXED-INCOME VALUATION
Cross-Reference to CFA Institute Assigned Reading #52

BOND PRICES AND THE TIME VALUE OF MONEY

Bond Pricing with a Market Discount Rate

- If the coupon rate offered on the bond equals the rate of return required by investors to compensate them for the risk inherent in the instrument, the bond will sell for its par value.
- If the coupon rate offered on the bond is higher than the required yield, the bond will sell for a **premium**.
- If the coupon rate offered on the bond is lower than the required yield, the bond will sell for a **discount**.
- The higher the discount rate, the lower the present value of each individual cash flow, and the lower the value of the fixed income security.
- The lower the discount rate, the higher the present value of each individual cash flow, and the higher the value of the fixed income security.

Yield-to-Maturity

The yield-to-maturity is the (uniform) interest rate that equates the sum of the present values of the bond's expected future cash flows (when discount at that rate) to its current price. It also represents the internal rate of return on the bond's cash flows given that:

FI

1. The investor holds on to the bond until maturity.
2. The issuer makes all promised payments on time in their full amount.
3. The investor is able to reinvest all coupon payments received during the term of the bond at the stated yield to maturity until the bond's maturity date.

Relationships between the Bond Price and Bond Characteristics

1. A bond's price is inversely related to the market discount rate (the inverse effect). When the discount rate increases (decreases), the price of the bond decreases (increases).
2. Given the same coupon rate and term to maturity, the percentage price change is greater in terms of absolute magnitude when the discount rate decreases than when it increases (the convexity effect).
3. For the same term to maturity, a lower coupon bond is more sensitive to changes in the market discount rate than a higher coupon bond (the coupon effect).
4. Generally speaking, for the same coupon rate, a longer term bond is more sensitive to changes in the market discount rate than a shorter term bond (the maturity effect). Note that while the maturity effect always holds for zero-coupon bonds and for bonds priced at par or premium to par, it does not always hold for long-term low coupon (but not zero-coupon) bonds that are trading at a discount.

Relationship between Price and Maturity

If the yield remains constant:

- A *premium* bond's value *decreases* towards par as it nears maturity.
- A *discount* bond's value *increases* towards par as it nears maturity.
- A *par* bond's value remains *unchanged* as it nears maturity.

Pricing Bonds with Spot Rates

The arbitrage-free valuation approach does not use the same rate to discount each cash flow, but uses the relevant spot rate to discount each cash flow that occurs at a different point in time. A spot rate (or zero rate) is the yield on a zero-coupon bond for a given maturity.

$$PV = \frac{PMT}{(1+Z_1)^1} + \frac{PMT}{(1+Z_2)^2} + \ldots + \frac{PMT+FV}{(1+Z_N)^N}$$

Flat Price, Accrued Interest and the Full Price

When the price of the bond is determined by calculating the present value of future cash flows as of the settlement date, the computed value is known as the full price (also known as the invoice or dirty price). This price includes accrued interest and reflects the amount that the buyer pays the seller. From this full price, the accrued interest is deducted to determine the flat price (also known as the clean price or quoted price) of the bond.

$$PV^{Full} = PV^{Flat} + AI$$

Accrued interest is the seller's proportional share of the next coupon payment. It is calculated as:

$$AI = t/T \times PMT$$

- For government bonds, the actual/actual day count convention is usually applied. The actual number of days is used including weekends, holidays, and weekdays.
- For corporate bonds, the 30/360 day-count convention is often used.

$$PV^{Full} = PV \times (1+r)^{t/T}$$

PV^{Full} = Full price of the bond (value between coupon payments)
PV = Price of bond at last/previous coupon payment date
r = Discount rate per period
t = Number of last coupon payment date to the settlement date
T = Number of days in coupon period
t/T = Fraction of coupon period that has gone by since last payment

FI

Matrix Pricing

Matrix pricing is used to estimate the market discount rate and price of bonds that are not actively traded. Essentially, prices of comparable (in terms of terms to maturity, coupon rates and credit quality) are used to interpolate the price of the subject bond. Matrix pricing can also be used when underwriting new bonds to estimate the required yield spread over the benchmark rate on the bonds to be issued.

Yield Measures for Fixed-Rate Bonds

The effective annual rate (or effective annual yield) on a fixed-rate bond depends on the assumed number of periods in the year, which is known as the periodicity of the stated annual rate or stated annual yield.

- An **annual-pay bond** would have a stated annual yield for periodicity of one. The stated annual yield would equal the discount rate per year.
- A **semiannual-pay bond** would have a stated annual yield for periodicity of two. The rate per semiannual period would be computed as the stated annual yield divided by two.
- A **quarterly-pay bond** would have a stated annual yield for periodicity of four. The rate per quarter would be computed as the stated annual yield divided by four.

Note that:

- Given the stated annual rate, as the number of compounding periods (periodicity) increases, the effective annual rate increases.
- Given the effective annual rate, as the number of compounding periods (periodicity) increases, the stated annual rate decreases.

FI

The stated annual rate that has a periodicity of two is known as a semiannual bond basis yield or semiannual bond equivalent yield. The semiannual bond basis yield is calculated as the yield per semiannual period multiplied by two.

Important: What we refer to as stated annual rate (SAR) is referred to in the curriculum as APR or annual percentage rate. We stick to SAR to keep your focus on a stated annual rate versus the effective annual rate. Just remember that if you see an annual percentage rate on the exam, it refers to the stated annual rate.

Converting Stated Annual Rates (SARs)

$$\left(1+\frac{SAR_M}{M}\right)^M = \left(1+\frac{SAR_N}{N}\right)^N$$

Bond Yield Quoting Conventions

- The street convention yield represents the internal rate of return on the bond's cash flows assuming all payments are made on scheduled dates regardless of whether any scheduled payment dates fall on weekends or holidays.
- The true yield uses these actual payment dates to compute the IRR.
- The government equivalent yield (usually quoted for corporate bonds) restates a yield-to-maturity based on a 30/360 day-count convention to one based on an actual/actual day-count convention.

- The current yield (also called the income yield or interest yield) is calculated as the sum of coupon payments received over the year divided by the flat price. The current yield is a relatively crude measure of the rate of return to an investor.
    - It neglects the frequency of coupon payments in the numerator.
    - It neglects any accrued interest in the denominator.
    - It neglects any gains (losses) from purchasing the bond at a discount (premium) and redeeming it for par.
- The simple yield is calculated as the sum of coupon payments received over the year plus (minus) straight line amortization of the gain (loss) from purchasing the bond at a discount (premium), divided by the flat price.

Yields for Callable Bonds

- The yield-to-call is computed for each call date (based on the call price and the number of periods until the call date), and then determine the yield-to-worst as the worst or lowest yield among the yield to maturity and the various yields to call for the bond.
- The option-adjusted yield is based on the option-adjusted price, which is calculated by adding the value of the embedded call option to the flat price of the callable bond. The option adjusted yield is lower than the yield to maturity on a callable bond because callable bonds offer higher yields than otherwise identical non-callable bonds to compensate investors for effectively selling the embedded call option to the issuer.

Yield Measures for Floating-Rate Notes

The effective coupon rate for a specified period is determined at the beginning of the period but actually paid out at the end of the period (in arrears).

If the quoted margin equals the required margin, the FRN will trade at par at each reset date, but if the quoted margin is lower (greater) than the required margin, the FRN will trade at a discount (premium).

Changes in the required margin can be caused by changes in the issue's (1) credit risk, (2) liquidity and/or (3) tax status.

Risk Exposure of Fixed- versus Floating-Rate Bonds

- Fixed-rate and floating-rate bonds respond very similarly when it comes to credit risk. An increase (decrease) in credit risk leads to a decline (increase) in the value of both types of bonds.
- However, fixed-and floating-rate bonds respond very differently when it comes to changes in benchmark interest rates.

Yield Measures for Money Market Instruments

Money-market instruments are short-term debt securities with maturities ranging from one day (e.g., repos) to one year (e.g., bank certificates of deposit). Money market yields differ from yields in the bond market in the following respects:

1. Bond yields-to-maturity are annualized and compounded. Money market yields are annualized but not compounded (they are stated on simple interest basis).
2. Bond yields-to-maturity can usually be calculated by applying standard time value of money analysis and using a financial calculator. Money market yields are often quoted in terms of nonstandard interest rates so users need to work with various pricing equations.
3. Bond yields-to-maturity are typically stated for a common periodicity for all terms-to-maturity. Money market instruments that have different times-to-maturity have different periodicities for the stated annual rate.

Pricing formula for money market instruments quoted on a discount rate basis:

$$PV = FV \times \left(1 - \frac{Days}{Year} \times DR\right)$$

$$DR = \left(\frac{Year}{Days}\right) \times \left(\frac{FV - PV}{FV}\right)$$

A money market discount rate understates the rate of return to the investor and understates the cost of borrowing for the issuer (because PV is generally less than FV).

Pricing formula for money market instruments quoted on an add-on rate basis:

$$PV = \frac{FV}{\left(1 + \frac{Days}{Year} \times AOR\right)}$$

$$AOR = \left(\frac{Year}{Days}\right) \times \left(\frac{FV - PV}{PV}\right)$$

The add-on rate a reasonable measure for the yield on a money market investment.

Typically money-market yields are converted to a rate known as the bond-equivalent yield or investment yield for comparisons. The bond equivalent yield is a money-market rate stated on a **365-day year** on an **add-on rate basis**.

Generally speaking, the lower the level of interest rates, the smaller the difference between the stated annual rates for any two periodicities.

The Maturity Structure of Interest Rates

The spot rate curve reflects spot rates for a range of maturities. The distinguishing feature of spot rates is that they are yields that have no element of reinvestment risk. Using spot rates provides a more accurate relationship between yields and terms to maturity relative to using yields to maturity on coupon-bearing Treasuries.

A yield curve for coupon bonds shows the yields-to-maturity for coupon-paying bonds of different maturities. To build the Treasury yield curve, analysts use only the most recently-issued and actively-traded government bonds as they have similar liquidity and tax status. YTMs for maturities where there are gaps can be estimated through a variety of interpolation methods.

A par curve represents a series of yields-to-maturity such that each bond trades at par. The par curve is derived from the spot rate curve.

Forward Curve

A forward rate represents the interest rate on a loan that will be originated at some point in the future. Forward rates are used to construct the forward curve, which represents a series of forward rates, each having the same horizon. Typically the forward curve shows one-year forward rates stated on a semiannual bond basis

Implied forward rates (also known as forward yields) can be computed from spot rates.

If the yields presented are semiannual bond basis:

$$\left(1+\frac{\text{6-mth spot rate}}{2}\right)\left(1+\frac{\text{6-mth forward rate 6 mths from now}}{2}\right)=\left(1+\frac{\text{12-mth spot rate}}{2}\right)^2$$

To calculate the x-period forward rate y periods from today, simply remember the following formula: Note that x and y here respresent the periodic spot rate.

$$(1+{}_yS_0)^y(1+{}_xf_y)^x=(1+{}_{x+y}S_0)^{x+y}$$

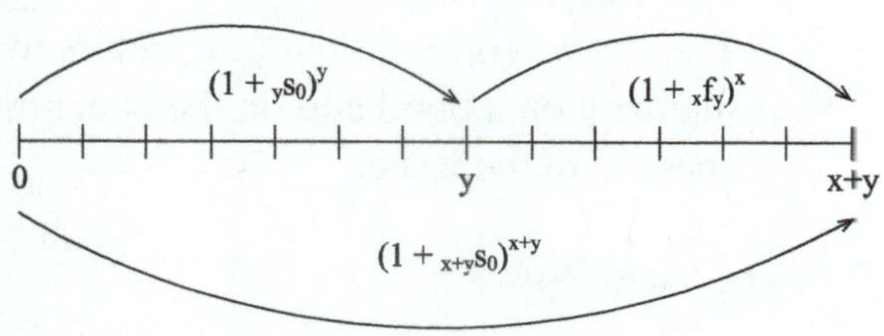

Example: Calculating Forward Rates

Calculate the 1-year forward rate 6 years from today if the 6-year spot rate is 6.25% and the 7-year spot rate is 6%.

Solution:

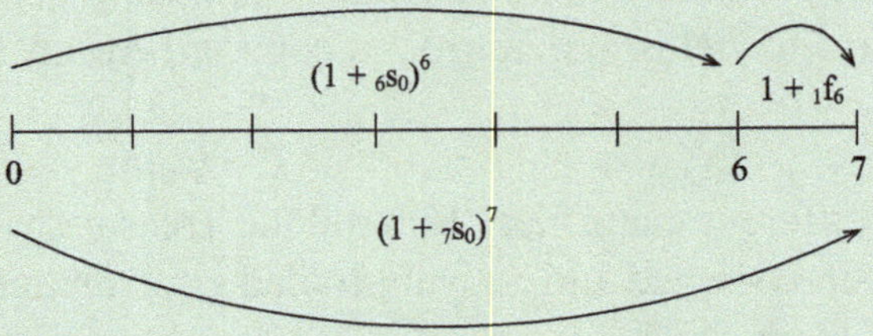

$$(1+{}_6s_0)^6(1+{}_1f_6)=(1+{}_7s_0)^7$$

$$(1+{}_1f_6)=\frac{(1.06)^7}{(1.0625)^6} \Rightarrow {}_1f_6=4.51\%$$

A forward rate can be looked upon as the marginal or incremental return from expanding the time to maturity by one more year or as a breakeven reinvestment rate. Forward rates are useful to investors in making maturity choice decisions.

Important: Please note that finance authors use different notation when it comes to forward rates. We use ${}_xf_y$, which refers to the x-period forward rate y years from today, or the interest rate on a loan that has a term of x years, where the loan will be originated y years from today. The CFA Program curriculum uses different notation. In the curriculum, the forward rate 2y5y refers to the 5-year rate 2 years into the future and 3y2y refers to the 2-year rate 3 years from now. We have stuck with our (different) notation because we feel it is easier to work with. You can work with either notation, as it won't affect your answers.

FI

YIELD SPREADS

Yield Spreads over Benchmark Rates

- The benchmark yield (or risk-free rate) captures **macroeconomic factors.** The benchmark can be broken down into (1) the expected inflation rate and (2) the expected real rate.
- The spread (or risk premium) refers to the difference between the yield-to-maturity on a bond and on the benchmark. It captures all **microeconomic factors** specific to the issuer.

Types of Yield Spreads

- The yield spread in basis points over an actual or interpolated government bond yield is known as the G-spread.
- The yield spread over the standard swap rate in the same currency and with the same tenor as the subject bond is known as the I-spread or interpolated spread to the swap curve.
- Note that the government bond yield or the swap rate used as the benchmark for a specific bond will change over time as the remaining term to maturity of the bond changes.
- For floating-rate bonds, Libor is often used as a benchmark. Note that Libor is an interbank rate, not a risk-free rate.

Yield Spreads over the Benchmark Yield Curve

Given the term to maturity of a security, the appropriate benchmark yield-to-maturity applies the same discount rate for each cash flow. Theoretically, this method is unappealing because each cash flow received from the bond carries a different amount of risk (typically, cash flows expected to be received further out into the future entail more risk). It makes more sense to use individual spot rate rates to discount each of the bond's expected cash flows as spot rates accurately capture the risk entailed by each corresponding cash flow (i.e., for each time horizon, there is a specific spot rate unless the yield curve is flat). Therefore, practitioners tend to favor use of the **z-spread** over the G- and I-spreads.

The z-spread (or **zero-volatility spread** or **static spread**) of a bond is a constant spread over the government (or interest rate swap) **spot rate curve**.

The z-spread is also used to calculate the **option-adjusted spread (OAS)** on a callable bond. The OAS is calculated by subtracting the value of the embedded call option (stated in terms of bps per year) from the z-spread.

$$\text{OAS} = \text{z-spread} - \text{Option value (bps per year)}$$

Stated simply, the OAS removes the cost of the option from the z-spread, so the OAS is the spread on top of the spot rate curve that the bond would offer if it were option-free. Since the embedded call option in a callable bond favors the issuer, the OAS (the spread that an otherwise identical option-free bond would offer) is less than the z-spread. An issuer would pay out more (in terms of yield) on a callable bond than on an option-free bond.

INTRODUCTION TO ASSET-BACKED SECURITIES
Cross-Reference to CFA Institute Assigned Reading #53

Benefits of Securitization

- It removes the layer between borrowers and investors.
- It allows investors to have a stronger legal claim on the collateral pool of assets.
- Investors can pick and choose the types of securities they want to invest in (in terms of interest rate and credit risk).
- Financial intermediaries are able to originate more loans (by using financing provided by outside investors to originate loans) than they would be able to if they were only able to issue loans that they could finance themselves.
- The increase in the total supply of loanable funds benefits organizations (governments and companies) that need to borrow.
- Since securitized bonds are sold in the public market, they enjoy much better liquidity (lower liquidity risk) than the original loans on bank balance sheets.
- Financial markets are made more efficient.
- Securitization encourages innovation in investment products, which can offer investors access to (otherwise directly unavailable) assets that match their risk, return, and maturity profiles.
- Even large investors, who may be able to purchase real estate loans, automobile loans, or credit card loans directly, would prefer to invest in asset-backed bonds since they would not be required to originate, monitor, and collect payments from the underlying loans themselves.
- ABS offer companies an alternative means of raising finance that can be considered alongside bond and equity issuance.

FI

Parties to a Securitization

Party	Description	Party in Illustration
Seller	Originates the loans and sells loans to the SPV	ABC Company
Issuer/Trust	The SPV that buys the loans from the seller and issues the asset-backed securities	SPV
Servicer	Services the loans	Servicer

In order for a securitization to serve its purpose, the SPV must be a bankruptcy remote entity, i.e., its obligations remain secure even if the parent company goes bankrupt.

RESIDENTIAL MORTGAGE LOANS

- A mortgage loan is a borrowing that is secured by some form of real estate.
- Upon initiation of the mortgage loan, the borrower's equity equals the down payment, but over time, the borrower's equity changes as a result of (1) changes in the market value of the property and (2) payment of periodic mortgage payments (that include a principal component).

- The lower (higher) the LTV ratio, the higher (lower) the borrower's equity, the less (more) likely the borrower is to default, and the more (less) protection the lender has for recovering the amount loaned in case the borrower defaults.
- Most mortgages around the world are structured as amortizing loans.
- A mortgage loan may allow the borrower to prepay (make a principal repayment that exceeds the scheduled repayment for the month) a portion, or the entire amount, of the outstanding mortgage principal at any point during the term of the mortgage.

RESIDENTIAL MORTGAGE-BACKED SECURITIES

- Agency RMBSs are issued by (1) federal agencies (e.g., Ginnie Mae, which is a federally related institution), and (2) quasi-government entities (e.g., Freddie Mac and Fannie Mae, which are government sponsored enterprises or GSEs).
    - There is no credit risk for agency RMBSs issued by Ginnie Mae as they are backed by the full faith and credit of the U.S. Government.
    - There is minimal credit risk for agency RMBSs issued by GSEs as they are guaranteed by the GSEs themselves.
        - Mortgage loans issued by GSEs must satisfy specific underwriting standards established by various government agencies to qualify for the collateral pool backing agency RMBSs issued by GSEs.
- Non-agency RMBSs are issued by private entities.
    - They typically come with credit enhancements to reduce credit risk.
        - There are no restrictions on the types of non-agency mortgage loans that can be used to back non-agency RMBSs.

FI

MORTGAGE PASS-THROUGH SECURITIES

- A mortgage pass-through security is created when shares or participation certificates in a pool of mortgage loans are sold to investors.
- The cash flow collected from the collateral pool includes scheduled principal and interest payments, and prepayments.
- The amount and timing of cash flows paid to investors in the pass-through securities are different from those of the cash flows collected from the collateral pool of mortgages.
- Payments made by borrowers pass through the government agency (and on to investors) net of servicing and guaranteeing fees. Therefore, the pass-through rate (coupon rate on the pass-through security, which is net interest/net coupon) is lower than the mortgage rate on the underlying pool of mortgages.
- Mortgage loans that are securitized to create pass-through securities do not all carry the same mortgage rate and maturity. Therefore, a weighted average coupon rate (WAC) and weighted average maturity (WAM) are calculated to describe the pool of mortgages that serves as collateral for the pass-through securities.
- Market participants use average life (the weighted average time it will take for all the principal payments, i.e., scheduled repayments and projected prepayments, to be received) as a measure of the interest rate risk of a mortgage-backed security.
    - The average life of an RMBS depends on the assumed prepayment speed—the higher the prepayment speed assumed, the shorter the average life of the mortgage backed security.

- The prepayment rate is measured in terms of the single monthly mortality rate (SMM). It is calculated as the amount of prepayment for a month as a percentage of the mortgage balance that was available to be prepaid that month.

Contraction Risk versus Extension Risk

Prepayment risk encompasses contraction risk and extension risk.

Contraction risk occurs when interest rates fall.

- Option-free bond prices increase when interest rates fall. However, for mortgage loans, the issuer (homeowner) has the right to prepay and can easily do so by refinancing her mortgage. This option to prepay is similar to the call option granted to the issuer of a callable bond. When interest rates fall, it becomes feasible for the mortgage issuer/borrower to prepay (just like it becomes feasible for an issuer to call a callable bond), so the upside potential of the pass-through security is limited. It experiences price compression at low interest rates and exhibits negative convexity.
- To make things worse, when interest rates fall, refinancing activity typically increases and leads to an increase in prepayments, reducing or shortening the average life of the pass-through. The (higher-than-expected) cash flows from the pass-through must then be reinvested at current (lower) rates.

Extension risk occurs when interest rates rise.

FI

- The price of a pass-through (just like the price of any bond) will decline when interest rates increase.
- To make things worse, refinancing activity and prepayment rates slow down when interest rates rise, increasing or lengthening the average expected life of the pass-through. Consequently, a greater-than-anticipated amount remains invested in the pass-through at the coupon rate of the instrument, which is lower than current interest rates.

COLLATERALIZED MORTGAGE OBLIGATIONS

Collateralized mortgage obligations (CMOs) redistribute the cash flows from mortgage pass-through securities into packages/classes/tranches with different risk exposures to prepayment risk.

- For CMOs, the mortgage-related products from which cash flows are obtained are considered the collateral, i.e., a pool of mortgage pass-through security serves as the collateral. For mortgage pass-through securities, a pool of mortgage loans serves as collateral.

Sequential-Pay Tranches

- Each class of bond is retired sequentially.
- Interest payments are periodically made to each tranche based on its coupon rate and principal amount outstanding at the beginning of the period.
- Principal payments are first forwarded to Tranche A, then to Tranche B (after Tranche A has been fully paid off) and so on.

- The principal payment pattern for each of the tranches is not known. However, the shorter-term tranches receive protection from extension risk, while the longer term tranches receive protection from contraction risk.

Planned Amortization Class (PAC) Tranches

- PAC bonds bring increased predictability of cash flows, as they specify a repayment schedule that will be satisfied as long as actual prepayments realized from the collateral fall within a pre-defined band.
- The greater certainty in payments for the PAC tranche comes at the expense of greater uncertainty for the support or companion tranche, which absorbs the prepayment risk.
- The average life of the support tranche fluctuates more wildly than that of the PAC tranche.
- The support tranche provides **two-sided protection** (i.e., protection against extension **and** contraction risk) to the PAC tranche.
- The greater the par value of the support tranche relative to that of the PAC tranche, the greater the prepayment protection for the PAC, the lower the PAC's average life variability, and the greater the support tranche's average life variability.

Floating-Rate Tranches

- Even though the collateral for CMOs carries a fixed rate, it is possible to create a floating-rate tranche (along with an inverse-floater tranche) from any of the fixed-rate tranches in a CMO structure.
- Since the floater varies positively with interest rates, and the inverse floater varies negatively with interest rates, they offset each other.

NON-AGENCY RESIDENTIAL MORTGAGE-BACKED SECURITIES

Non-agency RMBSs are not guaranteed by the government or a GSE, which make the evaluation of credit risk an important consideration when investing in them.

- Cash flows are distributed according to a set of rules that determines the distribution of interest and principal payments to tranches with varying levels of priority/seniority.
- There are also rules for allocating realized losses, with senior tranches having a priority claim over payments and subordinated tranches absorbing losses.
- When it comes to forecasting cash flows on non-agency RMBSs, investors must make assumptions regarding (1) the default rate for the collateral and (2) the recovery rate.

Internal Credit Enhancements

- Reserve funds:
    - Cash reserve funds: The entity seeking to raise the funds deposits some of the proceeds of sale of the loan pool with the SPV. This cash can be used to pay for potential future losses.

  - Excess spread accounts: The excess spread or cash that remains after the payment of net coupon, servicing fees, and all other expenses is kept in reserve to pay for future credit losses on the collateral.
- Overcollateralization: This refers to a situation where the value of the collateral exceeds the par value of the securities issued by the SPV.
  - The amount of overcollateralization for an issue changes over time due to (1) defaults, (2) amortization, and (3) prepayments.
- Senior/subordinate structure: This type of structure has senior bond classes and subordinate bond classes (also known as non-senior/junior bond classes).
  - The structure basically provides credit tranches as the subordinate bond classes provide credit protection to the senior classes.
  - To provide credit protection to investors in the senior bond classes, a shifting interest mechanism is added to the structure. This mechanism locks out subordinated classes from receiving payments for a period of time if the collateral performs poorly.

External Credit Enhancements

External credit enhancements are third-party guarantees for payments to security holders should the issuer not be able to meet payment requirements.

- Monoline insurers are the most common third-party financial guarantors.

Time Tranching versus Credit Tranching

FI

- Time tranching occurs when prepayment risk (or the timing of distribution of cash flows) is redistributed among the various classes of ABS as in a sequential-pay CMO structure.
- Credit tranching occurs when credit risk (or risk of loss from default) is redistributed among the various classes of ABS as in a senior/subordinate structure

COMMERCIAL MORTGAGE BACKED SECURITIES (CMBS)

CMBSs are backed by a pool of commercial mortgage loans on income-generating properties (e.g., apartments, warehouses, shopping centres, etc.). In the U.S. (and many other countries), commercial mortgage loans are non-recourse loans. Therefore, evaluation of credit risk for commercial mortgage loans requires examining the income-generating capacity and value of each property on a stand-alone basis.

Two measures are commonly used to evaluate the potential credit performance of a commercial property:

- The debt-service coverage (DSC) ratio is used to evaluate the adequacy of income generated from the property to service the loan. It is calculated as net operating income (NOI) divided by debt service. NOI is calculated as rental income minus cash operating expenses and a non-cash replacement reserve that reflects depreciation of the property over time.
    - A ratio greater than 1 means that cash flow from the property covers debt servicing costs adequately.
    - The higher the ratio, the lower the credit risk
- The loan-to-value ratio equals the loan amount divided by the appraised value of the property.
    - The lower the ratio, the lower the credit risk.

Basic CMBS Structure

- A credit-rating agency determines the level of credit enhancement required for the issue to attain the credit rating desired by the issuer.
- Different bond classes are created with each class having a different priority on cash flows. The various bond classes are retired sequentially with all principal repayments, prepayments, and proceeds from default (from selling repossessed properties) being used to repay the highest-rated tranche first.
- Losses from loan defaults are charged against the lowest-rated tranche first. If this tranche is not rated by credit-rating agencies, it is known as the first-loss piece, residual tranche, or equity tranche.
- The equity tranche typically has no specific interest rate (as it is the residual tranche). Investors price it based on the expected residual rate of return. Actual returns can be better or worse than expected depending on actual future interest rate movements and actual defaults.
- Interest payments are made to all tranches.
- Typically, CMBS investors have significant call protection, which actually results in these securities trading more like corporate bonds than like RMBSs.
    - Call protection at the loan level can come in form of prepayment lockouts, defeasance, prepayment penalties, and yield maintenance charges.
    - Call protection at the structure level comes from credit tranches.
- Most commercial loans that back CMBSs have balloon maturity provisions, i.e., they require a significant amount of principal to be repaid at maturity (as opposed to during the term of the loan). This exposes investors to balloon risk, which is more like extension risk as there is usually a workout period during which the borrower and lender try to modify the original terms of the loan to ensure eventual repayment.

FI

NON-MORTGAGE ASSET BACKED SECURITIES

The collateral backing asset-backed securities can be classified as either amortizing or non-amortizing assets.

Amortizing loans:

- The periodic cash flows include interest payments, principal repayments (in accordance with an amortization schedule), and (if allowed) prepayments.
- Examples include residential mortgage loans and automobile loans.

Non-amortizing loans:

- These only require a monthly minimum payment with no scheduled principal payment.
- If the payment received is less than the interest amount due, the shortfall is added to the outstanding loan balance.
- If the payment is greater than the interest amount due, the excess serves to reduce the outstanding loan balance.
- Since there is no scheduled principal payment amount, the concept of prepayment does not apply to non-amortizing assets.
- Examples include credit card receivables.

The type of collateral (amortizing versus non-amortizing assets) has a significant effect on the structure of the securitization.

- When amortizing assets are securitized, the total face value (total amount outstanding) declines over time due to scheduled repayments and prepayments, and the number of outstanding loans (composition of the collateral) declines as a result of (1) defaults and (2) full principal repayments or full amortizations.
- On the other hand, securitizations of non-amortizing loans usually take the form of a revolving structure, where the composition of the collateral can change over the term of the securities. This is because principal repayments can either be (1) reinvested by purchasing additional loans, or (2) passed on to security holders.
    - During an initial lockout or revolving period (which immediately follows the origination of the transaction), all principal repayments are reinvested in additional loans with a principal amount equal to the total principal amount received. While this can result in a fewer total number of individual loans comprising the collateral, the total face value outstanding remains the same.
    - During the principal amortization period (which follows the lockout period), principal repayments are not used to purchase additional loans, but are distributed to security holders.

Auto Loan Receivable-Backed Securities

These securities are backed by auto loan and lease receivables. Cash flows for auto loan-backed securities consist of regularly scheduled monthly interest and principal payments and prepayments.

- Generally speaking, auto loan-backed securitizations come with some form of credit enhancement.
- Typically, the securitizations involve a senior/subordinate structure (to provide credit protection to the senior tranches). Further, some securitizations also involve reserve accounts, overcollateralization, and excess interest on the receivables.

Credit Card Receivable-Backed Securities

- The cash flow from a pool of credit card receivables includes (1) finance charges collected (interest charges on the unpaid balance after the grace period), (2) fees (for late payments and membership), and (3) principal repayment.
- Interest payments are made to security holders periodically (monthly, quarterly, or semiannually). The interest rate may be fixed or floating (typically with no cap).
- During the revolving period (also known as the lockout period), any principal repayments from the pool of receivables are used to purchase additional receivables to maintain the size of the pool. During this period, the cash flow passed on to security holders consists only of (1) finance charges and (2) fees collected from the pool of receivables. Principal repayments are only passed on to security holders once the principal-amortizing period sets in.
- Even though receivables in a revolving structure may not be prepaid (since there is no concept of prepayment here), all the bonds may be retired early if an early or rapid amortization provision is triggered.

COLLATERALIZED DEBT OBLIGATIONS

A CDO is a security that is backed by a diversified pool of securities.

- Like an ABS, a CDO also involves the creation of an SPV.
- A CDO manager (also known as collateral manager) is responsible for managing the collateral portfolio of assets (consisting of debt obligations).
- The funds used to purchase the collateral assets are raised from the issuance of bonds to investors. Bond classes may include senior bonds, mezzanine bonds (with credit ratings between senior and subordinated bonds), and subordinated bonds (also known as the residual or equity class).
- Restrictive covenants are placed on the manager to ensure that the credit ratings assigned to the various tranches at issuance are maintained during the term of the CDO.
- Cash flows from the underlying portfolio of assets include (1) coupon interest payments, (2) proceeds from maturing assets, and (3) proceeds from sale of assets. These cash flows are used to make interest and principal payments to the various bond classes.
- From the asset manager/issuer's perspective, the aim is to earn a rate of return on the collateral pool of assets that is higher than the interest costs of bonds issued. This excess return accrues to the equity holders and the CDO manager. Effectively, issuing a CDO is like undertaking a leveraged transaction where the idea is to use borrowed funds (raised from bonds issued) to generate a return that exceeds the funding cost.
- From the investors' perspective, each class of bonds entails a different level of risk. Senior/mezzanine bond investors may be able to earn a potentially higher return than on a comparably-rated corporate bond by gaining exposure to debt products that they may not otherwise be able to purchase. Equity investors can earn an equity-type return by taking the (higher) risk associated with the subordinated class.
- Certain restrictions are placed on the manager (via various tests and limits) to ensure that the senior bond classes are adequately protected and the ratings issued to the bond classes are maintained. Failure to meet these tests may trigger an immediate payoff to the senior bond classes until the tests are satisfied. This payoff would have the effect of deleveraging the CDO (as the asset manager's reliance on its cheapest source of funding, i.e., senior bonds, would be reduced).

The major difference between an ABS and a CDO is that in an ABS the cash flows from the collateral pool are used to pay off bond holders without the active management of collateral. In a CDO, the manager buys and sells debt obligations (assets) to (1) generate the cash flow required to repay bond holders and to (2) earn a competitive return for the equity tranche.

Study Session 16: Fixed Income—Analysis of Risk

FI

UNDERSTANDING FIXED-INCOME RISK AND RETURN

Cross-Reference to CFA Institute Assigned Reading #54

Sources of Return on a Fixed-Rate Bond

1. Receipt of promised coupon and principal payments.
2. Reinvestment of coupon payments.
3. Potential capital gains/losses if the bond is sold prior to maturity.

If a bond is purchased at a premium/discount, it adds another dimension to the total rate of return.

Horizon Yield, Carrying Value and Capital Gains and Losses

The horizon yield equals the YTM at issuance if the following two conditions hold:

- The bond is sold at its carrying value, i.e., at a price that lies on its constant-yield price trajectory.
- All coupon payments can be reinvested at a rate that equals the bond's YTM at issuance until date of sale.

Carrying value refers to the value of a bond (at any time between the purchase date and maturity date) that entails the same YTM as when the bond was purchased. The carrying value reflects amortization of any premium/discount since the time of purchase. Capital gains/losses arise if a bond is sold at a price different from its carrying value.

FI

Interest Rate Risk

There are two types of **interest rate risk**, which offset each other:

- **Reinvestment risk.** The future value of any interim cash flows received from a bond (these could be coupon payments as well as principal repayments on amortizing bonds) increases when interest rates rise and decreases when interest rates decline.
- **Market price risk.** The selling price of a bond (at any point during its term or before maturity) decreases when interest rates rise and increases when interest rates decline.

Reinvestment risk matters more to a long-term investors, while market price risk matters more to short-term investors. Therefore, two investors who are holding the same bond can have different exposures to interest rate risk depending on their individual investment horizons.

INTEREST RATE RISK OF FIXED-RATE BONDS

Duration

Duration measures the sensitivity or responsiveness of a bond's **full price** (including accrued interest) to changes in **its yield-to-maturity** (or market discount rate). Broadly speaking, duration can be classified as:

- Yield duration, which measures the responsiveness of a bond's price with respect to **its own yield-to-maturity**. Yield duration statistics include Macaulay duration, modified duration, money duration and the price value of a basis point.
- Curve duration, which measures the responsiveness of a bond's price with respect to **a benchmark yield curve** (e.g., government yield curve, forward curve, or government par curve). Coupon duration statistics include effective duration.

Macaulay Duration

Macaulay duration represents the weighted average of the time it would take to receive all the bond's promised cash flows, where the weights are calculated as the present value of each cash flow divided by the bond's **full price**.

Macaulay duration (in terms of periods) can also be computed using the following closed-form formula:

FI

$$\text{MacDur} = \left\{ \frac{1+r}{r} - \frac{1+r+[N \times (c-r)]}{c \times [(1+r)^N - 1] + r} \right\} - (t/T)$$

Macaulay duration is typically not used as a measure of the interest rate sensitivity of a bond's price. However, it does have has some useful applications, including measurement of the duration gap.

Modified Duration

Modified duration is calculated by dividing Macaulay duration by one plus the yield per period.

$$\text{ModDur} = \frac{\text{MacDur}}{1+r}$$

Modified duration can be used to estimate the percentage price change for a bond in response to a change in **its yield-to-maturity**.

$$\%\Delta PV^{\text{Full}} \approx -\text{AnnModDur} \times \Delta\text{Yield}$$

- Modified duration only provides a linear estimate of the change in the price of a bond in response to a change in yields.
- It provides good estimates for bond prices in response to relatively small changes in yields, but its estimating accuracy fades with larger changes in yields as the curvature (convexity) of the price-yield profile becomes more pronounced.

If Macaulay duration is not already known, annual modified duration can be estimated using the following formula:

$$\text{ApproxModDur} = \frac{(PV_-) - (PV_+)}{2 \times (\Delta\text{Yield}) \times (PV_0)}$$

- This approximation basically estimates the slope of the line tangent to the price-yield profile for a bond at a particular yield level.
- The value for approximate modified duration obtained by applying this formula gives us the percentage change in the price of a bond in response to a 100 bps (1%) change in yields.
- The percentage price change if yields were to change by 50 basis points would be half the figure obtained from applying the formula.

We can also use the approximate modified duration (ApproxModDur) to estimate Macaulay duration (ApproxMacDur) by applying the following formula:

$$\text{ApproxMacDur} = \text{ApproxModDur} \times (1 + r)$$

FI

Effective Duration

Effective duration (also known as **OAS duration**) measures the sensitivity of a bond's price to a change in **the benchmark yield curve**.

$$\text{EffDur} = \frac{(PV_-) - (PV_+)}{2 \times (\Delta\text{Curve}) \times (PV_0)}$$

Note that:

- Effective duration is a **curve duration** statistic that measures interest rate risk in terms of a change in the benchmark yield curve (ΔCurve).
- Modified duration is a **yield duration** statistic that measures interest rate risk in terms of a change in the bond's own yield-to-maturity (ΔYield).

Effective duration is the appropriate measure of risk **for bonds with embedded call options**, including callable bonds (and mortgage-backed bonds).

- Modified or Macaulay duration (essentially, just one statistic) can be computed to estimate the percentage price change for a **traditional fixed-rate bond** in response to a change in the benchmark yield and/or credit spread.

- On the other hand, **for bonds with embedded options** (where there is no well-defined internal rate of return), a curve duration statistic must be computed to measure the effects of a change in benchmark yields, and a separate measure (e.g., credit duration) must be computed to measure the effects of a change in the credit spread.

Further, note that unlike modified duration, effective duration does not necessarily provide more accurate estimates for changes in a bond's price if we use a smaller change in benchmark rates.

Finally, although effective duration is the appropriate interest rate risk measure for bonds With embedded options, it is also used for traditional bonds to supplement the information provided by modified and Macaulay duration.

Key Rate Duration

Key rate duration (or partial duration) is a measure of a bond's (or bond portfolio's) sensitivity to a change in the benchmark yield for a given maturity. Key rate durations are used to assess shaping or yield curve risk for a bond, i.e., the bond's sensitivity to changes in the shape of the benchmark yield curve, or non-parallel shifts in the yield curve (e.g., the yield curve becoming steeper or flatter).

For parallel shifts in the benchmark yield curve, key rate durations will suggest the same interest rate sensitivity as effective duration.

FI

Properties of Bond Durations

Fraction of the coupon period that has elapsed (t/T):

All other things remaining the same, Macaulay duration falls as time passes through a coupon period, and then jumps after each coupon payment (creating a saw tooth-like pattern).

Time-to-maturity:

- For fixed-rate coupon bonds trading at par or premium to par, longer times-to-maturity correspond to a higher Macaulay duration.
  - However, Macaulay duration for these bonds never rises above a threshold level defined by MacDur = (1 + r)/r
- For fixed-rate coupon bonds trading at a discount, longer times-to-maturity **generally** correspond to a higher Macaulay duration.
  - Given a long enough time-to-maturity, Macaulay duration for discount bonds actually rises to a maximum level that lies above MacDur = (1 + r)/r.
  - However, after reaching its maximum level, as time-to-maturity further increases, Macaulay duration for discount bonds starts falling back towards (1 + r)/r if the coupon rate is low relative to the yield-to-maturity.
- The Macaulay duration for a zero-coupon bond equals its time-to-maturity.
- For a non-callable perpetuity (or consol) i.e., a bond that pays a fixed coupon forever, Macaulay duration equals the threshold level MacDur = (1 + r)/r.

Coupon rate:

All other things remaining the same, a lower-coupon bond has higher duration and more interest rate risk than a higher-coupon bond.

Yield-to-maturity:

All other things remaining the same, a lower yield-to-maturity bond has higher duration and more interest rate risk than a higher yield-to-maturity bond.

Callable Bonds

- The price of a callable bond is always *lower* than the price of an otherwise identical non-callable bond. The difference represents the value of the embedded call option.

When interest rates are **high** relative to the coupon rate:

- It is highly unlikely that the issuer will call the bond, so the value of the embedded call option is relatively low.
- Therefore, the effective durations (slopes of the price-yield profiles) of the callable and non-callable bonds are very similar.

When interest rates are **low** relative to the coupon rate:

- It becomes more likely that the issuer will call the bond (and exercise the option to refinance at a lower cost of funds), so the embedded call option gains value for the issuer.
- As interest rates fall, the callable bond suffers "price compression."
- The effective duration (slope of the price-yield profile) of the callable bond is *lower* than that of an otherwise identical non-callable bond – its expected life shortens as the weighted average time to receipt of cash is reduced.

Putable Bonds

- The price of a putable bond is always greater than the price of an otherwise identical non-putable bond. The difference represents the value of the embedded put option.

When interest rates are **low** relative to the coupon rate:

- It is highly unlikely that the investor will put the bond back to the issuer, so the value of the embedded put option is relatively low.
- Therefore, the effective durations (slopes of the price-yield profiles) of the putable and non-putable bonds are very similar.

When interest rates are **high** relative to the coupon rate:

- It becomes more likely that the investor will put the bond back to the issuer, so the embedded put option gains value for the investor.
- As interest rates rise, the putable bond does not lose as much value as an otherwise identical non-putable bond. The put price effectively serves as a floor on its value.
- The effective duration (slope of the price-yield profile) of the putable bond is lower than that of an otherwise identical non- putable bond- its expected life shortens as the weighted average time to receipt of cash is reduced.

To summarize, the presence of an embedded option (be it a call or a put) *reduces* the duration of the bond and makes it less sensitive to changes in the benchmark yield curve, assuming there is no change in credit risk.

Computing the Duration of a Bond Portfolio

1. Compute the weighted average of time to receipt of the portfolio's aggregate cash flows.

   Under this method, projected cash flows on all (1) traditional bonds and (2) bonds with embedded options held in the portfolio are aggregated to determine the portfolio's cash flow yield (i.e., internal rate of return based on those projected cash flows), which is then used to compute Macaulay and modified duration for the portfolio. While theoretically accurate, this method is difficult to implement in practice.

2. Compute the weighted average of the durations of the individual bonds held in the portfolio.

   Under this method, Macaulay and modified duration statistics for a bond portfolio are computed as the weighted average of the statistics for the individual bonds that comprise the portfolio, where each bond's weight equals the proportion of the total portfolio's market value that it comprises (based on **full prices**).

FI

$$\text{Portfolio duration} = w_1 D_1 + w_2 D_2 + \ldots.. + w_N D_N$$

Money Duration and Price Value of a Basis Point

Money duration (or dollar duration) is a measure of the *dollar* (or whichever currency the bond is denominated in) *price change* in response to a change in yields.

$$\text{MoneyDur} = \text{AnnModDur} \times PV^{Full}$$

The estimated (dollar) change in the price of the bond is calculated as:

$$\Delta PV^{Full} = -\text{MoneyDur} \times \Delta\text{Yield}$$

The price value of a basis point (PVBP) estimates the change in the full price of a bond in response to a 1 bp change in its yield-to-maturity.

$$\text{PVBP} = \frac{(PV_-) - (PV_+)}{2}$$

Bond Convexity

Duration *underestimates* the price increase caused by a reduction in yields, and *overestimates* the decrease in prices when yields rise. Therefore, price estimates of option-free bonds based on duration must be revised upwards to bring them closer to their actual values. This revision is performed via the convexity adjustment. The more the curvature or convexity of the price-yield relationship, the more significant the convexity adjustment becomes.

Annual convexity can be approximated using the following equation:

$$\text{ApproxCon} = \frac{(\text{PV}_-) + (\text{PV}_+) - [2 \times (\text{PV}_0)]}{(\Delta\text{Yield})^2 \times (\text{PV}_0)}$$

The percentage change in a bond's full price can be estimated as:

$$\%\Delta\text{PV}^{\text{Full}} \approx (-\text{AnnModDur} \times \Delta\text{Yield}) + \left[\frac{1}{2} \times \text{AnnConvexity} \times (\Delta\text{Yield})^2\right]$$

The money convexity of a bond is its annual convexity multiplied by the full price of the bond such that:

$$\Delta\text{PV}^{\text{Full}} \approx (-\text{MoneyDur} \times \Delta\text{Yield}) + \left[\frac{1}{2} \times \text{MoneyCon} \times (\Delta\text{Yield})^2\right]$$

Factors that Affect Convexity

- The longer the term-to-maturity, the greater the convexity.
- The lower the coupon rate, the greater the convexity.
- The lower the yield-to-maturity, the greater the convexity.
- The greater the dispersion of cash flows, the greater the convexity.

Given the same price, yield-to-maturity and modified duration, a more convex bond will outperform a less convex bond in both bull and bear markets.

Convexity for Bonds with Embedded Options

For callable bonds (and other bonds with embedded options) the first-order effect of a change in the benchmark yield curve is measured by **effective** duration, and the second-order effect of a change in the benchmark yield curve is measured by **effective convexity**. Effective convexity is a **curve convexity** statistic.

$$\text{EffCon} = \frac{[(\text{PV}_-) + (\text{PV}_+)] - [2 \times (\text{PV}_0)]}{(\Delta\text{Curve})^2 \times (\text{PV}_0)}$$

Negative convexity (also known as concavity) is an important feature of callable bonds. When the benchmark yield is high, callable and non-callable bonds experience similar price changes to changes in benchmark yields. However, as benchmark yields decline, there comes a point where the callable bond moves into negative convexity territory, where the embedded call option holds significant value to the issuer and is highly likely to be exercised.

Putable bonds always have positive convexity.

INTEREST RATE RISK AND THE INVESTMENT HORIZON

Yield Volatility

Changes in bond prices result from two factors:

1. The impact per basis point change in the yield-to-maturity. This factor is captured by duration and convexity; and
2. The number of basis points in the change in yield-to-maturity. This factor is captured by yield volatility.

Investment Horizon, Macaulay Duration and Interest Rate Risk

Given a particular assumption about yield volatility, Macaulay duration indicates the investment horizon for which coupon reinvestment risk and market price risk offset each other. This is one of the applications of duration where "years-based" interpretation is meaningful and where Macaulay duration is used rather than modified duration.

When interest rates rise:

- Money duration measures the immediate decline in the value of the bond.
- Over time, the value of the bond is pulled up to par.
- The gain in future value of reinvested coupon starts out small, but increases at an increasing rate over time.
- At a certain point during the life of the bond, the gain on reinvested coupon and the loss on the sale of the bond offset each other. That point is the Macaulay duration of the bond.

When interest rates fall:

- Money duration measures the immediate increase in the value of the bond.
- Over time, the value of the bond is pulled down to par.
- The loss in future value of reinvested coupon starts out small, but increases at an increasing rate over time.
- At a certain point during the life of the bond, the gain on sale of the bond and the loss on the future value of reinvested coupon offset each other. That point is the Macaulay duration of the bond.

Important Takeaways

1. When the investment horizon is *greater* than the Macaulay duration of the bond, coupon reinvestment risk dominates market price risk. In this case, the investor is concerned about interest rates *falling.*
2. When the investment horizon is *less* than the Macaulay duration of the bond, market price risk dominates coupon reinvestment risk. In this case, the investor is concerned about interest rates *rising.*
3. When the investment horizon equals the Macaulay duration of the bond, coupon reinvestment risk and market price risk offset each other.

The difference between the Macaulay duration of a bond and the investment horizon is known as the duration gap.

$$\text{Duration gap} = \text{Macaulay duration} - \text{Investment horizon}$$

As time passes, (1) the investment horizon falls and (2) the Macaulay duration of the bond also changes, so the duration gap changes as well.

CREDIT AND LIQUIDITY RISK

For fixed-income securities, changes in the components of the overall yield-to-maturity do not occur in isolation i.e., there is interaction between changes in benchmark yields and spreads, between changes in the expected inflation rate and the expected real interest rate, and between changes in credit and liquidity risk. Therefore, for a fixed-rate bond, "inflation duration" or a "credit duration" all refer to the same number and we can use modified duration and convexity to estimate the change in the value of a bond in response to any change in the yield-to-maturity regardless of the source of the yield-to-maturity change.

FUNDAMENTALS OF CREDIT ANALYSIS

Cross-Reference to CFA Institute Assigned Reading #55

Credit risk refers to the risk of loss resulting from a borrower's failure to make full and timely payments of interest and/or principal. It has two components:

- Default risk or default probability refers to the probability of a borrower failing to meet its obligations to make full and timely payments of principal and interest under the terms of the bond indenture.
- Loss severity or loss given default refers to the portion of the bond's value that an investor would lose if a default actually occurred. Loss severity equals 1 minus the recovery rate.

The **expected loss** is calculated as the probability of default multiplied by loss severity.

$$\text{Expected loss} = \text{Default probability} \times \text{Loss severity given default}$$

Spread risk refers to the risk of a widening of the yield spread on the bond. It encompasses:

- Downgrade risk or credit migration risk: This is the risk that the issuer's credit worthiness may deteriorate during the term of the bond, causing rating agencies to downgrade the credit rating of the issue.
- Market liquidity risk: This is the risk that an investor may have to sell her investment at a price lower than its market value due to insufficient volumes (liquidity) in the market. Two issuer-specific factors that affect liquidity risk are the size of the issuer and the credit quality of the issuer.

FI

Seniority Ranking

Companies may issue debt with different rankings in terms of seniority, where the most senior or highest-ranking debt has the first claim on the issuer's cash flows and assets in case of an issuer default or restructuring. Debt may be classified as:

- Secured debt: Holders of secured debt have a direct claim on certain assets and their associated cash flows.
- Unsecured debt or debentures: Holders of unsecured debt only have a general claim on the issuer's assets and cash flow.

In the event of default, secured debt ranks higher than unsecured debt in the **priority of claims**.
Further, within each category of debt, there are sub-rankings.

Recovery Rates

All creditors at the same level in the capital structure are treated as one class irrespective of (1) the coupon rate offered on their bonds, and (2) when their bonds are maturing. This is referred to as bonds ranking pari passu (i.e., on an equal footing) in right of payment.

Recovery rates are highest for the senior-most class of debt in the priority of claims and fall with each lower rank of seniority. Therefore, the lower the seniority of the bond, the greater the credit risk and this is why investors demand a higher yield to invest in lower ranked debt instruments.

Apart from the relative seniority of a particular bond, recovery rates also vary (1) by industry and (2) depending on when the default occurs in a credit cycle.

Priority of Claims: Not Always "Absolute"

In practice, holders of junior and subordinated debt and even shareholders may recover some value on their interests without more senior creditors being paid in full.

Credit Ratings

Rating agencies issue credit ratings, which reflect an opinion on the potential risk of default of a particular (1) bond issue or (2) bond issuer.

Issuer versus Issue Ratings

Rating agencies usually provide credit ratings for the **issuer** (referred to as a **corporate family rating**) and for different **issues** (referred to as **corporate credit rating**) as well.

- The corporate family rating (CFR) is based on the overall creditworthiness of the issuer.
- The corporate credit rating (CCR) applies to a specific financial obligation of the issuer and is based on factors such as the issue's relative seniority ranking in the priority of claims and covenants.

The existence of cross-default provisions implies that the **probability of default** for all the different issues of a particular company is the same. However, different issues can be assigned different (higher or lower) credit ratings due to a ratings adjustment known as **notching**.

Generally speaking:

- For more risky issuers (with lower credit ratings), a larger notching adjustment is applied across seniority rankings. For these issuers, the probability of default is higher, so the potential difference in loss from a lower or higher seniority ranking is a bigger consideration in assessing the issue's credit risk.
- For less risky issuers (with higher credit ratings), the probability of default is lower, so there is less of a need to notch ratings to capture any potential difference in loss severity.

FI

Risks in Relying on Agency Ratings

- Credit ratings can (and generally tend to) change significantly during a bond's term.
- Rating agencies also make mistakes.
- Certain risks (e.g., litigation risk faced by tobacco companies, environmental and business risks faced by chemical companies) cannot be anticipated in advance so rating agencies fail to capture these risks in assigned credit ratings.
- Ratings tend to lag market pricing of credit.

Further, credit ratings primarily focus on the risk of default, whereas (especially for low-quality credits) market price depends more on expected loss (i.e., default probability times loss severity). Therefore, two bonds with similar default risk, but different recovery rates will have similar ratings, but different market values.

The Four Cs of Credit Analysis

Capacity

Capacity refers to a borrower's ability to make its debt payments on time.

Industry Structure

Generally speaking:

- An industry that relies on just a few suppliers has greater credit risk than an industry that has multiple suppliers.
- Industries that rely heavily on just a few customers have greater credit risk than those that sell to a large number of customers.
- The higher the barriers to entry, the lower the level of competition in an industry, and the lower the credit risk of industry participants.
- Industries that offer products and services for which there are no good or cost-effective substitutes have greater pricing power and hence, lower credit risk.
- The greater the intensity of competition among companies in an industry, the lower the industry's profit potential, and the higher the credit risk.
- If an industry is characterized by high fixed costs (e.g., airlines and hotels), companies would find it difficult to cut down costs if they are unable to generate sufficient revenue.

Industry Fundamentals

Evaluation of industry fundamentals is based on:

- Industry cyclicality
- Growth prospects
- Published industry statistics

Company Fundamentals

Analysis of company fundamentals involves an examination of the company's:

- Competitive position
- Track record/operating history
- Management's strategy and execution
- Financial ratios

Collateral

Collateral refers to the quality and value of assets that are pledged against the issuer's debt obligations. Analysts focus more on assessing collateral when the probability of default is significantly high (as is the case with companies with low creditworthiness).

It is sometimes difficult to observe the value and quality of a company's assets directly so analysts should consider the following factors:

- The nature and amount of intangible assets on the balance sheet.
- The amount of depreciation an issuer takes relative to its capital expenditures.

Covenants

Covenants refer to the terms and conditions in a bond's indenture that place restrictions (negative or restrictive covenants) or certain requirements (affirmative covenants) on the issuer.

- While covenants protect bondholders by creating a binding framework for the repayment of debt obligations, they must offer management sufficient flexibility to run the business.
- Covenants provide only limited protection to investment-grade bondholders and slightly stronger protection to high-yield investors.
- Covenants tend to be stronger for bonds that are issued in weak economic times (to induce investors to purchase them).

Character

Character refers to the quality and integrity of management. When evaluating management's character, analysts should:

- Evaluate the suitability and reliability of management's strategy.
- Assess management's track record in executing strategies successfully, while keeping the companies they run clear of bankruptcy, restructuring and other distressed situations.
- Identify the use of aggressive accounting policies and/or tax strategies.
- Look for any history of fraud or malfeasance.
- Look for instances of poor treatment of bond holders in the past.

Ratios and Ratio Analysis

Profitability and Cash Flow Measures

- Earnings before interest, taxes, depreciation, and amortization (EBITDA)
- Funds from operations (FFO)
- Free cash flow before dividends
- Free cash flow after dividends

Leverage Ratios

- Debt / Capital
- Debt / EBITDA
- FFO / Debt

Coverage Ratios

- EBITDA / Interest expense
- EBIT / Interest expense

Issuer Liquidity

All other things remaining same, companies with ready access to liquidity represent lower credit risk. Generally speaking, issuer liquidity is a bigger factor when evaluating credit risk for high-yield companies than for investment grade companies.

FI

Factors Affecting the Yield Spread on Corporate Bonds

This yield spread is composed of the liquidity premium and credit spread.

$$\text{Yield spread} = \text{Liquidity premium} + \text{Credit spread}$$

Yield spreads on corporate bonds are affected by the following:

- Credit cycle: Credit spreads widen (narrow) as the credit cycle deteriorates (improves). They are widest (tightest) at or near the bottom (top) of the credit cycle when financial markets believe that risk is high (low).
- Broader economic conditions: Investors demand a higher (lower) risk premium in relatively weak (strong) economic conditions.
- Financial market performance overall, including equities: Credit spreads widen in weak financial markets, and narrow in strong markets. Credit spreads also narrow in relatively stable, low-volatility market conditions as investors search for yield.
- Broker-dealers' willingness to provide sufficient capital for market making: Credit spreads are narrow when broker-dealers bring sufficient capital to the market, but tend to widen when there is a reduction in broker-provided capital available for market-making purposes.

- General market supply and demand: Credit spreads tend to widen when there is an excess supply of new issues, and tend to narrow when there is excess demand for bonds.

Finally, note that yield spreads on low credit quality bonds tend to be wider that those on high credit quality bonds.

The Return Impact of a Change in the Credit Spread

For small, instantaneous changes in the yield spread, the return impact (i.e., the percentage change in price, including accrued interest) can be estimated using the following formula:

$$\text{Return impact} \approx -\text{Modified duration} \times \Delta\text{Spread}$$

For larger changes in the yield spread, we must also incorporate the (positive) impact of convexity into our estimate of the return impact:

$$\text{Return impact} \approx -(\text{MDur} \times \Delta\text{Spread}) + (1/2 \times \text{Convexity} \times \Delta\text{Spread}^2)$$

- Longer-duration bonds are generally more sensitive to changes in the yield spread.
- Longer-maturity bonds entail more uncertainly than shorter-maturity bonds This is why **spread curves** (also referred to as **credit curves**) are generally upward sloping.

FI

Evaluating the Credit of High-Yield Corporate Debt

High-yield corporate bonds (also referred to as **non-investment-grade corporate bonds** or **junk bonds**) are those that are rated below Baa3/BBB- by the credit rating agencies. High yield bonds entail a greater risk of default than investment grade bonds. As a result, credit analysts pay more attention to recovery analysis (or loss severity in the event of default) when evaluating these bonds.

Special Considerations when Analyzing High Yield Corporate Bonds

- Liquidity: While having cash or the ability to generate cash is important for all debt issuers, it is absolutely critical for high-yield debt issuers. High-yield companies only have access to limited sources of liquidity.
- Financial projections: Analysts should forecast earnings and cash flows several years into the future to assess whether the issuer's credit profile will remain stable, improve, or deteriorate. Analysts should also incorporate required capital expenditures, changes in working capital, and realistic "stress" scenarios in their analysis to identify any vulnerabilities in the business.

- Debt structure: High-yield companies usually have many layers of debt in their capital structures, with each layer having a different seniority ranking and hence, entailing a different potential recovery rate in the event of default. To evaluate the credit risk of a high-yield issuer with many layers of debt in its capital structure, analysts must calculate leverage for each level of the debt structure.

  High-yield companies with a relatively high proportion of secured debt (typically bank debt) in their capital structure are said to be "top-heavy." It is generally difficult for such companies to take on more debt in the event of financial stress because of (1) the stringent covenants associated with bank debt and (2) the relatively short maturity of bank debt relative to other forms of debt. Both these factors contribute to a higher risk of default for these companies and lower recovery rates for less secured creditors.
- Corporate structure: High-yield investors need to assess whether debt has been issued by the parent or its subsidiary, and how cash can move between the two. They should compute leverage ratios for each of the debt-issuing entities individually, and on a consolidated basis.
- Covenant analysis: Analysis of covenants takes on even more significance for high-yield bonds than investment-grade bonds. Some of the important covenants for high-yield issuers are:
  - Change of control put
  - Restricted payments:
  - Limitations on liens and additional indebtedness
  - Restricted versus unrestricted subsidiaries

FI

It is also important to analyze covenants in a high-yield issuer's bank credit agreements. Bank covenants can be more restrictive than bond covenants.

Equity-like Approach to High-Yield Analysis

An equity-like approach can be useful for analyzing high-yield bonds. One such approach is to calculate multiples (e.g., EV/EBITDA and debt/EBITDA) and compare them across several issuers. For a given issuer, if there is only a small difference between the EV/EBITDA and debt/EBITDA ratios, it indicates that the issuer has a relatively small "equity cushion," which means higher risk for bond investors.

Evaluating the Credit of Sovereign Debt

Sovereign debt refers to debt issued by national governments. Credit analysis of sovereign bonds entails an evaluation of the government's ability and willingness to service its debt. An assessment of willingness to service debt is particularly important for sovereign debt as bondholders typically have no legal recourse if a national government is unwilling to meet its debt obligations.

Credit rating agencies typically assign a local currency debt rating and a foreign currency debt rating to sovereign issuers. This is because defaults on foreign currency-denominated sovereign bonds have tended to exceed defaults on local currency-denominated sovereign bonds.

Evaluating the Credit of Municipal Debt

Non-sovereign (or sub-sovereign) government entities include local and state governments as well as various agencies and authorities created by them.

General Obligation (GO) Bonds

GO bonds are unsecured bonds issued with the full faith and credit of the issuing entity, and are supported by the taxing authority of the issuer. Credit analysis of GO bonds is quite similar to that of sovereign bonds.

Revenue Bonds

These are issued for financing a specific project (e.g., a toll road, bridge, hospital, etc.) and are serviced with revenues generated from the project. Therefore, analysis of revenue bonds is similar to analysis of corporate bonds. It focuses on the cash-generating ability of the particular project and on the economic base supporting the project (sources of finance).

A key ratio used to analyze revenue-backed municipal bonds is the debt service coverage ratio (DSCR). The higher the ratio, the lower the credit risk of the bond.

Study Session 17: Derivatives

DR

DERIVATIVE MARKETS AND INSTRUMENTS
Cross-Reference to CFA Institute Assigned Reading #56

A derivative is a financial contract or instrument that derives its value from the value of something else (known as the underlying). The underlying on which a derivative is based can be an asset (e.g., stocks and bonds), an index (e.g., S&P 500), or something else (e.g., interest rates).

Exchange-Traded versus Over-the-Counter Derivatives

Exchange-Traded Derivatives Markets

Exchange-traded derivatives (e.g., futures contracts) are traded on specialized derivatives exchanges or other exchanges.

- Standardization facilitates the creation of a more liquid market for derivatives. However, it comes at the cost of flexibility.
  - Liquidity is a function of (1) trading interest and (2) level of uncertainty. Little trading interest and a high level of uncertainty lead to low liquidity.
- Market makers and speculators play an important role in these markets.
  - Market makers stand ready to buy at one (low) price and sell at another (high) price in order to lock in small short-term profits (known as scalping).
  - Speculators are willing to take educated risks to earn profits.
- The exchange is responsible for clearing and settlement through its clearinghouse. The clearinghouse is able to provide a credit guarantee to market participants.
- Exchange markets also have transparency, i.e., information regarding all transactions is disclosed to regulatory bodies. This regulation does bring certain benefits, but also means a loss of privacy.

Over-the-Counter (OTC) Derivatives Markets

OTC derivatives (e.g., forward contracts) do not trade in a centralized market; instead, they trade in an *informal* market. OTC derivatives are customized instruments. Dealers (typically banks) play an important role in OTC markets as they buy and sell these customized derivatives to market participants, and then look to hedge (or lay off) their risks. Due to the customized nature of OTC derivatives, dealers are typically unable to find identical offsetting transactions. Therefore, they turn to similar transactions to lay off some of the risk, and use their specialized knowledge and complex models to manage any remaining exposure.

- Note that there is a tendency to think that the OTC market is less liquid than the exchange market. This is not necessarily true.
- OTC derivative markets are less regulated than exchange-traded derivative markets.
- OTC markets offer more privacy and flexibility than exchange markets.

Forward Commitments versus Contingent Claims

A forward commitment is a legally binding **obligation** to engage in a certain transaction in the spot market at a future date at terms agreed upon today. Forward commitments can be made on exchange-traded derivatives and over-the-counter derivatives.

- Forwards are customized and private contracts between two parties, where one party has an obligation to buy an asset, and the counterparty has an obligation to sell the asset, at a price and future date that is agreed upon signing of the contract.
- Futures are standardized derivative contracts where one party, the buyer, will purchase an underlying asset from the other party, the seller, at a later date at a price agreed upon contract initiation.
- A swap is an over-the-counter derivative contract in which two parties agree to exchange a series of cash flows whereby one party pays a variable series that will be determined by an underlying asset or rate, and the counterparty pays either 1) a variable series determined by a different underlying asset or rate or 2) a fixed series.

A contingent claim is a derivative in which the outcome or payoff is determined by the outcome or payoff of an underlying asset, conditional on some event occurring.

- Options are contingent claims because their payoffs depend on the underlying's value in the future. Options are derivative instruments that give their holders the choice (not the obligation) to buy or sell the underlying from, or to the seller (writer) of the option. Options can be customized, over-the-counter contracts, or standardized, exchange-traded contracts.
- A credit derivative is a contract that transfers credit risk from one party (the credit protection buyer) to another party (the credit protection seller), where the latter protects the former against a specific credit loss. Credit derivatives include credit default swaps (CDS), total return swaps, credit spread options, and credit-linked notes.
- An asset-backed security(ABS) is a derivative in which a portfolio of debt instruments is pooled, and claims are issued on the portfolio in the form of tranches, which have different priorities of claims on the payments that come in from the pool of debt securities.

Purposes and Benefits of Derivatives

- Risk allocation, transfer, and management
- Information discovery
- Operational advantages
- Market efficiency

Criticisms and Misuses of Derivatives

DR

- Destabilization and systematic risk
- Speculation and gambling
- Complexity

Arbitrage

Arbitrage opportunities exist whenever similar assets or combinations of assets are selling for different prices. Arbitrageurs exploit these opportunities and trade on mispricings until they are eliminated and asset prices converge to their "correct" levels. Arbitrage plays an important role in the study of derivatives. It is an important feature of efficient markets because it helps:

1. Determine prices
2. Improve market efficiency

BASICS OF DERIVATIVE PRICING AND VALUATION

Cross-Reference to CFA Institute Assigned Reading #57

Pricing the Underlying

The price or value of a financial asset is determined as the present value of expected future price plus (minus) any benefits (costs) of holding the asset, discounted at a rate appropriate for the risk assumed.

$$S_0 = \left[\frac{E(S_T)}{(1+r+\lambda)^T}\right] - \theta + \gamma$$

- The required rate of return includes the risk-free rate and a risk premium.

The Principal of Arbitrage

Arbitrage and Derivatives

When the underlying is combined with the derivative to create a perfectly hedged portfolio, all of the price risk is eliminated and the position should earn the risk-free rate.

Asset + Derivative = Risk-free asset
Asset – Risk-free asset = –Derivative
Derivative – Risk-free asset = –Asset

Risk Aversion, Risk Neutrality, and Arbitrage-Free Pricing

- Derivative pricing models discount the expected payoff of the derivative at the risk-free rate rather than the risk-free rate plus a risk premium.
- Further, the expected payoff is calculated based on what are known as risk-neutral probabilities (not actual or true probabilities of possible outcomes).
- While the risk aversion of investors is relevant to pricing assets, it is not relevant to pricing derivatives. As such, derivatives pricing is sometimes called risk-neutral pricing.

Limits to Arbitrage

- Significant transaction costs
- Large capital requirements
- The possibility of additional capital being required down the line
- Some assets possibly difficult to short
- Modeling risk

Derivatives Pricing versus Valuation

- Price, as it relates to forwards, futures, and swaps (note that options are not a problem in this regard), refers to the fixed price (that is agreed upon at contract initiation) at which the underlying transaction will take place in the future. These securities do not require an outlay of cash at contract initiation, so there is no concept of a price being paid at the beginning.
- The value of these contracts fluctuate in response to changes in the price of the underlying.

FORWARD CONTRACTS

A forward is a contract between two parties, where one (the long position) has the **obligation** to buy, and the other (the short position) has an **obligation** to sell an underlying asset at a fixed forward price (that established at the inception of the contract) at a future date.

- Typically, no cash changes hands at inception.
- The long position benefits when the price of the underlying asset increases, while the short benefits when the price of the underlying asset falls.
- If the party that is adversely affected by price movements defaults on its commitment, the counterparty with the favorable position faces default risk.
- Forwards are a zero-sum game—one party's gain is the other party's loss.

Pricing and Valuation of Forward Contracts

The price of a forward contract is the fixed price or rate at which the underlying transaction will occur at contract expiration. The forward price is agreed upon at initiation of the forward contract. Pricing a forward contract means determining this forward price.

The value of a forward contract is the amount that a counterparty would need to pay, or would expect to receive, to get out of its (already-assumed) forward position.

Valuing a Forward Contract at Expiration (t = T)

$$V_T(0,T) = S_T - F(0,T)$$

DR

Forward Contract Payoffs at Expiration

	$S_T > F(0,T)$	$S_T < F(0,T)$
Long position	$S_T - F(0,T)$ (Positive payoff)	$S_T - F(0,T)$ (Negative payoff)
Short position	$-[S_T - F(0,T)]$ (Negative payoff)	$-[S_T - F(0,T)]$ (Positive payoff)

Valuing a Forward Contract at Initiation (t = 0)

$$V_0(0,T) = S_0 - [F(0,T)/(1+r)^T] = 0$$

No-Arbitrage Forward Price

$$F(0,T) = S_0(1+r)^T$$

If the underlying asset entails benefits/costs:

$$F(0,T) = (S_0 - \gamma + \theta)(1+r)^T; \text{ or } F(0,T) = S_0(1+r)^T - (\gamma - \theta)(1+r)^T$$

- The risk premium on the asset does not directly appear in determining the price of a forward.
- Although the forward price is fixed for a particular forward contract, a new contract calling for delivery of the same asset at the same point in time will have a different forward price (depending on the current spot price).

Valuing a Forward Contract During its Life

$$V_t(0,T) = S_t - [F(0,T)/(1+r)^{T-t}]$$

If the underlying asset entails benefits/costs:

$$V_t(0,T) = S_t - (\gamma - \theta)(1+r)^t - [F(0,T)/(1+r)^{T-t}]$$

Value of a Forward Contract

Time	Long Position Value	Short Position Value
At initiation	Zero, as the contract is priced to prevent arbitrage	Zero, as the contract is priced to prevent arbitrage
During life of the contract	$S_t - \left[\frac{F(0,T)}{(1+r)^{T-t}}\right]$	$\left[\frac{F(0,T)}{(1+r)^{T-t}}\right] - S_t$
At expiration	$S_T - F(0,T)$	$F(0,T) - S_T$

Forward Contracts on Interest Rates (Forward Rate Agreements)

A forward rate agreement (FRA) is a forward contract where the underlying is an interest rate (usually LIBOR). Think about the long position in an FRA as the party that has committed to take a hypothetical loan, and the short as the party that has committed to give out a hypothetical loan, at the FRA rate.

- If LIBOR at FRA expiration is *greater* than the FRA rate, the long benefits.
- If LIBOR at FRA expiration is *lower* than the FRA rate, the short benefits.

DR

A borrower (who would like to lock in a borrowing rate) would take a long position on an FRA, while a lender (who would like to lock in a rate of return) would take a short position on an FRA.

Pricing a Forward Rate Agreement

The price of an FRA (forward price) represents the interest rate at which the long (short) position has the obligation to borrow (lend) funds for a specified period (term of the underlying hypothetical loan) starting at FRA expiration.

- Pricing an FRA is a simple exercise of determining the forward rate consistent with two (given) spot rates.
- Essentially, taking the long position on an FRA is equivalent to holding a longer-term Eurodollar time deposit and at the same time shorting (or owing) a shorter-term Eurodollar time deposit.

FUTURES CONTRACTS

Characteristics of Futures Contracts **Vol 6, pgs 17–21**

- Futures contracts are standardized.
    - The futures price is the only term set by the two parties involved in the contract; all other terms are established by the exchange including the expiration date of the contract, the underlying, the mode of settlement, and contract size.
- In the futures market, the initial margin is the amount that must be deposited by each party—the long and the short, into her account to be able to trade in the market.
- The maintenance margin is the minimum balance that must be maintained in an investor's account to avoid a margin call (a call for more funds to be deposited in the account).
- Marking-to-market is the process of adjusting the balance in an investor's futures account to reflect the change in value of her futures position since the last mark-to-market adjustment was conducted.
- The clearinghouse is the counterparty to every trade on the exchange. It acts as the short for every long position, and as the long for every short position.
- Taking the position as the counterparty to every trade combined with the ability to enforce periodic mark-to-market adjustments for all market participants makes for a very efficient mechanism for controlling default risk.
- Some futures contracts have price limits. These limits are set by the exchange to restrict the change in the settlement price of a contract from one day to the next.

Forward Prices versus Futures Prices

- If underlying asset prices are positively correlated with interest rates, the futures price will be higher than the forward price.
- If underlying asset prices are negatively correlated with interest rates, the forward price will be higher than the futures price.

- If interest rates are constant, forwards and futures would have the same prices.
- If futures prices are uncorrelated with interest rates, forwards and futures would have the same prices.
- Forward and futures prices would be different if the volatility of the forward price is different from the volatility of the futures price.

SWAPS

A swap is an agreement to exchange a series of cash flows at periodic settlement dates over a certain period of time (known as the tenor of the swap).

Plain Vanilla Interest Rate Swaps

- A plain-vanilla interest rate swap involves the exchange of fixed interest payments for floating-rate payments.
- The party that wants to receive floating-rate payments and agrees to make fixed-rate payments is known as the pay-fixed side of the swap or the fixed-rate payer/floating-rate receiver.
- The party that wants to receive fixed payments and make floating-rate payments is the pay-floating side of the swap or the floating-rate payer/fixed-rate receiver.
- There is no exchange of notional principal at initiation or expiration of the swap. The notional principal is simply used to determine the interest payment on each leg of the swap.
- Interest payments are not exchanged in full at each settlement date. Interest payments are netted, and the party that owes more in interest at a particular settlement date makes a payment equal to the difference to the other.
- As with forward contracts, there is an element of counterparty credit risk in swaps as the party that owes the lower amount can default.
- The floating rate is usually quoted in terms of LIBOR plus a spread. The floating rate for any period is known at the beginning of the period, while the settlement payment is actually made at the end of each period.

$$\text{Net fixed-rate payment}_t = [\text{Swap fixed rate} - (\text{LIBOR}_{t-1} + \text{spread})] * (\text{No. of days} / 360) * \text{Notional principal}$$

Pricing versus Valuation of Swaps

- At the initiation of the swap, the swap fixed rate is set at a level at which the present value of the floating-rate payments (based on the current term structure of interest rates) equals the present value of fixed-rate payments so that there is zero value to either party. This swap fixed rate therefore represents the price of the swap.
- Over the term of the swap, as there are changes in the term structure of interest rates, the value of the swap will fluctuate.
    - If interest rates increase after swap initiation, the present value of floating-rate payments (based on the new term structure) will exceed the present value of fixed-rate payments (based on the swap fixed rate).

DR

        - The swap will have a positive value for the fixed-rate payer (floating-rate receiver).
        - The swap will be an asset to the fixed-rate payer and a liability for the floating-rate payer.
    - If interest rates decrease after swap initiation, the present value of floating-rate payments will be lower than the present value of fixed-rate payments.
        - The swap will have a positive value for the floating-rate payer (fixed-rate receiver).
        - In this case, the swap will be an asset to the floating-rate payer and a liability for the fixed-rate payer.

Swaps and Forward Contracts

A swap essentially combines a series of forward contracts into a single transaction. For example, a plain vanilla interest rate swap is a combination of FRAs, where one FRA expires on each settlement date over the tenor of the swap, and the FRA rate (forward price) for each FRA equals the swap fixed rate (swap price).

Swaps and Bonds

The payoffs of the pay-fixed side of an interest rate swap are similar to those of a strategy of issuing a fixed-rate bond (on which fixed payments must be made) and using the proceeds to purchase a floating-rate bond (which will return floating-interest payments). On the other hand, the payoffs of the pay-floating side are similar to issuing a floating-rate bond and using the proceeds to purchase a fixed-rate bond.

- If interest rates increase, the fixed-rate payer benefits as there is a positive difference between her (floating-rate) receipts and (fixed-rate) payments.
- If interest rates decrease, the fixed-rate payer loses out as there is a negative difference between (floating-rate) receipts and (fixed-rate) payments.

OPTIONS

European versus American Options

- A European option is one that can only be exercised at the option's expiration date.
- An American option can be exercised at any point in time up to, and including, the option's expiration date.

DR

Moneyness and Exercise Value

Moneyness refers to whether an option is in-the-money or out-of-the-money.

- An option is in-the-money when immediate exercise of the option will generate a positive payoff for the holder.
- An option is out-of-the-money when immediate exercise will generate a negative payoff for the holder.
- An option is at-the-money when immediate exercise will result in neither a positive nor a negative payoff for the holder.

The intrinsic value or exercise value of an option is the amount an option is in-the-money by. It is the amount that would be received by the option holder if he were to exercise the option immediately. An option has zero intrinsic value if it is at- or out-of-the money.

Call Options

- A call option gives the **holder/buyer** the **right** to **buy** (or call) the underlying asset for the given exercise price at the expiration date of the option.
- A call option **writer/seller** has the **obligation** to **sell** the asset to the holder of the call option for the given exercise price, should the option holder choose to exercise the option.

Call Option Payoffs

Option Position	Descriptions	Payoff	
		$S_T > X$	$S_T < X$
		Option holder exercises the option	Option holder does not exercise the option
Call option holder	Choice to buy the underlying asset for X	$S_T - X$	0
Call option writer	Obligation to sell the underlying asset for X if the option holder chooses to exercise the option	$-(S_T - X)$	0

$$\text{Intrinsic value of call} = \text{Max}\,[0, (S_t - X)]$$

Moneyness and Exercise Value of a Call Option

Moneyness	Current Market Price (S_t) versus Exercise Price (X)	Intrinsic Value Max $[0, (S_t - X)]$
In-the-money	S_t is greater than X	$S_t - X$
At-the-money	S_t equals X	0
Out-of-the-money	S_t is less than X	0

DR

Put Options

- A put option gives the **holder/buyer** the **right** to **sell** (or put) the underlying asset for the given exercise price at the option's expiration date.
- A put option **writer/seller** has the **obligation** to **buy** the asset from the put option holder at the option's expiration date for the given exercise price, should the holder choose to exercise the option.

Put Option Payoffs

Option Position	Descriptions	Payoff	
		$S_T < X$	$S_T > X$
		Option holder exercises the option	Option holder does not exercise the option
Put option holder	Choice to sell the underlying asset for X	$X - S_T$	0
Put option writer	Obligation to buy the underlying asset for X if the option holder chooses to exercise the option	$-(X - S_T)$	0

Intrinsic value of a put option = Max [0, $(X - S_t)$].

Moneyness and Exercise Value of a Put Option

Moneyness	Current Market Price (S_t) versus Exercise Price (X)	Intrinsic Value Max [0, $(X - S_t)$]
In-the-money	S_t is less than X	$X - S_t$
At-the-money	S_t equals X	0
Out-of-the-money	S_t is greater than X	0

Put-Call Parity

$$c_0 + \frac{X}{(1+R_F)^T} = p_0 + S_0$$

DR

A fiduciary call, which is composed of (1) a call option on a stock and (2) a zero-coupon riskless bond that pays X at maturity (face value equals X) must have the same value as a protective put, which is composed of (1) a European put option on a stock and (2) a share of the same stock as long as:

- The call and put option, and the zero-coupon bond, have the same time to maturity/expiration (T).
- The exercise price of the call and the put, and the face value of the zero-coupon bond, are the same (X).
- The call and the put are options on the same underlying asset as the one held in Portfolio B (S). This asset makes no cash payments and has no carrying costs.
- The call and put can only be exercised at expiration i.e., they are European options.

Combining Portfolios to Make Synthetic Securities

Strategy	Consisting of	Value	Equals	Strategy	Consisting of	Value
fiduciary call	long call + long bond	$c_0 + \frac{X}{(1+R_F)^T}$	=	Protective put	long put + long underlying asset	$p_0 + S_0$
long call	long call	c_0	=	Synthetic call	long put + long underlying asset + short bond	$p_0 + S_0 - \frac{X}{(1+R_F)^T}$
long put	long put	p_0	=	Synthetic put	long call + short underlying asset + long bond	$c_0 + S_0 - \frac{X}{(1+R_F)^T}$
long underlying asset	long underlying asset	S_0	=	Synthetic underlying asset	long call + long bond + short put	$c_0 + \frac{X}{(1+R_F)^T} - p_0$
long bond	long bond	$\frac{X}{(1+R_F)^T}$	=	Synthetic bond	long put + long underlying asset + short call	$p_0 + S_0 - c_0$

Factors that Affect the Value of an Option

Value of the Underlying

- The greater (lower) the value of the underlying, the greater (lower) the exercise value of the call option, and the greater its price/value.
- The lower (greater) the value of the underlying, the greater (lower) the exercise value of the put option, and the greater its price/value.
- Note that the value of the underlying serves as an upper boundary on the price of American and European call options.

Exercise Price

- For call options, the higher the exercise price, the *lower* the exercise value of the option.
- For put options, the higher the exercise price, the *higher* the intrinsic value.
- The maximum value of a European put option equals the present value of its exercise price, $X/(1 + RFR)^T$.

Risk-Free Rate

- The value of a call option is *directly* related to the risk-free rate.
- The value of a put option is *inversely* related to the risk-free rate.

Time to Expiration

- The value of a European call option is *directly* related to the time to expiration.
- The value of a European put option can be either *directly* or *inversely* related to the time to expiration. Typically, the direct effect holds, but the inverse effect can prevail if a longer time to expiration comes with a higher risk-free rate, and if the option is deep in-the-money.

Volatility

- Greater volatility in the price of the underlying asset *increases* the value of both calls and puts.
- At any point in time before expiration, an option is worth at least as much as its exercise value. However, on top of its exercise value, there is also an element of speculative value in the option to account for the possibility that the underlying asset's price could move favorably over the remaining time to expiration and result in a payoff greater than the current exercise value. This speculative value is known as the time value of an option, which increases with volatility but decreases as the option nears expiration (known as time value decay). At expiration, no time value remains, and the option is worth its exercise value.

Payments from the Underlying and the Cost of Carry

- For call option holders, benefits from the underlying, which cause a decline in the value of the underlying, are a negative because they lead to a decline in the exercise value. For put option holders, on the other hand, benefits from the underlying are a positive (as the value of the underlying falls).
- Carrying costs have the opposite effect. They are a positive for call options, but a negative for puts.

Lowest Prices of European Calls and Puts

- The lowest value of a European call is the greater of (1) zero and (2) the value of the underlying minus the present value of the exercise price.
- The lowest value of a European put is the greater of (1) zero and (2) the present value of the exercise price minus the value of the underlying.

DR

Put-Call Forward Parity

$$p_0 - c_0 = \frac{[X - F(0,T)]}{(1+R_F)^T}$$

Assumptions:

- The price of the forward contract on the underlying is given by F(0,T).
- The put and the call options expire at the same time as the forward contract.
- X represents the exercise price of the call and put options.

- The options are European options.
- The options and the forward contract are based on the same underlying asset.

Payoffs

	Outcome at T	
	$S_T < X$ Put Expires In-the-Money Call Expires Out-of-the-Money	$S_T > X$ Call Expires In-the-Money Put Expires Out-of-the-Money
Protective put with forward contract		
Risk-free bond	F(0,T)	F(0,T)
Forward contract	$S_T - F(0,T)$	$S_T - F(0,T)$
Long put	$X - S_T$	0
Total	X	S_T
Protective put with asset		
Asset	S_T	S_T
Long put	$X - S_T$	0
Total	X	S_T
Fiduciary call		
Call	0	$S_T - X$
Risk-free bond	X	X
Total	X	S_T

The One-Period Binomial Model

In the one-period binomial model, the price of the underlying stock starts off at a given level, S, and can either:

- Move up by a factor of u to a new price, S^+, one period later with a probability of q; or
- Move down by a factor of d to a new price, S, one period later with a probability of 1 – q.
- Note that q and 1 – q are actual or real probabilities of the up and down movements respectively.

$S^+ = Su$
$c^+ = \text{Max}(0, S^+ - X)$

S
$c = ?$

$S^- = Sd$
$c^- = \text{Max}(0, S^- - X)$

t = 0 **t = T**

Value of a Call Option

$$c = \frac{\pi c^+ + (1-\pi)c^-}{(1+r)}$$

where

$$\pi = \frac{(1+r-d)}{(u-d)}$$

The value of an option under this approach is computed by discounting the expected value of the payoff (calculated using risk-neutral probabilities) at the risk-free rate.

American Option Pricing

- Minimum value of an American call option = Max $[0, (S_0 - X/(1+\text{RFR})^T]$
- Minimum value of an American put option = Max $[0, (X - S_0)]$

American Call Options

- There is no reason to exercise an American call option on an asset that offers no benefits before expiration.
- However, if the asset does offer benefits, early exercise of an American call option may be warranted.
- If there are significant costs of carry on the underlying, there is less of a reason to exercise the American call option early.

DR

American Puts

- It would be beneficial to exercise an American put prior to expiration when a company is in or nearing bankruptcy, and its stock price is close to zero.
- Dividends and coupon interest discourage early exercise for American puts.
- Carrying costs on the underlying encourage exercise for American puts.

Study Session 18: Alternative Investments

INTRODUCTION TO ALTERNATIVE INVESTMENTS

Cross-Reference to CFA Institute Assigned Reading #58

Alternative Investments versus Traditional Investments

Alternative investments differ from traditional investments (long-only positions in stocks, bonds, and cash) with respect to (1) the types of assets and securities invested in and (2) the structure of the investment vehicles in which these assets are held.

Investments in these special vehicles are generally characterized by:

- High fees.
- Large size of investments.
- Low diversification of managers and investments within the alternatives investment portfolio.
- High use of leverage.
- Restrictions on redemptions.

Other Characteristics of Alternative Investments

- Illiquidity of underlying investments.
- Narrow manager specialization.
- Low correlation with traditional investments.
- Low level of regulation and less transparency.
- Limited and potentially problematic historical risk and return data.
- Unique legal and tax considerations.

Portfolio Context: Integration of Alternative Investments with Traditional Investments

Historically, the returns on some categories of alternative investments have been found to have relatively low correlations with returns on traditional investments over long periods. Further, most categories of alternative investments have historically exhibited higher returns than traditional investments.

Considerations When Evaluating the Historical Performance of Alternative Investments

- Reported returns and standard deviations are averages, which may not be representative of returns and standard deviations for sub-periods within the reported period, or for future periods.
- The volatility of returns of alternative investments, as well as the correlation of returns with those of traditional asset classes may be underestimated.
- Hedge fund indices may be inherently biased upwards due to self-selection bias, survivorship bias and backfill bias.
- Differences in weightings and constituents in index construction can have a significant impact on the indices and their results and comparability.

CATEGORIES OF ALTERNATIVE INVESTMENTS

HEDGE FUNDS

General Characteristics

- Hedge funds are aggressively managed portfolios of investments.
- They are not constrained by any significant investment restrictions so they enjoy more flexibility in decision-making.
- They are set up as private investment partnerships, where the fund is the general partner (GP) and the investors are limited partners (LPs).
- Hedge funds are regulated to a much lower extent than traditional investments.
- Hedge funds usually impose restrictions on redemptions.

Funds of funds are funds that invest in a number of hedge funds, hence diversifying across hedge fund strategies, investment regions, and management styles.

Hedge Fund Strategies

Event-driven strategies: These strategies take a bottom-up view, i.e., they begin with company analysis and then aggregate and analyze a larger group. They focus on short-term events that usually involve potential changes in corporate structure (e.g., acquisitions and restructurings) that are expected to affect individual companies. Hedge funds following these strategies may take long and short positions in common stock, preferred stock as well as debt securities and options. Event-driven strategies include:

- Merger arbitrage
- Distressed / restructuring
- Activist
- Special situations

Relative value strategies: These strategies seek to profit from pricing discrepancies (or short-term mispricings) between related securities. Examples of relative value strategies include:

- Fixed income convertible arbitrage
- Fixed income asset backed
- Fixed income general
- Volatility
- Multi-strategy

Macro strategies: These strategies take a top-down view as they focus on the overall macroeconomic environment, taking long and short positions in broad markets (e.g., equity indices, currencies, commodities, etc.) that are expected to benefit based on the manager's view regarding overall market direction.

AI

Equity hedge strategies: These strategies take a bottom-up view and focus on public equity markets, taking long and short positions in equities and equity derivatives. Examples of such strategies include:

- Market neutral
- Fundamental growth
- Fundamental value
- Quantitative directional
- Short bias
- Sector specific

Hedge Funds and Diversification Benefits

It would be inappropriate to make generalized statements regarding hedge fund performance given the wide variety of hedge fund strategies. A specific strategy or fund may generate very high returns in some years, and then perform poorly in subsequent years.

- Studies that have analyzed data over long periods of time suggest that there is a less than perfectly positively correlation between hedge fund returns and equity returns.
- However, there have been (shorter) episodes during which there has been a strong positive correlation between the two.
- The correlation between hedge fund returns and stock market performance tends to increase in times of financial crisis.
- As the hedge fund market has become more crowded, funds have begun to take on more risk to generate competitive returns.

Hedge Fund Fees

Hedge funds usually charge two types of fees:

A management fee (also called base fee) is calculated on **assets under management**.

An incentive fee (or performance fee) is based on realized profits. They may be calculated on profits net of management fees or on profits before management fees. Further, incentive fees may be subject to a **hurdle rate**, or a **high water mark provision**.

Hedge Fund Valuation Issues

- When using market prices for valuing traded securities, it is common practice in the hedge fund industry to use the average of the bid and ask quote.
- For highly illiquid or non-traded investments, reliable market value data is unavailable, so values are estimated using statistical models.

Due Diligence Considerations When Investing in Hedge Funds

- Investment strategy.
- Investment process.
- Competitive advantage.
- Track record.
- Size and longevity.

- Management style.
- Key-person risk.
- Reputation.
- Investor relations.
- Plans for growth.
- Methodology used for return calculations.
- Systems for risk management.

PRIVATE EQUITY

Private Equity Structure and Fees

Private equity funds are also usually structured as partnerships, where outside investors are Limited Partners (LPs) and the private equity firm (which can manage a number of funds) is the General Partner (GP). Most private equity firms charge both a management fee and an incentive fee.

- Management fees are usually calculated as a percentage (usually 1% to 3%) of **committed capital**. Once the committed capital is fully invested, the fee is paid only on the funds remaining in the investment vehicle.
- Incentive fees are usually earned by the GP only after the LPs are paid back their initial investments. The GP typically receives 20% of the total profit of the fund as an incentive fee, while the LPs receive 80% of profits (in addition to the return of their initial investment).

Other private equity strategies include:

- *Development capital* (or *minority equity investing*): This generally involves providing financing to more mature companies to help them expand, restructure operations, enter new markets, or finance major acquisitions.
- *Distressed investing* usually involves buying debt of mature companies that are in financial distress (bankrupt, in default, or likely to default). Distressed debt typically trades at a deep discount to par and the idea is to benefit from an increase in the price of these securities as the company is turned around.

Private Equity Exit Strategies

- Trade sale
- Initial public offerings (IPOs)
- Recapitalization
- Secondary sale
- Write-off/liquidation

Private Equity: Diversification Benefits, Performance, and Risk

Studies have shown that:

- Private equity funds have earned higher returns than equities over the last 20 years.
- Based on the standard deviation of historical annual returns, private equity investments (including venture capital) entail higher risk than equities.

- Private equity returns are less than perfectly positively correlated with returns on traditional investments, so there are diversification benefits of including private equity investments in investment portfolios.

However, it is important to bear in mind private equity return indices are subject to survivorship and backfill biases, both of which lead to overstated returns. Further, in the absence of a liquidity event, private equity firms may not mark-to-market their investment portfolios on a regular basis, which leads to understatement of (1) measures of volatility and (2) correlations with other investments.

Evidence also suggests that identifying skilled private equity fund managers is very important as differences in returns between the top and bottom quartiles of PE funds are significant. Further, top-quartile funds tend to persistently perform better than others.

Portfolio Company Valuation Methods

- Market or comparables approach
- Discounted cash flow approach
- Asset-based approach

Factors That Must Be Considered When Investing in Private Equity

- Current and anticipated economic conditions.
- Interest rates and capital availability expectations.
- The quality of the GP.

REAL ESTATE

Forms of Real Estate Investment

Basic Forms of Real Estate Investments and Example

	Debt	Equity
Private	• Mortgages • Construction lending	• Direct ownership of real estate. Ownership can be through, sole ownership, joint ventures, real estate limited partnerships, or other commingled funds
Public	• Mortgage-backed securities (residential and commercial) • Collateralized mortgage obligations	• Share in real estate corporations • Shares of real estate investment trusts

Real Estate Investment Categories

- Residential property
- Commercial real estate
- REIT investing
- Timberland and farmland

AI

Real Estate Performance and Diversification Benefits

The performance of real estate may be measured using three different types of indices:

- Appraisal indices use estimates of value (based on comparable sales or DCF analysis) as inputs. Appraisal indices tend to understate volatility.
- Repeat sales (transactions-based) indices are constructed using changes in prices of properties that have sold multiple times over the period. These indices suffer from sample selection bias.
- REIT indices are constructed using prices of publicly traded shares of REITs. The reliability of these indices increases with the frequency of trading.

Studies have shown that:

- Real estate as an asset class enjoys less than perfect positive correlation with stocks and bonds, so there may be diversification benefits to adding real estate investments to a portfolio containing traditional investments.
- The correlation between real estate and equities is higher than the correlation between real estate and bonds because real estate and equities are affected similarly by the business cycle.

Note that the low correlation between real estate and other asset classes may be the result of the methods used in index construction so actual diversification benefits may be less than expected.

Real Estate Valuation Approaches

Comparable sales approach: Under this approach, the value of a property is estimated based on recent sales of comparable properties.

Income approach: Two income-based approaches to real estate valuation are the direct capitalization approach and the discounted cash flow approach.

- The *direct capitalization approach* estimates the value of a property by dividing expected net operating income (NOI) generated by the property by a growth implicit capitalization rate (also referred to as the cap rate).
- The *discounted cash flow approach* estimates the value of a property as the present value of its expected future cash flows over a specific investment horizon plus the present value of an estimated resale value (or reversion value) at the end of the holding period.

Cost approach: Under this approach, the value of a property is estimated as its replacement cost, which equals the total cost that would be incurred to buy the land and construct a new, but similar, property on that site. This estimate of current replacement cost is adjusted for the location and condition of the subject property.

REIT Valuation Approaches

Income-based approaches for valuing REITs are similar to the direct capitalization approach for valuing individual properties (described above) in that a measure of income is capitalized into a value using an appropriate cap rate. Two common measures of income used are Funds from operations (FFO) and adjusted funds from operations (AFFO).

AI

Asset-based approaches aim to determine a REIT's net asset value (NAV) by subtracting the value of its total liabilities from the estimated total market value of its assets.

Real Estate Investment Risks

- National and global economic conditions, local real estate conditions, and interest rate levels.
- The ability of fund managers to select, finance and manage the properties.
- Changes in government regulations.
- Regulatory issues, construction delays, and cost overruns.
- Leverage.

COMMODITIES

Investments in physical commodities entail costs for transportation and storage. As a result, most commodity investors prefer to trade commodity derivatives instead of actual physical commodities. Commodity derivatives include futures and forward contracts, options contracts and swaps contracts.

Other commodity investment vehicles include:

- Exchange traded funds (ETFs)
- Common stock of companies exposed to a particular commodity
- Managed futures funds
- Individual managed accounts
- Specialized funds

Commodity Performance and Diversification Benefits

Studies have shown that over a period from 1990 to 2010:

- Commodities earned a lower annual return than stocks and bonds.
- Commodity returns had a higher standard deviation (risk) than stocks and bonds.
- As a result, the Sharpe ratio for commodities as an asset class was much lower than for stocks and bonds.
- Commodities have a relatively low correlation with stocks and bonds, which suggests that there are diversification benefits from adding commodities to a portfolio consisting of traditional asset classes.

Commodity Prices and Investments

Spot prices for commodities are a function of supply and demand, costs of production and storage, value to users, and global economic conditions.

Pricing of Commodity Futures Contracts

The price of a futures contract on a commodity may be calculated as follows:

$$\text{Futures price} = \text{Spot price}\,(1 + r) + \text{Storage costs} - \text{Convenience yield}$$

The futures price may be higher or lower than the spot price of a commodity depending on the convenience yield.

- When futures prices are higher than the spot price (when there is little of no convenience yield), prices are said to be in contango.
- When futures prices are lower than the spot price, prices are said to be in backwardation.

Sources of Return on a Commodity Futures Contract

- Roll yield: The difference between the spot price of a commodity and the futures price, or the difference between the futures prices of contracts expiring at different dates.
- Collateral yield: The interest earned on the collateral (margin) deposited to enter into the futures contract.
- Spot prices: These are influenced by current supply and demand.

INFRASTRUCTURE

- The assets underlying infrastructure investments are real, capital intensive, long-lived assets. They are intended for public use and provide essential services.
- Typically, infrastructure assets are financed, owned, and operated by governments.
- However, increasingly, the private sector is getting involved in infrastructure investments with an intention to (1) lease the assets back to the government, (2) sell newly constructed assets to the government, or (3) hold and operate the assets.
    - Investors are tempted to hold and operate infrastructure assets when (1) there is relatively inelastic demand for the assets and services, and (2) the high costs of the assets create high barriers to entry, both of which result in a strong competitive position for the service provider.
    - Investors expect these assets to generate stable cash flows, which adjust for economic growth and inflation.
    - Investors may also expect capital appreciation depending on the type of investment.

Benefits of Investing in Infrastructure

Investing in infrastructure may enable investors to:

- Add a steady income stream to their portfolios.
- Further diversify their portfolios as infrastructure assets exhibit low correlation with other investments.
- Gain some inflation protection.

Since they typically entail investments in long-lived assets, infrastructure investments may also better match the longer-term liability structure of some institutional investors (e.g. pension funds and life insurance companies).

Categories of Infrastructure Investments

Economic versus Social Infrastructure Assets

- **Economic infrastructure** assets support economic activity. They include assets such as transportation and utility assets.
    - Transportation assets include roads, bridges, tunnels, airports, ports, and railway lines.
    - Utility assets include assets to transmit, store, and distribute gas, water, and electricity; generate power; treat waste; and broadcast and transmit information.
        - Note that assets that broadcast and transmit information may also be categorized separately as communication assets.
- **Social infrastructure assets** are directed toward human activities. They include assets such as education, healthcare, and correctional facilities.

Brownfield versus Greenfield Investments

- **Brownfield investments** refer to investments in **existing** investable infrastructure assets.
    - These assets may be currently owned by a government that wants to (1) privatize the asset, (2) lease the asset out, or (3) sell and lease back the asset.
    - Typically, some financial and operating history regarding the asset is available.
- **Greenfield investments** refer to investments in infrastructure assets that are **to be constructed**.
    - The intent may be to (1) hold and operate the assets or (2) lease or sell the assets to the government after construction

Direct versus Indirect Investments

Direct investments in infrastructure assets result in investors controlling the assets and having the opportunity to capture the entire value on offer. However, they entail a very large capital commitment, which gives rise to concentration and liquidity risk in investor portfolios. Further, investors then bear the responsibility of managing and operating the assets.

Indirect investments include shares of (1) companies, (2) exchange-traded funds, (3) listed funds, (4) private equity funds, and (5) unlisted mutual funds that invest in infrastructure. Investors who are most concerned about liquidity may choose to invest through (1) publicly traded infrastructure securities and/or (2) master limited partnerships.

In addition to liquidity, publicly traded infrastructure securities provide reasonable fees, transparent governance, market prices, and the ability to diversify across underlying assets. Unfortunately however, these securities represent a small segment of the infrastructure investment universe and tend to be relatively concentrated in categories of assets.

Master limited partnerships (MLPs) trade on exchanges and are pass-through entities similar to REITs.

- Regulations regarding MLPs tend to vary across countries.
- Most of the free cash flow is passed on to investors. However, investors are liable for taxes on that income.
- Typically, a general partner manages the partnership, receives a fee, and holds a small partnership interest. Limited partners own the remaining partnership interest.

Risks and Returns Overview

Low risk infrastructure investments have more stable cash flows and higher dividend payout ratios. However, they also typically have less growth and lower expected returns.

- An investment in an MLP with a brownfield investment in an asset that is being leased back to a government, such as a school, is a low risk infrastructure investment.
- An investment in a private equity fund with a greenfield investment is a riskier investment.

Risks of investing in infrastructure include:

- Revenues not meeting expectations.
- Leverage, which may give rise to financing risk.
- Operational risk.
- Construction risk.
- Regulatory risk. Since infrastructure assets often provide services that are very important to society, governments typically regulate certain aspects, including the sale of the underlying assets, operations of the assets including service quality, and prices/profit margins.

Other Alternative Investments

Collectibles include antiques and fine art, fine wine, rare stamps and coins, jewelry and watches, and sports memorabilia.

- They do not provide current income, but have potential for long-term capital appreciation, can diversify a portfolio and can also be a source of enjoyment for owners.
- They can fluctuate dramatically in value and can be relatively illiquid.
- Investors must have some degree of expertise to make wise investing decisions.
- Storage costs can be significant (e.g., for wine and art).

RISK MANAGEMENT

- Investments in certain types of alternative investments require long holding periods. For example, private equity funds and hedge funds have long lockup periods.
- Hedge funds and private equity funds are less transparent than other investments as they may consider their investment strategies to be proprietary information.
- Investments in many alternative investments are relatively illiquid.
- Indices are widely used to track the performance of several types of alternative investments. Historical returns on those indices and the standard deviations of their returns may not really be representative of the risk-return characteristics of alternative investments.
- Reported correlations between alternative investments and traditional investments can be very different from actual correlations.
- There can be significant differences between the performance of an individual portfolio manager or fund and the performance of the overall investment class.
- Large investors can diversify across managers/funds, but small investors cannot.
- Hedge fund managers who have incurred large losses tend to liquidate their funds instead of trying to offset those losses.

Risk-Return Measures

The Sharpe ratio is not an appropriate risk-return measure for alternative investments.

Returns generally tend to be leptokurtic and negatively skewed (positive average returns but with higher than average risk of extreme losses). As a result, measures of downside risk are more useful. These include:

- Value at Risk (VaR)
- Shortfall or safety first measures
- Sortino ratio

AI